Karl Benjamin Klunzinger

Upper Egypt

Its people and its products: a descriptive account of the manners, customs, superstitions, and occupations of the people of the Nile Valley, the desert, and the Red Sea coast; with sketches of the natural history and geology

Karl Benjamin Klunzinger

Upper Egypt

Its people and its products: a descriptive account of the manners, customs, superstitions, and occupations of the people of the Nile Valley, the desert, and the Red Sea coast; with sketches of the natural history and geology

ISBN/EAN: 9783337323943

Printed in Europe, USA, Canada, Australia, Japan

Cover: Foto ©Andreas Hilbeck / pixelio.de

More available books at www.hansebooks.com

UPPER EGYPT:

ITS PEOPLE AND ITS PRODUCTS.

A DESCRIPTIVE ACCOUNT

OF THE

MANNERS, CUSTOMS, SUPERSTITIONS, AND OCCUPATIONS OF

THE PEOPLE OF THE NILE VALLEY, THE DESERT, AND THE RED SEA COAST,

WITH SKETCHES OF THE NATURAL HISTORY AND GEOLOGY.

BY

C. B. KLUNZINGER, M.D.,

Formerly Egyptian Sanitary Physician at Koseir, on the Red Sea; Member of the Gesellschaft
für Erdkunde zu Berlin, &c. &c.

WITH A PREFATORY NOTICE

BY DR. GEORG SCHWEINFURTH,

Author of "The Heart of Africa."

NEW YORK:
SCRIBNER, ARMSTRONG, & CO.
1878.

AUTHOR'S PREFACE.

MIGHTY is the stream of literature which since ancient times, but especially in modern times, has flowed over the wonderful land of the sacred Nile, but we are still far from being able to boast of possessing a complete knowledge of even Egypt proper. For the truth and accuracy of his descriptions of its modern inhabitants Lane still remains unequalled, but he has almost exclusively confined himself to the people of the capital; on the subject of country life, and especially on Upper Egypt, we possess merely the reports of travellers. In the whole of Upper Egypt only a few Europeans have hitherto settled, and these are almost exclusively Greek traders, who are not in a position to utilize their experiences by giving them to the world; still less is this to be expected of the natives themselves. Accurate observations and judgments cannot be attained by a bird's-eye view, but only by living on terms of intimacy with the people as one of themselves (like Lane), gradually getting acquainted with their manners, customs, and religious observances, and especially their language, and for this a fixed abode and much time, study, and self-denial are necessary.

When in 1863 I left Europe with the special object of making zoological investigations and collections on the Red Sea, I resolved not to confine my observations to animals, but to become acquainted with my whole surroundings, for, as Humboldt says, one can only enjoy what one understands. Since that time, from 1863 to 1869, and, with a break of a few years spent in Europe, from 1872 to 1875, I lived at the little Upper Egyptian seaport of Koseir on the Red Sea, as sanitary or quarantine doctor, appointed by the Egyptian government, but was also much occupied both on private and official business in the neighbouring portion of the Nile valley, corresponding to the ancient Thebaid, and the present *mudiríyeh* of Keneh. As an inhabitant for many years of a small town, where, so to speak, I formed one of a family, as a doctor and government official, and as a naturalist, I had ample opportunities for thoroughly studying the language, and for becoming acquainted with the country and the people, while Europeans who dwell in the capital find it very difficult to pass beyond their own circles and enter those of the native inhabitants.

My lengthened experiences and observations I have now set forth in this book, and have attempted to clothe them in a dress that will have some attractions for the public. I have not adopted the plan of giving a descriptive account of my travels, since the personality of the writer always obtrudes itself in that form of composition, but have taken the inquirer by the hand, and thus we pass together from scene to scene. The comparison of the modern Egyptians with the ancient appears to me specially interesting, the more so as the inhabitants of Upper Egypt have preserved the ancient type and many customs with remarkable purity. The reader, therefore, may always have Wilkinson's *Ancient Egyptians* at his hand.

Portions of the present work were originally published in periodicals, such as "Ausland," Westermann's "Monatshefte," and the "Zeitschrift für Erdkunde," but these portions have been revised and greatly enlarged by observations made during my second stay in Egypt; other chapters are entirely new.

C. B. KLUNZINGER.

BERLIN, *November*, 1876.

NOTE BY THE PUBLISHERS.

This translation of Dr. Klunziger's Work has been prepared by arrangement with the author, and with his active co-operation and assistance. It is illustrated by additional engravings after his own sketches, which do not appear in the German edition. The Work has met with a very cordial reception in Germany, where the press has bestowed upon it the warmest encomiums.

GLASGOW, *October, 1877.*

PREFACE

BY DR. GEORG SCHWEINFURTH.

KINDRED intellectual tendencies and a like interest in science brought myself and the author of this work together in Cairo thirteen years ago, and in a short time united us by the bonds of a lasting friendship. When we first met in the city of the Caliphs, I, a novice on African soil, had still to make my primary studies, while the German physician and naturalist, whom I hunted up in an out-of-the-way Arabic quarter, was already far advanced in the language and in the knowledge of the manners and customs of the people.

While others who had come to appropriate one thing or another from the foreign world, unwilling to resign the home comforts of hotel-life, allowed this world to pass before their eyes as if on the stage of a theatre, and left chance to determine whither and how far their intellectual feelers should extend, Dr. Klunzinger, as formerly Burkhard, "the son of the Lutheran," and Lane of blessed memory, lived entirely among the believing heirs of paradise. In modern times the life of Europeans in the East has generally assumed such a form, that one may have lived his twenty years in Egypt without knowing much more about the country and the people than may be found set down in any one of a hundred books in which chamber students describe to us things they have never seen. To this class of people my friend did not belong. When I found him as above mentioned, in his house of unburned bricks, diligently practising among the poor, surrounded by blind and lame from whose lips issued many a blessing on the self-sacrificing and disinterested friend of man, while from the hands of others he received as his fee zoological materials for his studies, I found a companion to look up to, a model on whom to gaze with admiration.

Some months after my first meeting with the author, when I had begun those travels which were to lead me in the course of years from regions little known to others altogether unexplored, I arrived at that secluded seaport where my friend had meantime settled as sanitary physician. On three different occasions I was hospitably received in his house, and passed many weeks by his side, introduced by an incomparable teacher into the Arabic world, and at the same time made acquainted with the secrets of that subterranean wonder-world, the corals. For many years after that did my friend labour devotedly in this remote corner of the globe on behalf of science and for the good of suffering humanity. The inhabitants of Koseir still preserve towards him the most grateful remembrance, and a brilliant testimony to the love and respect which he was able to gain among them was given by the elders of this town, when in a special petition they prayed the supreme sanitary authorities to renominate him as physician on his return as a private individual after a few years' absence in Europe.

Solitary and without companionship in his researches, but by no means turning his back with self-sufficiency upon what society he could avail himself of, mean although the garb might be in which it showed itself, and far from puffing himself up with the pride of being "the only living man among shades," he lived here a man among men. Among fishermen and mariners, among pilgrims and camel-drivers, among petty dealers and lowly scribes, our friend of humanity has sacrificed the best years of his life. The man of learning, the naturalist above all, whose ideal everywhere is nature, can never degenerate in the wilderness.

If some of us view with disgust the life of the upper and

highest classes among the modern Egyptians, the cause is not far to seek. All their thoughts and actions centre on the vile greed of money and shameless bondage to Mammon; things which cannot find an equivalent in hard cash are beyond the pale of their understanding. Here we see men without character, without national feeling, without conscience, from cowardice as incapable of crime as from mean-spiritedness they are incapable of any noble action. But we should be guilty of manifest injustice in judging of the character of the people were we to allow our disgust for a class to set us against the whole. If the poor appear covetous, the oppressed cowardly, that by no means proves that in the totality of their good qualities they might not be placed far above us Europeans, who under a less favourable sky enjoy immensely more favourable social conditions. But in order to hold the balance quite true we must always, in forming our judgments, keep in mind to compare like with like; and in this most observers fail, for it is as a rule the fortunate lot of our middle classes that they have before their eyes when they venture to describe the manners and customs of the common people of Egypt. Such writers have often indeed no thorough knowledge of our own working classes. In fact, however, the Fellahin are only to be compared with the dregs of our lowest social strata, and looked at from this point of view, they cannot but appear to us worthy of admiration. Deprived of almost all means of self-cultivation, and without any pattern of morality above them worthy of being imitated, they grow up quite like savages; nevertheless, we see them excelling in several virtues which only the wisest among us practise, and that only with an effort. Their life is the most regular and orderly possible, and they are the most courteous and mannerly people in the world.

Apart from his intimacy with a large number of people belonging to the middle and lower classes in various parts of Egypt, the author naturally enjoyed also special privileges as government physician. It is part of the diagnostic penetration of a doctor to be able to sound the depths of the human heart. Such knowledge and experience as may be thus obtained ought not to remain the property of one man. As early as my first visit I recommended my friend to cultivate the field of Egyptian manners and customs so long lying fallow, advising him to take Lane as his model, and produce an appendix to the Bædeker of the future.

My wishes have been fulfilled. Egypt, too, has now got its Bædeker, a guide through the ancient land of wonders that puts all previous guide-books quite in the shade, and Klunzinger's descriptions will in future be an indispensable addition to the library of every Nile tourist, however small it may be.

More than forty years have elapsed since Edward Lane gave his *Manners and Customs of the Modern Egyptians* to the world. His descriptions are unsurpassed; they have acquired indeed in the course of years a certain reputation of classicality, and the best proof of the impossibility of superseding them is the circumstance that no author has ventured to follow his footsteps by an independent path.

Great, however, is the number of works which have appeared within the period mentioned, having for their subject the land of Egypt and its people. Whole ranges of volumes have been entirely filled with court histories and palace intrigues of the time of Mehemed Ali, narrated often by people who themselves had come to ruin in the empty show and bustle of the world of the great. Then came fantastically tricked out romances and gossipy anecdotes dished up in the hotels of Cairo, these productions appearing as "Secrets of Egypt," and running through the world as cheap railway reading. A flood of cursory Recollections of Travel, in which experiences during a three months' voyage by dahabiyeh were related—or even less than this—alternated with works on special subjects written by hands possessed both of knowledge and skill. The German literature of travel has no reason to be ashamed so far as concerns the latter class, and works such as those of a Von Kremer, a Lütke, or a Stephan have enjoyed a favourable reception in the widest circles; yet, in the study of popular customs, none of these could pretend to rival the descriptions of a man who, like Dr. Klunzinger, has devoted so much time and industry to this subject, and whose knowledge of the Arabic language of every-day life has rarely been equalled in Egypt itself.[1]

The present work, which, even in its external form and its arrangement of matter, is throughout new and peculiar, is indeed to be recommended as a gift to the inquiring public, and as filling up a still remaining blank in our knowledge of modern Egypt. Lane, however trustworthy and complete his descriptions may be, concerned himself in the main with such conditions of life as exist in a large town only. A weak point in his work is its insufficient description of the Egyptian Christians. His field of observation was the old and splendid city of the Caliphs, with the innumerable festivals and the pleasure-loving populace of an absolute monarch's capital. Ægypto-Arabic manners and customs are in Klunzinger's sketches clothed in a slighter garb, but the pictures appear all the more plain and natural.

It is not the author's way to obtrude himself upon his readers as a censor of morals, to draw judgments and conclusions from the relations he describes where the actual facts enable any one to form a judgment for himself. And he has done well in avoiding this dangerous rock, seeing the ideas of men are as multiform as their heads. At least he escapes in this way the scornful remark of the stay-at-home wiseacre who would tell him that there is no reason for censure, if one who has spent the best years of his life among

---

[1] Dr. Klunzinger is preparing for immediate publication an extensive work on the common Arabic idiom employed in Egypt.

people at such a stage of civilization shows himself but little practised in logical thinking.

The author's chief endeavour was that the facts should speak. A soul overflowing with poetry will perhaps miss the descriptions of nature which are usually employed as the setting for a picture of manners, and if so also the idyllic atmosphere with which our writers, often infected with the "world-pain," or some other superstition, think they enliven their descriptions. In the matter-of-fact eyes of an investigator, such as a physician or zoologist, the All has no permanence; as his scalpel separates the fibres of the most mysterious tissues in which the unconscious life pulses, so his microscope throws light on a world of riddles of which the common eye has no idea. I congratulate my friend that he has not fallen into the mistake of his contemporaries, namely, of ascribing to his characters too refined, and perhaps altogether imaginary feelings, such as in their lowly sphere of life, and in the fight and struggle for a subsistence, they could not find time to have. Let others copy him—and how easy will it now be to patch up a novel with Egyptian local colouring by copying such a model.

CONTENTS.

CHAPTER I.

FOUR DAYS IN A COUNTRY TOWN.

FIRST DAY.—General Survey, 1. Entrance into a Town—The Houses, 3. Street Traffic—Donkey boys, 5. The Great Man, 8. The Bazar, 9. Industrial Survey, 11. Survey of the People, 16. Dress, 17. Types of the Market, 20. A Street Quarrel, 23. The Market and the Women, 23. A Coffee-house, 24. Greek Tavern, 27. Native Beer-shops, 28. Dancing Girls, 30. Night and its Accompaniments, 32.

SECOND DAY.—Weekly Market, 33. A Slave Market.—Slavery, 34. Chance Meeting with Women, 40. Visit to the Interior of a House, 42. (The Courtyard, 42. The Kitchen, 43. Rooms on the Courtyard, 44. The Reception-room, 45. Taking Coffee, 47. The Terrace, 48. The Harem, 48.) Ancient Egyptian Dwelling-house, 49. Summons to a Sick Woman, 49. Revelations, 50. A Dinner, 54. Bill of Fare, 59. After Dinner, 60.

THIRD DAY.—A Public Office, 61. Coptic Scribes, 62. Officials of the Provinces, 64. Taxes and other Burdens, 67. Official Procedure, 71. The Country Judge, 75. The Hakim Pasha, 80. A Coptic Meal during a Fast, 83.

FOURTH DAY.—The Coptic Church and the Copts, 85. The Bath, 91. The Dogs, 94. Boys and Girls at Play, 95. School, 97. A Mosque, 98. A Saint's Mausoleum, 103. A Burial-place, 105.

CHAPTER II.

TRAVELLING BY LAND AND RIVER.

Preparations, 107. The Embarkation, 108. A Voyage on the Nile, 111. Eating and Drinking on Board, 116. A Journey by Land, 117. An Inn, 118. A Village, 120. The Country in the Circle of the Year, 125. The Overflow of the Nile, 125. After the Inundation, 129. The Egyptian Calendar, 130. The Time of the Small and of the Great Sun, 133. Chamasin and Early Summer, 133. Summer Culture, 134. Water-Raising Apparatus, 135. A Water-wheel, 136. Harvest, 138. A Palm Grove, 139. A Garden, 140. Field and Garden Plants, 142. The Gardens and Cultivated Plants of the Ancients, 143. The Wild Plants, 144. The Animal World, 145. Monuments of Antiquity, 155.

CHAPTER III.

WORKING DAYS AND HOLIDAYS, DAYS OF JUBILEE AND DAYS OF MOURNING.

Working-day Life of the Common People, 158. Life of the Women, 161. The Family, 166. Friday, 171. Ramadan, 171. The Great and the Little

Feast, 176. Feast of the Saints, 178. Easter Week, 182. The Night of the Drop, 184. The Nerus Day, 184. Birth-day Ceremonies, 185. Ceremonies Preliminary to Family Festivals, 187. Religious Entertainments, 191. Entertainments of the Women, 193. Circumcision, 194. Marriage, 195. Funeral Ceremonies, 199.

CHAPTER IV.

THE DESERT.

1. RIDE THROUGH THE DESERT.—Point of Departure, 204. The Camel, 205. Provender, 208. Loading and Saddling, 209. Mounting, 212. Caravan Donkeys, 214. On the March, 215. Camping at Night, 218. The Morning Camp, 220. Day March, 221. Marching at Night, 225. The Littoral Slope of the Mountains, 228.
2. THE NATURE OF THE DESERT.—Configuration of the Mountains, 229. Rain and Rain-water Streams, 230. Geological Constitution, 233. Springs, 235. Vegetation, 237. The Animals of the Desert, 240. The Naturalist in the Desert, 246.
3. INHABITANTS OF THE DESERT.—History of the Desert, 248. The Ababdeh, 250. Dress of the Ababdeh, 252. Of the Ababdeh in General, 254. Dwellings and Household Matters, 256. A Life of Hunger, 258. Employments, 259. Intellectual Qualities and Capacities, 262. Language, 263. Religion, 264. Family Life, 265. Wedding Festivities, 266. Funerals, 267.

CHAPTER V.

ON THE RED SEA.

The Red Sea, 268. The Desert Shore, 269. Ancient Settlements and Sea-port Towns, 270. History of the Sea-port of Koseir, 271. The Town, 277. Population, 277. The Markets, 278. The Water, 281. Industry, 282. The "Courts" and the Trade, 283. Custom-house, 285. The Government Grain-store, 286. The Port, 288. The Mole, 289. Arrival and Departure of Vessels, 290. The Vessels of the Red Sea, 292. The Ship's Company, 295. Navigation, 298. Use of the Compass and Stars, 300. Mariner's Calendar, 301. Traffic, 303. Fishermen, 303. Preparation of the Fish, 307. Other Marine Animals Made Use of, 308. The Pearl Fishery, 310. The Coast Bedouins, 315. The Pilgrimage to Meccah, 318. Quarantine, 328.

CHAPTER VI.

THE NATURAL TREASURES OF THE RED SEA.

The Tropical Sea—Ebb and Flow, 334. On the Shore, 335. Preparing for a Visit to the Reef, 340. The Reef, 341. Outer Shore Zone, 342. The Inner Shore or Sea-grass Zone, 345. The Division into Zones, 348. Stylophora or Coralline Zone, 348. Joys and Sorrows of the Naturalist, 349. The Inhabitants of the Stylophora Zone, 352. Life in the Pools, 353. A Nocturnal Visit to the Reef, 356. A Block of Stone, 356. Reef Pools, 358. Fish of the Pools, 360. Fauna of the Stylophora Bushes, 361. Transition or Præcoral Region, 362. Coral Zone Proper, or Surf Zone, 363. Fauna of the Surf Zone, 364. The Inhabitants of the Corals, 366. The Coral Slope, 367. The Corals, 370. The Fishes, 373.

CHAPTER VII.
POPULAR BELIEFS AND SUPERSTITIONS.

The Ginn, 382. The Man of Science and the Magicians, 383. The Magic-books, 385. The Compact with Iron and Lead, 385. Receipt for Summoning Spirits, 386. A Love-charm, 387. The Magic Mirror, 387. Other Magical Rites, 388. Fear of Spirits, 389. Talismans, 390. The Envious Eye, 391. The People of Blessing. The Saints, 392. States of Ecstasy, 394. The Sâr, 395. Popular Medicine, 397. The Animals in Popular Belief, 400. Alchemy, 403. Religio-astronomical Fantasies, 404. Astrology, 405. Geomantists and Gypsies, 406. The Future, 406. The Day of Judgment, 407.

LIST OF ILLUSTRATIONS.

PAGE ILLUSTRATIONS.

	PAGE
Koseir, looking over the Market-place,	*Frontispiece.*
The Caravanserai of Bir Amber,	204
Koseir from the Sea,	276
Travelling Dervishes and Free Negro of Darfur,	326

ILLUSTRATIONS IN TEXT.

Manfalut, on the Nile,	xvi
Shop of a Retail Dealer,	10
A Borer of Pipe Stems,	12
Woman and Child of Upper Egypt,	53
Coptic Scribe,	63
Mausoleum of a Saint,	104
Pigeon-houses,	120
Dancing-girl,	189
Camel's Saddle,	210
An Ababdeh Man,	251
Ababdeh Boys,	252
Ababdeh Woman,	253
Ababdeh Tent,	257
Ababdeh Tobacco Pipes,	267
Mariner's Lute,	297
Black Fisherman making Thread with the Spindle,	305
Native Fisherman spinning Twine,	305
Vessel used in the Pearl-fishery,	310
Tent of Coast-Bedouins,	316
Fellah Pilgrims at Koseir,	320

Manfalut, on the Nile.

UPPER EGYPT.

CHAPTER I.

FOUR DAYS IN A COUNTRY TOWN.

FIRST DAY.

WE are standing upon a mound of rubbish entirely destitute of vegetation, above us the deep blue cloudless vault of heaven; a gentle north wind guards us from being scorched by the glowing rays of a vertical sun; so dry and transparent is the atmosphere that the eye can wander unimpeded to the distant horizon, and take in every detail of the surrounding landscape. Verdant crops, interspersed at intervals by groves of palm-trees, clothe the level valley that stretches away towards the north; and through it a large river pursues its winding course, lending moisture and fertilization to the arid soil. Eastwards and westwards the green valley is bounded—the line of separation being sharply defined—by the bare, yellowish-gray desert, which sometimes loses itself in gently rising plateaus over which the eye cannot reach, sometimes terminates suddenly in precipitous rocky hills.

At our feet lies a confused and labyrinthine collection of houses forming a considerable town. The houses, built of crude unburnt bricks, are mostly one story high, flat-roofed pierced with few apertures for light, and often growing narrower towards the top in the antique style. Amidst these rise a number of tall minarets, large cupolas with their vaulted roofs, and neat quadrangular battlemented towers, the last having their walls pierced with numerous holes in which the pigeons carry on their busy traffic, while the grayish clay-colour of the houses is richly relieved by the perennial green of the palms and other trees interspersed among them. Most of the buildings show signs of decay, and a considerable portion of the town is in ruins. With difficulty we make out streets and thoroughfares in this labyrinth, the houses, standing apart from each other, and being arranged in rows; and here and there larger areas are left free from buildings. In these open spaces we next observe the thronging and movement of human traffic like the globules in the capillary blood-vessels.

In the general murmur arising from this mass of human dwellings the ear can distinguish the harsh barking of numerous dogs, the trumpet-like and painful bray of asses, the angry roar of stubborn camels, the shouts and calls of street-boys at play, and the warnings of the scampering donkey-boys; while from the markets rise the ceaseless cries of the brokers and petty dealers, from the battlements of the towers the clear voice of the muezzin calling to prayer, and now and again we catch also the quavering strains of some love-sick youth, or the feast-enlivening notes of a pipe with an accompaniment of drums and clapping of hands.

No rumble of carriages is heard as in the busy North; tall chimneys have not yet gained the victory over the towers of palaces, temples, and pigeon-houses; the voices of men and animals are not yet drowned by the buzz of machinery, or the knocking and hammering of manufacturing industry.

In a shady grove in front of the town a man with a full beard and expressive features is seriously and quietly spreading a carpet on the ground; his head is covered with a large roll of linen, the turban; his body, bronzed of a deep brown colour, is enveloped in a full toga with wide sleeves, reaching down to his feet; he takes off his red slippers, steps devoutly and composedly on the carpet, turns his face towards the south-east according to an invariable rule, and prostrates himself before the Almighty. In another spot sits or squats a son of the country, who in contemplative mood imbibes from a long pipe and a tiny cup the permitted luxuries of tobacco and coffee. Round the walls of the house before us a ghost-like being steals, the whole figure from the crown of the head to the feet—which are alone visible—carefully enveloped in a wide mantle, which falls in numerous folds; we are told that it is one of the fair sex.

We have seen enough, even though we had been carried away by a genie in the darkness of night and set down here on this mound of débris, to let us know that we are standing before a town in the Mohammedan East, far away from Central Europe, much farther even for the imagination to reach than the land of the West beyond the Atlantic. We are on the classic soil of the primeval Nile, far up in the south of Egypt, where the Mercury of the nineteenth century has indeed begun already to stretch out his wire feelers, where he goes and comes occasionally with his steam-pinioned sandals on road and liquid highway, leading after him the narrow-trousered bearers of civilization, but where he does not yet feel himself at home, and where the people rejoice in their aboriginal state of existence.

ENTRANCE INTO A TOWN—THE HOUSES

We descend and make our way towards the confused mass of houses. No rampart surrounds the town, but the outermost houses form a close barrier, in which here a regular archway, there an open street, there again a narrow doorway affords an entrance, or a ruinous building forms a breach which no one thinks of building up. The best way is to follow the raised causeway, which winds along towards the town, and during the time when the river is high and the country around covered with water, conducts the passenger without danger into the midst of the houses. The street into which we enter is not much broader than the causeway, which barely allows two riders to pass. It leads us gradually onwards, widening and narrowing, twisting and turning, sinking and rising. The walls of the houses display little of geometrical accuracy; the line of direction is often broken and bent, though each individual house has an approximately rectangular type.

In such a provincial town the houses are seldom of more than one story; nothing meets the gaze but a bare gray wall of clay, seldom plastered, and often common to a whole stretch of houses. Very different are the houses here from those of Cairo, with their numerous projecting windows; here we see little externally but a few small air-holes, and even these are mostly closed by a wooden lattice. In this way the interior is shut off and secluded from the outer world. Air and light enter the rooms from the court-yard, which is entirely surrounded by the house. The wall is constructed of rough unburned bricks of a longish rectangular form, such as those used by the ancient Egyptians for their private dwellings, and then always stamped with the government mark. These bricks, still called by their ancient name *tub*, are a material suited only for rainless districts such as this; a heavy rain of some duration would soon convert a town so built into a ruinous heap, a convincing proof that the climate of Upper Egypt in ancient times was quite as dry as at the present.

Two things, however, arrest attention—the gateway of the house and the pigeon-tower, which adjoins or surmounts so many of the buildings. The sides and top of the gateway must possess a certain amount of solidity, which is secured by the use of squared stones, burned bricks, and cross-beams, and advantage is taken of these to produce at the same time something of architectural ornament, by the interchange of colours and a kind of mosaic arrangement. Less success is attained when attempts at painting or sculpture are made, the Arabic artist only succeeding in producing hideous childish caricatures. The Hâdj, that is, one who has made a pilgrimage to Mecca, is fond of distinguishing his house by such bizarre gate-paintings. Among the ancient Egyptians also the pilgrimage to a temple was an exploit that was painted on the houses. To neutralize the glance of the envious it is common to put quotations from the Koran over the entrance to the house; and to turn aside the evil-eye, a stuffed monster, such as a crocodile, or it may be an aloe plant, is often fixed above the entrance. The ancient Egyptians were likewise in the habit of putting inscriptions and symbols of good omen in the same place. In the middle of the large gate, which is only opened to admit objects of large size, there is usually a small door through which persons and the smaller animals pass out and in.

The pigeon-towers, which are either placed in groups on the tops of the houses, or rise singly by themselves, now in the shape of cubes, now narrowing towards the top, after the style of the ancient temples, form a large—often indeed the largest—portion of the buildings. They give to the houses of the towns and villages of Upper Egypt a characteristic and distinguished appearance. Chimneys are wholly wanting, and in their stead are erected on the tops of many houses short sloping structures of boards projecting above the roof, and having a vertical side open towards the north, to catch the cooling wind and afford a shade; such was also the practice among the ancient Egyptians.

STREET TRAFFIC—DONKEY-BOYS.

In the provincial town the Old World and the New have not yet, as in the capital, come into dangerous collision. Here none of that hurried driving and running is seen, none of those carriages that whirl noisily along, and may have bumped the back of the pedestrian before he has had time to distinguish the warning cries of the driver. Everything proceeds at a measured pace; and if, at any time when lost in thought, a person suddenly feels the grinning jaws of a camel in his neck, or a donkey running lightly along treads on his heels, he has always time to step aside, if the circumspect beasts do not do so of themselves. The nearer we approach the chief centre of traffic—the market-place—the greater grows the bustle. A push, a kick, or a collision with some one of our fellow-men, demonstrates to us the existence of a non-ego. Behind us we hear youthful voices shouting nearer and nearer to our ear, and warning us to take care of our back, our legs, our head, and whatever about us is liable to be broken. These are the famous donkey-boys, who, themselves running behind, are driving a company of riders at a gallop through the bustling crowds and narrow streets to the place of their destination. The somewhat sluggish disposition of their long-eared charges is animated by continued cudgelling, or if the blows fall harmlessly on a hide rendered callous by long custom, a stick is driven into their sores, which are thus continually kept open. At the same time plenty of abuse is poured out upon the animal, the favourite epithets "son of a dog," "son of a Christian," "son of a Jew," being followed by a prolonged emphatic "Ha, Ha" such as only a genuine Arab is able to produce, and then by a strong push against the lean hind-quarters of the beast, which is thus driven forwards and sideways. The bold notion comes into our head that we will also mount a donkey; but the donkey-boys that have their stand hard by are quicker than the thought. Already half a dozen have surrounded us before we have made up our mind. Rescue or flight is no longer possible; a speedy choice alone remains. An angry glance around, a stick brandished threateningly, and the quarrelling, scuffling crowd around our person is scattered, towards which result the boy of our selection has effectively contributed.

The donkey-driver, throughout the whole of Egypt, is the same brazen-faced poltroon, but at the same time a really good-natured fellow so soon as one has become better acquainted with him. In the provinces of the interior he has fewer opportunities for cultivating his linguistic talent than in the capital; here he does not address us in the rich Alexandrian mosaic language of the *lingua franca*— "*Nigi ya musyo, voulez ride good esel, un abrico theyib, bono,*" which means "shall we come, oh sir; will you ride good donkey, a donkey good good." The donkey-boys are wonderfully quick at detecting the nationality of a traveller, and when offering their donkeys for hire regularly call them —of course only for the occasion—by the name of some public man belonging to the same country as the stranger. An Englishman accordingly may find himself urged to accept the services of "John Bright" as a German would be offered those of "Bismarck."

Well, we are now firmly seated, and shoot forwards with hanging reins, but require to be constantly on the alert to preserve our equilibrium, since the *vis a tergo* of the cudgel-wielder falls now to right, now to left, and the latter end of the beast we bestride always turns suddenly and instinctively to the opposite side to that on which the blows fall. Scarcely has our donkey begun to trip along in his not uncomfortable trot when a general stoppage of the current of traffic in the street brings him to a sudden halt. A camel that carries upon his ribs a load projecting at each side like a pair of expanded wings has failed to keep right in the middle when turning the corner at a bend of the street, allowing space only for the width of his own body, and so has struck against the corner. He has accordingly to be pulled back for some paces, and gradually led into the middle of the street. Immediately after the removal of this obstacle, and when traffic has again begun to circulate, we see a laden donkey lying on the ground at another corner; it has been the same with him as with the camel, but the collision with the corner has disturbed the equilibrium of the excessive load upon his back, and his burden being out of all proportion to his strength he has not been able to keep his feet.

Annoyed at the continual stoppages we dismount, and prefer to rely upon our own personal agility. We thrust a few copper coins into the hand of the donkey-boy, who is always discontented when he has to deal with a Frank, and besides what he ought to get always insists upon *Backshish*[1], that gratuity of so many significations, the name of which continues to haunt a stranger who has been in Egypt. According to humour and disposition, and in order to avoid a row, we satisfy the impudent demand either by giving something more or by making a threatening movement with our uplifted stick. A native who knows the charges gives him half what we have given; the youngster kisses the gift thankfully, and, without looking how much it

---

[1] This word is Persian, and is generally used in addressing Europeans only; it seems also to have entered the country with the Europeans, since at the French period the natives still used the words *Fáda, Fáda*, in begging.

is, thrusts it into his bosom, into the folds of his turban, or into his ear. The European, however, must at all times and in all places pay too much; but on the other hand, he is an object of the most abject outward respect throughout all Egypt, on account of his ability to pay, his power, his energy and acknowledged cleverness, less perhaps in virtue of his moral superiority.

THE GREAT MAN.

What is the meaning of this? Those who were walking rapidly stop and remain still, whoever was sitting stands up, pipes or cigarettes are taken from the mouth, animated conversation ceases, scolding and quarrelling are at an end, the parties bending their heads and remaining motionless, groups step aside, and right and left a wall of people is formed. Out of the multitude that parts on either side springs a swift-footed light-clad young fellow, with dress tucked high up, holding a rod in his hand; this is the avant-courier. After him, and seated high on horseback, or on a snow-white ass of noble race, as tall as a horse, trots a wide-trousered Turk[1], followed by a crowd of heavily-armed Turkish police-soldiers panting after him, and a number of domestics and slaves. The great man, after the manner of Islam, first graciously salutes the citizens standing rooted in reverence on either side of him, while they bending low raise dust from the ground as a mark of their subjection, and carry it to their mouths to kiss, testifying to the sincerity of their respect by laying their hand on their forehead and their heart. This Turk of high rank is the *Mudir*, the head man of the province. The pomp, without which he never stirs from his house, is the passion and necessity of the race to which he belongs, and clothes him at the same time, to the eyes of the people, in the precious nimbus of majesty.

[1] In modern times, however, officials of high rank must appear in a suit of European black.

THE BAZAR.

We follow the human current for a few steps farther and reach the centre of traffic, the market, or as the European and Turk, but seldom the Arab, are wont to call it, the bazar. The wide open spaces of the town are only intended for shady hours and on certain days of the week for the sale of provisions, the retail trade on the other hand goes on in the narrow streets, where the shops are situated. In these streets there is a continual twilight either from the closeness of the houses to each other or from an awning stretched above from side to side, so that the hottest periods of the day or year can here be passed in comfort. The shops consist of rows of low-roofed cells formed in the ground story of dwelling-houses, or situated in special long, low buildings. We have heard a great deal of the splendid bazars of the luxurious East, and there was perhaps some excuse for our ancestors waxing enthusiastic over them at a time when European industry and Europe generally was far behind the wealthy East in the production of costly merchandise; but at the present day a bazar, even in the larger towns of Upper Egypt, appears poor and insignificant when compared with the handsome shops of Europe. The Arab dealer is perhaps not altogether in the wrong in not giving to his little shop the splendid exterior which consumes a considerable part of the capital required to start the business, and behind which often enough hollow-eyed bankruptcy lies in wait. The finest and richest native shop in one of the towns of Upper Egypt is, as a rule, inferior in outward appearance to a petty retail-shop in the outskirts of a European town, or even to the booth that a wandering trader takes round with him to country fairs. In the provinces it consists at best of a quadrangular chamber, raised some feet above the level of the street, only high enough to let a person stand upright, so that prayers may be duly performed in it, and usually measuring less in the other dimensions. The few goods that are kept in stock are piled up openly on some rough shelves or benches in the back part. Some pieces of cloth and finery hang from the upper half of the door, which half is raised so as to project in the manner of a roof, while the lower half is let down, or is extended outwards tablewise in order to add to the surface of the shop-floor. Here and there also a case with a glass top displays a variety of small ornamental wares. Large bills and tickets need not be looked for here; while few can read a written announcement

Shop of a Retail Dealer.

what is in the shop can be seen by any one. The only pieces of writing that are stuck up are passages from the Koran. An outspread carpet and a few cushions are all that the easy-going shopkeeper requires in the way of comfort, and there he sits with his legs crossed, a long pipe or a paper cigarette in his mouth, and waits for purchasers in silent dignity. Another, who cares still less for show, drags his wares day after day out of the dark store-room behind into the doorless hole of a shop, fills his straw baskets with them, and sets them out for show upon old boxes or crates made of palm twigs, while lighter goods flutter picturesquely from extended cords and poles.

INDUSTRIAL SURVEY.

The workshops of the artisans differ little from the booths of the shopkeepers, and the occupations of these people are carried on in full publicity. By a very ancient rule the market people arrange themselves generally according to trades and guilds; but in the provinces, where the division of labour is not so well marked, this system is carried out to a less extent than in the capital. This arrangement does not seem to be prejudicial to the individual society. From the quiet district of the grocery and drug shops one can pass to the noisy quarters occupied by the tinsmiths and coppersmiths; from the savoury hearths of the cooks to the vile holes of the tanners. Let us make the round of the industrial establishments. At the present day any one who undertakes a journey of investigation with the view of adopting from the industries of foreign peoples anything that may be advantageous for his native land, will certainly turn his steps last to that country from which, in former times, the first light of civilization shone over the world. Still an industrial inspection is here by no means devoid of interest, seeing that we find, beyond doubt, a picture of the handicrafts practised by the venerable fathers of the human race, and very often living images of the ancient Egyptian forefathers themselves. The principle that prevails throughout the industries of the modern Egyptians is to produce from cheap readily procured materials articles that "will do," without regard to durability, accuracy, and taste.

We halt in astonishment before the stall of a workman who is using a strange kind of boring-tool. Holding in one hand a bow something like a fiddle bow, the string of which he has twisted round an upright rod, he gives the rod a rapid circular movement by urging the bow backwards and forwards. In this way a piece of iron wire projecting above the rod, and having a lancet-like point, cuts its way deeper and deeper into the heart of a reed which he holds down on the top of it with his other hand. With a few strokes, which produce a scratching, rattling sound, he produces an excellent tube for a tobacco-pipe. Beside him sits an assistant or brother, the *turner.* The whole of his portable apparatus consists in a foot-board, with two small boards rising perpendicularly from it, between which the object to be turned, be it wood, bone, or amber, is firmly fixed by means of projecting pins. By the bow in his right hand this object is made to revolve on its axis, while his left hand applies the sharp steel chisel

A Borer of Pipe Stems.

that cuts the object smooth. The apparatus is steadied by planting the naked right foot upon two cross-bars, the left upon the foot-board.

The cabinet-maker or carpenter—in Arabic there is but one name for both, *neggâr*—has neither a bench, nor in general a vice. What would be the use of such an expensive appliance? He squats upon the board that he is to plane and hew, supports his log with his foot, or in the case of finer work takes the object between the second and the great toe of his prehensile foot, as the ancient Egyptians did; his teeth even serve instead of a tool. Instead of a rule he is generally satisfied with a cord or a palm twig, on which he marks his measurements, and for a pair of compasses he uses a cord with a piece of wire stuck through it as a centre. His boring tool resembles the instrument of the pipemaker, and like it dates from ancient Egyptian times. It is a piece of iron wire with one of its ends flattened to a lancet shape, inserted in a wooden cylinder. The upper end of the wire enters into a hollow knob, which in most cases consists of a doom-nut (the fruit of the doom-palm). The cylinder is made to revolve by the bow already mentioned. The manipulation of this boring-brace in the hands of the Arabic artisan seems easy and playful; the unaccustomed Frank prefers a gimlet. The chief tool of the carpenter is the small axe, in the use of which he displays great dexterity.

The tinsmith, the locksmith, and the silversmith use a remarkable kind of bellows. A little heap of earth is pierced by a piece of an old gun barrel, one end of which is directed towards the fire, this consisting of a little heap of coals kept together by a few loose stones. The bellows part consists of a goatskin, probably an old water skin, of a conical form, ending in a point, which is attached to the other extremity of the tube. In the posterior part of the skin is cut a transverse slit, the edges of which are strengthened by slips of wood. In the back of the stall squats the plump-cheeked apprentice boy, who with the fingers of one hand works the valve of the bellows, raising it so as to open the slit, and then depressing it so as to close it, when the air, being expelled, passes under the heap of earth through the tube and acts upon the fire.

The bellows of the blacksmith is somewhat more complicated. Behind a sloping wall of boards are two large cylindrical leather bags, strengthened by a number of wooden hoops, and both closed posteriorly by a wooden bottom, with an air-hole and with a valve. By a very simple arrangement —namely, several wooden bars fastened perpendicularly to the wooden bottom of the bellows, and having a kind of hinge movement on a foot-board below by means of an iron ring —the two air-holders are alternately made to take in and give out air through the backward and forward motion given to them by a young fellow standing upon the foot-board. The air-bags converge, and terminate first in two separate tubes, then in one common one, and the air-current is directed upon the front part of the hearth, which consists of an earthen mound surrounded with rough stones. The Arabic Vulcan has on his raggedest clothes, or it may be is bare to the thighs on account of the heat. The ceiling of the roomy smithy is festooned with hanging rags or fragments of straw matting, for it is his belief that elegance of appointments does not help work forward. A knotty undressed piece of wood, as it grew from the soil, contents him for a handle to his hammer as well as if it were of the most finished kind.

We cast a glance into the open booths of the tailors, shoemakers, saddlers, lacemakers, tinsmiths, coppersmiths or braziers, the mat and basket weavers, and enter the more retired and half-open premises of the tanners, indigo-dyers, weavers, bakers, and potters. A bed-cover maker is loosening into a fleecy mass, with the tightened string of a bow-shaped instrument, a quantity of old cotton which has become lumpy. The silver and gold smith melts down the fine gold of old zechins and Austrian ducats as well as the silver mixed with tin of the Maria Theresa dollars, and manufactures from them very handsome and highly prized trinkets by the help of some matrices, a simple conical blow-pipe, pincers, and hammer. The fondness of the Egyptian women for gold and silver ornaments enables such a goldsmith to do a thriving trade in every small town. The manufacture of glass, which had its native country in ancient Egypt and not in Phœnicia, and here was once so famous, has greatly declined, and now only a few wretched productions are turned out Almost all goods made of glass, as well as of porcelain, even the coffee-cups in such general use, and which are scarcely to be had in Europe, are now brought from the land of the Franks. The manufacture of pottery, on the other hand, in some places of Upper Egypt, as Keneh, Balas, Siout, is in a very flourishing state, the processes scarcely differing from those employed in Europe. The products are a porous, unglazed ware, and the vessels still have the same shapes as those depicted in the ancient Egyptian tombs. The large handled jars of Balas, named after that village, are fastened together into rafts and by this means are transported by water.

We observe also the dexterity of the barber, here as elsewhere always loquacious. He scrapes bare all craniums that come under his hands, and has, therefore, acquired a quite astounding facility in shaving; his customer complacently views his magnified features in the concave mirror which is held before him by its handle. A patient may here get himself cupped, the barber making cruciform incisions with his razor on any affected part, and the cup being formed of a conical-shaped horn with a leather valve at top, from which the air is sucked by the mouth so as to make the blood flow freely.

In the mill, located in the lower part of a house, we see a horse walking round in a circle; he carries a rough trunk of a tree on his neck, and with it sets in motion a cylinder, a toothed wheel, and a millstone. The latter receives the grain from a hopper, and lower down the flour and bran, ground and mixed together, stream out. We learn that the wind-mills formerly introduced by the French, and still visible at a distance on many an elevation, do not generally succeed, and that the "steam flour," that is, the fine flour of the steam-mills, already enjoys a continually increasing sale. Much flour is also made in the houses by means of a hand-mill, the basis of which is also the millstone. It always demands great strength, and the grinding is done by strong female slaves, or by women of the lowest ranks. The work begins at the first dawn of day; and the women are fond of joining in grinding parties, at which they sing peculiar monotonous grinding-songs, and keep hands and tongues both going.

A *kafaz-maker* manufactures from the fresh twigs of the date-palm a multitude of cheap articles in basket-work, such as bedsteads, chairs, benches, cages, and crates for all kinds of brittle wares, as glass, clay pitchers, &c. From the prevailing scarcity of wood, palm twigs are very serviceable for this purpose. These articles, however, have the unfortunate peculiarity of furnishing excellent lurking-places for bugs.

The Egyptian artisan is dexterous and quick at learning. He excites astonishment indeed when we consider the rudeness of his implements. It can at once be told, however, whether an article has been made by an Arab or a European. The natives know this very well themselves, and have a keen sense of their own inferiority in such matters. An Arab chair never stands quite firm on its feet, a table or a door is always a little off the truth, a trunk or box always gapes about the lid, a tin-case has always the joints smeared with solder, the corners too sharp, or has a small hole somewhere.

The native artisan learns from his childhood onwards; so soon as he can walk and speak he passes the greater part of the day in his father's workshop, and helps or hinders as much as he can. The son becomes apprentice as a matter of course, then journeyman, and lastly his father's successor in business. When a man has no son he buys himself a slave and teaches him his trade. As soon as the young fellow is as far advanced as his father he is master of his trade; to wish to know more would be presumption. If the master becomes old and feeble he is supported by the gratitude of his apprentices and sons.

We may add that every one can drive what trade he pleases, since industrial freedom has always prevailed in the Mohammedan East. Among the ancient Egyptians, on the other hand, trades were rigidly exclusive; no artisan could, on peril of punishment, encroach upon the trade of another, and the son always followed the calling of the father.

SURVEY OF THE PEOPLE.

Having become acquainted with the general features of bazar life, let us step aside and enter some shop or other in order that we may quietly, and at leisure, observe how the current of street life flows on. The owner gives us a friendly invitation to seat ourselves beside him on the shop-bench, quickly orders refreshments from the neighbouring coffee-house, and offers us a chibouk. Man after man crosses the open doorway as we gaze; our thoughts begin to become dreamy, we see passing bodily before us all the figures that stirred our enthusiasm in our youthful days when we read the Arabic stories of the Thousand and One Nights. There is Ali Baba, who discovered the cave of the Forty Thieves; there the old cobbler Baba Mustafa; there the merchant Ali Chuge, who concealed his money in olives; there the fortunate Aladdin, who found the wonderful lamp; there are they all, the Hassans, the Hossens, the Ibrahims, the Ahmeds. It is more than ten hundred years since Harun er Rashid rustled past; many a thing is changed in the great world since; no mighty Khalif rules any longer over the faithful; but the people, at least those who speak the Arabic language and profess the religion of Islam, do not differ notably in speech, dress, and habits from the type of their ancestors. We shall even go farther. Let us pick out at random a man belonging to the common people of Upper Egypt and divest him of his modern outer dress (loose shirt and turban), let us strip him of his undoubtedly thick varnish of Mohammedanism, or it may be of Christianity, take from him his pipe, his coffee, and his beard, and there stands before us a genuine native of Kemi. He will be sure to exhibit the same slim yet strong limbs, the broad chest, the same type of face with its broad cheeks, projecting lips, wide nostrils, and almond eyes; also the same solid shaven head, and in spite of all the buffets of Fate, at bottom the same inherited nature. In Upper Egypt, too, we find, lastly, a multitude of individual customs and usages dating from the great Pharaonic period, which have partly been transmitted directly by tradition, and partly have become naturalized in Islam indirectly through Judaism.

DRESS.

In his dress the oriental does not allow himself to be tyrannized over by the despotism of fashion; taste has the fullest play subject to certain unchangeable rules. It is only the higher officials, from the head clerk and the doctor upwards, who require in modern times, even in the provinces,

2

to follow the dictates of a higher will, and provide themselves with a black Europæo-Turkish suit (with a standing collar on the coat), this being regarded as the basis of all civilization. The man of the lower ranks in the towns wears a kind of loose shirt or blouse of cotton reaching to the feet, or somewhat shorter, with or oftener without a girdle. Underneath this he has a kind of short, light drawers, or only a thigh-cloth round his middle. The shirt is only laid aside when the wearer is engaged in hard, wet, or dirty work. The ancients were still less particular about this matter; the workman, the warrior, even the king in the heat of battle exposed himself with nothing on but a short loin-cloth or apron. The well-formed hairy breast is seen through the broad triangular opening in the front of the shirt, or is concealed by a bright-coloured, striped waistcoat, which is put on under, or even over it. The colour of the shirt that is worn by the black natives of Soudan and the light-tinted Bedouins is white; but the thrifty Egyptian of the towns, who is never in a hurry to change his linen, more prudently wears generally a blue one. The peasant of Upper Egypt, on the other hand, wears even in summer a wide, coarse woollen shirt of a brown colour—a mark by which he may be at once recognized—and his sleeves, which are wide enough to admit the body of a man, hang down almost to his ankles. Countryman as well as townsman, when he goes afield, always carries with him his *milayeh*, a kind of plaid or shawl of a striped pattern, fringed at both ends, and worn round the shoulders. This article of dress serves for many different purposes, being used to keep its owner warm in winter, as a cushion for his head when lying down, as a carpet, as a screen from the sun, as a wrapper to put purchases into, as receptacle for provender, and as a table-cloth.

The feet, hardened by early practice, are bare, or are covered with bright-red leather slippers, generally somewhat peaked in front, or sometimes sandals are used. Stockings or boots, as being obstructive to the practice of religion, are little worn; the head is all the more carefully attended too. Youths and many of the labouring class must be contented with a white cap of cotton stuff fitting closely to the head, and leaving the ears free. Youths of a more advanced age or higher standing wear above this a red cap of fine cloth, called *tarbush*, in Turkish *fez* (those of European cloth are not liked by the natives), from which hangs down a bold tassel of blue silk. The tarbush or fez is usually bought only once in a lifetime, or descends by inheritance from generation to generation, till no trace of its original colour remains. Grown up men wear besides the fez the turban, which is usually white or red; among the descendants of the Prophet green, among the Kopts black or blue. The turban, which may be regarded as the symbol of Islam, consists of a piece of gauzy material of immense length wound round and round the fez a great many times. It forms a picturesque and imposing but somewhat heavy head-dress. Some Fellahs, as well as the dervishes, wear a thick felt cap of the form of an inverted flower-pot or of a sugar-loaf. The Bedouin of the East, and many of the inhabitants of the towns, have bright-coloured cloths, often of silk, fluttering about their head and shoulders as a protection against the sun and weather. In the stormy days of winter the native is concerned before everything about the protection of his bare shaved head, since, in spite of the turban, it is only about his head and neck that he seems to feel the cold, his lower extremities being left naked as usual. The winter mantle of black, or white, or striped woollen cloth is then drawn over the head, or only the hood, which is attached to the mantle above. The long striped kaftan, which hangs loosely from the neck down to the heels, and is confined by a Tripoli silk or cashmere girdle, belongs to the better classes. Above it is worn a wide-armed blue-black garment like a toga. The elegant Arab gentleman puts on above the costly and brightly-striped silken kaftan, a coat of fine cloth, simply but generally brightly coloured, open in front, as long as the body, and mostly of a very simple cut. The Turk, with all who affect the title of Effendi, flings himself into a jacket, and those wide many-folded trousers, the superfluous cloth of which dangles coquettishly like a sack behind. In his girdle the warlike Turk sticks daggers and pistols, the peaceful "son of an Arab" (so the Egyptian calls himself, Arab meaning Bedouin) an ink-bottle. There is a comfortable dress worn, especially by semi-orientals, such as Levantines, Jews, or Syrians, and even regarded as fashionable on the street and in the reception-room, consisting in a combination of the kaftan (usually a simple white one) with the Turkish jacket or the European coat, and when this is worn the turban must give way to the tarbush. The official also, so soon as his position allows, and especially in summer, exchanges his uncomfortable uniform for this easy suit, under which drawers alone are worn. Arabs even of good position do not recognize the value of proper underclothing; they wash and bathe much, and carefully; but their shirt consists of a flimsy, semi-transparent, gauzy material, which is ill-adapted for absorbing the perspiration. The costume worn by the ancient Egyptians, so far as we can judge from the figures in outline shown in their paintings, was considerably different from that of the present day. The common people wore, as already mentioned, only a cloth round the loins, or a short coat reaching to the knees, and on their heads (bare-shaven like their cheeks) a close-fitting cap like that still in use; those of higher rank had a longer coat, with a fringed skirt hanging in many folds, and confined round the thighs by a girdle, and above this again a wide woollen mantle, similar to that now worn by the people of Marocco. They wore a wig on their heads, and a carefully trimmed beard on their chin, while they had no shoes, but only sandals.

TYPES OF THE MARKET.

The loudest voice to be heard in the chorus of market people is that of the broker or auctioneer. Unweariedly he runs up and down, right and left, through the market, lifting up his arm to show off his wares, consisting, for example, of a carpet, a pistol, or an amber mouth-piece for a pipe, which he is commissioned to sell for some invisible owner. Formerly one might see a slave disposed of in this manner. A would-be purchaser at one end of the market calls out, "A hundred piasters." "A hundred piasters," he shouts, and runs down to the lower end of the market-place, where another buyer has offered $99\frac{3}{4}$ piasters, in order that the latter may know the advance. Some one in the middle now offers $100\frac{1}{4}$, and again he runs up and down proclaiming the new price. For his trouble he receives 1 meyti or 1 para per piaster, that is, one-fortieth of the selling price. He is the lion of the market, all listen to him, he knows everything and everybody, and no small part of the traffic passes through his hands. The merchant himself makes use of the brokers when he wishes to dispose of his goods quickly; or the latter may buy at a low price the goods of a person who is pressed for money, in order to sell them at a profit when an opportunity offers. When he has important sales on hand the broker goes through all the town, visiting the coffee-houses, warehouses, inns, and other places of public resort, knocks at the doors of private houses, and even penetrates within the sacred precincts of the harem. His rivals in trade work hard against him, but the strongest voice and the greatest cunning gain the day.

In the second rank comes the cry of the pedlars, who sell nick-nacks on their own account. The pedlars consist mostly of children with lucifer-matches, cigarette papers, fruits, and sweets. The stationary dealers, and even the substantial merchants, also find it necessary from time to time, publicly and by word of mouth, to make known to the crowd passing the existence and excellence of their wares. This they do in stereotyped, laconic phrases, which are often in rhyme, and frequently quite poetical, and are chanted to a melody set apart for each class of goods. These cries lose their charm when translated, for example: *Ya tin ya akl es salatin*—"Figs, the food of sultans;" or as the seller of liquorice juice cries, "Oh, refresher of the body;" and so on. In a corner sit some money-changers beside a money box jingling their dollars. Scribes are to be seen everywhere, mostly Christian Kopts, who try to derive a livelihood from the ignorance of the people; even the higher class merchants make use of their services for their calculations, partly because they feel they are not equal to the task themselves, partly because it is considered the correct thing to keep a clerk.

Water-carriers, with earthen water-jar on their backs, are always ready to present the refreshing fluid in a brazen cup such as the ancient Egyptians used, and very often gratis, being engaged by some pious institution. The clinking together of two of these cups is a regular element in the hubbub of the market. Another kind of water-carrier bears on his back a large leathern bag with stumps projecting from it which vividly recall the form of the goat, its former owner. From the opening of the neck he squirts the water over the dusty street. To sprinkle smaller areas, such as the floor of a room, water is taken into the mouth and spirted out again, so that the sprinkler resembles the figure of a triton on a fountain.

A porter skips groaning along the market with a huge chest weighing more than a hundredweight on his back; he believes he makes the work easier by skipping. Heavier burdens are sometimes carried upon two wooden staves connected by cords crossing between them; this mode requires four men, who sing to keep time as they bound along. Everything is carried, and that mostly on the back, partly by men, partly by beasts of burden; wheeled carriages are not met with in any country town. The ancients made much use of carriages, but, as appears, only for war and the chase. Lighter burdens, such as water-jars, were carried by them attached to bars of wood laid across the neck and shoulders, an equal weight being hung at either end, whereas now they are carried on the head or shoulders.

Numerous beggars, mostly blind, steer boldly and safely through the stormy billows of street and market, feeling their way with their stick, and asking the reward of their poverty in words almost of command, though only indirectly addressed to the people, such as—"I ask of God the price of a loaf of bread;" or, "I am the guest of God and of the Prophet, oh God that givest abundantly!" Others stand in one spot and chant melodiously from morning to night a passage which they have learned by heart from the Koran in the expressive old Arabic tongue. A few lunatics or imbeciles, filthy and with only a few rags to cover their nakedness, wander restlessly up and down. Nobody disturbs them in their aimless occupation, and whoever attracts a friendly glance from them thinks himself lucky. For they are considered saints, favourites of God, and their blessing works wonders.

A STREET QUARREL.

A crowd suddenly collects. Some persons have come to words about an insignificant matter of business, and the affair soon degenerates into an open quarrel. Offensive words are used, gradually rising to the highest pitch of opprobrium, such spicy expressions as, "son of a dog," "brood of the Pharaohs," "infidel," "son of a monk," "pimp," "mongrel," "accurst be your father, your beard, your mother's womb," "may the grave seize you," "mischief upon you," follow one after another. A bloody issue seems unavoidable, and no police are to be seen, when an old man passing by, a sheikh, steps solemnly within the circle, and the parties separate respectfully. He makes them tell him the cause and history of the quarrel, and passes sentence or calms the contesting parties with the words *ma 'alesh* (never mind), and in a few moments the deadly enemies embrace each other, and after kissing the old man's forehead, or his hand, or the hem of his garment, march away hand in hand. Such a result, of course, does not always happen, but happens often enough.

THE MARKET AND THE WOMEN.

But what has become of the other sex all this time? Woe to her who should dare, however closely muffled up, to set foot in any part of the public market; she would lose her good name for ever. Even the charmers that flutter past from time to time, and belong to a class who set but little store by a good name, here find it necessary for decency's sake to veil themselves partially. Only here and there a solitary old peasant woman, who has lost all her charms, wanders unveiled. The strictness with which the fair sex are treated in public increases in direct proportion as we approach the sacred land of the Prophet, in saying so, however, we do not mean to say anything as to the strictness of the people's morals. The farther north we go the more these phantoms swarm, especially in the chief towns; indeed they sit there (veiled of course) like ordinary merchants in their shops.

A COFFEE-HOUSE.

The tumult allayed we proceed on our wanderings again, and find ourselves before a café. The places so called, which correspond still less than the shops to Frankish ideas of elegance and comfort, may be found in abundance in every small town and village. In style they range from the simple straw covered shed to the spacious pillared saloon not altogether devoid of architectural ornamentation, especially when they are owned by well-to-do private persons, or belong to a mosque. Elegant waiters, showily-dressed barmaids, glittering wall mirrors, are not to be seen. Even the carpet, the basis of all oriental comfort, has disappeared, and in its stead simple straw mats are spread upon the earthen floor, or on the seats of clay and stone. Or one may seat himself in front of the shop and next the street upon a seat made of palm twigs, or upon a clumsy chair woven basket-fashion. It savours somewhat of *mauvais ton* to visit a common café, and the guests belong chiefly to the lower classes; still for our good money we may venture upon one draught. For a few paras we receive a tiny cupful of the bitter muddy beverage. The native almost always drinks unsweetened coffee; the sugar is said to take away or lessen the exhilarating effect of the beverage. If we ask for coffee "alla Franka" we are not likely to get a cup of coffee with milk, or brandy, such a mixture is to a native quite inconceivable, but merely black coffee with a small lump of sugar in it. The landlord of the coffee-house is always thrown into a state of excitement by such an order, and has to send some of his satellites expressly to the market for the lump of sugar. For the future it will be better to follow the example of some of the natives who have got a sweet tooth and carry always a bit of sugar in our pocket to sweeten the bitter cup for ourselves when we pay a visit to a café. Since such a café could not afford a clerk or book-keeper, and as the proprietor himself belongs to the lowest ranks, and cannot write, he marks up each man's score with strokes upon the wall, using coffee-grounds instead of ink. The house itself is not exactly dirty, but the landlord always is so, since he sits at the fire in the middle of the room like the stoker of an engine. A large pot with hot water is always on the fire; a panikin, either without a cover or with a fragmentary one, serves to make ready any single order. The beverage prepared is excellent in spite of the fact that much of the aroma has escaped through the holes in the lid. Mokha is near, and chicory almost unknown. Roasted chickpeas are the common substitute with the thrifty, and they do not taste badly, especially when a few cloves are added, as is often done, to improve the flavour. The crushing of the roasted coffee-beans with a heavy pestle, which reduces them to a fine flour, such as coffee-mills never produce, no doubt contributes essentially to the satisfactory extraction of all the elements in the coffee. Coffee-grinding or rather pounding forms a distinct trade. At every blow of the long and heavy pestle, wielded in the two hands, the workman emits a loud groan from his chest.

The frequenters of the coffee-house, as already stated, are of the poorer sort, such as artisans, petty shop-keepers, attendants on public offices, Turkish soldiers, seldom a peasant. The civilian prefers the floor, and despises the chair standing beside him, leaving it to the more honourable customers, the Turkish soldiers to wit. One man finds it exceedingly comfortable to assume a crouching position intermediate between sitting and standing, with his knees much bent, so that his hams come within a few inches of the floor, but do not touch it; another in a similar position supports himself on the floor with his legs bent and his arms clasped round them; a third sits with his legs crossed in the well-known position in which tailors sit. This, as well as the squatting position on the floor, was common among the ancient Egyptians, and is a genuine oriental custom. They, however, were fonder of sitting upon chairs and tasteful fauteuils, and were likewise accustomed to sit resting upon one knee, a practice which is never observed now, possibly for religious reasons, since it is held that one ought to kneel and prostrate himself before God alone. In the one hand the guest holds the small cup containing the hot coffee, tasting and sipping the beverage, in the other the long pipe stem with the broad smooth amber mouth-piece to his mouth. Here a customer has laid himself down on his side, resting his head upon his elbow, the feet carelessly stretched out, there another has sunk into a deep slumber. Over there is a group of domino players lying on their bellies; in the background a rakish fellow may be noticed dallying with a hetæra.

From time to time a peculiar gurgling, bubbling sound is heard; it proceeds from the nargileh or hookah, a kind of tobacco-pipe which has scarcely established itself anywhere but in the East. A person who gives himself up to this enjoyment smokes from the chest. The smoke from the tobacco rises with a slight noise through the water in the hollow of a cocoa-nut, and being thus purified is sucked through the tube or stem, which is either flexible or made of a reed. It penetrates deep into the lungs of the smoker, and only a small portion issues from the chest again in the next expiration. It may be suspected that many, indeed most, of those who smoke the hookah put into their pipes, in addition to the innocent Persian tobacco, a little pill of hashish, the well-known narcotic prepared from Indian hemp. The peculiar odour wafted from the café betrays this unmistakably. The keeping of hashish has, to be sure, been again forbidden lately; generally, however, such ordinances are strictly enforced only for a short time after they are promulgated. Already a few may perhaps have smoked themselves into a state of the most rapturous happiness, yet the intoxication is of a mild and good-natured, often humorously loquacious kind, and is mainly characterized by mental delusions. On the whole there reigns in these resorts of the common people a stillness and gravity peculiar to the oriental. Here are never heard the wild shouting and noise which issue from the beer-shops and pot-houses of the "civilized" world. Unintentionally we have fallen into conversation with a neighbour who proves talkative. We have to smoke a pipe alternately with our friend, receiving it with the mouth-piece wet from his lips; but finally break off the conversation, as the good nature of our comrade threatens to degenerate into unblushing inquiries regarding our person and concerns.

GREEK TAVERN.

In most Egyptian towns, large and small, even in the remotest provinces, shopkeepers are to be found, almost exclusively of the Greek nation, who sell some European or Levantine commodities, such as olives, olive-oil, cheese, preserved fruits, gunpowder, toys, and nick-nacks, but especially spirituous liquors. These goods being much in request their shops become taverns. We enter one of them. It is a dark dirty place, with necessarily more room in it than in an Arab shop, since it has to serve as store as well, and barrels, boxes, and bags lie heaped in wild confusion. Arab comfort is discarded, and European has not yet taken its place; we find very few seats for the guests, and still fewer tables—the counter excepted. The owner wears the Græco-Turkish costume, with long blue trousers of coarse linen, or he may have procured a European dress, in which, however, the former barbarian still remains. An orthodox Mohammedan will not use a glass in which there has been a drop of spirits until it has been cleaned with the utmost care, and, though lying on a sick-bed, will refuse a medicine in which he scents a few drops of an alcoholic tincture, since indulgence in alcoholic liquors is one of the most awful offences possible; it is natural, therefore, that he should view with horror the establishment of such a tippling-house in the provinces, as yet but little contaminated by the Franks, and look down with the deepest contempt upon the person starting it, even though little else could be brought against the character of the latter. One may often hear abusive expressions testifying to this feeling, the epithet "tavern-keeper" figuring along with "pimp" and "hashish-smoker." Were a Mohammedan to start a spirit-shop he would soon be compelled by his fellow-believers to give it up. This "disreputable" occupation is left to Christians, and almost exclusively to Greeks. But we by no means intend to say that the Moslimin always abstain from spirituous liquors. On the contrary, they are extremely ready to learn to drink them, and soon surpass their teachers the Christians. Where the teacher sips a few glasses the follower of the Prophet swallows as many bottles of strong spirit, and the charm of forbidden indulgence leads directly to unbridled and vicious excess. One after another becomes a prey to the habit, as the steady rise of new drink-shops and the prosperity of their owners show: to be sure the taverns are never found full, for people are ashamed to show themselves there openly, so the guest slinks into a corner and sits down, or he makes a number of successive visits, in order to refresh the thirst of the inner man. So much the more drink is carried outside, especially to places which will presently be mentioned. The liquors to be had are mostly grain-spirit mixed with mastic and aniseed, and therefore becoming turbid when diluted with water; more seldom a Greek red wine, also cognac, burgundy (at least so the labels on the bottles say), and even champagne. The dear and mostly soured beer of Europe is not much thought of.

NATIVE BEER-SHOPS.

The common people, including the peasantry, more frequently drink a native beer (*búza*), which is sold in very primitive reed-huts in towns and villages, and in the time of harvest also in the field. The beer-seller, generally a Nubian, serves his guests by pouring it out of a large cauldron into a wooden dish which passes from mouth to mouth. This beer is made from malt, and is a milky, acidulous, half fermented, and therefore non-intoxicating mash, resembling the German "white beer;" it is one of the luxuries that are not forbidden. Still these shops often present a very lively scene; playing and singing are heard in them, and daughters of Eve of doubtful character may be seen going out and in. The women also drink this beer at their peculiar curative meetings, when they put themselves into an ecstasy, in the so-called *sar*. (See Chap. VII.). The beer of the ancient Egyptians, called *zythus*, was intoxicating, like that which is still so largely drunk in the Soudan and Abyssinia. On the whole, however, the drinking of alcoholic liquors is rare among the temperate and thrifty people of Egypt, in so far as the Mohammedans are concerned, while the native Christians, almost without exception, are greatly addicted to this indulgence. The peasant knows almost nothing of this luxury, and is therefore preserved from much evil. "Wine has many good qualities," says the Prophet in the Koran, "but also many bad;" indeed, as even the faithful relate, Mohammed himself is said at one period to have sometimes got tipsy, and on one such occasion to have stabbed his beloved teacher. Hence the strict prohibition. The common people of Islam indeed are distinguished from the same class in western countries essentially by their temperance and sobriety, and through the absence of drunkenness, by less rudeness, and a certain staid and dignified air. The very considerable portion of their income that western people, even the temperate among them, expend upon their gullets, keeping body and soul together only with the "necessaries," the Moslim expends on the maintenance of a family, and though drinking only water, he finds himself as healthy, strong, and capable of the severest labours as the workman of the North with his constant craving for stimulants. And this craving, when it has established itself, is not less powerful in the warm South than in the cold North. Indulgence in opium, and still more in hashish, however much the custom is reprobated, is more widely spread among the Moslimin, and that too in the class that have to represent the religion, namely, the Kadis, the Ulemas, and the Dervishes. The ancient Egyptians, as is well known, were very fond of wine, and it was not uncommon even for women to get tipsy.

DANCING GIRLS.

From the dram-shops to the quarter where live the frail sisters of the dancing profession is but a step—both actually and mentally. The occupants of both work into each other's hands; neither thrives without the other. Under the influence of alcoholic liquors a man forgets the considerations and scruples that actuate him at other times, and falls into the arms of the tempting siren beside him; once under the power of his hetæra he sends for bottle after bottle, and it becomes an easy matter for her to induce her companion, intoxicated by drink and sensual desires, to sacrifice his ready money. These dancing girls, an Egyptian institution from the earliest, even from Pharaonic times, ply their trade in large numbers in all the towns of Upper Egypt, both great and small, especially since they were expelled the capital. They boast to be descended from Barmek, the well-known favourite of the Khalif Harun er Rashid; according to some they are genuine gipsies; but with such loose morals as theirs purity of race is out of the question, and their ranks are certainly recruited from the rest of the population. They are called *Ghawâzi* (sing. *Ghazîe*), a name said to be derived from the fact that they sported before (?) the Ghus, as the old Mamelukes are called. Many writers speak of them as *Almeh*, but these are singing girls of somewhat better fame. They are not tolerated near the houses of respectable citizens, but certain streets or quarters are assigned to them, which, it must be stated, are often the very ones most frequented. Their trade is not wholly put a stop to, both because they are employed to dance at feasts, and because the wise Arab regards them as "a protection for the women," that is, they serve to keep the rakes from running after "the forbidden ones," the *harîm* or virtuous women.

Discarding scruples let us wander through the headquarters of this tolerated immorality, and, selecting afternoon as the best time, let us seize an opportunity seldom occurring of admiring the charms of the Egyptian female world in all its splendour and adornment, for otherwise the few muffled figures seen would scarcely lead us to imagine it existed. Here, then, we are met at once by three ladies, the highest of their class. Classically wide and pleasingly coloured upper garments of silk flutter around them, and a narrow, closely-fitting gown, with narrow sleeves, and made of costly materials, falls perpendicularly from the thigh to a few inches above the ankles, so as to display the bright-coloured baggy trousers, followed by a shoe of glazed leather, or a yellow slipper. The whole person from head to foot is hung and bedizened with gold ornaments, so that such a dancing girl is rendered thereby really a very valuable object. Though poor little girls only a few years ago they have made, in their line, such a skilful use of their charms and advantages that they can now show themselves off in this costly guise, and their money-box is perhaps better filled than that of many a merchant, or even a Turkish pasha. The first of the three graces is full, robust, strong as an oak, with Semitic-Arabic lengthened profile; the second, small, pale, and slender, is built in the famous full-moon style of the Arabic fables; the third, dark almost as a Moor, is modelled after the broad-cheeked sphinx type (the Egyptian sphinxes are said, however, to represent male beings) of the Fellah women, the direct descendants of the ancient Egyptian women.

We hasten away, for already we hear their peacock-voices and vulgar language which destroy the illusion. We work our way successfully through among the siren-voices of all the fair ones, whose skin varies in colour from the deepest black through coffee and nut brown to clear lead colour, but is never so fair as that which belongs to the blue-eyed, rosy-cheeked blonde. We rather admire their purple mantles, their yellow trousers, and emerald jackets, than are attracted by the fineness of their features. Convinced of the ugliness of the greater number, we endeavour to escape from the scene of their activity.

All at once a hideous fury holds her Medusa-head right before us; our footsteps thus arrested, we stand staring at her, hair on end. The woman, a member of the same trade already in the late autumn of her years but unable to believe in the loss of her charms, has attempted to smear a second youth upon her cheeks by reddening them with cinnabar; while on nose, brow, cheeks, lips, and chin, a great number of round black spots of colour show themselves very distinctly. Her thin hair, which is either her own simply smoothed down or may be false, shows here and there a clot of grease not yet melted; the rancid smell is smothered in the strong odour of a kind of musky perfume that exhales from the surface of her skin. And thus she cowers by her doorstep, puffing thick clouds from a long pipe, in the company of her gray-haired mother, who sucks away at her hookah.

With horror we turn away from her allurements and look to the other side of the street. There our glances light on a pretty childish face that smiles towards us. Fancying we have found innocence at last, we nod in a friendly manner. The dark-skinned maiden darts towards us and clings to us; we soon learn that she is an Abyssinian slave, lately purchased by a Ghawazi mother. But imagine our astonishment when we see and hear, as we must, how this lovely young thing four feet in height, and scarcely nine years of age, points to her little room, and with a bold smirk makes known her desire to receive us there. The class of dancing girls, now when the slave-trade is being abolished, is more generally than ever recruited by purchase from among such young Galla maidens.

NIGHT AND ITS ACCOMPANIMENTS.

Meantime it has become dark, and we betake ourselves to our domicile, musing on the plasticity of the human soul.

A nocturnal walk offers us little. The streets are deserted as soon as the last rays of daylight have disappeared, except at full moon and during Ramadan. Whoever now walks out carries a glass or paper lantern, otherwise he runs the risk of being taken by a night watchman to the nearest watch-house. Here and there perhaps a fruit-seller still stands, endeavouring by the scanty light of an oil-lamp to dispose of his fast decaying wares at any price they will bring; or we come upon some peaceful citizens of the poorer class conversing together as they lie stretched out on the dust in some open space. From a neighbouring dram-shop some late topers raise a sound of mirth or quarrelling. The last glimmer of human intercourse dies out round the above-described grottoes of Aphrodite and Terpsichore.

SECOND DAY.

WEEKLY MARKET.

The Moslem is a child of the day. Unlimited dominion over the dismal night he gladly leaves to the dogs, the owls, and the ghosts. But no sooner can a black thread be distinguished from a white than activity reigns everywhere, and the rising sun already sees the tide of public life in full sweep.

We too rise early and proceed to a pretty large open space. Here there is an unusual crowd of brown-skinned country people bustling about. It is the weekly market. The sellers, many of them having their wives along with them, sit on the ground, with the products of the fertile soil before them— a soil which gives two or three crops in the year, and does not cease to bear even in winter. Thus there is no lack of fresh vegetables all the year through, though there is much to be desired on the score of variety. Their wares are stowed in baskets, or are heaped upon their shawls, which are spread on the ground for the purpose. According to the commodity they sell their goods by the piece, or they have them parcelled out into little heaps, or weigh them on home-made scales, using stones previously weighed to serve as weights. Country pedlars sit there too, who try to attract the rustics by offering trinkets of little value, pocket-knives, &c. There are not wanting also geomantists, soothsayers, amulet-writers, and so forth.

A SLAVE MARKET.—SLAVERY.

In a corner of the square, beside the cattle-market, we observe a group of raven-black, scantily-clad children of both sexes; they are slaves exposed for sale. In the capital and its neighbourhood the slave-trade has of course been greatly curtailed in recent times through the vigilance of the higher authorities, and the inhabitants themselves are now chary of buying slaves, as they have no longer any recourse when they run away, since every slave on reporting himself to the police becomes at once free. From time to time whole caravans of slaves are confiscated, and the slaves escorted to the capital, where the government takes charge of them. The boys, as soon as they become strong enough, are generally turned into soldiers, though some of them are distributed as domestic servants, and a few of the cleverer sent to the government schools. The girls are also sent into service. But as there is nothing more certain to bring a foreign bird to an unhappy end than suddenly giving it its freedom in a foreign land, so too for these slaves freedom is not the best lot, as long as they are unaccustomed to it. A male or female slave is to his or her master always a valuable which he guards and takes care of; the free servant is not to be depended on, and stands in a looser relationship towards his master. He is no longer fed, but must himself struggle for his bread in a country of whose language he is quite ignorant. In the present transition state of matters mere anti-slavery societies, or societies having for their object solely the rescue of men from slavery, are not sufficient; humane societies should be formed for the purpose of sending back to their native lands those who have just been made free, a task which in those days, when the interior of Africa is becoming more and more accessible, can at any rate be partly accomplished, although at a great expenditure of time and trouble.

In Upper Egypt the slave-trade on the whole still remains pretty much as of old. The public sale of slaves in the market-place has by no means entirely ceased, although sales are no longer so extensive as formerly. The government officials themselves lend a hand when an escaped slave is to be tracked out, and more than that, it is an open secret that the native Christian or Mohammedan consular agents of European powers often invest their money in the slave-trade, though not under their own names! In the ordinances which are issued for the purpose of putting a stop to this traffic, and which are renewed from time to time, permission is given for people of respectability and position to purchase one or several slaves for domestic service. But so long as slaves can be bought so long will they also be sold.

The slave-dealers have ordinarily their depôts in the public hostelries. We intimate our intention to make a purchase, and are conducted into the court of such an establishment. There we find some Sauahli girls, with skins of a deep-brown colour, occupied in pounding in a large wooden vessel the kind of grain called *duchn*, which forms the basis of the Soudan bread, and which has been brought by their masters from their native lands. They do not much concern themselves to cover the nude portions of their persons, which are already pretty fully developed. A smaller negro girl wears nothing else than a girdle of tufts. A carefully veiled Abyssinian miss is brought before us, a Galla girl, the noblest of all coloured races; the owner points to her graceful limbs, uncovers her agreeable brown face with its large speaking eyes, and is prepared for all the investigations of the purchaser. He next opens the mouth of a little Moor who is among them that his white teeth may be inspected, and draws our attention to his plump and firm thighs. The prices mentioned to us are: for a male slave of black race £8 to £14, and for a female £12 to £16; for a male Abyssinian or

Galla (of brown colour) £16 to £20, for a female of the same race £18 to £26; for a white Circassian woman not less than £100 to £200. Slaves are valued most highly some years before or at puberty, when they are still pliant, and "their brain is not yet dry."

Are these creatures really so unfortunate? An account of their lives as given by some of themselves will show. A child in a tropical village in an evil hour, when darkness has come on, removes to the distance of a few steps from the hut of its parents. Suddenly it finds itself seized by a strong hand, a gag is thrust into its mouth to prevent it from crying out, and away it is carried on the shoulders of a man for many miles in the dark. It is taken into a house and food and drink set before it, but it refuses these and cries for its mother. Grief, anxiety, and fatigue struggle for the possession of the poor little creature; the last conquers, and the child falls into a profound slumber. It awakes, finds the hut like that of its parents and hears the language of its village, though the faces are strange. A swarm of youngsters of every age, forming part of the body of stolen children here assembled, gathers round and makes friendly advances to the new comer; there is no lack of food and drink, there is no work to do, and in a short time the child, being still at an age when feeling is not yet deep, forgets its home and parents. The stealing of children is, however, a mild form of procuring slaves; far worse are those well-known forays or razzias, which often assume the appearance of open warfare, when bands of armed slave-dealers surprise whole villages, carry into slavery women, children, every one who is worth the trouble, and tear asunder all family ties.

The period of rest does not last long. The full complement of slaves being made up they are dragged over hill and dale, field, and desert; the mule, the horse, the ox, and the camel alternately assist them on their journey; they are conveyed down a swollen mountain stream in a crowded boat; tropical heat and torrents of rain vie with each other in their assaults upon their tender, ill-protected bodies; one child after another is attacked by fever, the sick and the healthy lie huddled together; the dead are buried in the sand; ceaselessly the caravan moves onwards. Some rashly make a desperate attempt at flight, but are immediately caught, and, being beaten and bound, are dragged still onwards. The girls, however small they are, are sacrificed to the lust of their drivers, so that an unviolated female slave is a great rarity. At last they reach a town. The captives are shut up in confinement, from which they are brought out fettered at night for a promenade; on the market day they are sold by public auction, the would-be purchasers feeling their limbs, making them leap about, and opening their mouths as if it were a horse market. The highest bidder gets the goods that please him, singly or in groups. The companions in misfortune, who have become friends on the journey, separate in tears; though in the more civilized localities the Mohammedan slave-dealer commonly avoids parting brothers and sisters, parents and children. The new owner acts pretty much like the old one: he gives the slave children plenty of food for a time till they have recovered from the fatigues of the journey, and then sells them; and so they pass from master to master, and from place to place, or they are fattened in the same house for years and left without work—especially the girls. This and the tedium of their position have both a moral and a physical effect, the girls develop early, and now is the time to sell them at the highest price. Indeed they are eager for this themselves, and lay warm dough upon their bosoms, which is said to hasten the swelling of the breasts. Meanwhile they are also civilized, that is, they are made to veil themselves and not appear forward; they must learn to believe in Islam, Mohammedan names are bestowed upon them, and all trace of their native ideas as far as possible swept away.

The semi-mature maiden is now sold, and if she is merely brown and of good race, if she is, for instance, a Galla or Abyssinian, her lot is generally by no means hard. If a man in good circumstance takes a fancy to her, she shows no reluctance, since she is not thereby dishonoured, but proud of playing the part of a wife or *sitt;* her owner provides her with clothes, ornaments, and sweets to her heart's content, gives her male and female servants, allows her the management of the house, nay, often neglects or puts away through his passion for her his own wedded wife. And their little ladyships know how to play their part very well, and are fond of acting the tyrant. They are ambitious enough, but their love is mostly deep and ardent; they are faithful, tidy, domesticated, and have fine sensibilities. They are therefore preferred by many to the native women. Their position is by no means that of a mistress, since, on the one hand, no stigma of immorality attaches to it, though the free women are accustomed to despise a woman who is merely a slave; and on the other hand, as soon as they become mothers, they are free, or at least cannot be sold. While in certain countries the gallant is wont to make himself scarce when he perceives that his victim is *enceinte,* or as soon as his child is born, here such a result serves as a closer bond of connection, for the Moslem is not allowed to deny or to sell his own children. Such a slave has even this advantage over a free women, that she cannot be divorced and sent away, seeing that she has no relatives. It is not rare for a female slave who has presented her master with a child, especially with a boy, to be raised to the position of actual wife.

Of course fortune does not smile thus upon every female slave, especially if she has the ill luck to be plain or black, to belong to one of the inferior races, or to prove unfruitful. Then she passes often from hand to hand, she has to allow the finery that has been presented to her to be torn from her person—calamity hard to bear—when it is not sold along with her, and she sinks, with the decrease of her charms and her price together, lower and lower in the scale of society. Or, as we have already seen, the slave girl is bought by a procuress, who gives her an education according to her own taste. By far the greater number of slave women, most at least of the true negresses, are employed as domestic servants, and the highest position they attain is the dominion of the kitchen.

If their behaviour is good their master gets them a black husband, and any children that may spring from this black marriage become the vendible property of the slave-raiser—of course with this restriction, that the family must be sold together. It is the rule, however, for such a family to remain, and to wish to remain, for life in a household, constituting the serving element in it perhaps for several generations.

The male slaves enjoy a brilliant career more seldom than the girls. When they fall into the hands of masters who are in a good position they are generally well fed and dressed, and often look down with scorn upon men who are free, but are also hungry and ragged; still they are nothing but servants who may be sold at any time, and have not their future in their own hands. Many, however, gain the full confidence of their masters, transact commercial and other business for them, and frequently inherit all their property. Slaves are often set at liberty, an act recommended as praiseworthy by the Prophet, and when liberated they generally receive a gift of some kind. Such persons usually retain all their lives a kind of dutiful feeling towards the family to which they have belonged, and often prefer to remain in the house of their masters though free. Slaves are seldom ill treated in these parts, and punishment is rarely greater than what is deemed necessary to train them. In the patriarchal Mohammedan system the slave has more the position of a member of the family (whose duty, of course, is merely to serve), and an injury to the slave is an injury to the family. But there are exceptions, and cruel masters may be found who are more liberal with their whip than with their bread, and who kick the poor slaves and load them with heavy fetters to prevent them from running away. On the other hand, there exists that excellent law of the Koran, that a discontented slave may demand before a court that he shall be sold. Their treatment is less harsh too for the reason that they may become dangerous, or, as not seldom happens, may commit suicide, whereby the slaves themselves lose little, but entail a loss upon their owners.

The white slaves, male and female, are the best off. They

are now almost exclusively of Circassian race (formerly they were often Greeks). On account of their price they come into the hands only of the rich. The males (Mamelukes) often receive a superior education from their masters, are treated like sons, and generally pass comfortable lives. A considerable number of the higher officials at present acting in Egypt were once such slaves. They frequently receive in marriage the daughters of their masters; indeed it sometimes happens that a father purchases a good-looking Mameluke for a daughter he has got to marry, and makes him his son-in-law.

The white slave women are an essential ornament of the harem of the great. They are said to be ambitious of power and fond of finery. The colour of the skin, in this country as elsewhere, is generally regarded as pointing to superiority of race even among the natives themselves. But there is no such thing as contempt for a dark skin, whether free or in slavery. That would be contrary to religion; besides, the population is already so commonly dark skinned that it would have to despise itself.

CHANCE MEETING WITH WOMEN.

We now step aside into a dark and narrow lane. Our way twists and turns, so that in its course it follows all the points of the compass. Without plan or guide we fearlessly wander about in the labyrinth. Pistol and dagger we may allow quietly to rest in our pocket; the poor people who have settled here have none of the Græco-Alexandrian bandit proclivities about them. They are rather inclined to suspect us of such a character, timidly retiring from us, while the little children regard us with mistrust and terror, and run off screaming.

After a time the street forks, and we turn to the left by way of experiment. An invisible female voice issuing from a house suspiciously asks us what we want. We find we are caught in a *cul de sac* and turn back. We now come upon a creature entirely enveloped in a large brown or striped gray cloth, and as our glance lights upon it it darts in at an open door. Another creature of the same kind that does not at once find a place of refuge squeezes itself close to a wall till we have passed by, drawing the cloth together firmly over its face. Turning a corner we suddenly come upon a third, and catch a glimpse of the face, but quick as lightning its head is shrouded in its mantle. Wishing to act with propriety we behave as if we had observed nothing, and turn aside to let it pass. After a few minutes both of us—we and this being —seized with curiosity, turn round at the same moment; our eyes again meet, and the two large black beaming orbs betray to us that under the uneasy covering a heart warm as our own is beating, perhaps beating for us. Wherefore then this fear, this flight, this anxiety; what crime have we committed; are we robbers or enemies; are we hunters laying our plans to catch the gentle gazelle? Modesty will have it so; we are men, and unbelievers to boot, and the creature we have just seen is a woman. We meet quite a drove of such modest walking suits of clothes, who lay their heads together, like cows before a wolf, and form square against us with their backs. The veil which the bolder ladies of the capital wear, and which allows the eye, the mirror of the heart, to be seen, is not worn by the fair sex in the provincial town, and they have always their hands ready at both sides of the slit in front of the face, in order that they may at once conceal their features with their outer wrapper in times of danger, that is, when a man's form becomes visible. A woman that does not do this is certainly of doubtful character, or else we have become intimately acquainted with her, and have seen her fully on some former occasion as in attending her medically, in which case veiling before us is no longer thought of. It is not the case that good-looking women are ready to let themselves be seen, while old ones, on the contrary, when neither dangerous nor likely to run any danger, are not so particular.

We were surprised at the walking suits of clothes, but we now light upon one riding. The ladies of the East are still as good equestrians as formerly in the time of the Virgin Mary, and sit so firm and secure on the saddle of their donkeys, with stirrups buckled high up, that the business of suckling is never interrupted even while they are riding. The eastern lady, unlike the European lady, has no scruple about riding with legs astride. These respectable women are rarely met with in the principal streets, and never in the markets, but chiefly in the minor streets. In other countries a state of matters the reverse of this may be remarked.

VISIT TO THE INTERIOR OF A HOUSE.

We meet a well-dressed native gentleman with whom we are acquainted, and are soon engaged in a discursive conversation with him, which it seems desirable to carry farther undisturbed and in comfort. *Tefaddal* ("If you please"), he says to us, shaking and rattling the bar of a gigantic wooden lock on the door of a handsome house. We hesitate to accept his abrupt invitation to dine with him, but the adherent of the Bedouin religion is in earnest. While we stand hesitating, he takes us kindly by the hand and half pulls us over the threshold of the small middle door, that is just opened from behind. "Your faces! Cover yourselves!" he calls out, gently detaining us, and clapping his hands, as he enters alone the sanctuary of the house. We hear some half-uttered cries of fear, whimpering children's voices, whispered scolding, and smothered giggling. In a few minutes the inmates of the harem, thus taken by surprise, have fled to their hiding places, and our host invites us to step into the interior of the house, now no longer debarred to us. He might, in accordance with custom, have preferred to order soft carpets to be spread for his guest on the stone bench, or floor of the entrance hall, without disturbing his family. We follow him, and passing along the narrow lobby and round a corner that prevented us from seeing farther enter a spacious courtyard.

THE COURTYARD.—This open, airy space, and the half-covered-in sheds and porticoes (*sufa*) open on the side next it, serve, at least among the middle and lower classes of the provincial population, as the general family-room. Here both women and children, in company with sheep, goats, fowls, and pigeons, spend the greater part of their time, not troubling themselves about the common belief, according to which they pass a monotonous existence imprisoned in the harem. Here the wife who has to work takes her meals along with her children, eating the scraps which her husband—and his friends if he has had guests—has left over; here is the sitting-room for the female gossips of the town; here the merry daughters and their playmates sing their songs to the accompaniment of the inevitable *darabuka* (a kind of small drum). Among the richer class the date-palm or something green is planted in the courtyard where possible.

THE KITCHEN.—One of the side rooms is occupied by the kitchen, which is almost wall-less towards the court. The fireplace is either built of clay, the favourite form being that of a low stair with holes containing the fire let into the top; or all the needs of the household are satisfied year after year by a fireplace of loose stones such as one might improvise in the open air when travelling. The fire must be low, since the women squat before it when cooking, as standing is highly unpleasant to them. The use of any kind of stove does not seem to be appreciated anywhere. In cooking, a copper pot, without a handle, or an earthenware saucepan, is used, and these vessels do not appear very secure as they sit half on half off the fire. Only a portion of the fire above the gradually rising heap of ashes touches the pot and slowly cooks the victuals, a large square-shaped fan being used to make it burn more briskly; the rest of the fire crackles merrily up without having any useful effect, and escapes outside by a small opening in the roof, which is formed of reeds and beams, black with soot, but apparently incombustible. The kitchen utensils, the plates and other dishes of tinned copper, wood, or earthenware; the iron pans, the wooden spoons and ladles, lie scattered over the earthen floor of the kitchen; or the earthen kneading trough, and the copper washing tub, in shape like a gigantic plate, have been placed over them in order to preserve them from being meddled with by the sportive goats and pigeons. Those utensils not intended for immediate use are placed upon an open shelf, or put away in a picturesque clay cupboard. The turbid muddy water of the Nile is kept in a tall cylindrical vessel of clay hung upon a frame, rounded buckets of wood or leather, or tin-plate mugs being dipped into this vessel when necessary; sometimes also it is kept in large narrow-mouthed heavy pitchers with handles (*balas*). A small portion trickles pure and clear, drop by drop, through the pores of the cylindrical clay vessel into a vessel placed below it, in which, if the whole does not stand in a close wooden box, ants, centipedes, perhaps also lizards and serpents, refresh and bathe themselves. The drinking water is poured into porous vessels of clay, in which it is cooled by the rapid evaporation that takes place from the dryness of the air. Water for washing is drawn up by a rope and bucket from wells in the court of no great depth, and always brackish. After it has been used for washing utensils, or for cleansing the person, it is either poured out in the court, the soil of which soon absorbs it, or it is carried off by a deep narrow funnel-shaped sink.

ROOMS ON THE COURT-YARD.—In the middle of the court rise cylindrical structures of clay, usually having rounded dome-shaped tops. These are intended for a pigeon-house, a house for fowls, an oven, a corn-store, or a pantry. The rooms situated on the ground-floor in the irregular mass of buildings surrounding the court, and which are almost devoid of windows, serve for magazines, or in winter for warm sitting and sleeping rooms. In the clothes-room the articles of dress hang openly upon cords, or are shut up in green boxes along with the ornaments and valuables. Wardrobes and chests of drawers are scarcely to be found, though wall-presses with doors are sometimes met with. In these rooms, therefore, the greatest disorder usually reigns. One of the rooms opening on the court, cleaner, more spacious, and better lighted than the others, and usually fitted up with some elegance, is the *mandara*, in which many receive their guests; it is thought preferable, however, to have this room in an outer court, separate from the inner one where the women are. In the warm but dark sitting-room opening to the court the family circle gathers in the winter evenings before the open brazier, in the dim light of a cup-shaped hanging lamp of glass, or of a small shallow lamp of antique shape supplied with viscid, sooty oil, and standing in a niche of the wall blackened by its smoke. In recent times, however, petroleum has been extensively introduced. The sleeping rooms are almost entirely without windows, or if there are a few slits by way of window they are papered over in order to keep out the cold night air. The sleepers lie upon a portion of the earthen floor at the side of the room purposely raised above the rest, and on which a straw mat and a carpet are spread, or less frequently upon a wicker-work bedstead of palm branches; such bedsteads, however, are quite useless in summer on account of the multitudes of bugs they harbour. Mosquito curtains and European bedsteads of iron are sometimes found in the houses of the wealthy. The sleeper keeps half his clothes on, and in summer, therefore, requires no covering; in the colder nights he draws his ordinary wrapper (*milayeh*) over him, in winter he adds a woollen coverlet and a heavy quilted cotton one besides. So soon as the spring sun shines into these dark rooms their human occupants desert them to sleep in airier apartments or in the open air, and, wakening from their winter sleep, the army of bugs, flies, mosquitoes, fleas, lice, sugar-mites, ants, cockroaches, black beetles, scorpions, serpents, geckos, rats, and mice celebrate their entry.

THE RECEPTION-ROOM.—Having cast upon all these surroundings a passing glance, we observe the restless and suspicious looks of the hospitable lord of the harem, who cannot attribute our survey to mere curiosity, and at his earnest invitation we mount the stair, which is jammed in between the walls, and consists of high steps covered with wood. We enter a well-lighted and spacious saloon, the *ka'a*, called also *tábaka*, as being in the first story, the *salamlik* of the Turks. The floor consists of slabs of stone, or of a mass of clay and sand smoothed on the surface and hardened almost to the consistency of marble. The walls are white-washed or show an earthy surface, have numerous niches, and are adorned with a few verses of the Koran framed and glazed, here and there also with sheets of pictures of Arabic or Frankish production. The ceiling is composed of longitudinal and transverse layers of the midribs of palm fronds, with a coating of clay and lime above, and is supported by rough palm stems stretched across and bending downwards a considerable distance into the room. In the houses of wealthier persons we find an artistic panelled ceiling of mosaic. We are glad to observe there is no glass in the windows, and much prefer the cool air streaming in through the unglazed apertures, or conveyed down through the roof by the ventilator above. When it becomes too cool we have simply to close the shutters on the side next the wind.

Across the far end of the room runs a low bench of stone or clay projecting several feet. Over the mattress that covers it, and is stuffed with wool or cotton, is spread a bright-coloured cloth or a carpet hanging down in folds in front. The cushions, which are of the same material and colour, but without any breach of propriety may be different, lie at fixed intervals free and resting against the wall, and thus the famous *divan* is formed. On the floor along the sides of the room a splendid Persian carpet is spread over a straw mat, and on it next the wall are laid cushions on which to recline. No other furniture or utensils are here except some water-coolers on window ledges, shelves, or niches in the wall, and religious manuscripts with black, red, and gold letters. Our host invites us to seat ourselves beside him on the divan, but we cannot succeed in finding a comfortable position, since the cushion behind lies too far backwards. To try to touch the cushion with our back and then stretch our legs straight out does not seem either becoming or convenient; the best we can do is to lay a cushion at our side and rest the forearm upon it. Our oriental friend looks with a smile upon our straining trousers and our cumbersome boots, while he himself, taking off his slippers, steps upon the soft couch, and crossing his legs, seats himself at the very back of the divan with the wall cushions to support him behind. In his hand he holds a fan, that is, a flat piece of straw-plait with a handle, and with this he fans himself and drives away the flies, the great plague of southern countries.

TAKING COFFEE.—A servant, a slave, or an obedient son enters, and with his left hand on his heart hands us the pipe of ceremony, the stem of which is five feet long, richly adorned with silk and silver-wire, and hung with tassels. The tiny dish of red clay at the lower end of the stem, that forms the pipe bowl, is already filled above the brim with fine cut Syrian tobacco, mixed perhaps with the raw green tobacco of the country; a live coal carried with a pair of tongs or in the hollow of the bare hand sets the narcotic in a glow (if the careful attendant himself has not already set the pipe agoing), we place to our lips the costly amber mouth-piece, smooth as glass and almost large enough to fill the mouth, and "blow a cloud" with all the dignity of an oriental. In a little the attendants again appear, halting respectfully at the door of the chamber. One carries a tray, in the middle of which there is a coffee-pot, picturesquely surrounded with minute porcelain cups without handles, placed in as many small stands of brass or filigree, shaped like egg-cups. The second attendant pours the black-coloured beverage into the cups, the third takes hold of the metallic support which receives the cup and hastens to us with it. We grasp the elegant apparatus carefully with our fingers, but as we hold it up before our eyes and turn it round and round admiringly, the law of the conduction of heat is more and more feelingly brought home to us through the metal support. The heat at last becomes so great, that we give our hand a jerk and spill a little of the boiling hot liquid which fills the cup to the very brim, and if we had not the presence of mind to change our fingers alternately we should run the risk of burning our hand, breaking the cup, and staining our clothes, the divan, and the floor. When we succeed in sipping the remainder, our mouth being now more inured to the heat, and as we and our host exchange expressions of thanks by mutual movements of the hand to the forehead and mouth, the attendant takes the cup from us, covering it with his hand, and retires backwards to the door without turning his face away from us.

In the meantime dinner has been got ready, having been delayed a little in order that some more fowls should be roasted, and various additions made to the ordinary meal, in honour of the unexpected guest. But of the meal we shall treat elsewhere.

THE TERRACE.—After dinner our host conducts us up to the *terrace* or *platform*, which is half roofed in, seldom entirely roofless, open towards the north, and surrounded by walls. We express our desire to mount to the flat and entirely open roof above in order fully to enjoy the prospect; but with this wish he does not comply, as he might thereby incur the displeasure of his suspicious neighbours, whose harem might thus be exposed to our view. Besides, there is no stair leading up to it. We content ourselves, therefore, with the view from the terrace. Here in winter some little sunny and sheltered spot may always be found where the limbs stiffened with the morning frost may be warmed and strengthened in the sun as he gradually rises in the heavens. Here the inhabitants withdraw in summer, and enjoy their siesta under the shade of the roof, and fanned by the cool north wind. And in summer nights, after the toil and trouble of the day, what can be more agreeable than to stretch one's self out here on the soft couch of carpets, under the starry splendour of the southern sky, with a loving wife and merry crowd of children around, and to sink into the land of dreams with pleasing thoughts of the delights of earthly existence.

THE HAREM.—There are not many upper rooms, but they are more pleasant and spacious than the holes of rooms on the ground floor. No second stair leads to a higher story. Those closely-grated windows that look into the court opposite to us conceal no doubt many of the secrets of the harem; the occupants have certainly ascended from the court and observed us, but we try in vain to obtain a sight of anything except darkness through the narrow openings between the crossed bars. A private stair leads from the court to these apartments to which no stranger can have access.

The plan of the houses is naturally very different according to the taste and the means of the owner or builder. The above arrangement is in general the rule in these parts. The use to which the different apartments are put also varies according to taste and the season of the year; at one time the door room, at another the mandara, at another the tabaka or the sufa, opening to the court being used as reception room; while others allow no male guests into the house, but entertain them in their warehouse, situated elsewhere.

ANCIENT EGYPTIAN DWELLING-HOUSE.

A general survey of the house and its arrangements reminds us how closely the plan corresponds with that of an ancient Egyptian dwelling-house. That, too, had a general wall of unburned bricks, a court, court-room or mandara, store-room, and other chambers round the court, folding doors with wooden lock, ventilator on the roof, rooms in the first story, and grated windows. But the ancient Egyptians had more taste and more artistic feeling than the moderns. They did not, like the middle classes of the present day, content themselves with bare walls, but applied ornament everywhere, painted all the walls, and were fond of decorative furniture. Guests received on entering a small cup of wine instead of coffee, and instead of the pipe a nosegay.

SUMMONS TO A SICK WOMAN.

In the meantime the neighbourhood has become aware of the presence of a Frank. In the eyes of the common people every Frank is still a doctor. A neighbour comes to our host and begs him to use his good offices with us for some medicine to his "house," that is, his wife. We ask to see the patient first, to which he demurs, but latterly consents. We are fortunately not without some skill in the art of Æsculapius, and gladly embrace this single opportunity allowed us of becoming more closely acquainted with "the forbidden ones" without incurring any risk.

The patient has already gone through a variety of cures;

she has had to swallow the ink of many verses of the Koran; she has been be-read, be-written, be-danced, fumigated, disenchanted, rubbed, and worked all over, till the master of the house has resolved as a last desperate step to call the doctor. All the way to the house we have to listen to encomiums on the true art of medicine and on our own kindness and wisdom, for the oriental is a master of flattery and compliment. We enter after the inmates have been made aware of the sight that is to be presented to them. The court is filled with a great crowd of women who have come out of sympathy to check and shorten with the gift of eloquence the patient's attack of fever. All that we see, however, is a lot of bundles of clothes lying together, and resembling a bird's-eye view of a crowd of people holding up umbrellas. We march on to our examination, and find the patient, who is veiled, lying in an open apartment next the court. Her hand has to be almost forcibly drawn forward to let us feel her pulse, and it is only after our repeated request, which is supported by the master of the house, that a very foul tongue is protruded through a slit in the robe enveloping her, which is otherwise quite close. The slit is shifted when the cheek, the eye, the forehead, the other half of the face, has to be examined, in order that the whole countenance may not be shown. When we ask the patient how she feels the answer sounds like the oracle of a sibyl from the recesses of a closed temple.

REVELATIONS.

At last one of the cloths in the heap opens out wider and wider; a frightful face, above whose brow there projects a tuft of hair dyed with henna of a bright fox-red, but showing also in parts its natural silver-gray colour, looks boldly round, and thereupon the old woman begins in a shrill screeching voice the endless story of her sufferings. Soon the younger generation also acquire sufficient courage to uncover here a hand, there an eye or a foot, only to withdraw them, however, with the slightest movement on our part. But gradually we inspire more confidence; our medical utterances afford consolation and hope; the figures uncover themselves more completely, and for a longer period; two coal-black eyes are fastened upon us, each encircled by a black ring produced by painting the rims of the eyelids with antimony, the eyes themselves large and fiery, but with a somewhat squinting look on account of a spot on the pupil. The large eye is the strong point with Egyptian women, but also the weak point, as it is commonly affected with some disease or marked by some defect. The blackening of the eyelids was a general custom among the ancient Egyptians also, not only with the women, but even, as is still sometimes the case, with the men. The well-shaped and not too small mouth of the beauty now regarding us smiles upon us with innocent frankness. The covering for the head, made of a coloured woollen stuff of light texture, over which Egyptian women throw before going out the mantle which is in universal use, has meanwhile become loose, and has to be again tightly wrapped round the hair, ears, neck, and upper part of the breast, so that the oval countenance, the hair above the forehead, and the side-lock alone remain visible. During this process of rearrangement we catch a glimpse of that which oriental women keep concealed with the most sensitive delicacy, namely, the hair that crowns the head, with the numerous slender tresses, black as the plumage of the raven, that flow down on all sides. The coiffure of the women of ancient Egypt was exactly similar to this; even the side-lock was not wanting. The locks behind are allowed to hang freely down the back, and are tied at the extremities with long cords of red silk adorned with spangles and gold coins. Curiously shaped trinkets of gold, precious stones, or pearls depend from the ears; golden arrows and combs are stuck in the hair, which, where it meets the brow and sides of the face, is fringed with a row of ducats, sequins, little bells, and flakes of pure gold prettily wrought into the most singular forms. An oriental woman is thus somewhat expensive in her ornaments, for she disdains to wear sham trinkets. These ornaments are procured in times of prosperity before or after her marriage, and are worn all her life as unemployed capital yielding no interest. In seasons of misfortune the woman may pawn them, but she never sells them unless reduced to the utmost need. As they last her whole life they are ultimately cheaper than the fashionable gewgaws of European cities that are destined to be cast aside at the end of a few months. The breasts are covered, but hardly concealed by a chemise of transparent gauze. Over this the women wear a narrow-sleeved garment, which fits tightly round the body, being fastened in front by a close series of silken knots reaching from beneath the breasts downwards, and which falls in folds straight from the hips to the feet. (See cut of Dancing Girl in Chap. III.) Oriental women are fortunately unacquainted with the confining instrument called a corset, and are still so backward in civilization as to be unable to appreciate a waist of wasp-like tenuity. The legs are encased in a wide sort of drawers, which are fastened under the knee, but are continued down to below the edge of the frock, between which and the feet they move about in a rather picturesque manner. This style of drawers is not, however, in universal use. Instead of them a kind with legs gradually tapering towards the foot is often worn. In addition to the close-fitting dress above described, the women belonging to the towns of Upper Egypt (see the accompanying cut) wear a loose garment of light cotton of a blue colour, or with bright blue stripes and sometimes embroidered. This garment has no sleeves, but on each side there is a long slit extending from the shoulder nearly to the bottom of the robe, so that the arms can be uncovered at any time. In the hot summer months the under garments are too tight for comfort, and this loose robe and the drawers are all that are worn in the house. Often, indeed, the drawers are forgotten, and the arm being carelessly lifted, the woman's whole profile from the shoulder to the ankles is disclosed to view. These women, while careful to conceal their charms out of doors, are careless on this matter inside the house, where they think they do not need to mind who sees them. It is therefore advisable that warning should be given before a stranger enters the house.

The feet have either no covering at all to prevent one

from admiring their beauty, or they have their natural nimbleness impeded by clumsy slippers. Silver clasps, with little bells attached to them, are worn round the ankles. Bracelets of pure gold or silver are worn on the wrists, and still more commonly on the upper arms. Numerous rings,

Woman and Child of Upper Egypt.

either with or without stones, deck the fingers, but the forefinger, with which they attest their faith, is always kept free of them. The shocking nose-ring is not intended, as with the camel, to serve as a means of keeping the wearer in check, but the women themselves desire it from their husbands as a charming ornament. Lastly, we manage to see many other proofs of an abnormal taste in the form of temporary as well as indelible skin-painting on the face, hands, feet, and other parts of the body.

A number of little light-footed girls run about in the court. They are dressed like their elders, except that the innocence of their youth spares them the infliction of the heavy outer mantle. Already, however, they begin like their maturer sisters to practise concealment with the corners of their head-covering, and even the youngest of them could not be induced to expose her head to view completely.

A child which seems too old to be still receiving suck has firmly fastened on the open breast of his tender mother.[1] A thick cape keeps the cold air from his head, which is thus early concealed from view. Sequins and ducats are clustered on his brow, and there are little packets on his breast containing precious spells to thwart the baneful look of the envious.

On leaving, according to traditional practice in the case of a medical visit, we are treated to sherbet, that is, a sweet liquor made from the juice of fruit and water, and served in a crystal cup. This we drain at one draught, as expected by the servant, who attends with a fringed cloth which he holds underneath while we are drinking, and with which we afterwards wipe our mouths (exactly as among the ancient Egyptians). We also receive perhaps a handkerchief embroidered by some fair hand, but as a rule nothing else, unless it may be some trifle wrapped up in the handkerchief.

A DINNER.

Meantime evening has come on, and we return to our dwelling; for we must keep ourselves in readiness for the dinner that a well-to-do citizen intends giving this evening in celebration of some such event as a betrothal, a circumcision, or a wedding, and to which we, as being among the persons of most distinction, have received an invitation in the course of the day. The host comes in person to our residence, for it is his duty to conduct the guests to his house. The reception-room is already filled with a considerable number of people, who have settled themselves down on the richly carpeted floor in front of the cushions placed against the wall.

All present rise up to welcome the newly arrived guest,

---

[1] According to the injunction of the Prophet children must be suckled for two years.

and after we have adjusted ourselves to our satisfaction on the carpet, so far as that is possible, and have cleared our throat, we receive a separate salutation from each of the other guests, which greetings must severally be returned along with a movement of the hand to the forehead, mouth, and heart to give emphasis to our replies. We are asked regarding our health, and we do the like. The inquiries follow one after another in stereotyped and often very ingenious phrases, which imply a bosom friendship that has lasted for years, but which, at the same time, have no other result than that nobody receives any enlightenment as to the health of the other, for the answer is always an expression of thanks or a blessing, and nothing more. After a good deal of time has been spent in such compliments and ceremonies we begin to talk. From the weather, of which there is in this region, properly speaking, none at all, or which, at least, only changes from cold to warm or warm to cold, we pass to the prices of articles of food and other commodities. We express our opinions upon individuals, all the more gently and flatteringly the nearer the persons spoken of happen to be, relate stories and adventures, astonishing feats and tales about ghosts, criticize the government with a surprising freedom of speech, and propound rather sweeping and, in truth, horrible political schemes. The conversation is agreeable, at the same time polite and ceremonious, lively, fanciful and eloquent, with a certain picturesque circumstantiality, a frequent use of similes and comparisons to make the speaker's meaning clearer; often with a degree of pathos and demonstrativeness of gesture, which contrast strikingly with the apparent apathy that the Egyptians preserve on other occasions. In short, the conversation at such parties is often in the highest degree brilliant and intelligent in spite of the amount of ignorance it betrays, and the superstition, fanaticism, and fatalism which are seen in every action and breathe in every word.

During this talk that precedes dinner the guests make use of nothing to invigorate or stimulate the physical system, except perhaps a mouthful of cold water, a little coffee, and tobacco, which last each smoker brings rolled up in a fine woollen or silken pouch along with his pipe. The rising vapours, the sound of frying and similar noises in the kitchen, the running hither and thither of the servants, the whisperings of the host, and other signs, indicate that the affair is not going to end with the small cup of coffee that had been promised us either by word of mouth or by means of a note of invitation. Soon the large lamp which rests in the middle of the hall on a polygonal stand with four or eight feet (among the ancients only one foot) is removed, and the stand is covered with an enormous circular tray or plate of metal (usually tinned copper, and there are usually engraved on it some arabesques and pentagrams). A basket containing round flat cakes cut in two sufficient in number to satisfy a company of twice the size if they were to get nothing but bread and water, is now brought in, and the cakes are placed round the tray, which is not covered with a table-cloth. Living caryatids of the male sex hold lamps high above the heads of the guests; a cup-bearer passes round, carrying a water-bottle on his arm; there is also a servant whose duty it is to sweep away the vermin. The guests arrange themselves on a carpet round the tray, usually in companies of from ten to twelve, never thirteen. If the company is too large for one table similar arrangements are made in other parts of the room as may be required. A servant goes round to each guest with a vessel of water, and all wash their hands, or at least have water poured over the tips of the fingers of their right hand. They all then lay their napkins across their knees, and turn up their right sleeve. The left hand hangs down by the side, and is kept dry for use in drinking or for other incidental purposes.

To-day the dinner is Turkish (alla turka), that is, one viand is brought in after the other. The menu is a long one. Were the dinner after the Arabic fashion, according to which all the viands are laid on the table at once, so that the guests may help themselves at pleasure, there would not be room for the great variety of dishes. A large bowl of soup being served, the host, after squeezing into it the juice of some green lemons or citrons the size of walnuts, and pronouncing the word "bismillah" (in the name of God), dips his wooden spoon into the bowl, and is followed by all the other guests. In traversing the distance between the common dish and the mouth many a drop and solid fragment fall upon the table and the cakes of bread. In the well-spiced soup lies a bit of boiled meat or a fowl, which the master of the house now takes out, and offers in pieces to his guests. They show, however, no great relish for it; for already a colossal breast of mutton stuffed with chopped flesh, onions, rice, raisins, almonds, and hazel-nuts, is beheld in the hands of a servant in the background. Scarcely is it placed on the metal plate when all the twelve guests fall upon it with their right hands. Each tears off a piece of the flesh, which has been first boiled soft and then roasted. Where it is found rather tough two guests sitting opposite one another begin pulling at the same piece until it gives way. In a few minutes the breast-bone is stripped of flesh, and the precious stuffing lies dispersed over the dish from which the diners convey it to their mouths by means of wooden spoons. This practice of all eating out of one dish in common, and using the hands in doing so, usually appears to Europeans one of the most barbarous usages of the East. Yet the same practice was followed by the ancient Egyptians, who were a people of refined and formal manners, as well as by the Jews. To the Oriental, on the other hand, it seems barbarous in Europeans not to wash their hands before and after eating, although the utmost care and nicety are often insufficient to prevent them from being greased.

The breast of mutton serves as a foundation, and is followed by a number of trifles, such as vegetables of different sorts, and onion sauces with small pieces of flesh, usually, as among the ancients, small legs of mutton with the bone. These are brought in on small plates, and each guest takes what he can get either by dipping a piece of bread into the dish, or by forming a sort of pincers with his piece of bread, so as to be able to seize on some of the solider contents of the dish. Some farinaceous article, roasted maccaroni, vermicelli, or pastry now appears. We have already seen perhaps six different dishes. Our appetite is quenched, and after the farinaceous course we should like to rise; but we have not even yet reached the beginning of the middle of the banquet. Dish still follows dish, butcher-meat alternating with farinaceous preparations. The master of the house offers us, with exclamations of delight, a fowl's leg prepared with quite extraordinary skill. The other guests also encourage us to eat, offering choice morsels to us as well as to one another; but the climax is reached with the sweet tart (*santeh bakláua*). The whole of the worshipful circle of gourmands salute its entry with a delighted Ah! How wonderfully does it lie imbedded in the deep pie-dish. The use of knives to cut it up is forbidden, but the host digs out a great hole with his fingers, whereupon all the guests plunge in their fingers at the breach and tear out fragments of the firmly baked composition, until the whole artistic structure falls in ruins. The ancient Egyptians adopted at their feasts another way to remind the feasters in all seriousness of the transitoriness of everything earthly. At this stage of the feast servants used to drag round the room the image of a mummy.

We have now struggled on to about the middle of the banquet. The small plates again appear, and gratify our palate with a continually ascending scale of excellence and sweetness. Greatly do we regret having so soon spoiled our appetite. We are becoming giddy with our exertions, but we are not yet at the end; for a huge, massive, and juicy roast still remains to be vanquished. Even experienced guests, who have prepared themselves for the sumptuous repast by fasting from early morning, and have cautiously climbed up step by step, sit despairing and exhausted before this object of Titanic magnitude. The company at last hasten towards the close of the repast. Several plates now offered are mercilessly rejected, and the pilau of steamed rice, which invariably concludes the feast, is placed on the table along with a cooling sweet rose-scented jelly. To crown the whole the guests now take a good supply of this delicate preparation into their well-crammed paunches, and then each after the other rises with a "Thank God" (which serves as a grace after meat as the "bismillah" does for a grace before meat), and makes his way as quickly as possible to the washing-vessel. The host is the last to rise, as he was the first to make the attack.

The foundation of the feast is always *mutton*. The animals are slaughtered for the purpose on the day of the entertainment, not the day before, and if possible in the house itself in spite of the prohibition of the government. No important feast can be held without animals being specially slaughtered for the occasion, for the consumption of flesh is then so considerable. By the ancient Egyptians mutton was not relished, perhaps was not eaten at all; and their numerous flocks of sheep were kept chiefly for the wool. Beef and the flesh of geese, which at the present day are but slightly esteemed, formed in ancient times the basis of the Egyptian banquets, which were then at least as lavish and frequent as they are now. At the grander entertainments now-a-days a turkey appears on the table instead of a goose.

BILL OF FARE.

We cannot omit to furnish our readers with the entire *menu* of our feast.

1. Rice soup.
2. Döl'a mahshi: stuffed breast of mutton. (See above.)
3. Bâmieh burâni: the bâmieh fruit (*Hibiscus esculenta*) boiled and roasted entire with flesh and a great deal of clarified butter.
4. Kauirma (Turkish): roast meat with whole onions.
5. Wárak mahshi. In making this dish vine or cabbage leaves are filled with pounded leaves of the same sort, minced meat, onions, rice, and pepper, and fried with clarified butter.
6. Kunâfa or vermicelli. A dough of water and flour not very tenacious is pressed through a perforated mould, which forms it into worm-like threads. It is then fried with clarified butter, then sugar and dripping are sprinkled over it, and lastly it is boiled above a coal fire.
7. Moluchîch. This is a mucilaginous vegetable resembling spinage, and is prepared for the table by boiling with flesh-meat.

8. Kufta or meat-dumplings. Minced roast-meat, rice, and onions are made into little balls and fried with clarified butter.

9. Batingân kûta: tomatoes boiled with flesh.

10. Sémak makli: fish baked in oil.

11. Sambûsek. Dough made with water and flour is rolled out into round flat cakes, on which is placed minced roast-meat with rice; half the dough is then folded over, and the edges are pressed together. The whole is cooked by baking.

12. Kabâb: small pieces of flesh roasted on a spit.

13. Jachni: roast-meat with onion sauce or made into a ragout.

14. Fakûs mahshi. The soft contents of the fakus fruit, which is of the gourd family, are taken out of the shell or rind and mixed with minced meat and the other ingredients mentioned in no. 5, and then replaced, when the whole is boiled.

15. Batingân iswud mucharrat. The black batingan fruit (fruit of the egg-plant) is cut into small pieces, and added with onions to broiled meat and boiled.

16. Sanîeh baklâua or sweet tart. (See above.) A number of flour cakes are placed in the dish, and between each pair is spread a layer of butter. Honey is spread on the top one, and the whole is baked in an oven.

17. Sälk: beet boiled with flesh.

18. "Milk-rice:" rice and milk with some water and clarified butter boiled, to which are afterwards added sugar and rose-water.

19. Mumbâr mahshi: pieces of intestine filled with the mixture already mentioned more than once and boiled.

20. Kabab bi déma: meat roasted on a spit with a plain sauce.

21. Ful achdar: green horsebeans (both pod and kernels) boiled with flesh.

22. Láhma muhámmara: a large roasted joint. (See above.)

23. Balûsa: sweet jelly; sugar boiled with water and farina, to which honey and rose-water are added while cooling. Almonds are afterwards stuck in the jelly. (See above.)

24. Rus mufälfäl, Turkish pilâu: steamed rice saturated with clarified butter. (See above.)

AFTER DINNER.

The Mussulman washes himself only with pure running water, and does not splash about in a basin. A servant pours water upon the hands of the guest from a large metal vessel having a spout, and generally of an elegant shape. The dirty water falls down into a large metal bason, having a broad rim and a perforated bottom, through which the water passes into a cavity at its base. These utensils are exactly like those which were in use among the ancient

Egyptians. Much soap is employed, but they do not use it properly, for they allow the lather to be washed off the hands before it has time to act upon the skin. The mouth is next carefully cleansed inside and outside, and all this goes on quite openly in the dining-room. The unused cakes are now collected, and the numerous crumbs on the table and floor are carefully gathered up. Bread is reckoned by the Mohammedan a sacred gift of God, which should not be wasted; and if he finds a small piece of bread anywhere on the ground he picks it up and kisses the hand in which he holds it. Last of all, the metal table is removed.

The company, who, without any breach of propriety, give frequent indications of satiety by loud eructations, again take their places on the carpet before the wall-cushions, and conversation is resumed under the influence of the chibouk. The attendants now have their turn for dining (of these there is no small number, inasmuch as each of the guests brings along with him his own servants, slaves, and dependants), and during their dinner no one disturbs them except for some pressing need. At last, when the servants have satisfied themselves, coffee is brought in; and from this time the company have no more peace, for they all begin to feel uneasy in the stomach. The most important of the guests gives the signal for breaking up. All seek for their slippers, which lie about at the threshold of the door, and depart to their homes overburdened in stomach but with brain quite clear. Each guest is preceded by a servant carrying a large lantern, and is accompanied on his way by the host, for every step taken for the sake of a guest is accounted a step in the ascent to paradise.

THIRD DAY.

A PUBLIC-OFFICE.

The duties of those who have to provide for the people's weal and woe begin with the bustle of trade and other business at an early hour of the morning. Already the fierce-looking bands of Turkish police stand armed to the teeth at the open gate in the wall of the extensive seraglio (which, be it noted, signifies a palace or official residence, not a harem). Only a few drunken fellows, overcome by the hashish or liquor of the preceding evening, still lie snorting on their palm-twig couches or stretched out on the stone-bench in the portico. No one hinders us from entering the spacious court, which is surrounded by the plain white-washed irregular buildings of the palace (Mudirîeh). Some very old sycamores, dating, like the palace itself, from the time of the Mamelukes, spread a broad shadow which is very grateful during the hot hours of the day. Under the protection of their foliage the head of the province is accustomed to transact his business when he finds the air of the court hall too oppressive.

COPTIC SCRIBES.

A man arrayed in a voluminous black toga with wide flowing sleeves, his face well covered with hair, a black turban on his head, and an ink-stand of massive silver in the girdle of his caftan, hurries past us with a friendly greeting. We take him to be a Christian priest wearing his official robes and ornaments; but what is he doing in a secular court of the Moslem rulers? We feel drawn to the man by his courteous demeanour, and make his acquaintance. We soon learn that he is "of our kindred," for we certainly believe like him in the Messiah, read the gospel, and abhor the false prophet Mohammed and his accursed brood. Our remark, that to the Christian all men are brothers meets with no acceptance, and turns the conversation to another topic. We are informed that he is not a priest, but belongs to the strictly exclusive guild of Coptic scribes. He conducts us with every mark of politeness into the scribes' hall, where we find a number of our "kindred" of this class. He bids us be seated, hands us a chibouk, and causes us to be supplied with a few small cups of the coffee of the seraglio. These scribes sit cross-legged on the ground or on a stone-bench. In front of them lies the desk, which is more used for holding documents than as a support in writing. One of them now opens the lid of his club-shaped ink-vessel, from the long tubular part of which he draws out his broad-pointed reed-pen. After trimming his pen he begins to

Coptic Scribe.

paint thick lines on the long narrow strip of paper that he holds up freely in his left hand without any other support. The pen is dipped with remarkable frequency into the ink-vessel, which has an absorbent flap that gives out sufficient ink to impart strength to the letters, but not so much as to make a blot. The strip of paper has frequently to be adjusted for the convenience of writing, in consequence of which it becomes a good deal folded and crumpled.

The Coptic scribe is a master of style, and, while he has almost entirely lost the language of his own race, no genuine Moslem Arab excels him in the employment of the language imposed upon his ancestors. The official style is somewhat diffuse and archaic. There is no lack of expressions like "seeing that," "inasmuch as," and of labyrinthically involved phrases. It forms the connecting-link between the old language of the Koran and the dialect of the people. The ancient Egyptians in like manner used to write, for example, in drawing up treaties, with an extremely precise and formal circumstantiality.

Another scribe is employed in transferring some official

letters to his large folio, which he finds it more convenient to rest on his knees than on the writing-desk before him. A brother official or a private assistant, who is his pupil, and who is likewise a Copt and of his own family (strangers, and especially Mussulmans, are not admitted into the caste of scribes), reads out to him in a drawling sing-song the prosaic contents of the letters, with all the titles, names, and numbers, his head and upper part of his body swaying all the while backwards and forwards with a rhythmical regularity. A fellah stands before a group of idle scribes, who are deep in some conversation that has no connection with their official duties. He timidly requests that the document he carries in his hand should be attended to. He receives neither a word nor a look in answer, and becomes more urgent. "Be off! We have no time just now." The unfortunate peasant then bares his shaven head, and with a heavy heart rummages about in the folds of his turban, which usually serves as a purse, opens a knot with his teeth, and places a silver coin in the half-open hand of Master Gerges (George), who eagerly seizes it. Now the business goes on like clock-work. The paper is passed from desk to desk, from room to room, from one official to another, until it is covered with seals and scribblings. The cashier, usually a Mussulman, opens his coffer and pays the amount due to the peasant. A small sum, however, wanders into the private chest of the treasurer, which the countrymen silently beholds with rueful astonishment.

OFFICIALS OF THE PROVINCES.

Our new acquaintance the scribe favours us with a variety of information regarding the business of his office. The higher and highest circles we here pass over, confining ourselves to the provinces. Each province is subject to a governor, with extensive powers, called a *Mudîr*, who corresponds to the "nomarch" of ancient times. Administration, finance, the royal domains, the armed forces of the district, and to a certain extent also the judicial proceedings, are in his hands; but the Damocles sword of mightier overseers, and still more of informers, hangs over his head, and frequent changes of these officials are made with the view of checking abuses.

A provincial court of justice according to present arrangements, which have come into force at a comparatively recent date, is composed of the kadi, who merely gives his opinion in accordance with the laws of the Koran, and of some of the leading citizens, who act as assessors. No trace of legal learning is to be looked for in these officials; although since the introduction of the present organization of courts of justice, an attempt is being made to train up some of the natives to be real jurists, who are to give their decisions according to the French code. The presidency of the court belongs of right to the Mudîr; but his whole attention is taken up with the collection of the taxes and the management of the vice-regal estates. Neither citizen nor peasant places any confidence in the fairness of the judgments of these courts; though the government does all it can to provide for the security of the people and the punishment of the offenders.

The large province (Mudirîeh) is divided into several smaller administrative districts, the heads of which are entirely under the control of the governor of the province. The towns are governed by their own prefects of police, who stand either directly under the Mudîr or under the heads of the districts. The communes likewise have their own petty magistrates. These are chosen from among the inhabitants of the several communes which they preside over. Their dignity, according to the old patriarchal system, is mostly hereditary, but also depends upon property; for they are bound to answer for their charge with their life and their whole estate. In the towns, where there are royal officers, the local mayor, if there is one at all, has hardly any voice in the management of affairs. In the communes the local magistrates are the only persons with official authority. Trade and industry have their guild-masters, with whom alone the government has any dealings. In the towns where trade is active it is usually the merchant's sheikh who plays the part of mayor.

All the more important officers of government, who have any administrative duties, have the right of "sealing." They are always Turks, or at least 'abdelâui, that is, natives of the country with Turkish blood in their veins. This rule, however, does not apply to the more innocent departments of government, especially those for which some little scientific knowledge is requisite, such as medicine, architecture, and engineering. These Turks thus form a privileged aristocracy. A large proportion of the higher officials consist of liberated white, mostly Circassian, slaves (Mamelukes). But the Coptic scribes, the living law-books of the province, the masters of the "uzûl" (tradition), constitute, although not possessing the right of the seal, the soul of official life. For those Turks and descendants of Turks and slaves have passed through no school of law, and being mostly taken from the army or the fleet, and from the higher circles of society generally, they have little inclination and little leisure to occupy themselves in their new position with deep studies. They acquire a certain knowledge of their duties by practice, and get along as best they can, trusting either to their own unlearned instinct or to the counsel of their omniscient scribes. There are many advantages but far more disadvantages connected with this state of matters, and hence, in quite recent times, there has been a steady endeavour on the part of the supreme government to have a regular system of official training introduced. The progress of business, where the affair takes its regular course, and is not settled by some arbitrary and, so to speak, instinctive declaration of Turkish law, is very slow, and in modern as was the case in ancient Egypt there is a great, a very great, expenditure of ink.

Some years ago an attempt was even made to replace the Turkish officials from the Mudîr down to the gendarmerie by native Egyptians. But the experiment did not succeed. The new officials displayed no energy, and showed themselves accessible to all sorts of private influences. The administration of justice and the maintenance of order suffered. The natives of the country were soon indeed the loudest in their complaints. They had no respect for one of their own sort, a "Fellah;" and a return was therefore speedily made to the old system of Turkish governors. Even the native soldier is unable to secure respect for his authority in the same degree as the violent Turk, and is not adapted for his most important duty, that of enforcing the payment of taxes.

TAXES AND OTHER BURDENS.

The Fellah has been habituated from the earliest times to the bearing of all sorts of burdens. The load of taxation increases from year to year. The old taxes are retained and sometimes increased, and new ones are devised under the most various shapes and designations. The nineteenth century is in this respect also, and not in Egypt only, the age of inventions. Years ago it was thought that the milk must soon dry up, but the Fellah is an inexhaustible milch-cow. As in every country, there is in the first place a *land tax*, here amounting to from 70 to 100 Egyptian piastres on the acre of farm-land (100 government piastres are equal to about 22 shillings, and one piastre accordingly to something more than $2\frac{1}{2}d$.). This tax is leviable on a larger or smaller area, according to the extent of the inundations of the river. Further, there is a pretty moderate *trade* or *income tax*, which is fixed for each individual by a council of government officers and natives having the necessary experience; for no reliance can be placed upon the declaration of the person taxed. The large number of palms in the Nile valley makes the *palm-tax* of 20 piastres for every fruit-bearing date-palm a very productive one. Boats employed on the Nile pay from 100 to 700 piastres. Everything brought to market is liable to a duty of from 2 to 9 per cent. of its value, in addition to which weighing dues of from 1 to 2 piastres per cwt. have to be paid, whether the article be capable of being weighed or not. Even firewood and cattle are subject to these dues. In the case of cattle there are likewise slaughter-house dues of from 4 to 10 piastres per head, even when there is no slaughter-house. Among the ancient Egyptians also the same practice was in vogue of weighing everything in public, and there were special clerks whose duty was to mark down the particulars. Cattle-owners pay $3\frac{1}{2}$ piastres for small cattle, and from 10 to 20 for large, among which asses have latterly been reckoned. Fisheries are in some cases leased out, in other cases the fishermen have to hand over at least a fourth of the proceeds to the government. Salt also is leased out; but as the lessees found that it did not pay, since the people found that they could procure salt cheaper from the desert and the sea, this article is now distributed among the inhabitants at a fixed price per head. Tobacco, which a short time ago was duty free, is now highly taxed. The plaintiff in an action has to pay a few piastres before being allowed to state his case; and 20 piastres must be paid before a petition in writing is received. The house-owner contributes to the government a month's rent annually. Quite recently the burden of taxation has been increased to the general consternation by the imposition of a poll-tax of 45, 30, or 15 piastres, according to the supposed means of the tax-payer. In answer to our inquiries the scribe estimated (in 1868) that his province, which has about 200,000 inhabitants, yields annually from 67,000 to 83,000 purses (a purse is 500 piastres, or about five guineas), from which about 10,000 purses have to be deducted on account of the cost of collection. The palm-tax yields 7000, the land-tax 40,000 to 50,000, the trade and income tax 4000, the fisheries' tax 250, the market-tax 500, and the tax on the Nile boats 12,000 purses. The figures may now indeed be very different, since, as already mentioned, many new taxes have been imposed since that date, while on the other hand the steadily increasing stagnation of trade may have had the effect of bringing about a reduction in the yield of each tax.

Still more oppressive than the number and amount of the taxes, is the irregular manner in which they are levied. As a rule indeed they are collected gradually, and every month a steamer appears to convey the sums raised, less the amount required to defray the provincial expenditure, to the central treasury; but this treasury is subject to frequent and sudden ebbs, and in such cases has to be replenished in a few days. The governors of the provinces then receive the command to pay into the treasury within so many days a certain and often a pretty large sum of money; and if any of the governors or mudîrs is thought to be of too mild a temper to take steps of the necessary severity a successor is often sent along with the order for the special purpose of carrying it into force. This new governor then makes a tour through the province with his scribes and other officers, and with the utmost politeness "requests" the richer citizens to make advances, which they are obliged to do even if they should have to borrow the money at high interest from Greek usurers, while the poorer tax-payers are compelled to pay at once the sums due for the whole year; and whoever is in arrears, and is still not ready to pay, is treated to the lash. This instrument, although abolished by law, is on such occasions rigorously wielded till late in the night. The grain that the farmer is now obliged to sell to pay his taxes in these circumstances sinks for some days considerably in price, greatly to the advantage of the corn-buyers. The truth is that even in ordinary times the balance of state revenue and expenditure could not be maintained without the aid of the *kurbâg* or scourge of hippopotamus hide. The Fellah (and it was the same among the ancient Egyptians, at least in later times) will rather be beaten till the blood flows than voluntarily pay the detested taxes to the government; and he boasts of this as an act of heroism. Not unfrequently, after getting all the flesh of his body made tender by repeated scourging, he slowly drops the money demanded of him out of his mouth, where he had concealed it. An extortionate system of taxation has been the order of the day in the land of the Nile from the earliest times; but while formerly the sums extorted only went to benefit the rulers, now it must be confessed a large share of them is expended for the good of the country. The peasant, to be sure, is unable to see of what use the schools are, and scarcely appreciates the value of the new canals, bridges, and railways. His children and children's children will get the benefit of them; he knows only the suffering that he has to undergo to meet the demands of the government.

Forced labour, people in Egypt say, is quite as indispensable as the kurbâg. It also is formally abolished, but is nevertheless maintained even more actively than ever. To be sure the services exacted by the government ought by law to be paid for by the government officials. For carrying goods through the desert, for example, the camel-driver receives the medium pay current at the time. But the country people, who are from time to time levied *en masse* and forced to labour on public works, assert that they receive either none at all or very little of the pay due them, which passes through the hands of the government officers and the village mayors. Without resorting to compulsion, or paying excessively high wages, the government could not get labourers for public works, for the peasant and the labourer carefully avoid as much as they can all connection with the government. Those who can read and write are declared to be exempt from liability to forced labour, at least in their own persons.

The officials also have to bear a large share of the burdens of the state. The pay of the lower grades is in itself very small, and is calculated according to the wants of a time that is now past. It is out of all proportion to the great increase in price of the necessaries of life since the introduction of the cotton cultivation, an increase so great that Egypt is now one of the dearest countries in the earth to live in. The happy times of Mohammed Ali, when one could get a whole handful of eggs and fowls for a few paras, are gone. To take a few examples of the rates of official pay, the keeper of a prison receives 75 piastres (that is, about 16s. 6d.) a month, an hospital attendant 100 piastres, an ordinary scribe 200 to 400 piastres, an officer of the rank of a lieutenant, for example an ordinary doctor, an architect, an assistant, 500 piastres (a purse), an officer of the rank of a captain (*yus báschu*) a purse and a half, one of the rank of a chief captain (*sakolaghási*) three purses, a lieutenant-colonel (*kaimakâm*) five purses. From this grade upwards salaries rapidly increase. An officer of the rank of a bey or colonel, for example the mudîr, has from 8 to 10 purses, a pasha 15 to 20 purses monthly. While in other countries schemes were devised for increasing official salaries as the prices of necessaries became higher, in this country a resolution was suddenly come to a few years ago to reduce salaries by a fifth, a reduction still in force, so that a government servant who formerly received 1500 piastres now receives only 1200. This measure, however, does not apply to the lower grades of government servants receiving a salary of 500 piastres or less. The government officers are not even exempt from the poll-tax recently imposed. A day's salary is regularly deducted from their monthly pay. The copper-tax, which was levied for a considerable time, and which consisted in paying a tenth of their salary in almost worthless copper piastres, is now at last abolished.

From time to time an attempt is also made to reduce the number of the officials, especially the inferior ones; and when this is done those whose services the government thinks it can dispense with are simply discharged with nothing more than the hope of the next permanent appointment that may become vacant. Only the privileged Turks often receive in such cases compensation in the form of an allotment of lands. But these measures are in reality more impolitic than cruel; for, as a general rule, the official during his term of office lays past his salary to form a permanent capital, defraying his current expenses "from without."

OFFICIAL PROCEDURE.

The head of the province is generally absent on a tour of inspection through his long district, or visiting the royal sugar-refineries and domains, and his deputy, the "wekil," despatches the ordinary business. We get ourselves introduced to him through a suitable medium. He receives us in a manner at once courtly and proud. His strongly marked features and the clear colour of his skin betray the Turk; a certain want of polish in his behaviour and the fluency of his Arabic reveal a large admixture of native Egyptian blood. He is sitting in his official room or divan on the richly cushioned couch or sofa (divan in the narrower sense). He sips coffee, which is included in the charges of the court, takes a cigarette from his box, or has the gilded chibouk brought to him. Some privileged persons, among them several priests, have seated themselves on the divan at some distance from him; less highly honoured persons sit cross-legged on the carpets that are laid on the floor next the walls. No furniture enlivens the clean and well-kept hall. The windows are hung with costly curtains adorned with elegant tassels. On ledges all round the hall lie a few books, among which there is a book of laws of the time of the great Mohammed Ali, which perhaps has never been opened, and also without fail a copy of the Koran.

The chief of the scribes, the Bashkâtib, Master Hanna (John) enters, and brings under his arm a great heap of official documents just drawn up. With a frowning look the man of authority snatches the papers out of the hand of the accomplished scribe who stands before him with his head hanging down. He makes as if he were reading and could read the writing, which swims before his eyes, and dipping the tip of his finger in the ink-vessel which the chief scribe holds up before him he applies it to the surface of the silver seal on which his name is engraved, and stamps therewith all the documents in succession. Twenty documents are despatched in this way before the learned scribe could have read out five lines. He throws down one after the other before the author, who patiently picks them up, and retires with a profound and silent obeisance. In this way is shown before the public the mighty difference that there is between the exalted Turk and the Christian scribe. In private, however, there is a perfect understanding between the two.

There is always a great bustle in the court of the Mudirîeh, especially in the morning hours. Here the parties to a suit sit squatting on the ground awaiting the decision of the court. There a criminal is handed up in fetters, and is cast into the dark dungeon. At another spot some who have to receive payments wait for days till the scribes find the necessary leisure for the purpose. In the same court deeds of surrender and leases are prepared; and here also the mudîr or wekil keeps a supply of camels.

Gradually the court becomes more and more crowded with brown-skinned and brown-mantled country people. The village mayors and village patriarchs (sheikhs) are summoned into the divan. With a deep obeisance they go through the usual form of lifting dust from the smooth marble floor and pressing it to their lips as a mark of respect. In these countries, however, the Mussulman never, except in extreme cases, prostrates himself before his ruler. That sign of reverence is reserved for the Almighty. A decree is read, and the people are required to signify their assent to it, and bind themselves to obey it. "Right willingly," answer the honourable village mayors with one voice, "as your excellency commands; we are thy slaves and the slaves of our sovereign; nothing but good comes from thee; thy opinion is our opinion." "Then seal the document," says the governor; and the heads of the communes, one after the other, give their brass seal to the scribe, who smears it with ink, and fills the sheet with their important names. When the sheikh has sealed, the villager does so likewise, although he has only a faint glimmering of what it is that he has pledged himself to. In the country, where very few can write, the seal takes the place of a signature. To lend a person a seal is a mark of the highest confidence. When an official has lost his seal and has to provide himself with another, the fact is made known by public notices. Official seals, properly so called, are not in use except for stamped paper, and where doors have to be sealed up on behalf of the government. For example, on the occasion of a death a large official seal made of clay and chopped straw is placed on the door of the house where the deceased person lived, and similar seals are placed on the doors of the government magazines every evening, as was customary also among the ancient Egyptians.

We are now about to quit the buildings in which the business of the state is carried on, but remain a little longer to cast a glance at the ecclesiastical court, in which the *kadi*, the representative of the clergy, assisted by advisers well versed in the Mohammedan Scriptures (muftis or ulema), dissolves ill-made marriages, arranges the inheritance of deceased persons, administers oaths, and now and then in difficult cases gives the benefit of his opinion to the secular court. On the whole, however, all that he has saved from the ruins of his former splendour is a certain moral influence among his religious brethren, an influence that is daily declining. His rôle is in fact now almost confined to that of a notary. "Par ordre du moufti" is a phrase that has become of no effect, unless by mufti a pasha is understood.

By and by we see the government post darting past us, in the form of an express runner, with a little bell at his foot or on his stick, and a knapsack, which he carries to the next post-station, where he is relieved of it by another runner. Many a piece of intelligence is brought by these nimble-footed men, before the snail's post of the electric telegraph has worked its way through the intermediate stations filled with a set of young officials whose chief occupation is to dream and loiter away their time. The postal system is now organized on a European plan even in Upper Egypt. Where there are as yet no railways the functionaries are Arabs. Scrupulous punctuality has never been the leading virtue of the natives, and an Arab post-office of the kind we are now speaking of is not exactly a model institution. In recent years there has been much improvement, although even orders and decorations are occasionally lost. Ordinary people make but little use of the government postal service. They prefer to trust their letters, which are written on ribbon-shaped strips of paper and then rolled up, to some chance visitor to the place for which they are destined. In this way their transmission costs nothing. There is never any hurry, and the people are afraid the government might learn their secrets. On this account the Egyptian post-office always works at a loss.

A company of regular troops marches out at the gate of the seraglio, preceded by a band of fifers. The light, slim-built beardless youths, among whom many negro heads with ivory teeth are conspicuous, are dressed in loose trousers, like those worn by the Zouaves, fastened high on the body, a short military coat made of ticking, and a red cap with a tassel to it, a uniform which suits them admirably. A squadron of irregular Turkish cavalry (Bashi Bazouks), ride into their barracks, headed by their aristocratic commander seated on the gold-fringed housing of his high-bred horse. Their wild countenances, their motley self-chosen dresses, their arms, bearing, and character—everything about them in short, betrays almost unbridled license. Their commander is their patriarch. He has himself raised them, and has to maintain them out of the funds placed at his disposal for the purpose. They lead a restless, wandering life.

THE COUNTRY JUDGE.

Less important actions and cases arising out of trifling disorders in the town come before the police or town prefect's court, which lies in a different part of the town from that of the mudîr. Nevertheless its proceedings are always influenced and restrained by the authority of this powerful functionary, and Turkish justice is not here to be seen in its peculiar and original features as it is in a small country town where the local judge is absolute. We will therefore travel in spirit for a few hours to the divan of such a local judge or hâkim. His portrait essentially resembles that which we have given of the wekil of the mudîr. In his court we have the opportunity of witnessing the following scenes.

A loud wrangling is heard on the stairs. Two lads, with rolling eyes, and looking as if they would like to transfix each other, are dragged in by the police. One of them shows his torn shirt and bloody nose.

"What do you want, you fellows?" cries the tyrant on the divan.

The accuser all at once empties his overcharged heart before the assembled divan or judicial assembly. Nobody understands him. The accused interrupts him long before he has finished his little speech. A storm of abuse breaks out between the disputing parties. The police and soldiers do their best to quiet them by advice as well as by blows; the judge commands, nobody hears; the air is rent with intermingled Arabic and Turkish phrases. Witnesses are called, and these make the chaos complete. At last quietness is obtained. The judge asks the accused:

"Did you strike anyone?"

"No, I did nothing. Nothing has happened at all."

"And that nose?" asks the judge.

"God knows all," replies the accused.

"Bring the cord; bind him, the liar, the pimp!"

"Thus was it fore-ordained for me by Fate; I submit."

As a lamb that is led to the slaughter, the poor sinner lays himself flat on his face on the floor of the court. The police tie his legs with an apparatus which they have had in readiness. Two pieces of wood keep the ankles together, and two executioners armed with scourges of hippopotamus hide deal out terrible strokes on the uplifted soles of the prisoner's feet. An anxious stillness prevails in the room, interrupted by the regular smack of the whips, and by the tortured man's supplications, which become always more urgent and penitent. He appeals to the grace of the prophet, then to that of some saint, next to the heart of the judge's little son and the sweet mildness of his wife (*faardak, ya sitt el bey*). But there is no mercy, until at last a word from one of those present makes the rigorous judge aware that a severe enough punishment has been inflicted. The poor wretch is carried away like a corpse.

"The other now; that brawler, that dog!"

The accuser meets with the same fate at the hands of justice as the accused, but being of a stronger constitution shrinks away unassisted, resolved never again to go to law.

Not only the hippopotamus-hide scourge, but corporal punishment generally, has been legally abolished for a considerable time, though only upon paper. The ancient Egyptians likewise resorted freely to beating as the most effective means of carrying out the ends of justice. To judge from the monuments they made use of a rod for the purpose, applying it to the hips, not to the soles of the feet. Even women were not spared the bastinado, but in their case the strokes were laid on the back, and they received them sitting. The practice of inflicting blows on the soles of the feet was probably brought by the Turks from Asia; and it is not so cruel as it looks; for the sole of the foot of a man belonging to the lower classes is almost as hard and thick as the sole of a shoe. It must be admitted, however, that a man occasionally dies while undergoing this punishment.

A case such as that above described, in which both accuser and accused are punished, does not indeed form the rule (for if it did no one would ever be an accuser); yet it is by no means rare. The very common practice of interceding for some offender with the words, *ma alesh* (do nothing), inattention to which is taken by the interceders as a personal insult, is one of the weak sides of justice, and often makes every law illusory.

Another accuser appears, his case being that some women of the neighbourhood have ill-treated his wife. The accused, namely, these women's husbands, who, while the female war had been raging, were quietly and peacefully attending to their work in the town or the fields, now warmly take the part of their wives, who remain at home anxiously awaiting the decision of the judge. For only in exceptionally grave cases are women required to appear personally in court. A hot wordy warfare arises between the accuser and the accused as champions of their respective wives, but is speedily and energetically stopped by the judge, who orders the husbands of the offenders, or it may be, as in the last case, both accusers and accused, to receive one after the other a sufficient number of strokes on the soles of the feet, and then dismisses them with the warning that for the future they keep their wives better in check. The private consequences of this procedure in the apartments of the harem may be left to the reader's imagination.

The parties that have thus far been dealt with are common peasants, who are only to be kept in order by the cudgel.

But now persons of position appear. The grown-up son of one of the leading merchants, and at the same time of a *sherif* or descendant of the prophet, has knocked out with his fist some of the teeth of a highly respected citizen of the town, who appears as accuser. The man in power listens to the important case with severe gravity. He scratches himself behind the ears, strokes his whiskers and beard, invests his figure in impenetrable clouds of tobacco-smoke, and calls for his scribe. What's to be done? According to law or tradition (*uzûl*) a record of the case must be taken. Dozens of messengers and police-officers traverse the town in all directions. The court is gradually filled with the venerable and patriarchal forms of the muftis, the oldest of the citizens, the leading traders, the native or foreign representatives of other powers or consular agents, the dignitaries of the bureaucracy, the commanders of the armed forces. Silently the exalted assembly hears the accusation. The accused denies the charge, or stammers out a few words in defence. (Advocates there are none.) The father of the youth represents to his petulant son the whole extent of his manifest guilt, and taking hold of his own silvered beard asks him how he could bring such sorrow upon his old father. The son remains dutifully silent, and looks shamefaced upon the ground. Nevertheless, the father attempts the defence of his son with all the animation and dexterity he is capable of. The party of the accused make some remarks. The persons present sometimes give tokens of their approval of what the speakers say. The record becomes rather lengthy. A physician is called and gives his opinion on so serious a case.

"To prison with the offender!" is the decision of the judge, which resounds through the hall.

"My son sent to prison, the son of a sherif? I will become surety for my son."

An anxious silence follows. The judge hesitates. Civil justice demands the punishment of the wrong-doer without respect of persons. Personal and religious considerations and patriarchal laws do not allow of any disrespect to an honourable descendant of the Prophet. A pause occurs. Those present sip a little coffee out of small cups, and make a few observations for the general good about the weather and the time of day. Some go out and in, and occasionally the clink of coins is heard. The kadi, the ecclesiastical judge, who in truth has no say in the matter, now puts in his word:

"First of all a fatiha!"

All those present thereupon, with uplifted hands, solemnly utter the prayer of prayers, ending with an earnest Amen. Then the kadi goes on to say:

"Serious things have taken place; but God is the all-pardoning, the all-merciful. The prosecution of the action would lead to incalculable consequences. Accusers and accused will become reconciled; I pledge myself to that. For your part, your grace, desist now; God will reward you."

But the civil judge will not yet yield, and hurls reproaches and accusations against the unapproachable sherif. He, for his part, throws in a number of taunting observations. Little is wanting to make the parties begin fighting again. The kadi now stands up with all the dignity of his person and office and requests the civil judge for his sake at least to grant pardon to the offender. To this solicitation the pious judge, the strength of whose moral resistance has already been broken at anyrate, at length yields. The parties, who are already prepared for this, become reconciled. The record of the case, along with the opinion of the physician, is solemnly torn in pieces, and the scene closes with a round of embraces, a cup of sweet coffee specially prepared and flavoured with cloves, and a fatiha.

Many civil judges, it is true, use much less ceremony with a sherif or a kadi, and decide strictly without respect of persons; but with all their uprightness these are precisely the judges who are most unpopular. To show partiality and indulgence in particular cases is a practice which has passed into the flesh and blood of the people to such an extent that the inexorably just judge passes for a tyrant, a "bad man," while the epithet of "good" (*ragel theyib*) is applied to one of more yielding nature, even when his indulgence may be purchased with gold. Among the ancient Egyptians rectitude and deep seriousness characterized the administration of justice, and that was the firmest support of their long-lived empire.

THE HAKÎM PASHA.

We now pay a visit to the Hakîm pasha, or, if you like, the chief official doctor, who has to look after the physical well-being of the province. We find him in the hospital in the midst of his medical duties with his sleeves turned up and wearing an apron. By his dress he seems a Turkish effendi, but otherwise he is body and soul a true son of Egypt. The year or two's training he has had under European teachers, or even perhaps in some famous *alma mater* of Europe, has caused many a seed of medical science to germinate greatly to the benefit of the suffering in his fatherland, but has not shaken the foundation of the character he has inherited from his ancestors or influenced his most deeply rooted ideas. The endeavours of the government of Mohammed Ali and of the present government to fit the youth for their callings by the institution of a superior class of schools cannot be too highly appreciated. But the way in which these efforts are carried out must be pronounced a failure, for all that these schools supply is a slight professional training. The minds of the learners are not prepared by a course of study in literature and philosophy, and hence they do not possess any genuine cultivation or tendency towards independent thinking. After being received by the doctor with the most engaging affability we accompany him through the airy rooms, where the patients, almost exclusively soldiers and prisoners, lie on their tolerably clean and tidy iron beds. A numerous body of attendants, all native soldiers who have served their time, wearing white or blue blouses, such as are worn by the people generally, follow his steps. The chief attendant, with a club-shaped ink-vessel like that already spoken of under his arm, stands ready to commit to writing the instructions of the physician as soon as they are uttered, holding his reed-pen always wet with ink above the prescription paper, and making movements with his hand as if he were writing. Another attendant carries the metal boxes with the ointments used in bandaging, and a casket containing the plasters, lint, spatulas, and scissors. The junior surgeon and the apothecary catch up every word and observe every gesture of their chief. The Arab Æsculapius goes round the beds of his charges, now all gravity and solemnity, now overflowing with humour, and always spicing his remarks with a plentiful dose of sparkling expletives (in which, however, there is not, as among Europeans, any profane mention of sacred things). The knife is swiftly passed through bleeding human flesh, and no such costly anæsthetic as chloroform is employed to relieve the pain. Inflammatory swellings are never soothed by the application of leeches, but streams of venous blood save the life of the inhabitants of the south. The denunciations of certain pathologists against the *medicina crudelis* find no echo on the hot soil of Africa.

While the doctor retires to his private room to write out for some court of justice the opinion that he is officially required to give on some case, we accompany the apothecary into a small room, which contains the principal collection of drugs and medicines in the province, whence all the state-appointed physicians, male as well as female, in the sub-districts receive their supplies. For as male physicians are not readily permitted to attend on women and children, there are some women who pass through a course of medicine and midwifery (though not a very extensive one) at the medical school at Cairo, and are then distributed through the provinces to treat those whom men are not allowed to visit. In this sort of emancipation, therefore, Egypt is already in advance of most western countries. By these arrangements those who are afflicted with diseases have always medical aid within their reach, and that free of cost. Even medicines are supplied by the government gratis, the doctors merely having to keep a register of what they give out.[1] Truly a humane idea worthy of "the great pasha"[2] who conceived it. Yet the peasant flies with horror from the offered hand and throws himself into the arms of the amulet writers, dealers in charms, soothsayers, saints, fumigators, spice-mongers, and stroking-women. The fatalist does nothing but quietly awaits the result. Those who have some glimmering of intelligence do indeed go to the doctor, but ask from him by name the medicine they want, for they know all about medicine themselves. They are already acquainted, for example, with carbonate of soda and *yodur el potassa* (iodide of potassium). And when they do leave it to the doctor to prescribe they will never take any medicine unless they are first satisfied as to the names and proportionate weights of the ingredients of which the mixture is composed, and so suspicious are they that they often insist upon the doctor himself trying it first. A patient of this description is standing at this very moment at the apothecary's counter. He stirs the witches' broth round and round, murmuring the while a *bismillah er-rahmân er-rahîm* ("in the name of God"), and at last with a look of valiant resolution empties it at a single draught down his throat. The native prefers, however, to get the separate ingredients of a mixture from the apothecary and mix them for himself at home. Purgatives are very commonly used among the people, emetics and clysters very little. In their own native trained doctors they have very little confidence. But a Frank travelling through the country, whether he be a medical man or not, is always a wonder-worker in the medical art, and is asked to cure the blind, lame, impotent, and all sorts of incurable—though seldom curable—persons. In pathology those of the common people who interest themselves at all in medicine render homage, like the old Arab physicians, to vague theories such as those of Galen. Thus peas are said to be "hot," coffee dries up the brain, a pain proceeds either from the blood or from cold (in which latter case it is to be quite differently treated), &c.

---

[1] This last provision has, however, recently been abolished.
[2] So Mohammed Ali is generally called.

The fact that these humane efforts of civilization in medicine do not succeed is not entirely the fault of the dark superstition in which the people are buried. The central repository of drugs, and still more the supplies that are drawn therefrom by the district physicians, are very deficient both in quantity and quality. The doctor must select for his patients medicines that he happens to have. When the rhubarb is done the patients' bowels are always loosened with Epsom salts. Many doctors, too, have no conception of the humanity naturally belonging to their profession. Their whole aim is to make money. They are ill-paid, and cannot make money in the honourable practice of their profession, since they are required by law to give their services free, and in fact no one will consent to pay them. They accordingly abuse their official authority, which is by no means limited. The doctor has to watch over the sanitation of his districts, and to see to the condition of all articles of food; on his decision often depends that of the judge; and the unprofessional man, however high he may be above the doctor in rank, in many cases cannot interfere. This powerful official has the key of the people's treasury, and he will use it unless he has the necessary moral restraint, whose place no babbling of prayers, washings, and prostrations before the Deity will supply. Thus it happens, that, although they are not wanting in outward marks of respect to a hakîm pasha, the medical profession is utterly detested by the people, and the provisions made for the maintenance of public health, by which their old habits are interfered with, are regarded by them merely as a mode of extortion devised by the Franks. They fear the hospital almost more than death; and hence its inmates, as already said, consist only of those who are there under compulsion—soldiers, prisoners, and pilgrims found half dead on the roads.

A COPTIC MEAL DURING A FAST.

We spend the evening in the house of a Coptic scribe, with whom we have made acquaintance in the morning in the mudirîeh. He invited us to become his guest, but gave the invitation in a very hesitating manner; for it happens to be a period of fasting, which it is during nearly half the year. Before every one of the greater festivals (Christmas, Easter, the feast of the apostles, the assumption of the Virgin) there is a fast of several weeks, in addition to which every Wednesday and Friday is a fast-day. On our entering the house the females are warned and got out of sight as in the house of the Moslems. We must seat ourselves either in the reception-room or on the terrace or verandah on a carpet on the floor, where some guests of the same race and religion as our host have already settled themselves. The proceedings are pretty much the same as those we formerly witnessed in the house of the Moslem; but the stomach is not immediately satisfied, being treated for several hours with date-spirit, which we get to drink in small bottles like medicine bottles. Our thirst is kept alive by all sorts of provocatives, such as roasted chick-peas or maize, salted *tirmis* (or lupines), hazel-nuts, and sweetmeats, while we smoke and talk. The conversation turns chiefly on religion, which in the East takes the place of politics.

The preparation of the liquor just mentioned, to which one must be accustomed before one can like it, may be taken as a characteristic example of Arab industry, and we shall therefore stop to give an account of it. After the dates have lain in a suitable quantity of water for weeks, during which period they have been stirred several times every day, and have thus undergone the process of fermentation, the resulting liquor is distilled. An ordinary copper caldron with a narrow mouth forms the retort, which stands on a few stones placed round the fire. The head of the still is formed by a large earthenware jar, such as is used for carrying water, a so-called *balâs*, the handles of which have been sawn off, and which has been cut away at the mouth so as to fit that of the caldron exactly. Towards the top a round hole has been pierced in the side of the jar, and in this hole a straight hollow piece of dry sugar-cane is inserted horizontally instead of the ordinary worm. Near the extremity this horizontal piece is intersected by a similar vertical piece, the lower end of which enters the receiver, which is a copper vessel of moderate height closed at the top by a pad. The receiver is kept cool by being placed in a wide vessel sunk in the earth and filled with cold water which is constantly renewed. The gaps and joints are stopped with rags and dough. The pieces of cane especially are wound round with rags several times. A great deal of the spirit of course escapes. The joints cannot be often enough cemented. There is always some new hole out of which the spirit bursts, not unfrequently taking fire in so doing.

At last, when the guests have imbibed a sufficient quantity of the spirit, and feel themselves in the happy state of mind and body which they call *kef*, the eatables are served. They consist of steamed marsh-beans, lentils, preserved olives, a syrup of sesamum, fish, and several sweetmeats, fruits, and vegetables, such as radishes (the leaves of which are preferred to the rather insipid root), raw purple-red carrots, and whatever other green vegetables the season produces. But all animal food except fish, and even such animal products as butter, milk, and eggs, are rigorously eschewed. Soon after the meal is over the party breaks up, having consumed a great part of the evening with gossiping and disputing, in the course of which the standpoint of most of those who took part in the discussion had become far from clear. We return to our abode in the opposite condition to that in which we had left the Moslem's feast the evening before—with empty stomach but overburdened brain.

FOURTH DAY.

THE COPTIC CHURCH AND THE COPTS.

Sunday morning has just dawned. A number of men exactly resembling the now familiar scribes, being dressed in dark-coloured clothes, and mostly wearing a black turban on their head, and also a considerable number of closely-veiled women as well as children, are streaming into a narrow lane. In that lane stands a plain building in Gothic or Byzantine style, not with a lofty tower but with a modest ridge-turret. We follow. No one hinders the Frank, the fellow-Christian, from entering; indeed, the entrance is not closed even against a Mussulman, although it is closed against a Jew. We are in the Coptic church. The interior is simple, not in any respect overloaded with ornament. In the choir, within an area which the congregation is forbidden to encroach on, stands the high altar with the image of the Virgin, and some tapers and missals. The aisles each terminate in a smaller altar consecrated to some saint, and are adorned with a few oil-paintings brought from Europe. The congregation occupy the nave and the forepart of the choir, which is separated from the other part by a latticed partition. They sit cross-legged man to man on straw mats laid on the floor. Some are in Sunday dress, some not. All keep their heads covered, and most of them take off their shoes. From the gallery over the door of entrance we hear women's voices, and the still shriller voices of little children. In front of the gallery is a lattice to prevent the occupants of it from being seen, as the devotions of those below might thereby be disturbed.

The mass has begun. Among the congregation in the fore-part of the choir are some of the inferior clergy dressed like the rest of the people. These stand at a reading-desk, and with furious rapidity read the gospels of the day in a sort of chanting style, first in the old Coptic language, which is still kept up for that purpose, and then in Arabic with a commentary for the edification of the people. Meanwhile a man goes round the congregation and distributes the host in the form of small loaves of white unleavened bread stamped with a cross, each person receiving one. A priest of very reverend aspect with a long silvery beard, which suits a priest so well, and wearing an embroidered white chasuble, now rises and goes through some operations in the most holy place beside the high altar, and then reads something to the people. The boys of the choir strike large metal disks or cymbals together, making a great noise, which has, however, a very solemn effect. At the same time they as well as the congregation sing a psalm in a subdued tone and in rather quick time. The priest arrayed in a long gown raises the crucifix or pyx in sight of the people, and every one bows and crosses himself to the beat of the cymbals. Towards the close of the mass, the symbolism of which we must admit that we did not understand, the congregation rise up and crowd round the priest, who lays his hands with a blessing on the head of every one, not excepting us strangers. The Christian brethren give their hands to one another, and after having lasted about an hour and a half the service is over.

The Coptic Church, a heretical offshoot, as is well known, of the Greek, formed in the fifth century under the emperor Marcianus after the Council of Chalcedon, also called the Monophysite or Jacobite Church, is found only in Egypt, Abyssinia, and to a smaller extent in Syria. It has preserved many echoes or relics of ancient Christianity, perhaps more than other churches. It has maintained itself to the present day in spite of the most bitter persecutions carried on through many centuries. Millions of Copts have indeed gradually passed over to Islam; but those who have remained faithful compel our esteem by the firmness of their faith and by their endurance. The church is entirely independent of the state, and is subject to a patriarch, who is likewise head of the Abyssinian Church. Formerly the Mohammedan rulers attempted to force their submission by oppression, but they never made any direct efforts to convert them. But now there is no greater example of toleration to be seen anywhere than that which is exhibited at least on the part of the government in all these lands as far as the Nile reaches. And even the individual Mussulman is at least outwardly remarkably tolerant, and never carries on religious conversations with a proselytizing tendency. As long as an unbeliever keeps himself on a proper social footing with a Moslem he is his friend and fellow-citizen. In daily intercourse the religious distinction is hardly noticeable. If, however, the unbeliever renders himself guilty of any offence he incurs a double disgrace.

The poison of slumbering fanaticism breaks out, and the offender is not only called a scoundrel, but also has the name of unbeliever thrown at him in contumely; precisely as among Christians and Jews in the civilized West. In disputes among native Christians of a purely ecclesiastical nature, for example those connected with marriage, priest, kadi, and governor may be seen sitting amicably together on the judicial bench. The kadi gives the benefit of his wisdom and experience towards the settlement of the question, the priest pronounces the decision of the court, and the governor executes it.

The Coptic priests, whose dress does not differ from that of the laymen, but is always, including the turban, of a dark colour, actually live in apostolic poverty, having no regular salary, and being entirely dependent for support upon their congregation. Articles of food are sent to their house, and they get a little money on occasion of baptisms, marriages, and funerals. Like the Moslem kadi, they have various judicial functions to discharge, especially in connection with marriages and inheritances. The want of money makes them very ready to accept equivocal presents, and they are easily induced by such a gift to remit a few penances, which usually consist in prayer and fasting. In Cairo, so at least it is generally asserted, many of them act the part of match-makers, betrothing Coptic girls, though not without the consent of their parents, after the manner of the Moslems, by proclamation, which is totally contrary to their laws. The Copts show great respect to their priests, outwardly at any rate. They kiss their hands to them; but at bottom they seem to hold many of the priests in very little esteem, no doubt on account of such malpractices as that above mentioned. There is a seminary for Christian priests, but of the higher theological knowledge, or even of general culture, there is no trace, hardly even among the bishops. Intending priests may be married before they are consecrated; but after their consecration, if their first wife dies, they are not allowed to marry again. The higher clergy are required to remain unmarried.

The Copts read the gospels, which, like the Mussulmans with the Koran, they also outwardly hold in great reverence, and by which they swear. They baptize children by immersion, have monasteries, and practise auricular confession and worship of the Virgin. The chief expression of their Christianity consists in fasting. The pope is their detestation. Besides a faint resemblance in feature, and many customs still prevalent among the Egyptians generally, the Copt, the true descendant of the great nation of the Retu, has inherited little from his remote forefathers. In fact he turns yellow when we tell him about the splendour and magnificence of the land of Kemi, of the quadriune God Amun, and the deeds wrought by the son of the sun. He knows the idolatrous and accursed race of the children of Pharaoh only from the opprobrious epithets which his enemies the Moslems bestow upon him, and from the representations inspired by national hatred given of them by the lawgiver of the Jews. The bad repute in which the excellent and high-minded Retu stand among the Moslems can be explained only by the degenerate effeminacy of their descendants at the time of Mohammed. Even the reproach of idolatry is at bottom not altogether justified; for there is no doubt that we must distinguish between the deep philosophic religion of the initiated and the symbolical idol and animal worship, which barbarous form of religion was inculcated by the hierarchy on the common people. In the ancient Egyptian religion there was in fact only *one* God; the others were merely attributes or energies of the one, though each had his own emblems.

As for the modern Copt, he has become from head to foot, in manners, language, and spirit, a Moslem, however unwilling he may be to recognize the fact. His dress is like that of the rest of the people, except that he prefers darker materials. The black turban, formerly the brand of the Christians (who were obliged to wear a black or blue turban to distinguish them from the Moslems), is now voluntarily and gladly worn by them, and especially by the Coptic scribes as a badge of honour. The Copt smiles at the Moslem, who, in going through his prayers, turns his face towards Mecca, while he himself with his face turned to Jerusalem mumbles out psalms by the yard in a regular paternoster gallop.

Unabashed he pollutes the virgin air of the Mohammedan great month of Ramadan with clouds of smoke from his pipe, but crucifies his own flesh during three quarters of the year with the scanty juices of vegetable, fluviatile, and marine aliments. Like the Moslem and the Jew, he has a horror of blood and swine's flesh,[1] but in addition has an equal abhorrence of camel's flesh, which the Bedouin Mohammed permitted. He clings with excessive tenacity to the privileges he enjoys in the case of his favourite spirit. He never tastes his evening meal until his mind is clouded by the vapours of this water of life, which he prepares for himself from dates. To this spirit alone he owes the rotundity of his body, and perhaps the existence of his race, which would otherwise have died out long ago under the regimen of pease, beans, and fish without fat or butter, which form almost his whole diet during the seasons of fasting. For the noble juice of the grape the descendant of the ancient Egyptians has no taste. The vine is much cultivated in Egypt, and the grapes are excellent, but are only used for eating. All the wine used in the country is imported, and the quantity consumed by the natives is very insignificant. The drinking of spirits is a characteristic sign of the degradation of the descendants of the wine-loving Retu.

The Kopt as a good Christian must live till his death a strict monogamist, but, like the Moslem, is allowed to taste the joys of married life in early youth. His spouse is generally chosen for him by his father from among his own near relations, and when he has married her he closely secludes her from the male world without. Like the early Christians, he loves to pray in domestic association with his fellow-Christians, and seals the prayer with a fraternal pressure of

---

[1] By one religion or another pretty nearly all domestic animals are forbidden; thus the cow is forbidden by the Hindus, and was so by the ancient Egyptians, who also apparently interdicted the sheep; the Abyssinians interdict the goose. Among the ancient Egyptians the swine was entirely forbidden as an article of food only to the priests; the other orders ate it, at least occasionally, as at the sacrifice of Typho. This animal was, however, thoroughly despised. Swineherds were not permitted to enter a temple, and no one having a different employment would marry one of their daughters.

the hand. He does not readily allow his Christian brethren, to whatever confession they may belong, to suffer want; but his love for his neighbour is generally confined to those who own the name of Christian. In proof of his Christianity he will often turn up his sleeves, and show a blue cross indelibly tatooed upon his arm. The Kopt is fanatical, servile, and avaricious, but more accessible to enlightenment than the Koran-bound Moslem.

As the missionaries scattered over Egypt accomplish virtually nothing with the Moslems, who are too firm in their faith to yield to such efforts, they have long turned their eyes on the wandering Koptic sheep, and Catholics and Protestants vie with one another in attempts to gain them over. The former had at one time some success, since the adoption of the Catholic faith brought them at least the moral support of a Catholic foreign power, namely Austria. In quite recent times, however, the Protestants have been making a great stir, and they have many avowed and still more secret adherents. The remission of fasting, a practice which causes so many Kopts to suffer from stomach complaints, may have not a little to do with this success. The Protestant mission is an organization of the American Methodists; but the work is chiefly carried on by a native converted Kopt (belonging to Kus), who is a successful reformer, and knows how to convince his fellow-countrymen and inspire them with enthusiasm. The sect which calls itself Protestant spread so rapidly, that the Koptic patriarch was compelled to interfere, and the Protestant agitator was condemned with the help of the government to be deported to Fazogl, the Egyptian Cayenne, and would actually have been sent there had not the American consul exerted himself in his favour. In some districts the Protestant zeal that fired a portion of the people led them even to plunder the ancient Coptic mother church, and the Moslem government had to restore order.

THE BATH.

After hearing the Sunday morning mass in the Coptic Church we determine to have a bath. We walk through a few lanes and stop at a door, surmounted by a projecting pediment, painted in rather childish style in a variety of colours. We pass from the street into a large hall, where the proprietor of the bath receives us sitting upon his divan. The hall serves as the office of the bath, for drying linen, and for dressing and undressing in. The master of the bath points us to a platform at the side, covered with straw mats, where we exchange our clothes for a bathing costume, which consists in a cloth put round the loins, with the addition perhaps of a bathing turban. An attendant similarly attired gives us his hand to lead us through a dark passage, along whose wet polished marble floor, smooth and slippery as ice, we have no little difficulty in tottering with our naked feet. This passage conducts us to the steaming-room, where the sultry vapour, that rises from a hot fountain bubbling up in the middle of a large marble octagon, condenses on the cooler dome-shaped roof of the hall, and descends in drops. Light is admitted by a number of small openings in the roof closed with glass. We seat ourselves on the octagon, and observe the bathers who pass in succession. We have already had sufficient opportunity on the public streets of noticing the great breadth of the upper part of their bodies and the slenderness of their limbs, but we have never had the chance of seeing them without a head-covering of some sort. The men who are now moving about in the bathing establishment, however, are mostly bare-headed. A bald head has been an object of timid reverence on our part ever since the prophet Elisha caused the children who reviled him to be consumed by bears, and we accordingly pay due respect to the old bald-headed bathers. But most of these bald heads seem to possess abundance of vital force, and have a youthful often child-like appearance. Here comes one whose head is crowned by a luxuriant tuft of hair on the summit; here is another from the upper part of whose brow spring two long horns like those of the lawgiver of the Jews; this one wears a tuft of hair in front like Peter, that one has only the back part of his head overgrown with a shaggy covering; in short, locks of hair may be allowed to grow at any point of the skull that the wearer pleases, but never over the whole skull, for that would stamp a man as an unbeliever. All this is the result of the tonsure, recommended by the forethought of the prophet for the sake of cleanliness, but not invented by him, since the original inhabitants of the land of Kemi always had their heads shaved smooth. In modern Egypt the men shave the hair off their whole body except the face, which is seldom shaved at all even by the peasants. The women keep their hair. In a room adjoining there is a small pond where one can stand breast-deep in water and parboil his limbs in company with the lame, the leprous, and the syphilitic. We, however, are led by another attendant into a dark ante-chamber and subjected to a tedious purifying process. One attendant first pulls at our limbs as if he wished to tear them off. We hear with alarm all our joints crack, yet we feel the operation so pleasant that we calmly let him proceed. Our flesh is then firmly stroked, kneaded, and worked. A douche of hot water now wets the whole surface of our body, and with such suddenness that the heart and breathing are checked. Thereupon the attendant, enveloping his hand in a sort of bag-shaped glove made of coarse cloth, begins to stroke us all over, thoroughly cleansing the pores of impurities, which become rolled up into spindle-shaped and cylindrical masses and fall down to the floor. We look with astonishment upon the heaps of refuse with which our skin was loaded. After the body has been soaped from head to foot, and played upon by streams of hot water, the shampooer leaves us to our fate, and we quit the scouring-room cleaner than marble. The steaming-room, on first entering which we were like to suffocate, now seems to us like an ice-cellar, and after getting a short dry cloak thrown round us by the attendant who conducted us into this room, we hurry, shivering and with chattering teeth, into the still colder outer room. A young man receives us in the dressing-room, and rubs us for a considerable time with dry warm cloths, an operation which we find very agreeable. Meanwhile we enjoy our pipe and sip a small cup of coffee. Finally we dress, pay the master of the bath his fee, and give a trifle to every one who has rendered any services to our body.

THE DOGS.

After our bath we make the best of our way into the fresh air, and ascend one of the many eminences outside the town which have been formed by the gradual accumulation of the refuse carried thither. In Upper Egypt those eminences near the towns are the homes of the dogs, which seldom venture into the streets except by night, while they remain both night and day in the larger towns of Lower Egypt, the members of each family strictly confining themselves to their own locality, and clearing the streets from filth. These dirty jackal-like and mostly ugly red-haired animals, which have neither property nor master to guard, evidently look upon our appearance, which is very unexpected, as boding no good to them. Their first feeling is one of cowardly fear, manifested by the way in which their tails curl down between their legs, and then by the manner in which they sneak round about us in an arc of a circle, while they steadily eye us with a look of distrust. When they are beyond the reach of any immediate danger they set up a hoarse yelping and a most disagreeable barking. These sounds communicate themselves to the families of dogs on the next eminences of the same kind, and spread in ever widening circles, proclaiming to the whole town that something extraordinary must have taken place, and the din returns to our suffering ears like a hundred-voiced echo. The dog, the faithful friend of man, has degenerated in the towns of the East to a cowardly misanthrope, and we cannot blame him for it when we consider the numerous little attentions that the Mohammedan in his zeal against uncleanliness has bestowed on him, and which have resulted in the limping legs, the broken ribs, and ulcerated skins to be seen everywhere. A few bitten noses and torn ears must be laid to the account of the exclusiveness which these creatures exhibit among themselves. Woe to the dog which a roving spirit, hunger, or any other impulse has brought among the inhospitable members of a neighbouring pack. Among the ancient Egyptians the dog met with an entirely opposite treatment. In those times he was highly esteemed, and in some places was worshipped. Mummies of dogs have been found at Lycopolis, near Siout. Cats enjoy a certain consideration even at the present day.

In our peregrination we pass a place where building is going on. A large number of people, mostly quite naked boys and half-naked girls, but also men and poor women pretty well advanced in years, are engaged in carrying earth and stones from one place to another. An overseer is set over each division of these labourers, and goes about with an uplifted rod in his hand keeping his gang diligently at work by word and deed. But that is hardly necessary, for the loud never-ending song which old and young sing to their work, a song embracing a comparatively small number of notes, with a regularly recurring refrain, and accompanied by clapping of the hands, is in itself sufficient to maintain their activity. Every division sings in its own way, and so they go on humming and bustling like a swarm of bees. Loads are carried in baskets on the head or shoulders, often also upon a sort of tray which they hold in front pretty high on the body grasping the outer edge with their hands which are bent well back. Similar scenes down to the minutest details are represented on the pictures of the ancient Egyptians.

BOYS AND GIRLS AT PLAY.

At a little open space near by we hear the confused shouts and cries of boys at play. Some bold warriors, holding up one foot and hopping on the other, try to knock each other down, and in order to play at this game they have taken off their only garment, a blue shirt, and bound it round their loins. Before long a weakling is thrown down, and kissing the ground, raises a frightful cry and begins to abuse his conqueror worse than Thersites. The latter in retaliation makes violent clutches at the only tuft of hair that has been left on the boy's shaved head, from which his cap has fallen during the scuffle. At last the boy gets free and runs off, casting all sorts of opprobrious epithets, among which that of "bastard" is never wanting, at his antagonist, and his father and forefathers.

Here also some boys have laid themselves down on the dusty ground, on which they have improvised a draught-board by drawing lines at right angles to one another, and are playing a game like draughts with stones picked up from the street for men. The men are called Moslim and Nusrani (Christian), and these names are always cried aloud. Others drive a ball by means of a club, or mounted on each other's backs play the ball-game of which the ancient Egyptians, and especially the Egyptian women, were so fond. Some are chasing a humble bee, setting off crackers, or firing small pocket-pistols. Some animal just caught, for example, a prickly fish, or, it may be a dog, is dragged along the ground with some life still in it, and is beaten to death amid loud cries of *yistáhel!* (it deserves it). The same cry is heard on the evening before the slaughter of any large animal, such as a camel or a buffalo, which is always an event in small places. The seller or slaughterer marches with his beast through the whole village followed by a band of boys, sometimes paid for the purpose, sometimes not, crying out incessantly *yistáhel!* which in this case is equivalent to: "it is good value." The buyers can thus see with their own eyes, while the animal is still alive, whether its flesh is sound and fat.

Another group of boys are engaged in the imitation of those well-known religious gymnastic exercises, called *Zikr*. A choir of little songsters, who are not yet fully able to speak their words correctly, sing with a loud voice and rapt expression in honour of the Prophet, repeating the phrase: "*la illah ill allah, Mohammed l(r)asul allah.*" A diminutive pair of human beings still at the very entrance of life, and wearing the innocent and simple dress of paradise, where man and beast still lived a quiet life at peace with one another, roll themselves on their mother earth in silent enjoyment; for numberless flies have found an undisturbed resting-place on their oily countenances and little watery eyes. The little children are playing with a "bride," that is, a doll scarcely bearing any resemblance to the human form, with shells, a clay camel, and the like. But there are not many kinds of toys in the children's hands, for they are considered as articles of luxury, and as such indeed toys are pretty good standards of civilization.

As soon as we are observed by the boys, they begin chirping in our ears *Bakshish yâ chauageh*. In vain we try not to hear them. The further off we remove, the more the little fellows feel themselves out of our reach, all the louder and more general do their demands become, and they now also bestow upon us the title of "*Nusrani*" (Christian), and every epithet that rhymes with that appellative.

SCHOOL.

We continue our wanderings through the streets and lanes of the town, expecting to fall in with other interesting scenes characteristic of the East, and before long a horrible confused noise arising from boys' voices and proceeding from a small house like a chapel forces itself on our ears. We put our head in at the open door, and see a worthy schoolmaster sitting with a cane in his hand in the midst of his scholars on the floor of the school-room, which is bare of furniture. All stages of boyhood are represented, from that at which the lisp and stammer of childhood are scarcely given up to that at which the youth becomes a man. One of the crowd, holding up a wooden or metal tablet close in front of him, is practising himself in reading aloud the venerable basis of all science, the alphabet, which the master has written out for him with large strokes; another makes his first attempts in writing; a third, more advanced, is reading or rather singing from the "pre-eminent book," the Koran, and accompanies his reading with an energetic oscillation of the upper part of the body. The master assists the efforts of every individual scholar with his superior knowledge, and not rarely also with the weight of his cane.

Nor does he lose sight of the general body of scholars, for his cane comes down with the speed of lightning on the knuckles of some inattentive boys, who were carrying on all sorts of games behind his back. An assistant, chosen from among his best pupils, aids him to the best of his ability in the practice of his pedagogic calling, instructs the younger ones with a manifest consciousness of his own importance, and makes no scruples about letting those who have been placed under his charge feel the weight of the cane intrusted to him. In the case of one of the learners the customary blows on the various members of the body have no effect, and, like the offender in the court of justice, he is stretched out upon the floor by his fellow-pupils, who act with great readiness the part of officers to their master, and is treated to the bastinado.

From sunrise till the evening call the schoolmaster is required to keep his pupils employed, allowing, however, a suitable period for relaxation at the time of the morning and mid-day meals. Every Thursday morning there is a public examination, during which the teacher remains a passive observer, and leaves the entire management of the school to his youthful assistant. The teacher receives a weekly fee of one piastre for every pupil. Friday is always a holiday. If the pupil after several years' schooling is able to drone off a few chapters of the Koran, the happy father is satisfied, the skilful teacher receives from him a few crowns as an honorary recompense for his labours, and the learned son leaves the school for ever. The high fees obtained by the numerous professional scribes shows how far from general, and how imperfect is the education of the people. It hardly needs to be mentioned that the teachers cannot live on the insignificant fee that they get from their pupils. They accordingly take upon themselves various other functions, such as those of text-writers, public readers of the Koran, hymn-singers, and attendants at the shrines of the saints.

A MOSQUE.

High in air above us there sounds a wonderful melody. It is the call to prayer, an institution peculiar to Mohammedan countries. On the parapet of a tower which rises like a pillar from the midst of the dense mass of houses, we see the *Muezzin*, the functionary who warns believers to bow themselves in adoration before the "highest and only God, and Mohammed is his prophet." We allow ourselves to be carried along by the streams of people who are now proceeding from all quarters in the direction in which the cry was heard, and we soon find ourselves before the temple.

Although we cannot here expect the majestic splendour of one of the mosques of the caliphs in the capital, yet we feel attracted by the peculiar taste of the modern Arabic architect. On the simple basis of a wall built with square-cut stones, he has employed all those artistic devices on which his religion, prohibiting the imitation of anything having life,[1] permits him to exercise his creative ideas; namely, mosaics, arabesques, geometrical figures, and alphabetical writing All these modes of decoration are lavishly employed, sometimes with elegance sometimes altogether tastelessly, on every part of the walls, but more especially on the portals and windows, which here, where there is no harem to hide, can be made more numerous. In making these openings the builder is not content with carrying out a single system, but forms a new style by the simultaneous use of all figures in which a wall can be imagined to be regularly pierced. The curve of the ass's back is seen in familiar juxtaposition with the camel's hump; the horse-shoe of the Moor appears in amicable alliance with the round arch of the Byzantine; the pointed arch soars aloft alongside of prosaic rectilinears. Points, lines, triangles, rhombuses, polygons, circles, arcs, undulations, and zigzags in all colours are chaotically distributed over the walls. The natural freedom of the Arabic writing has furnished the means of producing true works of art in the form of inscriptions, which are scattered over every part of the edifice.

---

[1] A rigid Mussulman cannot easily be induced to have his portrait painted, or to get himself photographed; it is only those who have come in contact with Europeans who have no scruples on that score. The view of the Prophet is that in painting anything having life something is abstracted from the soul of the object portrayed.

High above on the flat roof numerous generations of cupolas sprout round the great mother dome.

However marvellous and fantastic the outside shell of the temple may be, the interior is just as simple and puritanically devoid of ornament. In its essential features it differs so little from that of a Christian basilica that one is led to ask whether the founders of Islam, who displayed as little original genius for art as the Vandals, did not get their mosques built by conquered renegades. The high altar, where the Mohammedan lay-priest celebrates mass on Fridays, has become a wooden table supported by a few pillars. The pulpit has been retained. Instead of the blasphemous crucifix the eyes of the congregation are diverted to the niche in the wall, behind which lies Mecca. Besides these furnishings and a few framed inscriptions on the walls the interior spaces contain nothing but the invisible spirit of God. The old Arabic style of building has nothing in common with the ancient Egyptian. At the most a few columns of ancient temples are occasionally inserted in the more modern structures. According to some art critics the fundamental idea of the mosque is the Bedouin tent, and that of the arabesques the texture of a carpet.

We have the audacity to slink into the interior and place ourselves behind a pillar, and this we have accomplished by slipping a piece of silver into the hand of the door-keeper, who wished to preserve the sanctuary from being trodden by the unclean Frank. On another occasion we obtain entrance through meeting with a friend who closes the eyes of his fanatical fellow-believers by observing that at the bottom of our heart we are a Moslem. In any case we have, in common with the Moslems themselves, to take off our shoes.

Before prayer the Moslem must always carefully wash with running water all those parts of his body liable to become polluted by contact with the outer world; though it may be that he does not always at the same time purify his heart, which the washing symbolically represents. The priests of the ancient Egyptians were almost as particular in this respect, being likewise accustomed to perform religious ablutions several times a day.

By the time the last notes of the chant of the crier on the minaret have died away the whole congregation has arranged itself in rows before the Lord of hosts, with naked feet but covered heads. Each one visibly fills his soul with a purpose of devotion, energetically throwing aside for this solemn moment all joys and sorrows, all the hate and love belonging to earthly life. Under the guidance of an imam they then go through a series of observances, consisting in bending the body, falling on the knees, kissing the ground, turning the head, and performing a number of movements with their arms, hands, and fingers with all the precision of soldiers exercising, and all according to fixed regulations, in which the ambassador of God has been able to declare with accuracy what movements of the foot and hand, and what particular arrangement of the fingers, are most pleasing to God in any operation that has to be performed. As in the Christian Church the boys in the choir heighten the solemnity of the chief ceremonies of the mass by the sounding of cymbals; in the Mohammedan service the minaret-crier, who has by this time descended from his elevated station, sings out the exalted names of God and the Prophet, which from time to time are uttered in a loud voice by the otherwise silent worshippers. At the conclusion of the fatha, the Mohammedan paternoster, the whole congregation join in a prolonged Amen, which is pronounced in a low tone, and has a very impressive effect. Finally, after the worshipper has discharged the devotional duties common to all, he kneels upon the ground and lays the wants of his own heart before his creator, his mediator Mohammed, and Mohammed's holy family, and as he does this he holds his hands outstretched as if on them he had written his wants and were thence reading them off. All these ceremonies are performed without the assistance of any priest. Even the sermon on Fridays is delivered by a layman, it may be an artisan. In the Christian sense of the word Islam has no clergy, unless this name is given to the ulema and the kadis or ecclesiastical judges, who have studied theology. It is in fact the grandest thing in Islam, that its strength lies not in the hierarchy but in the people.

As if awakening from a long and beautiful dream, in which he believed himself to have seen the face of God, the Moslem at the end of the hour of prayer takes leave of the spiritual world and the angels who stood at his side, wipes his face with his hands, and steps out into the world of every-day life, proud to be adorned with the dust of the mosque which has stuck to his moist brow as he kissed the earth. Those who cannot so easily set their minds at rest find their way out of their difficulties by means of their rosary, as Theseus made his escape from the labyrinth with the help of a clue of thread. They mutter some unintelligible verses, and counting off one knot after another they pour out their feelings thirty-three times in honour of the glory of God (*subhan allah*), thirty-three times they render to him praise and thanks (*el hamdu lillah*), thirty-three times they acknowledge his supreme greatness (*allahu akbar*), and with the ninety-ninth knot they have once more happily arrived on this side of existence, and pursue their good or evil ways exactly according to their old proclivities.

But scarcely has the sun begun to descend in the heavens when the crier again ascends the minaret, and everything follows in the same order as in the morning; and the same is the case also when the last streak of day has disappeared and the vault of heaven is sprinkled over with stars. The Moslem thus prays at the first dawning of the day, as soon as a white thread can be distinguished from a black, again at mid-day when the sun has reached the culmination of his daily course, and again at evening when the length of a man's shadow is equal to the height of his body. It is no slight labour that Islam exacts of her followers. Their prayers may, however, be performed in their own houses, on the street, or wherever the worshippers may be, for God is everywhere. It is also free to the Moslem to give himself up to prayer at any time in the interval between one hour of prayer and another. The Moslem does not care to pray in the stillness of his chamber.

He prefers publicity and the companionship of his brethren at these exercises. In this way he gains not a little as a pious man in the esteem of his fellow citizens.

A SAINT'S MAUSOLEUM.

We again seek the open air, and are met by a band of men, who hurry past us laughing, disputing, and singing. Suddenly one cries out: "A Fatha to our lord Abdallah," and all stop before the lattice-window of a chapel. The noisy band is converted into a group of pious worshippers holding their hands before their faces. After a minute's pause they proceed on their way with the same boisterous noise as before. The sacred edifice, resembling in its fundamental conception the mausoleum of Hadrian, is built of stone or clay, and is in the form of a cube surmounted by an octagon terminating in a cupola. On each of the four corners of the cubical portion is erected a small tower or minaret, and the finial of the dome is crowned by a crescent moon, lying so that the points are turned upwards. The half-moon is never used, for it has lost interest for the adherents of Islam, and there is not even a name for it in the language. Nor is it the imaginary new moon of the calendar, but the newly risen narrow sickle-shaped strip as it first shows itself after the beginning of each lunar month, which is the symbol of Islam and the badge of its rulers. The appearance of this on the western horizon every believer watches month by month like his Sabæan forefathers in order to obtain from it, or at least by means of that sign, prosperity and bliss. The buildings already mentioned form the whole of the sanctuary, unless perhaps there is an open court adjoining with a number of outbuildings, and surrounded by a quadrangular wall. On the flat roof of these outbuildings we observe a frame made up of wooden bars, which, on the annual festival of the saintly patron of the mausoleum is carried in procession splendidly arrayed, and is called a *máhmel*. We boldly enter in at the gate. A few nods suffice to dispel the scruples of the guardian of the sacred spot; and in a short time, in consequence of the singular indulgence displayed to us, even the mysterious domed hall is trodden by our Christian feet after they have been deprived of their unclean covering. A large stone carved in the form of a sarcophagus takes up the greater part of the narrow space. The stone is covered with a bright

Mausoleum of a Saint.

green or red cloth with inscriptions embroidered on it in gold and silver, and with banners of a similar colour and similarly inscribed stuck round it. The walls are filled with pictorial representations of the holy places of Islam, including the city of David. In this picture-gallery red, green, and yellow are the most prominent colours. There is also no want of silver leaf and Dutch gold. Mount Sinai and other sacred mountains as depicted resemble a mound erected by white ants. The minarets make one think of gibbets. The sacred temples appear like tables, and their domes like balls rolling on the upper edges of the tables. The palms are like branched candlesticks; hell, paradise, and the river of life like the card of a compass.

In the corner of the sanctuary stands a wax candle as long and thick as an elephant's tusk. Beside it gapes a crocodile's mouth, while the rib of a gigantic fish menaces visitors like a drawn sword. Attached to the roof are a number of interlacing cords, and from these as from the branches of a Christmas-tree are suspended various glass lamps, little ships, ostrich eggs (which were also hung up in their temples and sanctuaries by the ancient Egyptians), but above all numberless little bundles of sacred earth from Mecca carefully wrapped up in sugar-loaf form.

We quit the most holy place, and take a look at the court and all that belongs to it, the niches for prayer, and the graves of the favoured dead, who must sleep in this consecrated earth a more blessed sleep than the common herd who people the graveyard without; and in passing out we cast a parting glance at the little room, from which we hear the sound of the strokes of a schoolmaster's cane and the cries of his young pupils. For schools and other foundations are often connected with these spots. But who was the great man to whom such a mausoleum has been built, and such reverence is paid? He was, according to Mohammedan ideas, a saint, who was endowed by God during his life (or perhaps only after his death) with miraculous powers as a compensation for his weak intellect, and who is accordingly regarded as a "favourite of God." In godless Europe, except in some districts such as Switzerland, where the idiots enjoy a high degree of respect, individuals of this class are called fools and imbeciles.

A BURIAL-PLACE.

Not far from this sanctuary, on the border of the desert, on the dividing line between living nature and dead, is the place allotted to those who have passed from life to death. No wall incloses the wide field, which is rather to be called a city of the dead than a graveyard. For, beside the mounds of earth and low flat gravestones, many considerable structures rise into the air; mausoleums, chapels, and mosques for the numerous miracle-working saints and other estimable God-favoured men, and in addition to these buildings a number of dwelling-houses where mourning families spend some days and nights, especially at the time of the great feasts beside the resting-place of their beloved dead. No living green thing, no fragrant flower, adorns the grave in the desert. Instead of a wreath a palm branch stuck in the grave in those days of mourning bespeaks a pure love and faith unconquered by death itself.

The army of the dead of all times and of all countries in which the language of the Koran is heard, is marshalled by the Prophet in orderly array, ready to stand armed in the faith before the Judge of the other world. The dead champion of Islam always lies with his head inclined to the right in such a manner that his face looks towards Mecca, the town which stands at the centre of the earth, and of all earths, that is, of all the heavenly bodies. The Egyptian, Turk, and Moghrebin look to the south-east; the Tartar looks to the south; the Indian to the west; the inhabitant of Sudan to the east. All grave-stones are laid in the same direction, and to show that the corpse has had the proper position given to it, the spot beneath which the head lies is marked by some external sign, for example, a turban carved in stone, an upright stone, slab, or merely a heap of stones, some wands stuck in the ground, and so forth, and often the place of the feet is correspondingly indicated. As if to make up for the want of a coffin,[1] the grave-stone is made in the form of one. It is oblong in form, and has a rounded or sharp-edged longitudinal ridge for men, and a longitudinal depression for women. The inscription, which gives some details regarding the person lying beneath, concludes with an invitation to pray a fatha over him:

For his sake a Fatha!

---

[1] The corpse is not inclosed in a coffin, but is placed in a kind of vault cut in the side of the grave at bottom.

CHAPTER II.

TRAVELLING BY LAND AND RIVER.

PREPARATIONS.

In order to make a journey of a few days in the valley of the Upper Nile, one requires something more than the quarter of an hour between resolve and starting that is sufficient for an active German gymnast, who is about to set out on a tour in the provinces of the Fatherland, and at the end of that brief space of time stands ready for the tramp with his travelling wallet by his side, and two or three thalers in his pocket; setting out in such a way one can go as a begging-pilgrim, and knock at the door of every farm-house on the road. Here there are no houses of reception or entertainment where a man can have for his money a furnished room, a bed, food, and drink. Such a thing is quite foreign to the ideas of Islam and its Bedouin hospitality. An Arabic inn in the European sense is not found even in the largest towns. Establishments of this kind present nothing but an empty room, the traveller having to provide his own food and bed. In such circumstances a journey by land must take another form than in the land of the Franks—even the smallest assumes more or less of the character of an *expedition*.

Since the termination of our journey lies in the narrow Nile-valley of Upper Egypt (in the Thebais, in the first place, or district of the city of Thebes of old renown, corresponding to the present mudirîeh of Keneh), and since this valley is nowhere broader than from 5 to 10 miles, and consequently no part of it far from the river, the most convenient and common mode of travel is by water. We have no hopes of a steamer, as these stop only at the larger towns, and have no certain times for arriving and departing. To hire a vessel for ourselves, since there is not a large company of us, would be very expensive, and we would also like to take for once a trip in the same way as the native citizen. We proceed accordingly to the landing-place to see if we can secure a passage, and soon find a well-laden craft that is to sail "to-morrow if it please God." We hasten home and hastily collect such things as are absolutely necessary, namely, a carpet, cushions, coverings, bread and biscuit, clarified butter, flesh, cheese, onions, salt, coffee, spirits or wine, pease, rice, dates, and fresh fruits, wood or coals, tobacco, and also cooking, eating, and smoking utensils, with the necessary bags, chests, and boxes.

THE EMBARKATION.

We get our baggage on board by earliest morn, with the assistance of a pack-donkey, but do not find the master of the vessel, who does not turn up by noon even, nor yet till late in the day. At last, however, he does make his appearance, and coolly meets our angry remonstrances with his, "Never mind; to-morrow if God pleases." But as we cannot start next day we determine to look out for another opportunity, and have our baggage again brought ashore. Vessel after vessel sails past in mid-stream, and call as we may they steer proudly onward with swelling sail, taking advantage of the favourable wind. At last we succeed in catching a small bark without a cabin, to which we gladly transfer ourselves and our belongings, and endeavour to make ourselves comfortable and at home by spreading our carpet beneath us, or by digging out an abode in the piled-up cargo of corn or dates, protecting ourselves against the rays of the sun by following the shadow of the huge sail, or by constructing a tent of rugs, wrappers, and spare sails.

The above means of travelling is only a make-shift; the Arabic public that make long voyages use the dahabiyeh, a vessel with a cabin. These vessels are constructed on the model of a floating house; but the house, which is built to rest upon the ship's bottom, does not occupy the middle, as it appears in fancy drawings of Noah's ark, nor as it did in the ships of the ancient Egyptians (which, strangely enough, have

THE EMBARKATION. 109

no resemblance to those of the present time, not even in the sail); it occupies the after half of the vessel. As a forty days' or even a single hour's rain is in these regions and in these days an improbability a ridged roof can easily be dispensed with, and accordingly the roof of the house takes the form of an open platform. The fore-part of the vessel carries the rigging, the simple mast, the slender yard swinging round its top, and the huge trapezoidal sail, which, during a stoppage of any length, is fastened round the yard in undulating folds. The communication with the platform and the beaked stern is effected by a plank that is placed like the scaffold used in rough-casting a house, running externally along the flanks of the cabin, from which a single false step would precipitate a person into the stream. During the voyage the captain of the vessel stations himself aft upon the platform with the long tiller in his hand, so that he can keep his eye on the crew while they are occupied about the rigging in the forepart of the vessel below. The crew are the more ready to obey his commands from the fact that he usually combines the dignity of captain with that of head of the family, those under his direction being generally his brothers, cousins, children, and grand-children. For the smaller class of vessels of this kind a crew of three or four men is considered sufficient, in cases of difficulty the friendly aid of the passengers being called in and immediately given, partly from self-interest, partly because the bargain is so made at starting.

The more fortunate among mortals when travelling in the cradle-country of mankind make use of saloon-vessels built on the same principle, but much more handsomely fitted up. These vessels alone deserve the name of *dahabiyeh*, that is, "little golden ship" (though the name may also be derived from *sahab*, to go or move). In these the dingy cabins are converted into fine saloons, fitted up with everything which the luxurious son of northern civilization has accustomed himself to require; the platform has become a pavilion, on which the consumptive foreigner from a colder clime drinks greedily into his damaged lungs the air warmed by the winter sun of the south, while in spite of wind and tide a crew of rowers urges the light galley to any point it is desired to reach.

The public has little opportunity for availing itself of the results achieved in this age of steam, since a regular river passenger service is not yet organized. An attempt was indeed made some years ago to set agoing such a scheme by the Viceregal River Steam Navigation Co. of the day. The fare charged was small, *viz.* about four shillings per day, or what was the same thing, per mudirîeh. But even that was too much for the common people, who continued to sail as before in their slow-moving dahabiyeh along with their baggage, which they cannot let out of their sight, so suspicious are they, while they do not know the value of time. Accordingly the company, like the post-office, worked at a loss on account of not being sufficiently patronized by the public, and soon gave up its regular passages. The principles of political economy are unknown in Egypt, and there was no thought of persevering in spite of loss. At present regular trips are made by the Nile steamers only during the winter months for the rich travellers from Europe. Still the river is continually navigated by a great many steamers, which are employed for government purposes, and receive occasional passengers. The crew, including the captain and engine-driver, is entirely composed of natives, who have emancipated themselves from their teachers in a gratifying manner, yet not without a previous mingling of the Anglo-Frankish and the Arabic element. This is seen in the narrow Frankish trousers and bare feet of the sailors, in the European uniform combined with the general unbuttoned state and red slippers of the captain, and in the Anglo-Arabic words of command, such as "stop," "halfy speed," "turn head," &c., which an uninitiated scribe could never unriddle.

All kinds of craft navigate the Nile besides these—larger and smaller cargo boats without cabins, great black tow-boats forming long lines behind the steamers, ferry-boats, fishing-boats, and rafts consisting of clay jars with handles fastened together; at the present day, however, the light and portable papyrus boats, once so celebrated, are no longer seen.

A VOYAGE ON THE NILE.

Thus we glide over the stream of streams. It is the height of summer, the period when the fresh north wind that then prevails drives the little vessel with bellying sail southwards through the flood now swollen with tropic rains. We revel in contemplation of the landscapes that fly past us and rivet our attention less by richness and brilliancy than by their strange solemnity. Bare steep banks of soft clay with beautifully regular strata alternate with gentler slopes, now clothed in a uniform manner with sown plants, now producing in separate clusters a natural growth of herbs which serve as pasture. At one time the steep bank is on the right at another on the left side, or, as the native always expresses himself, on the east or the west side; it is always at the point where the strongest current is, and may change with this in the course of time. The steep bank, with the land next adjoining it, always stands high and dry above the river and the inundated country, even when the river is at its highest, and is picturesquely dotted with palm groves, often also with towns and villages; but where it is not protected by blocks and dams of stone it is always in danger of being undermined and washed away by the summer flood. The valley-bottom is everywhere arable land; it usually exhibits a level surface, though on the outer edge towards the desert it is generally somewhat depressed. From the surface of the stream, however, the eye cannot reach far beyond the bank, the more distant stretches being hidden by herbaceous stems, trees, and bushes. From the evergreen surface of the valley, which is rich in cultivated fields but without meadows, rise on elevated points many small scattered palm groves, and behind these we may usually conjecture human habitations to exist, a farm, a village, or a small town. We make the same conjecture when a great number of vessels have brought to at any place, and the slender daughters and sturdy wives of the peasantry are going up and down the steep pathway on the bank, balancing the heavy earthen jars on their heads. They form along with the bathing buffaloes, and the shadoof men raising water from the river, the inevitable figures in every Nile landscape.

The river god, periodically causing his waters to overflow, has permitted few of the Egyptian founders of cities to settle immediately beside his bed. The greater number of the eminences that rise above the level of the valley, and stubbornly withdraw themselves from his annual bounties, are generally artificial, and are as a rule only sufficient to serve as sites for farms, villages, and hamlets; the roots of a town of any size, a town that would have occupied a great part of the comparatively small area of cultivable soil, had only the ever dry desert soil wherein to develop. Still the town-dweller, though thus repelled, has dug for the period of inundation a channel which conducts the sweet flood, with all that therein lives and moves, quietly and safely into the very heart of the town, so that for a few months he may draw from it refreshment and new strength, like the poor desert plant from the single shower of winter. For the remainder of the year he must send crowds of porters and beasts of burden in order to avail himself of the boon conveyed by the distant stream.

As we proceed our attention is forcibly attracted to the banks of sand or clay in the stream and at the edge of it, which, now when the summer is at its height, are becoming more and more covered by the water, while in winter and early summer they lie bare in great stretches. They form a rendezvous for innumerable water-fowl, from the pelican, the crane, the heron and the marabout, down to the lapwing and sandpiper. In the midst of these the great vulture, the little vulture, and the raven feed peaceably together on some piece of stranded carrion. Nor is it impossible for us to see there the sacred crocodile sunning himself. The countryman, however, is not deterred by that fact from planting the banks with melons and cucumbers as soon as the water withdraws and leaves them uncovered.

At the edge of the valley on both sides, now at some distance, now abutting perpendicularly on the river, rise the mountains, a term equivalent to desert, whitish-gray, treeless, without verdure, almost without soil. These mountains, which are calcareous in composition, belong on both sides of the valley to the tertiary formation; at Assouan (Syene), in the southern part of Egypt, they first become formed of primary rocks, especially syenite. High up, the precipitous rocky walls are often penetrated by great numbers of regular quadrangular holes like windows, along with natural clefts and crevices, where now only the creatures of the air fly in and out. But, strange fact! man in the form of mummies has dwelt here for thousands of years, and has selected these inaccessible tombs as eternal resting-places, here at least deeming himself safe from the profane investigations of treasure-digging Epigoni. But in many places at the foot of these desert mountains temple-palaces with splendid pillared halls, gigantic statues, richly painted and sculptured walls extend afar, bearing noble testimony to the mighty minds of the primeval dwellers in the land. Another and intellectually poorer time has built churches and convents on and with their ruins; while above them stand mud heaps hollowed out to serve as the dwellings of the race of modern Troglodytes. Thousands of years are thus piled above each other.

Not less pleasure and delight are experienced, especially in a clear still night with the moon at full, when the stream is high, and the vessel glides downwards assisted by the splashing stroke of the oars, accompanied with the peaceful sound of the monotonous songs of the crew. Among the passengers or the crew an accomplished singer may always be found to lead, beginning either with a popular song or one improvised by himself for the occasion, and being followed after every verse by the chorus of the rowers. The songs are such as the following:—

> "I entered your garden, best beloved,
>   And wished to pluck dates.
> By the thorn of the ripe, ah, the ripe fruit, dearest child,
>   Was my finger wounded."

Or,

> "I enter the garden,
>   And the rose shadowed me,

> Oh, my mistress, lead me about
> And be gracious to me.
> Oh leave me no longer alone and forsaken."

Less poetic is the song,

> "The gardener has been confined because he has stolen pomegranates,"

and the invocation of saints, such as

> "Oh, God! oh man of Damanhur, &c."

With or without sense, varied or the same for hours, the song soon causes a kind of intoxicated excitement which kindles a sort of demonic energy in the rowers, so that the power of poetry acts like that of steam. Between whiles a disciple of Clio with enviable eloquence, such as is here naturally cultivated among people of all ranks, narrates his adventures or all kinds of drolleries and tales for the common entertainment. Many also, while themselves out of reach in mid-stream, find a lively source of amusement in hurling at the boat-men, the peasants, and especially the water-raisers ashore, a flood of the choicest abuse in which the Arabic language is so rich, while these send back every epithet with cent. per cent. interest—all in mere harmless humour, forming a scene quite similar to those amusing colloquies between the students and the miners of the Black Forest in the Neckarhalde at Tübingen. Similar contests are related to have taken place among the ancient Egyptian women when on the pilgrimage to Bubastis.

The Nile voyage is quite different during winter and early summer, when the feeble waters glide languidly along and not a breath of air moves, or what wind there is is contrary and unsteady and idly sports with the flapping sail. Against this state of matters nothing avails but the unspeakable patience of the Mussulman with his trust in Providence. Fired with the thousand-fold repetition of the name of Allah and his prophet (*Ya Muhammed, sála 'alé*, "Oh, Mohammed, pray to him"), the crew drag by a long rope the floating burden, marching along the pathless bank with its endless windings, through the bushes and over the hollow projecting ledges of the clayey slope that are hurled downwards by the slightest footstep, and stopped by the cuttings made in the bank for irrigation purposes, while still the wished-for point that seemed so near is far from being reached. Contrary winds may compel them to bring to for days, even for weeks, at a desert part of the bank, far from civilization and exposed to the attacks of robbers. And when at last a good strong breeze takes pity on the traveller the pilot steers the vessel right upon a sand-bank, from which it cannot be got afloat again till the boatmen have been heaving at it for hours with their Titan shoulders to the rhythmic accompaniment of their *Eleza, ya eleza*.

The genial winter's sun quickly accomplishes his short course, and already the day's work that has advanced the vessel so little is at an end. Darkness, and even in these latitudes a very sensible degree of cold, drives everybody to some lurking place, in which, cowering under his mantle or rug, he sleeps through the long winter night till roused by the nipping frost of morning. Whoever has hired the after cabin is the most fortunate, for although it is little suited to freedom of movement it yet affords a close shelter; the youngsters, who have crept into the hold under the deck, between the bales of goods, and among rats and mice, are likewise not badly off; but the man that has taken up his quarters upon the narrow wooden bench of the main cabin is indeed to be commiserated. The folded wraps beneath him soon slide gradually outwards, drawing his body with them; and no sooner does he fall asleep than he has to start up again as his centre of gravity reaches the edge of the bench. At the same time the warm covering slips off, and the icy wind blows through the holes and crevices that are never wanting in the half broken window-shutters right upon his naked members. Only the native peasant and the Berberin or Nubian, indifferent alike to the glowing heat or the winter's frost, is able, enveloped in his plush, to fall asleep on the open deck or platform. At the period of early summer, when the south and west winds prevail (*Nau* and *Samum*), a voyage on the Nile is torture by day on account of the oppressive heat and the contrary winds, by night on account of the vermin and the frightful row that the rats and mice kick up. Whoever, therefore, can manage it takes his trip at the height of summer when the Nile is highest.

EATING AND DRINKING ON BOARD.

Amid such observations, considerations, and recollections, from which a general impression remains to us of the monotonous character of the landscape, the fauna and flora, and the people, time passes on, and hunger begins to make itself felt. One man begins to empty his sack, in which he had stowed away his provisions, and now every one is called by name and urgently invited to join him. It is easy to see that the invitation is a serious matter for him, even though his store were only spread out for the first time. On the other hand, there is a common understanding that those first invited ask their former host to join them at another time, namely, when his provender is all gone; or every one contributes something to the common meal in the manner of a picnic. Thus the whole company eat together or in groups, but never alone, that would be un-Arabic. By this hospitable practice a certain brotherliness is soon developed among those on board; differences of rank cease, and intimacies are formed that last perhaps for years. To have eaten salt and bread together is sufficient ground for avoiding or terminating quarrels. To be sure an excellent field is thus afforded to parasites, who flourish greatly in this country; and, on the other hand, the prudent host prefers to keep costly dainties at home. Any one who wishes to cook sets his sauce-pan on the clay vessel full of earth that serves as the caboose and stands in the fore part of the vessel. But when the vessel is moored to the bank, as is done in the evening, every mess does its cooking ashore, gathering dry reeds, stems of plants, and brushwood, and often plundering the neighbouring fields of their fruits and vegetables to supplement their meal.

Feeling thirsty, we let down a pitcher with a cord into the stream. Before we set it to our lips, however, all kinds of considerations crowd upon us: the water is turbid and muddy; we have already by means of the microscope detected in it animalcula, small crustacea, and minute worms; we have seen cattle bathing in it, and men washing their bodies and their clothes above our vessel, and emptying various matters into the stream; the carcass of an ox is floating past with a raven standing on it and pecking it; and such ingredients have been received by the stream from the whole of the immense country above. Shall we drink a mixture of the filth of the whole of North Africa! We venture; the Son of the Sun has done so before us, and all his sons continue to do so up to the present day, and are quite healthy notwithstanding. And indeed it is pure nectar; the soft cool water so refreshes us that we quite agree with the natives of the country, especially those from the desert, who consider a draught of Nile-water one of the greatest blessings the world can give.

A JOURNEY BY LAND.

In taking a trip entirely by land one has the advantage of not being dependent upon the wind and the humour of the crew, and of often being able to take a shorter route to his destination, though a land journey certainly has the disadvantage of being more fatiguing. From the condition of the roads the only means of travel are beasts for riding and for carrying burdens, *i.e.* either camels, asses, horses, or mules. A person can only go short distances on foot from the necessity of always having baggage with him. Broad highways there are none in this region, and of course no carriages, scarcely even a donkey-cart here and there. However suitable the camel may be for riding in the desert, riding on it in the cultivated Nile valley is not pleasant. Sitting aloft on a camel, we move along the narrow path on the bank which scarcely allows two such animals to pass, certainly not if they are carrying loads. One beast tries to get before another in front of it, or we are met by a herd of these or other animals. The camel on which we are riding is pushed close to the edge of the path, where there is a steep slope or a deep hole. Perhaps we have to take a still narrower field-path which suddenly strikes off right across the fields, down the slope of the embankment, over a clay field dried into great lumps, or over a wet and slippery patch of mire. Here there is a rivulet, at which the beast would fain drink, there a tree, a corn-field, or a bush, towards which it greedily stretches its neck.

The smaller and lighter donkey, with its nimble trot, is much better suited for this district. No path is too narrow for it, no way too steep, and it can be guided by the rein without any driver. A good Nile donkey trots and gallops for miles; it is distinguished from the mountain and pack-donkey as the dromedary or riding camel from the common camel. The ass is by far the most common and agreeable means of communication in the whole of the Egyptian portion of the Nile valley; hardly the poorest peasant cares to go on foot. People of higher rank ride higher, using a white ass of the genuine Arabic race of Nejd, a mule, or a horse. The ox or the buffalo is not yet commonly used for riding, as in the Soudan, though here peasant boys and even peasant women have begun to ride them to the field or to the watering-place.

When travelling by land it is customary to take a siesta during the day under some shady tree or grove where there is water; at night the practice is as described below. It is seldom that any one ventures to make a lonely night march, or to camp out by night in the fields, as is the custom in the desert, where there is no danger; this would give robbers and murderers too good a chance, and even would not be free from danger on account of the dogs roaming about everywhere and guarding the fields and farms.

AN INN.

At last we reach, if we have travelled by water, the haven of our destination; we disembark, while the vessel we have chanced to catch sails farther on. We load our baggage on the back of a donkey or a porter, such as may be found at all the more important landing-places, and ride to the nearest chief place. There we take up our quarters in the public lodging-house (caravanserai, Arabic *Wekáleh*) if there is one. It is merely a place of shelter, where one can get a roof to cover him and protect him from the terrors of night. All thought of finding in it comfort even approximating to what may be found in a regular Frankish inn we have long ago discarded. The furniture sufficient for a night's lodging according to Arabic notions we have ourselves brought with us, namely, a carpet, a cushion, a rug or mantle. The caravanserai has a spacious court round which, on the ground floor and the upper story, are a number of rooms; these are small and entirely without windows, having only a door which opens on the court, or in the upper story on the gallery which runs round the court. Before the large main door, and with an out-look on the street, sits the doorkeeper, or the goodman of the house here serves out coffee for his guests or any one who may come, coffee, in addition to water, being the only refreshment to be expected in this establishment. For our table we have ourselves to cater, and either try the productions of the dirty cook in the market, or make our servant prepare a simple meal with the materials contained in our travelling-bag, our fire-place being formed with two or three stones in a sheltered spot in the court-yard, or in the gallery. At nightfall we seek our rest on a carpet spread out in the open gallery, or if it is winter, withdraw into our little room.

Such lodging-houses exist only in the towns and larger market villages. If we find none such we must have recourse to the friendship of some acquaintance, or to some one to whom we are recommended, or we encamp, under the protection of the village guardians, on an open place in front of the houses. If we do not wish to do that, especially when it is winter, we knock boldly at the door of the village magistrate. Without being exactly an innkeeper, he is bound to receive strangers, he has almost every day to entertain various kinds of officials, providing food for them and their beasts, and he is not allowed to ask anything for so doing. However, he takes care afterwards to repay himself with the moneys that his servants often receive from the guests (the officials as a rule give nothing), and takes what meat, fowls, eggs, &c., he requires now from one member of his village flock now from another, and thus prudently shares the burden of quartering strangers.

A VILLAGE.

After dismounting somewhere and drinking some coffee, either as a ceremony of our reception or for refreshment, we take a tour through the village. While even in the town the lines of direction of the streets are not very correct, in the village there is in this matter perfect freedom. The better houses of the country people differ little from the buildings that the provincial town offers; they are clay-built blocks, one-story high, without windows, and pierced with

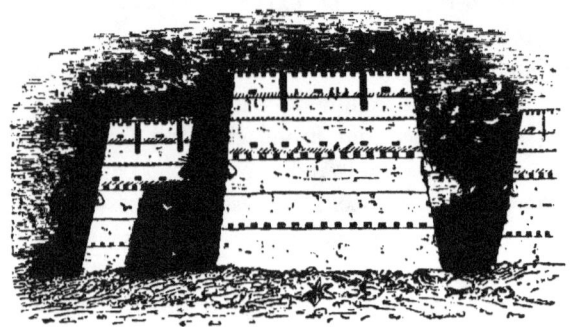

Pigeon Houses.

only a few holes for light, often narrowing towards the top in the ancient style; upon them, or beside them, frequently rise small quadrangular battlemented towers serving as pigeon houses. The house of the common Fellah degenerates gradually to the most wretched mud-hole, compared with which a nest of termites is a work of art. The Fellah does not use shaped bricks of dried clay, which give to a structure a neat regular appearance and sufficient stability for this rainless district, but he kneads for himself a hovel out of the clay left by the Nile in every hollow, mixed with some cut straw. A room is thus formed, which may be entered by creeping through a hole. It is covered over with reeds, straw mats, and rags. Round it he then builds a wall of clay about as high as a man, which incloses a yard. Cylindrical hollow spaces (*sûmaa*) are let into the wall at intervals and serve for keeping grain, which is poured into them from above; these were also in use among the ancient Egyptians. Other similar cavities serve as a pigeon house, a fowl house, an oven, and a cupboard, or the same purposes are served by certain columnar structures with dome-shaped tops, which stand detached in the middle of the court-yard. In particular there is seldom wanting a thick pillar about 5 feet high, having on the top a large round platter-shaped disk of clay with a high border round the outer edge, similar to a pillar with its capital.

That is the fundamental plan; when carried farther the walled-in farm-building is divided into several portions, such as stables, sheds, places for the poultry, especially the pigeons and a comparatively small portion added for the people. Commonly only a small part of the house is covered; the roofed portion being for winter, while in summer nothing but the blue vault of heaven is over people, cattle, and grain. On the roof and the crenellations of the walls promenade the dogs, which in the village have become domestic animals, though only in like degree with the cats; the relationship between man and the village dog is still very cold. The village dog is not quite wild and masterless like the town dog, but the master of the house throws him some scraps, for the sake of which the dog remains beside the house, watches the field, barks at the stranger, and guards the house from sudden attacks. Besides the common red-haired dog the Erment dog, a fine long-woolled race, with a thick head and similar to our sheep-dog, is not uncommon in our district. It was formerly introduced by the French conquerors, and is one of the few institutions that have kept their ground since their time. In walking through the fields a person has to be on his guard against these dogs, which often gather in a pack to attack a strange intruder.

The village is inhabited by the *Fellah*, that is, countryman, and here in Upper Egypt by a variety almost as dark as an Ethiopian, which has remained, comparatively speaking, very little affected by the international race-crossings through which the people of the Pharaohs has gradually passed. The dress of the peasant of Upper Egypt is no longer the blue cotton shirt of the inhabitant of the lower country, which at most serves him for an under garment; but a wide robe of brown unbleached woollen stuff, the sleeves of which, wide enough to admit his whole body, hang down almost to his ankles. This race is very well formed, almost always spare and at the same time muscular and full of endurance. The youth of both sexes have as a rule agreeable and even elegant forms. To be sure old age comes on early, and a maiden is not to be blamed if she prefers a beardless young fellow as a husband, or a man if he courts, when he can, a mere girl. The women of many places are celebrated far and wide for their good looks; those of Balas for instance, where the well-known large earthen pitchers for carrying water—the *baláseh*—are made. Indeed a slim, brown Fellah girl, twelve to fifteen years of age, and just arrived at puberty, dozens of whom stroll every evening from the village to the river for water, is really a charming sight, as she balances upon her head with rare dexterity and grace the above-mentioned *balás*, with its convex bottom and eccentric centre of gravity, carrying herself along lightly on her naked feet, unhampered by anything in the shape of a shoe. To be sure the figure is seen to less advantage under the brown woollen dress, the *hulalieh*, than under the thin light-blue cotton shift of the Fellah women of the lower country; the veil too that floats down over the back, or the kerchief, is apt to be drawn over the face at the sight of a man, or at least a corner of it is taken into the mouth. But still a finely rounded arm adorned with bracelets is often visible up to the shoulder, supporting from time to time the pitcher on the head, and the greater number do not think of aping the "forbidden ones," as those of the towns must, by concealing their faces. Golden ear-rings, silver nose-rings, a string of beads of small value or of gold coins, a silver band on the upper arm, tattooing of a blue colour on the face, arms, and hands are the ornaments that even the poorer peasant women would not like to deny herself. In later life those Graces usually became frightfully ugly; the nose-ring, the painting, the now unsparing exhibition of the naked skin, heighten the shocking sight. The full beard of the man, which early becomes grizzled, covers and conceals the wrinkled features of age and gives him the venerable appearance of the sheikh.

The Fellah, at least of the poorer class, is almost exclusively a vegetarian, and pastures his tongue mostly on coarse, heavy, and raw substances.[1] To his black millet-bread or his cakes of unleavened flour he eats salt, caraway, garlic, onions, and other vegetables, raw and uncooked, by preference, and in addition the many kinds of fruits he possesses, especially dates and melons. With his sharp teeth he eats into the rind of the doom-nut and the stems of the sugar-cane, which lacerate the gums of a person unaccustomed to them and make them bleed, and he chews grain and legumes slightly roasted, maize, beans, chick-peas, and half ripe wheat. He does not allow himself many dainties; any of this sort that he has, such as milk, eggs, fowls, pigeons, or cattle, he sells, though on a few days of the year, at family or religious feasts, when impelled by religion, he does allow himself the indulgence of a good piece of mutton. Spirituous liquors he never tastes. It is only with tobacco that he is not niggardly. A wife and family too are quite indispensable to him, he would rather starve, and allow those dependent on him to starve also, than remain unmarried. From the political pressure weighing him down, he cannot easily raise himself from his condition of poverty, and from indolence he has no great

[1] The people are fond of telling the story of a Fellah whom Napoleon I. is said to have taken with him, and who became a celebrated general. Becoming sick he tried all the doctors in Europe in vain. At last he returned to Egypt, and meeting one of the friends of his youth told him of his sufferings. This friend advised him to fall back upon his old Fellah diet, and lo and behold, after a short time he completely recovered!

desire to do so (most of the Fellahs are mere day labourers or tenants, not land-owners); yet from his contentment and domesticity he is always merry, he chats, jokes, and sings, is healthy, and incredibly efficient and assiduous in working.

The Fellah people are everywhere held in the lowest estimation as a degenerate race; indeed they apply to themselves the degrading names of "brood of the Pharaohs" and "Fellah." Poverty of course breeds dirt; in an earthen burrow which has to shelter a numerous family, which has a roof consisting of rags, which stands in a court-yard where all kinds of domestic animals and children mingle pell-mell, and which at the same time serves as sitting-room and bed-room, as kitchen, dining-room, and stable, it is not to be expected that wall and floor should shine, the dishes glance, and every utensil be in its proper place. The curious visitor will probably find the external walls thickly plastered with cow-dung, which serves as fuel for baking and cooking; pot-bellied, blear-eyed, naked children, with flies and mosquitos swarming upon them, are creeping about; the women in scanty clothing are catching the vermin on themselves, while the men and boys of the house are stretched on the ground clothed in the single woollen garment that serves them for both a summer and a winter dress.

A general view of the village shows us sights of the same kind. In spite of all the oft-repeated sanitary ordinances carrion of many kinds still lies about the village or floats in pools and canals; the Nile is still regarded as the most suitable burying-place for cattle; refuse and rubbish, with intermingled animal remains, have accumulated till they form veritable mountains round the village, and the hollows between have been selected as cess-pools for the commune, the houses never possessing such conveniences.

However, let us recall to mind the filthy yards and rooms, the dung-heaps and puddles, the streets only passable with tall boots, the glazed coat sleeves and leather hose innocent of washing, the natural timidity at water of the inhabitant of an out-of-the way village in our own country; let us reflect that animal refuse in the land of Egypt is quickly consumed by hungry dogs, vultures, and insects, and then completely and quickly dried up in the dry hot atmosphere; that, farther, the Fellah, as a Moslem, washes himself five times a day, and in addition has from time to time to take a bath, and the comparison may prove to be entirely in favour of the poor decried Fellah.

In many respects we must give the Fellah even a high place. Though belonging to the very lowest rank, he knows how to conduct himself with propriety, almost with polish, in society; he may be often rough, but he is never rude and boorish, a main reason for this being that he never gets drunk. Compliments flow from his eloquent tongue till they verge on flattery and falsehood. He is entertaining, witty, full of fancy, good-humoured in ordinary intercourse, and if at all well treated; but he is mendacious, deceitful, avaricious, fond of begging, and even thievish, when there is any question of *meum* and *tuum*. Patiently, like the camel, he bears the burden laid upon him; but if it seems too heavy he becomes stubborn and self-willed, until he has received a due number of official blows upon the soles of his feet, whereupon he immediately becomes obedient again and bends slavishly before his Turkish master, his superior in energy. Such endurance and stubbornness are also said to have been qualities of his ancestors at least in later times.

THE COUNTRY IN THE CIRCLE OF THE YEAR.

The appearance of the country, like that of its inhabitants, is for a visitor from the North new and strange, quite different indeed from that of any other on the face of the earth, and varying radically according to the season of the year. The seasons, spring, summer, autumn, winter, are here almost entirely astronomical conceptions; this division and succession is not known to agriculture, scarcely to language, or at least in another sense. Let us follow the year in its course.

THE OVERFLOW OF THE NILE.

According to the most ancient Egyptian mode of reckoning —and Islam, with its lunar months, quite impracticable for agriculture, has not been able to effect anything against this arrangement—the year begins on the 1st of the Coptic month Tut, corresponding to the 11th of September, when the Nile is at its highest. The land of Egypt is now a freshwater archipelago, and the waters cover the ground like the winter snow in the North, spreading their blessing over the greater portion of the fields. The swollen stream has flowed over them, but not destructively, man having tamed the wild element for thousands of years. The great main artery, full to overflowing, pours its nourishing fluid into large, deep, lateral canals constructed by the hand of man, which reach to near the edge of the desert, and sometimes return with a bend to the main channel, taking advantage of the fall of the valley. At intervals the canals are crossed by dams, behind which the water collects and flows through sluices down upon the adjacent land. When the land lying behind the first dam has been sufficiently covered by the overflow from the river, an opening is made in this dam, the water then runs along the canal to the next dam, overflows the district belonging to it, and so on and on. If the river does not rise sufficiently high, as is the case in many years, the water scarcely reaches the remotest parts of the valley, which accordingly remain for this year dry and fallow. The water is not allowed to touch those fields upon which a crop is still standing till after harvest. When the river falls the fertilizing water is still retained for some time on the field by damming it up.

Scattered over the inundated country there are a number of elevated points, which experience has proved to be above the reach of the water; these remain like islands rising above the great lake, and are used as sites for human habitations, and for growing such productions as cannot endure an inundation. In order that they may be still more secure, they are surrounded with an earthen dyke, especially the gardens, which the owners would be sorry to see overflowed. Such elevated points may either be alluvial formations dating from the original formation of the Nile valley, or are partly formed artificially by piling up rubbish.

At these times communication is often possible only by

boats and rafts; the principal places, however, are connected by earthen causeways, which, directing their course according to the configuration of the ground, have usually extensive windings, and cause the traveller upon *terra firma* to take very roundabout roads. It sometimes happens, too, that the flood advances rapidly with great force and in extraordinary volume; the dyke, which is nowhere strengthened by stonework, is broken through at some point of least resistance, the land beyond, which was intended to be kept dry, is overflowed, and the communication is interrupted. This happens almost every year at individual points, and in many years, as in 1863, 1869, and 1874, much mischief is thereby occasioned.

The period of high water is the crisis for the country. The people are in a state of excitement, and, "How much has the Nile risen to-day?" is the daily question of every one who thinks about the future. For, if the overflow is too scanty, a multitude of fields remain uncultivable and fallow, as so much added to the neighbouring desert, and the consequence is scarcity, if not actual famine. If, on the other hand, it is too abundant, then it is almost impossible to keep the element within bounds, and great damage is everywhere caused by the bursting of dykes, the devastation of cultivated land, the laying under water of dwellings, the washing away of embankments, and the drowning of cattle and human beings. On these occasions there are a multitude of hydraulic engineers, if we may call them so, provincial officials of all kinds, high and low, magistrates, burgesses, and peasants, constantly on their legs, examining whether the dams and sluices are in good order, and if any rupture occurs the people are forced to set to work. Even the animals are in an excited state. The cattle must be driven from the low grounds over which the water is spreading; the wild animals, such as mice and the like, have to leave their holes and find new ones on higher ground; the creeping creatures, such as lizards, insects, and worms, take refuge where the water has not yet reached, but at last are drowned. The grain-eating birds, especially the pigeons, can no longer procure their food, and migrate to the desert and the great caravan route; while the water-birds now find their food abundant in the waters, in which swarm innumerable frogs, fish, and water-insects, and they arrive in crowds.

If, however, the river god has filled his horn of plenty exactly to the brim, and the fact of its having done so has become clear by New-year's or Nerûs day, everybody is in a state of joyful excitement, "fantasies" are indulged in as well as the pleasures of masquerading, and whoever can so arrange it now gets married.[1] For after this time scarcely a moment injurious to the harvest need be feared. The countryman has now more rest than at other seasons, and has time for festivities. At this time the ancient Egyptians also indulged in all sorts of sports and pastimes, and held great annual feasts, such as that of Hermes or Thôt, on the 19th of the month of Tut, which was sacred to him. Along with the water an agreeable coolness has been diffused over the land, previously glowing with tropical heat; the oppressive Samoom of summer yields before a cool north wind; it is the "Nile-autumn," the most agreeable season in the land of Egypt. The vessels move about more than at other times, and the voyages are considerably shortened, up stream by the force of the strong north wind, which seldom intermits, down stream by the strong current. Desert towns become river ports, and the products of the country can be loaded and unloaded outside and inside of their gates. Lastly, that the measure of delights may be full, the Nile water, that drink divine, is cooler and more palatable, although more turbid than before, and dates, melons, pomegranates, lemons, cucumbers, and all kinds of fruits have just become ripe. Accordingly, now is the time when any one who can recruit his health once a year does so, by enjoying a change of air, or taking a course of bathing in the open water or in the public steam-baths, or by trying the fruit-cure.

According to the common opinion the Nile now remains

---

[1] For the three days' rule of Abu Nerus, see Chap. III., The Nerus Day.

standing at its height, neither rising nor falling, till the Christian festival of the invention of the cross (end of September). Even the Mohammedan countryman in this case follows the Christian in reckoning by the cross—at other times so reviled.

AFTER THE INUNDATION.

Although even during the inundation the operations of agriculture do not stand quite still, since the fields not reached by the flood must be continually watered artificially, yet the labour mainly begins only after the Nile has withdrawn, and the fields begin to dry. The plough in the first place has to turn up the soft and clayey soil, which is covered with a fresh layer of clay and deeply sodden with water. The implements of agriculture, still more than those employed in handicrafts, have preserved their primitive character, most of them being exactly the same as those employed by the ancient Egyptians; with the plough that is completely the case. This instrument, which is quite without wheels, is formed essentially of two pieces of timber meeting at an obtuse angle, the lower piece terminating in the share, which is of a rounded wedge shape and shod with iron, seldom entirely of this metal, while the upper or hinder piece rises obliquely, forming the stilt. From the opening of the angle rises the beam, which is fastened to the plough at its extremity directly, and farther up by means of a perpendicular timber. At the fore end of the beam a long cross-bar is let in or attached, and this, lying over the necks of the oxen, and fastened to them on each side by pieces of wood hanging down, or by cords, forms the yoke. The different parts are by no means neatly jointed, cut, and turned, but are mostly made of rough branches just as they grew, with all their knots and bends, clinched together, or merely tied with cords of palm-bast. Place behind this the brown-coloured Fellah, having his bald head covered with a skull-cap, and the upper part of his body or the whole of it bare, except for the loin-cloth;[1] and place

[1] The loin-cloth, often only in the form of a piece of cloth drawn through

in front the team, either oxen, asses, buffaloes, horses, or sometimes though more rarely camels, or it may be a camel on one side, a buffalo on the other, and then we have a true picture of the primeval ploughman. The implement suffices for the soft, slimy, stoneless soil, in which it draws only very superficial furrows, and no one thinks of improving it. For many fields the hoe alone is sufficient.

The ploughing is followed by the sowing, and the harrowing or smoothing of the soil, the latter being usually accomplished by causing draught cattle to drag a palm branch over the surface, more seldom by a toothed roller. The ancients drove swine and other beasts to the fields when the seed was put in. The manuring of the soil has been excellently performed already by the overflowing river; the dark rich soil comes chiefly from the mountains of Abyssinia by the Blue River, the White River contributing little. Only a few cultivated plants require a special manuring, for which pigeons' dung is the kind chiefly used.

Thus gradually does the year wear round to winter, that is, the time when the human body often experiences, especially at night before and at sunrise, a very sensible degree of cold, even in the most southerly parts of Upper Egypt; when a person is glad to take a seat beside the brazier, and wrap himself up in warm coverings (since the temperature often falls to 39° Fahr.); but when the growth of plants, upon the soil thoroughly penetrated by moisture, is most luxuriant, and the Nile valley at its greenest. Every month there is something to sow as well as to gather in, and accordingly always something fresh to eat.

THE EGYPTIAN CALENDAR.

The Arabic calendar for Egypt, little known among us, supplies a variety of interesting information relating to

---

between the thighs, is fastened to a leathern thong, which, being plaited by the hand of a woman, serves as a talisman for masculine vigour, and is worn by every peasant. Such an article was also worn by the ancient Egyptians, judging from representations.

THE EGYPTIAN CALENDAR. 131

agriculture, and we give a short extract from it. The Mohammedan, Coptic, Greek, Frankish, and even Jewish feasts and systems of reckoning the months, all which are conscientiously and harmoniously set down in it side by side, as well as the astronomical information regarding the sun's position and the length of the day, we omit, but we do not leave out the scattered sanitary recommendations. The times given for sowing and reaping are more suitable for Lower Egypt; Upper Egypt is ten to fourteen days earlier on the average.[1]

SEPTEMBER. 15. Cotton harvest (little cotton is planted in Upper Egypt). 16. Dew begins to fall. 17. Pomegranates sown. 19. Olive gathering (in Lower Egypt). 20. Time of Limunes (or small Egyptian citrons). 21. Dates (also as early as August). 24. Pomegranates. 27. Fresh fruits, best kind of food. 29. Eat *tunke* (*terid*, that is, bread in broth made with meat).

OCTOBER. 1. Good is it to glance towards the clouds (?). 8. The fruit (the bamujeh fruit) ripens (?). 9. (Sowing of clover, which gives three or four crops; in Upper Egypt instead of it the chickling vetch and liquorice vetch are more commonly sown as fodder and pasture plants). 10. (Maize harvest.) 15. Rice harvest (only in Lower Egypt). 16. End of high water in the Nile. 18. Drink cooling drinks (juice of fruits?). 23. Flax sown. 25. Wheat sown (also barley). 26. Avoid sleeping in the open air. 27. Beginning of morning coolness.

NOVEMBER. 2. Do not drink at night. 5. Roses. 7. Violets sown. 16. Saffron gathered. 17. Rain. 18. South winds. Drink warm water fasting. 21. Durra harvest (autumn crop, which stood during the inundation). 24. Horses pastured. 25. The whole night becomes cold (in the course of November most of the winter crops are sown— lentils, chick-peas, wheat, barley, beans, peas, lupines, safflower, lettuce, flax, poppy, winter durra).

DECEMBER. 1. Caraway, anise, black cummin sown. Time of the black crabs. 4. Olive-pressing. 5. Eat everything hot. 10. (First cutting of clover.) 11. Insects perish, serpents and mosquitos disappear. 15. Sugar-cane ripe. (Winter melon sown.) 16. Drink nothing out of open vessels for three nights. 17. The ants penetrate deep into the ground. 18. Vapours rise from the soil (mist). 23. First frost. 25. Late wheat sown. 29. Vines pruned.

JANUARY. 3. Avoid eating fowls. 11. Tobacco sown. Strong cold. 10. (Chickling vetch and liquorice vetch cut or eaten off). 17. Baptismal feast. Greatest cold of winter (called baptism-cold; at this time the Christians in their pious zeal take a cold plunge-bath). The Nile water becomes sweet and clear. 18. The depths of the earth

---

[1] The statements in parenthesis are taken from other sources.

become warm. 22. Eat hot (that is, heating) articles of food (such as legumes). 28. Last severe cold.

FEBRUARY. 1. The sap rises in the stems; cattle in heat. 3. Plums sown; trees planted. 10. Young lambs. 13. The cold is broken. 16. Violets. 18-20. The little sun (see below). 21. Birds pair. 22. Young cucumbers. 25. Avoid sitting in the sun.

MARCH. 2. Water-fowl in great multitudes. 10. Indian cotton (and rice) sown; silk-worms gathered (all this only in Lower Egypt). 10. (Barley harvest.) 12. Locusts develop. 14. Sesame sown. 17. Violent hurricanes and whirlwinds. 18. Swallows. 20. Large sun (see below). 24. Sugar-cane sown; (winter melons ripe). 25. Egyptian cotton sown. Flax reaped. 26. North winds. 29. Caraway sown. 30. Eat the flesh of goats and fowls.

APRIL. 1. Avoid eating cheese. 5. Time for blood-letting. 6. Trees in blossom (dates in blossom; summer durra and indigo sown). 8. Time for purging. 10. (Wheat harvest in Upper Egypt.) 12. The almonds form fruits. 16. Colds prevail. 17. First harvest in Cairo. 20. Preserve roses. 29. Easter Monday; beginning of Chamasin (Easter varies, however).

MAY. 2. Henna sown. 4. Make use of acids. 6. Strong gusts of wind from the north. 7. Blood-letting, and blood purifying drinks. 11. (Summer) cucumbers sown. 12. Late wheat harvest. 14. Avoid salted meats. 17. (Summer) durra sown in Upper Egypt. 21. Poppy heads gathered. 22. Falling of manna and quails (?). 22. Safflower blossoms gathered. 27. Beginning of the strong heat. Sirius sets. 31. Time of apricots.

JUNE. 1. The sap of the trees begins to diminish. 2. According to Hippocrates medical treatment should be avoided for 75 days from this time. 5. End of the "Nile-burning" (drought). 7. Rice sown. 8. The Nile water changes. 9. Rise of the Pleiades (*Tureya*). 10. Great heat in men's bodies. 11. The soil becomes cracked. 14. Stinking miasmata. 15. Honey taken from the hives. 16. Drink no water from the Nile for 15 days. 16-17. Night of the drop (see below). 19. First grapes. 20. Water melons. 22. Strongest heat. 23. The Nile begins to rise. 24. Bathe in cold water. 25. Use tamarinds. 26. Press juice from unripe grapes (*husum*). 27. Use acids. 29. Peaches and plums. 30. Last time for sowing sesame.

JULY. 3. The height of the Nile proclaimed. 4. Avoid purgatives. 5. The locusts perish. 7. The Nile becomes rapid. 9. Rather strong north winds. 10. Chief time for honey. 11. The air becomes temperate. 14. Maismata and fleas vanish; the plague ceases where it prevails. 19. Strong winds. 20. Mustard seed gathered; (summer durra harvest). 21. Samoom winds for forty days. 25. Eye complaints common. 26. Avoid washing clothes for seven days. 27. Grapes, figs. 28. Black cummin. 29. Grape-must.

AUGUST. 1. Summer melons. 3. Sirius rises. 9. Radish sown; cotton picking. 10. Pistachio-nut ripe. 12. First of the pomegranates.

15. (Autumn durra sown.) 17. Beware of the stings of insects. 18. The leaves of the trees changed. 19. Avoid eating sweets; garlic and onions sown. 20. Weaning of the domestic animals. 24. Vermin, mosquitos. 25. Morning coolness; young lambs. 29. Drink thick curdled milk; avoid the warm bath. 31. Rape-sowing; Fish-fry; Drink less water.

THE TIME OF THE SMALL AND OF THE GREAT SUN.

The general seed time, the short and verdant period of winter, follows, then, the period of inundation. Already by the 19th–20th of February, four weeks before spring begins astronomically speaking, the cold is broken by the approach of the "small sun," and judging from one's sensations, spring is begun. The name *robī'a* (spring) means literally "pasture," just as the German *Wonnemonat* (May) is properly *Weidemonat* ("pasture-month"), and under this title the native of Upper Egypt includes a part of January and the whole of February, when all the cattle are allowed to pasture for some weeks upon clover and vetches, and are only in exceptional cases, and usually against the wish of the owner, made to do any work. On the 20th–21st March appears the "great sun," which forms the dividing point between the winter and the summer half-year, the time following it being looked upon as belonging to summer. The period "between the suns," that is, between the little and the great sun, is important for gardening operations; whatever has to be set or planted is then put into the ground.

CHAMASIN AND EARLY SUMMER.

In April, at a time which varies, but does not agree with the Gregorian reckoning, occurs the Easter of the Copts, an important point in reckoning among natives of every faith. With Easter-monday, on which everybody goes abroad in order "to smell the good air," begins the dreaded season of *chamasîn*. By that term they do not understand, at least in Upper Egypt, a certain kind of wind, but the fifty days between Easter and Pentecost, when unwholesome winds, especially south winds, prevail, and diseases commonly invade the country. This and the period immediately succeeding it, the dry and hot early summer, when also the Nile has least water, are for Egypt the gloomiest times. Towards the summer solstice the rise of the Nile begins to be noticeable, accompanied by an agreeable and healthy coolness, north winds becoming at the same time more and more frequent. But some time before this, according to the popular belief, on the night of the 16th–17th June, a "drop" has fallen into the Nile and impregnated it, thus gradually producing high water. The period during and after the inundation is among the healthiest and most agreeable, although one would naturally suppose the contrary, and there are, in Upper Egypt at least, no intermitting fevers. In July and August a hot west wind called *samoom* or *samum* (poison-wind) often blows.

SUMMER CULTURE.

Agriculture does not stand still in the dry warm summer; on the contrary, the countryman now really works for the first time; this is the period of summer culture, after which comes the short period of autumn culture during the inundation, when a few fields from which the overflowing Nile is kept back are made to grow durra and maize, and in Lower Egypt also cotton and rice. The work at this time consists chiefly in irrigation. The field that is artificially watered gives two, often three, harvests in the year, the land that is merely overflowed only one. In Upper Egypt the latter forms by far the greater portion and remains fallow in summer, but in recompense the crops, especially the wheat, are much better and more highly prized than those in Lower Egypt, where the greater number of the fields are made to bear crops in summer also. In order to water all these fields once more much labour, money, and above all much water, is necessary, which in Upper Egypt is hard to be got. When it can be managed, however, it is managed, and such fields as can be subjected to an irrigation of both kinds are the best and dearest. Fields that are watered entirely by artificial means serve chiefly as gardens or grounds for growing vegetables.

WATER-RAISING APPARATUS.

The methods and machines for irrigation most commonly used in Upper Egypt are the well-known water-wheel, and especially the shadoof or water-raising apparatus, to which in Lower Egypt, where the water does not require to be raised so high, the swinging basket and a kind of chambered wheel are added—all instruments of ingenious simplicity that fulfil their object very well. Large and skilfully constructed pumping apparatus exist only in the plantations of the pashas, the people will have nothing to do with them; if a private person ventures upon any of these novelties he is sure to let it stand again in a few months and return to his old practice, since something will soon become broken or choked up, and no one can be found for hundreds of miles who is able to put it to rights. The shadoof, as it is still constructed, the Fellahs received from their forefathers, the people of the Pharaohs. In the soft and steep bank of the river, or of a canal, a number of trenches, with terraces behind them, are dug above each other, the number depending on the height of the bank; at the top a reservoir is constructed, the bottom of which is often strengthened by layers of reeds or palm stems. The principle of the apparatus for raising the water is similar to that of a draw-well, perhaps still more practical. On the upper ends of two pillars formed of rough palm stems, or more commonly of clay, a cross-beam is firmly attached, and under the middle of this a long beam is balanced by means of a cord-and-bar joint (so that it may move freely up and down). Behind, that is, at the shorter end, the end farther from the river, this beam terminates in a colossal ball of clay; from the other end hangs a palm twig, to the lower extremity of which a bucket, usually of leather, is fastened. It is the duty of the labourers standing on the terraces to fill the bucket in the lowest basin and to empty the contents into the next above it; the bucket is raised by the weight of the clay ball on the arm of the lever, and the workman has only to guide it. Thus even in ancient times did men discover how to save labour by mechanical means.

Having reached the highest basin, the water flows by a small channel on to the border channels of the fields that are to be watered.

When the river rises one terrace after another is swept away, and when it sinks again as many new ones are constructed every year.

The motive power in these water-raising apparatus is a class of men called "fathers of the shadoof," who in classical brown nakedness enliven at intervals the banks of the Nile, and every now and then utter shrill and plaintive cries, while the beams groan and the buckets splash.

A WATER-WHEEL.

The water-wheel is a far more complicated apparatus, and appears not to have been known to the ancient Egyptians, or only in later times. In Upper Egypt it is almost solely used for gardens. The chief condition for the existence of such a wheel is a well that contains spring water all the year round at a certain depth, and that may be the case some distance out in the desert. Such water, like all in Egypt obtained by digging, is always brackish, often scarcely drinkable. Two small walls standing opposite each other carry a large undressed palm stem lying across them. This forms the upper support, while several pieces of timber form the lower support of a vertical wooden cylinder pointed at both ends, and made to revolve by means of oxen or other animals yoked to a pole projecting from it either horizontally or obliquely. The cylinder turns a toothed-wheel of wood which is immovably attached to it below, and this turns a second toothed-wheel sunk deeply into the ground, the lengthened subterranean axis of this latter wheel again driving round the water-wheel proper. On the water-wheel is laid a so-called endless cord which below dips into the water. To the cord at short intervals clay pitchers are attached, and so ingeniously disposed that they fill themselves with water in the well below, and then being carried up and over the top of the wheel empty themselves one after the other into the reservoir standing there, the empty pitchers going down the other side again. The driving beam, which projects from the cylinder, and has at the outer end diverging pieces of wood forming a seat for the driver, often comfortably padded, is now pulled round in a perpetual circle by the animal attached to the draught-tree. In order to prevent the beast from diverging from the circular course, its head is also separately attached to the main cylinder by a cord or yoke, and for a similar purpose, or to prevent giddiness, its eyes are tied up. The animal—an ox, a cow, a horse, seldom a camel or an ass—once set in motion revolves, like a planet, in its strictly defined orbit, so long as the *vis a tergo*, namely, the voice of the driver or the lash, or still more commonly the goad, continues. The work proceeds with the greatest briskness when the driver, commonly a naked Fellah boy, seats himself on the above-mentioned frame, and going round himself with the machine keeps his team on its mettle. At the same time there is a collateral duty that he performs; whenever the beast he is driving is about to drop its excrement the boy catches it in his hand and lays the collected material beside the course. This is done less perhaps to keep the course clean than to get a supply of the important fuel that is formed by the dried dung of cattle, and cakes of this material are abundantly plastered on the little walls in order to dry.

The water thus raised is collected in a basin, and thence conveyed by a small channel to the land, which may be laid under water by means of a net-work of capillaries drawn at right angles, and surrounding small square fields lying at a lower level. The whole site occupied by the water-wheel is always shaded by an arbour, or by a sycamore, and such spots are among the most delightful that are to be found in this country. The tree (formerly sacred), the arbour, the shade, the splashing water of the well spreading coolness and freshness around, often the only water to be had for a long distance, and therefore supplying men, cattle, birds, and all kinds of creeping things, as well as the vegetable kingdom, the cattle quietly treading their circular course, the pleasing clack of the toothed-wheels, and sounding above all, the friction-music of the revolving cylinder, now harshly groaning and creaking, now playing in impure but often in pure concord—all these taken together excite the feeling of a deep idyllic peace.

HARVEST.

The chief time for the corn harvest is April and May. Then young and old, accompanied by beasts of burden and other domestic animals, proceed to the field, though the women, having chiefly the household matters to attend to, are less often seen there. The stalks are cut below by the sickle, or pulled up by the roots. The cattle brought with them then scatter themselves over the shorn fields, as also the poor people for the purpose of gleaning, while the farmer piles up his bundles of ears into a great heap in the middle of the field. There the wheat lies till there is time to subject it to farther operations. The ancient Egyptian, in place of thrashing his corn, which he cut at the top below the ears, had it trodden out by cattle. That plan is but seldom employed now, and thrashing is quite unknown. The separation of the ears and the husking of the corn are much more commonly effected by the *norag*, that is, a kind of waggon with cutting iron wheels, which, mounted by a peasant and drawn by cattle, goes round and round the heap of sheaves in a path strewed with corn-stalks, and chops ears and stalks into innumerable small pieces. These pieces being dexterously thrown up and winnowed in a breeze of wind, in the manner practised also by the ancients, the heavy grain separates from the chaff and chopped stalks, which are lighter and therefore fly farther. A farther sifting is finally carried out by the corn sieve, which allows the grain only to pass through. It is not to be wondered at that after this process impurities of many kinds remain among the grain, and the ordinary market grain consists, besides the grain, of a considerable mixture of chopped straw, lumps of clay, pieces of weed, and pellets of dung, all of which go to make up the measure, and it must be subjected to the industry of the women at home before grinding or baking is to be thought of. The grain is put into sacks and baskets, the chopped straw (long straw is scarcely to be had in Egypt) into net-work bags, and carried by asses and camels to the barns in the village.

A PALM-GROVE.

We long to escape from the open field and obtain rest, shade, and a draught of forest air. "Forest—what is that?" the native asks us with astonishment. He understands the word (*hersh*) no more than, as we have seen above, he understands spring (*robi'a*) or meadow (*merg*). None of these are to be met with in the land of Egypt. But instead we have something far finer, we think—the palm, crowned the queen of trees, and whole palm-groves. To wander under palms appeared to us from youth up the highest pleasure of the tropic world. We sought for rest; but instead of a soft grassy carpet we find in the grove a clayey soil dried, cracked, and dusty, or if watered, muddy, with scrubby, prickly bushes, and dry and thirsty weeds. We wished for shade; but the shadow cast by the lofty slender stem of the palm-tree is scarcely so broad as our body with arms and legs kept close together, and whoever lies down in this position is again in a quarter of an hour fully exposed to the rays of the never-halting sun; the individual stems stand too far apart for their shadows to meet together; the covering afforded by the crown of leaves proudly waving at a dizzy height above is of no avail on account of the distance, and the few loose feathery fronds that form it let through a thousand beams of light. We wished to breathe pure air; a palm has nothing aromatic about it; stem and leaves are dry and stiff; when we breathe we cannot avoid inhaling the dust that is suspended in the air of Egypt, that here in the grove has settled down more thickly on the pale green leaves and twigs, and now when the least breath of air stirs falls down on our heads and clothes, and even enters the lungs. How much more poetical, then, than a palm-grove is a pine-grove, which in other respects has some resemblance to it! There are many, too, perhaps even more, who are enthusiastic about the date-tree. Its usefulness in all circumstances we must admit. Its stem, either whole or split longitudinally, serves for beams, but the timber is of no farther use in building, nor is it esteemed as fire-wood. The ribs (*gerid*) of the branches or fronds are much employed in all kinds of wicker-work, for lining the ceilings of rooms, in inlaying and mosaic work; the leaves are woven into mats and baskets, and used also as brooms; the bast furnished by the sheaths of the leaves is made into cords and matting, and serves also instead of bath-sponges for cleaning the body. The broad ends of the leaf-stalks, split up into their component fibres, are also used as brooms. The fruit forms an important article of food; its sweetness even enables it to take the place of sugar; and a spirit is distilled from it. Lastly, by piercing into the heart of the crown, palm-wine is obtained, but the death of the tree is the result.

A GARDEN.

We do not here mean to speak of the fine gardens of many pashas and Europeans in the capital, where plants of the temperate and torrid zones of the Old and the New World, tended by Frankish gardeners, display in charming array their rich perennial verdure, flourishing in the open air under a mild sky and in fertile soil; it is of the gardens of the country people that we shall speak, and these afford scarcely more satisfaction than a palm-grove, and also differ but little from one, since here also, in these areas, surrounded by a mud-wall and watered by a water-wheel, it is the useful palm that forms the most prominent and striking object. To be sure fruit and foliage trees, which closely occupy the intermediate spaces, give shade, coolness, and an atmosphere smacking more of vegetation, but the poetic charm of blossoming flowers is wanting. For flowers the Egyptian countryman has no feeling, he thinks only on dry utility. In this respect the ancient Egyptians were much more poetical, as are at the present day the Moslems of other regions. The laying out of the whole, too, is as a rule confused; it is scarcely traversed by a path, and the visitor has often literally to bore his way through the thick shrubbery and prickly undergrowth. The rose is the favourite flower; but one does not see many attempts at cultivating either this or other plants so as to produce varieties or fuller and finer flowers. Other plants cultivated are jasmine, rosemary, mignonette, mint, and sesbania, and the people have a special fancy for basil. Besides these the garden always offers a rich variety of vegetables that bear the stamp of the South, and is therefore well worth visiting.

Alongside of the diœcious date-palm stands the doom-palm, remarkable for its repeated dichotomous branchings, and for its edible fruit resembling a cocoa-nut; it is called *Cucifera Thebaica*, because the Thebais is its head-quarters, beyond which (that is, beyond lat. 27° N.) it never extends northward. Genuine acacia trees of several species, with highly ornamental feathery leaves, and rather a low stem, from which oozes the well-known gum Arabic, some of them with very astringent fruits, commonly used in tanning, form dense thorny thickets or groves that cannot be approached. Among other trees we do not fail to remark the stately Labbach acacia (*Albizzia lebbak*), first introduced from the East Indies under Mohammed Ali, the myrtle, a willow, and the St. John's bread tree. Of the pine tribe only the cypress can be made to spring from the southern soil; while on the other hand the tamarisks, their representatives, flourish luxuriantly. The Hegelig tree (*Balanites*), a native of the South, also thrives, and the Tamar-henna (*Lawsonia*), which produces the henna pigment in so common use here; while the tropical banana sometimes brings its fruit-cones, the finest of all fruits, to the condition of luscious ripeness. Quite at home here is the *Zizyphus spinæ Christi*, with its miniature apples; the pomegranate-tree, and the wild fig-tree or sycamore, the stateliest tree of this zone. The real fig-tree produces only a middling kind of fig, the citron-tree only a small citron of the size of a walnut, the orange-tree only a green and not very sweet orange. It is too hot here also for the olive, the mulberry, and the Indian fig (*Cactus opuntia*), which as far south as Middle Egypt thrive well enough. Apples, pears, quinces, peaches, plums, damsons, belong to a colder zone, and though often planted the trees do no good. The kindly vine, however, has spread even as far as this, and is much cultivated in the gardens in the form of arbours; its sweet and abundant berries are merely eaten, scarcely ever converted into wine—not even by the Christians, who prefer to get drunk on date-spirit.

FIELD AND GARDEN PLANTS.

The vegetables most common in gardens are the *bamiyeh* (*Hibiscus esculentus*, one of the mallow tribe) and the *moluchîyeh* (*Corchorus olitorius*, a tiliaceous plant, tasting somewhat like spinage), *kulkâs* (*Arum Colocasia*, with a taste like that of a potato), the egg-plant (*Solanum melongena*) and paradise apples (*Solanum lycopersicum*); while *Solanum tuberosum*, that is, the potato, is not planted at all in Upper Egypt, and in Lower Egypt only here and there, as, *e.g.*, at Alexandria. It is brought almost entirely from abroad, is dear, does not keep well, and therefore is little used in Egypt. There are also turnips, mangolds, purslane, spinage, mallows, cabbage, celery, carrots (a purple-red kind), sorrel, rockets, beet, lettuce (eaten raw or cooked, seldom with vinegar as a salad), lastly, radishes (a peculiar kind, of which as a rule the leaves only, and not the small sharp root, are eaten), onions, garlic, cives, parsley, cress, and mustard. Of plants for seasoning there are caraway, coriander, anise, dill, fennel, black cummin, and red pepper. Our district is specially favoured as regards plants of the order Cucurbitaceæ. There are no fewer than five kinds of those cooling fruits the melons, which enable us easily to put up with the absence of many other kinds of fruits, cucumbers from dwarf to giant size, gourds that may be made excellent vegetables with plenty of cooking, often of extravagant form and dimensions.

The following are mainly cultivated in fields: of the cereals, wheat, barley (but not oats), durra, maize, seldom the Soudan millet (*duchn*) and Indian millet; in Lower Egypt, rice; of legumes, lentils, beans, chickpeas, lupines (*tirmis*), lubias, and several other kindred legumes; of green fodder, clover, fenugreek, lucerne, and chickling vetches. Farther, of dye-plants, indigo, henna (mostly shrubby), safflower, saffron, madder; of oil-plants, rape, lettuce, castor-oil plant, sesame, safflower, poppy; of fibrous plants, flax, hemp, cotton (more in Lower Egypt); of narcotic plants, tobacco, hemp, poppy (but opium and hashish are mostly imported from abroad); lastly, the sugar-cane, partly for the preparation of sugar, partly (a smaller kind) for eating.

THE GARDENS AND CULTIVATED PLANTS OF THE ANCIENTS.

The ancient Egyptians bestowed much attention upon their gardens. These contained flowers in the richest abundance, partly growing in the ground, partly in pots standing in the beds near the garden walks. The larger gardens included alleys lined with trees of various kinds, parks for game and poultry, special kitchen-gardens, arboretums, and vineyards. In the last the vines, which were formerly much more extensively grown, were trained on bowers or trellises; in gathering the grapes, if we can trust to the representations, apes were made use of, whose dexterity in such matters, though unquestionable, must have been of rather hazardous application. Instead of employing the water-wheel, the ancients conducted abundance of water from the Nile by special canals, and usually constructed ponds and lakes in the gardens to serve not only for irrigation, but for sailing and fishing.

The cultivated plants of ancient Egypt were in great part those of to-day. Not the smallest difference can be detected between the fruits and plants found on the oldest monuments and those of the present time. Many were employed and cultivated to a greater extent than now, as the castor-oil plant; of some, as the lotus and papyrus, which were once so famous, the native at the present day hardly knows the name. The lotus, like the Egyptian fig-tree, was a sacred plant; its blossom was esteemed the most beautiful of flowers, and its root-stock and seeds were used as food; of papyrus all kinds of plaited work were made, such as mats, curtains, ropes, sails, and light canoes, while its spongy pith, besides being eaten, was used for making paper. Other plants were not introduced till later, some only in modern times; among them we may specify cotton (already mentioned by Pliny), the sugar-cane (in the time of the Caliphs), rice, indigo, tobacco, and maize.

THE WILD PLANTS.

In our rural wanderings we take care to examine and collect also the plants growing wild. Here we find very few of those with which, in our tours in the Fatherland in former times, we filled our vasculum, since we have already left "Linné's, and even Decandolle's kingdom" behind us, and now stand in that of Forskal and Delile, in the sub-tropical zone of palms and myrtles. We find very little, however, of any kind, less than in most other parts of the world, scarcely more than in the desert, and what we do obtain is dry, rigid, bulky, prickly, hairy, and downy, so that it is ill suited for the herbarium. The scarcity of wood in the country is so great that dung forms the chief fuel, and all goods which can be so treated are packed in crates formed of palm branches instead of boxes and cases, while timber is little used in building. A large proportion of the timber used for building, even for ships, has to be imported from abroad. The whole known flora of Egypt, inclusive of the deserts belonging to it, comprises 1140 species, of which again 400 at least belong to the strip of coast on the Mediterranean. In floral wealth, therefore, Egypt will not compare at all with any district of equal size belonging to the temperate or tropical zones. In this country, wherever there is a spot where a wild plant can grow, especially where the soil is watered, there forthwith comes the countryman and sows a crop on it, extirpating the wild plants as so many weeds. There are here only two soils

—the cultivated clay-soil and that of the desert. In the desert the plants grow almost exclusively in the valleys, since the slopes of the hills, with the exception of a few watercourses, are devoid of soil or moisture. In this country there are none of the plants whose habitat is rocks, alpine heights, woods, moors, meadows, mounds of debris, swamps, and lakes, since such localities either do not exist or do not enjoy shade and permanent water. Consequently there remain only the fields, whether cultivated or fallow, steep and uncultivated river margins, hedgerows, the river, and the bed of an inundation canal. In such places there springs up of course a considerable number of plants, but even then only in a scattered fashion, never forming a continuous covering. Not even the grasses, which appear in tolerable variety, unite to form a carpet of verdure; there are therefore no meadows, which elsewhere lend such a charm to the landscape, the only substitute for them being the clover-fields, which serve as pastures, and the corn-fields so long as they are green. The leaves of the plants in the dry, glowing, dusty atmosphere never attain that fresh rich green which so delights the eye, and even the flowers want for the most part the deep fiery colours. Perennial plants, and especially the trees, are evergreen; they have no period of rest, and between the falling leaves of last year new ones already sprout again in January. Mosses, ferns, fungi, and cryptogams in general are extremely few. In the wild-growing flora orchids are entirely wanting. The clayey valley of the Nile possesses some, though not many, of the wild plants in common with the desert, and it has been observed that such plants as in the desert send out long fibrous roots in order to imbibe the scanty, deeply-seated, and widely-spread moisture, when settled in a moist and cultivated soil acquire shorter roots and become more tender, so that even biennials turn into annuals.

THE ANIMAL WORLD.

We have still to glance briefly at the fauna that is to be met with in Egypt. The remarkable form of the camel, the most important domestic animal of modern Egypt, we see everywhere in large numbers and performing the most diverse functions; still more numerous is the useful ass, once sacred to Typho, not held in high esteem, but belonging to an excellent race. Compared with it the horse plays, we may almost say, a subordinate part. The latter is used for riding by a very few personages of the highest rank, or it drives the mill, but rarely draws the plough. The common Egyptian country horse has not much in common with the celebrated Arab; it is rather heavy, gallops well, trots little, but is said to have good powers of endurance. Many horses also are imported from Arabia, Syria, Nubia, Darfur, Barbary, and Europe. The mule is much employed for carrying loads, as also the horse and the ass.

Not long ago Egypt was rich in cattle, but the epidemic of 1863 and the following years, which still continues to rage, has almost entirely annihilated the old long-horned race represented on the monuments. The imported foreign cattle, the ox of Soudan and European races, become acclimatized with difficulty; the Indian and African zebu, likewise introduced, which even the ancient Egyptians employed, is, in the opinion of the country people, ill suited to the agricultural labours of this region, consisting, so far as cattle are concerned, in ploughing, and turning the water-wheel and the norag. Fortunately the grayish-black buffalo, which loves a kind of amphibious life, has been spared by the disease, as likewise the camel, and it forms a substitute for the ox, being strong though rather slow to work, and yielding rich and good milk, nourishing but somewhat coarse and tough flesh, and strong leather. The flesh and milk of the camel are little esteemed. Neither buffalo nor camel is represented by the ancients. Flesh meat is mainly furnished by the Nile sheep, which belongs to the fat-tailed race, and is mostly of a dark-brown colour, with thick wool and a tuft on the head. When the poorer classes eat flesh it is that of the goat. Both animals were once sacred. The so called Egyptian goat proper, with the long ears and the curved nose, is oftener seen in Lower Egypt. The unclean swine, once an emblem of Typho, may be heard grunting at most in the stye of a Roman Catholic monk or a Greek tavern keeper. The strict prohibition of its flesh by Moses and Mohammed is based, however, more on a prejudice borrowed from the ancient Egyptians than on superior wisdom, since the Europeans in Cairo and Alexandria, and the Greeks in Upper Egypt, partake of it without bad effects, and the natives themselves eat the fattest mutton even in the hot season. Besides, pork was eaten by the ancient Egyptians at least once a year, when sacrificing to Typho.

Of the existence of the half-wild jackal-like dog, which, like the jackal, was once sacred, and at Lycopolis was embalmed in multitudes, we have already had occasion to convince ourselves. The cat, whose progenitor is believed to be the *Felis maniculata* of Upper Egypt and Nubia, leads a very dainty and thievish life, and is also half wild. It is much preferred to the dog by the adherents of Islam, and is also to some extent regarded with superstitious awe and therefore well treated, the ginns or spirits being supposed frequently to make use of it as form and medium. The ancient Egyptians held it as sacred. The striped hyæna is not at all uncommon, both in the desert and among the ruins and quarries on the edge of the Nile valley; it is only at night that it visits inhabited districts in search of carrion. The jackal (*Canis aureus*), called in Upper Egypt *dib*, which means strictly wolf, also frequents the borders of the desert, but always in the neighbourhood of inhabited localities; during the night and before daybreak its "hideous howl" is heard in concert with the not very different barking of the country people's dogs, whose duty it is to guard the farms against the predatory excursions of the jackal, which is not contented with carrion, but is still fonder of poultry, lambs, and goats. The Nile fox also (*Canis Niloticus*) is fond of poultry; but it is most successfully hunted in the gardens, especially at the time when the grapes are ripe. In the western desert it is represented by the little-eared fox or fennec, in the eastern by the *Canis famelicus*, which is similar to it. Of beasts of prey there are also sometimes found the swamp-lynx, the wild cat (*Felis maniculata*), several other species of jackal (*Canis mesomelas* and *C. variegatus*), the genet and the zorilla (*Rhabdogale mustelina*). The Pharaoh's rat or ichneumon belongs, like the wild boar, to Lower Egypt. Of the antelopes that inhabit the desert the gazelle (*Antilope dorcas*), which also occasionally approaches the Nile, is the most common; this very clean little animal is not seldom kept in a tame state by the inhabitants. The hare (*Lepus Ægyptiacus*) is common in the Nile valley and in the desert, especially in tamarind groves. It is not hunted, and the genuine Mohammedan despises its flesh. The dwellers on the Nile, in general, are no great sportsmen, although there are here no restrictions. There are, however, some professional hunters, especially hunters of the hyæna, commonly Bedouins. Among the ancient Egyptians hunting was a favourite amusement. Hedgehogs are not uncommon, but the porcupine, which is figured on the monuments, is no longer to be met with. The once sacred hippopotamus too has long been driven from Egypt proper; that he still exists, however, in the neighbouring countries in the Upper Nile is made feelingly manifest by the judicial lash which is prepared from his hide and is in common use.

Besides the innumerable mice and rats that infest the dwelling-houses, ships, and store-houses, large thick-headed field-mice frequent the fields and earthen dykes, and in many quarters are esteemed as dainties by the peasants. A shrew, which was deemed sacred by the ancients, also occurs. Grottoes, old temples, and tombs are haunted by bats of many genera and species, and in fabulous numbers; one of the most interesting is the date-eating, but not blood-sucking, vampyre (*Pteropus Ægyptiacus*).

Monkeys, which were sacred animals among the ancients, are nowhere found wild in Egypt proper, though they may be seen often enough in the possession of professional monkey tamers; a "right man" would have nothing to do with monkeys, as they bring ill-luck upon a house, or at any rate disorder and uncleanliness. Indeed there are scarcely any other animals kept but gazelles, as no advantage is derived from them. It is only the great pashas in the capital that care to keep lions and such like in their courts. The large animals of Soudan (giraffes, antelopes, ostriches) are often met with during the time of high water in late summer and autumn on the vessels of the Soudan traders (*gellâb*), who sell them in Cairo.

Of the 360 species of birds the greater number are old acquaintances from Europe. In the hot, dry, early summer this class of animals is almost entirely absent, and on a hot summer's noon the few that are left conceal themselves and become dumb. Even the shore-birds are mostly identical with European species, though they are also to some extent distinctly Egyptian, or at least African species. Among birds of prey we may mention the great white-headed and eared vulture. the little vulture, some species of eagles and falcons (especially the little kestrel and several noble falcons, which are still employed in falconry as they were among us in the middle ages),[1] the kite that may be heard everywhere, and several owls. Of scansorial birds there are the lark-heeled and the crested cuckoo, while woodpeckers are absent; of Clamatores there are several peculiar goat-suckers and swifts (of the latter a *Cypselus parvus* frequents the region of the doom-palm), the hoopoe, which is common in all Egypt, also bee-eaters and a kingfisher; of the order of singing birds (in the wider sense) there are the hooded crow (?), while the great black Noah's raven (*Corvus umbrinus*) belongs to the desert; also the crested lark, the sparrow, which is here common, a butcher-bird, peculiar species of swallows, the wagtail; and of singing birds proper, the Egyptian nightingale and the stone-chat; but on the whole the singing of birds is not heard in Egypt, as the birds that pass through or winter in the country do not sing in the winter season. Of the partridge tribe the cackling sand-grouse occurs in the Nile valley, but is more common in the desert; quails are only birds of passage. Native wading birds (exclusive of those frequenting the lakes of Lower Egypt) are the curlew, the cattle-ibis

---

[1] A falcon was sacred to the sun-god Ra.

(*Bubulcus ibis*), which always marches after herds of cattle at pasture, and was formerly sacred, the two egrets, the crested lapwing, the Egyptian plover (the celebrated *trochilus* of the ancients), and the marabout; lastly, of water-birds that belong to Egypt there are the Nile goose, and several gulls and sea-swallows. On the other hand, the country becomes in winter the rendezvous of a considerable number of the large and active tribe of birds. Those that migrate come from the North to the land of Egypt, almost the only possible highway to the interior of Africa, in order either to pass the winter here or to go still farther south, and again pass through in the end of winter. As soon also as the Nile has spread itself over the fields, the water and marsh birds of the Mediterranean and the lakes of Lower Egypt visit Upper Egypt in immense flocks.

Of the poultry tribe fowls and pigeons in particular are kept. The rearing of the former is facilitated by the hatching stoves, which were known even in the time of the ancients; for the latter dwellings, often more roomy and elegant than those of the people, are everywhere provided, and in these they dwell in immense numbers, both the tame particoloured or white breeds, and the bluish-coloured wild breeds, to which we may add the elegant turtle-doves, also abundant. Geese, ducks, and turkeys, here called malta-cocks, are less numerous.

The brilliant birds of the torrid zone remain within the tropic, which does not touch Egypt proper at all. Some few of them, however, during the tropical rains, that is to say, in early summer, migrate northwards, but here only reach the south of Egypt; among these are the sacred ibis, the tantalus, and an African honey-sucker.

The Reptilia are represented by some remarkable genera and species. The Nile crocodile, though it has become scarce, is still found in Upper Egypt, and every year demands some human victims. A lizard, which from its Arabic name of *waran* has been called the warning-lizard (*monitor*), and which resembles, though smaller, the crocodile, to whose eggs it is very destructive, may not unfrequently be seen roaming about the sloping banks of the river and its canals; the mountain waran (*Psammosauros*), on the other hand, belongs to the desert. Of tortoises and turtles there occurs in Egypt, in the Nile, a fine river-turtle (*Trionyx Niloticus*). Gaily-coloured lizards may be seen everywhere sunning themselves on banks, and into the lower part of the wall of almost every house the slippery scinc, which was formerly used in medicine, has penetrated. On the walls of rooms glide and squeak the small nocturnal geckos, the pilfering but otherwise harmless "fathers of leprosy." Here and there upon trees the chameleon, so celebrated for its change of colours, may be observed, while the ground agamas and harduns, which are sometimes prettily coloured, several feet long, and with long ringed tails, prefer the desert.

Egypt has been since early times renowned as a land of serpents. There are about twenty poisonous and non-poisonous species. As in the days of Moses there are still at the present day a considerable number of serpent-charmers. If any one wishes to collect serpents he must have recourse to these people, who display great skill in discovering these creatures and enticing them out of their lurking places. The serpents with which these Psylli give their exhibitions, and which consist chiefly of the once sacred African cobra (*Naja haje*), are always deprived of their poison fangs. The horned viper, which is also very poisonous, is oftenest represented by the ancients.

In the stagnant waters left behind by the inundation millions of frogs and toads are developed every year; as the land dries they all perish except a few that remain to keep up the race, having either taken up their quarters in a spot that continues moist, or penetrated to a deeper and moister stratum of the soil. Salamanders are entirely absent.

Among the most highly-prized gifts of the bounteous Nile are its fishes. These are mostly peculiar forms, having little affinity with the fishes of European waters, but more with those of other African rivers, for example, the Senegal. The number of species hitherto found in the Nile over its whole course amounts to about eighty. Their geographical distribution is very interesting. Seventeen species are found in the lower Nile, that is, below the cataracts. Among these are some unmistakably Mediterranean fish which periodically migrate up the river from the sea, such as several mullets (*mugil*), the Twait shad (*Clupea finta*), and the eel; they are naturally most common in Lower Egypt. From the former the Arabian cured herrings (*fezîch*) are chiefly prepared. Thirty-six species have been found in the upper and lower Nile; in the latter many occur only at the time of the inundation. Nineteen species are characteristic of the upper Nile, of which eight also occur in the west African rivers, and are genuine tropical forms. Altogether the Nile has twenty-six species in common with West Africa, but with East Africa only five or six. In the lower Nile, besides the above-mentioned Mediterranean forms, there are representatives of the family of the perches, of the carps, and in especial richness of the sheat-fishes, to which also the electric Malapterurus or thunder-fish belongs; also of the purely tropical family of the Characinæ and Chromidæ, and of the Mormyridæ, which are confined to Africa. The *Polypterus bichir*, one of the few living representatives of the ganoid fishes so numerous in the ancient world, is an interesting species, as is also the balloon-fish (*Tetrodon Fahaca*), a marine form occurring in the Indian Ocean and the Red Sea, but not in the Mediterranean. During the overflow the fishes, which are now pretty numerous, swim into all the canals and over the inundated surfaces. When the water begins to dry the poor creatures cannot get back, and a great part of the young fry, like that of the frogs, perishes; they are now taken in immense numbers, with very little trouble, even by children. The ancient Egyptians were very well acquainted with the fish, as with animals generally; and many Nile fishes, as also those of the neighbouring Red Sea, are very cleverly represented either in paintings or sculptures, particularly such as were sacred, the Oxyrhynchus for instance, with its remarkable snout, the Lepidotus (probably a barbel), the Phagrus or eel, and the Latus, which is perhaps the Malapterurus.

Of the innumerable race of insects Egypt exhibits a great

many South European forms, but also some that are specifically African, especially in Upper Egypt. The country is remarkably poor in large butterflies, but it possesses those citizens of the world the painted-ladies. Small moths are much more abundant, and at night swarm about a light. Among the beetles, which also are not very numerous, the commonest are the black beetles and dung-beetles. The best known is the sacred ball-rolling beetle (*Ateuchus sacer*), the *Scarabæus* of the ancients, which was so often represented by the ancient Egyptians on monuments and on gems. The ball that it forms is in the almost pantheistic mythology of Egypt compared with the matter of the world, which is also regarded as a ball. The principle of light and of the creative power of nature, the Chepera, whose symbol is the same beetle, and that too always in connection with the sun's disk, places in this world the germs of being and of light, as the beetle lays its eggs in its ball. The divinity Ptah, that is, the formative and quickening power, gives to these germs form, and produces the structure of the heavens and the earth. There are also beetles of very splendid appearance (*Buprestis*), sand-beetles (*Cicindela*), beetles that love putrefaction (*Hister*, *Dermestes*), and during the overflow numerous water-beetles.

The wasp-like or hymenopterous insects appear in fine large forms. The Egyptian bee is a mere variety of our own, and has also already been introduced into Europe. The ancient Egyptians were celebrated bee-keepers, but apiculture is now of little importance. The inhabitants eat a great deal of "honey" to be sure, but it is the "black honey" or molasses of the sugar-cane; "white" honey is mostly imported from Arabia, and is dear. The bee-keepers are said to convey their hives by boats and camels to suitable localities, even into other provinces; and after the period of gathering is over to bring them home again. To this order of insects belong also the ants, which contrive to gain entrance into all houses; and articles of food, sugar in particular, must be hermetically sealed, hung up, or protected by a circuit of water.

Of the Orthoptera locusts have proved a scourge to Egypt from the most ancient times, having been the eighth of the ten plagues in the time of Moses; among the most troublesome vermin are cockroaches, including the American in addition to native species.

Among neuropterous insects there abound everywhere on the Nile and canals ephemera and beautiful dragon-flies, especially a red-coloured species. Termites also belong to this region, but it is hardly their proper habitat, and they are not dangerous.

The Diptera or two-winged flies play an important part, there being several hundred species known. The common house-fly is nowhere bolder than here, and adds a decided element of unpleasantness to a residence otherwise so agreeable in this warm country. Equally annoying is the mosquito (*Culex*), more, perhaps, through the nocturnal hum of its multitudes, which almost drives the novice to despair as he attempts to sleep than through the smart and soreness produced by its sting. At certain periods all pools of stagnant water are full of its worm-like larvæ, and they swarm also in drinking-water, which must be strained through a cloth before drinking, the common people managing this by placing their coat-sleeve between their lips and the pitcher.

More than enough of other vermin also exist in the land of palms—such as fleas, bugs, and lice in all known forms. To these must be added also scorpions, tarantulas, and centipedes, and those scourges of the cattle, gad-flies and ticks.

Among Crustaceæ, instead of our crayfish, there occur in the Nile several kinds of crabs (*Telphusa*); and we found in the Thebais multitudes of a kind of shrimp (*Palemon*), a genus which otherwise is found only in the sea or in the lower course of the river. At the time of the overflow a multitude of minute crustaceans are developed in cavities that are gradually filled by the percolation of the Nile water, such as Phyllopoda, water-fleas, and soldier-crabs, with Rotifera and Infusoria. In a few weeks, on the drying of the soil, they disappear again, apparently without leaving a trace behind.

Lastly, fresh-water bivalves also are absent, while fresh-water univalves and Annelida (among these latter the Egyptian leech), though they do occur, are not found in any great variety of forms. We were already struck with the monotonous character of the country; the same characteristic runs through its fauna and flora, which display a remarkable poverty of species in almost all classes.

MONUMENTS OF ANTIQUITY.

We have approached the desert; before us lies a field of ruins. Half-dressed blocks of stone, shattered colossi and their members, fallen pillars, walls deeply embedded in debris there lie sown; everything transportable has been scattered through all the world. But here and there there still stand high and sublime the most wonderful architectural monuments of a noble and hoar antiquity, reaching back thousands of years. Many are even yet so well preserved that we can trace the plan, and by putting together this and that ruin gain an accurate picture of the former condition of the whole. The buildings we find are almost without exception works of piety. Of private buildings, even of royal palaces, hardly any now exist; they were built of materials easily destroyed, the former indeed of dried clay in the form of bricks. The dwellings of the eternal gods, however, and of the dead, are so strongly built that even the barbarians were not able to master them completely, though their rudeness and zeal for destruction were almost as grand as the art and the constructive skill of those who erected them.

We shall not enter upon particulars, we shall relate nothing farther of the hundreds of sphinxes which form the entrances to the temples, of the gigantic monolithic statues of polished granite standing or sitting like guardians of the sanctuary; of the graceful high-soaring obelisks, the gate-towers or pylons towering over all; of the pillared courts and halls, sometimes with no fewer than thirty-six columns 70 feet high and 37 feet round, and hewn from a single block; and lastly, of the building in the rear forming the holy of holies, where stood in mystery the image of the god. And what we have just mentioned is only a scheme, a system of a temple. As many as four such systems may lie behind one another, and the great whole, a temple city, is surrounded by a wide inclosure-wall. No description, no painting, can reproduce the overpowering impression that these buildings, matched by no others on the earth, produce upon even the most uncultivated spectator. The people themselves ascribe them to the ginns or to the people of Pharaoh, who, like the ancestors of the human race from Adam and Noah down to Abraham, are assumed to have had a stature above what men now have. Others think that the fathers of the Franks once lived here, and that the reason why the Franks visit these cities so often is that they may look upon the native country and the works of their ancestors. The Franks alone are believed by them capable of producing works of such grandeur.

However, it is not merely the colossal in size, but also the tastefulness in style—the buildings of all kinds narrowing to the top, the columns far from clumsy notwithstanding their thickness—as well as the almost inconceivable care and industry displayed in the execution of details (almost all the surfaces of the walls, towers, and pillars being entirely covered with painted or sculptured figures), that compel our admiration. No doubt these sculptures and paintings do not altogether please us. We expect more from an artist than caricatures and lay-figures. We are reminded of the antediluvian saurian dragons, the megatheriums, and all those attempts of the 'prentice hand of Nature, in some respects incomplete and generally colossal. The figures impress us as being horribly stiff, showing no natural power, formed on one model, and drawn without any knowledge of perspective.

But if we get over our original aversion, if we consider the narrow limits that were imposed upon the talented artists by the hierarchy, that power which raises rude peoples but keeps down those that have raised themselves; if we go more deeply into the study of those artistic productions; if we turn our eyes with toleration from that which is unbeautiful, we shall still find much that is beautiful, but especially much that is true, and that is the reason why these things have so great a historical value. By means of these representations, in connection with the hieroglyphics now generally deciphered with ease by the learned, and with the assistance of a few truth-loving historians of antiquity, especially Herodotus, we know ancient Egypt, particularly as regards the development of its civilization, better than we know many peoples now living, even better perhaps than the people living on the Nile at the present day.

Still finer and more distinct do we find the pictures and scenes in the sepulchral chambers where the colours have not faded and become obliterated, but are as bright as if painted yesterday. There we meet also with the men of ancient Egypt and many animals in bodily form as mummies, as well as vegetable products and implements of all kinds which had been put into the tomb along with the dead. Although these are met with in the sepulchral chambers accessible to all, they do not lie open to inspection like the wall-paintings, the statues, and the buildings; they must first be found or dug up, or bought from the natives and Europeans that drive a trade in them; the finest specimens are to be seen in the national collections in the capitals of Europe, and within very recent times also a splendid collection has been formed at Cairo (Bulak) by the Egyptian government, which now wishes to carry on this new kind of treasure-digging alone, and has forbidden all private persons to engage in it, though naturally without success. Such tombs are exemplified above all by the pyramids, the loftiest, the oldest, the most enduring of all the architectural structures erected by man. They are nowhere to be met with, however, in Upper Egypt proper—only in Middle Egypt, and again far up on the banks of the Nile in ancient Ethiopia.

Thus do we finish our wanderings in the wonderful Thebais, and return to the point from whence we set out, rich in observations on the country, on its natural phenomena, and on its inhabitants both of to-day and of former times.

CHAPTER III.

WORKING DAYS AND HOLIDAYS, DAYS OF JUBILEE AND DAYS OF MOURNING.

WORKING-DAY LIFE OF THE COMMON PEOPLE.

In Upper Egypt the life of the ordinary inhabitant of the towns is passed in a simple and uniform manner. Before sunrise he leaves his couch, performs the morning ablutions enjoined by his religion, and repeats his early prayer. To say his morning prayer after sunrise is forbidden by the ordinances of his religion, and to allow the sun to rise above one's slumbering head is universally regarded as prejudicial to health. He then drinks his cup of coffee and smokes his pipe, either at home or in the public coffee-house. His breakfast, which he takes after his coffee (though sometimes before it), consists of the remains of his meal of the previous evening, or of cakes and milk, or for a trifle he procures from the market the ever ready national dish of *ful*, that is, stewed beans. He then engages in his vocations, buys, sells, writes, works, or moves about, all in the most comfortable, quiet, and deliberate manner. "What is not done to-day may be to-morrow"—in good Arabic, *bokra in shah Allah* (to-morrow if God please)—stands written on his forehead in large letters. The most urgent affairs leave always a quarter of an hour free in which to gossip with acquaintances over coffee and a pipe, be it in retail-shop, workshop, or office. And if many acquaintances turn up the more numerous grow these quarters-of-an-hour. Now and again he has no work, or no desire to do it, and then he drags himself from one friend to the other. Bread for himself and his family will no doubt turn up; *robinna kerim*—"the Lord is gracious (or liberal);" it is but little he requires, and in case of necessity his soft-hearted neighbour will not allow him to go supperless to bed. Even before the mid-day call of the muezzin from the minaret, he has made his preparations for the hour of prayer, and after the performance of his devotions he returns home and enjoys his simple dinner. This consists for the most part only of bread with fruits or with white country cheese, milk, salt fish, or molasses (the so-called black honey).

He takes care not to make his mid-day sleep too short, especially in the long warm days of summer, and he lies down in his house or in his shop, in the café, or in any shady spot in the open air; at this time the streets and markets become deserted. Not till well through the afternoon does he again move, when he begins the second portion of the day as he did the first, with ablutions, prayers, and coffee, afterwards bestirring himself with some energy to make up during the remainder of the day for the time he has dreamed and trifled away. For this remainder is but short, and with the last rays of the setting sun the call from the minaret is again heard, the trader shuts his shop, the workman flings by his tool, the scholar, the writer, and the man of learning shut their books. This dawdling habit, which, in the province, at least, is the rule, is not, however, solely the result of indolence, but arises more from the fact that little trade or industry exists, and the want of a regular weekly day of rest is also not without blame. The natives when necessary often display the greatest ardour and even steady perseverance.

The cultivation of the fields allows the countryman less leisure for the *dolce far niente*, but even he does not overwork himself. From the mellowness and fertility of the soil his labour is light enough when compared with that of a northern peasant, and chiefly consists in the artificial watering of the land, effected mostly by the labour of young people or of cattle. When he can the countryman also takes his hours of idleness, and sleeps, and gossips, and sings. He too is never in a hurry. This slowness of action, intimately connected as it is with fatalism, is as intolerable to a European who is in haste, as it is beneficial to one who wishes to rest a little from the hurry and scurry of the West.

After his evening devotions the dweller in the town moves

homeward to his house, where his supper is already awaiting him. At this meal, which is generally the principal meal of the day, he quite acts the gourmand. His wife brings it to him on a round wooden board elevated on pieces of wood or short feet (*tablieh*); among richer people a shield-like metal plate (*sanieh*) is used instead. The basis of the meal is bread made of wheat or millet flour, or hot unleavened cakes—of which he devours incredible quantities—baked over a fire of dung. His wife has also boiled or fried for him a fish with onions and oil, or there lies in the pot a young pigeon or a fowl, the juice of which tastes excellently when the cakes are dipped in it. Sometimes also a small piece of mutton, buffalo, camel, or goat flesh has been procured, with which the soaked *bamiyehs* or the viscous-juiced, spinach-like *moluchieh* are cooked. These, however, are the more expensive viands, and in the evening also people on ordinary occasions are satisfied with the *ful*, which has become so much a national dish, and which (beans in general), according to Herodotus, was forbidden to the ancient Egyptians, or at least to the priests, and hence also to the Pythagoreans. Other dishes are such as lentils boiled in water without flesh, ful with moluchieh, a thick flour paste, coarsely ground barley or wheat, a cake made with butter, an omelet, fruit, roasted grain, salt, and caraway, and especially raw onions. All these except ful were also eaten by the ancient Egyptians, with the addition of papyrus and lotus. The consumption of lentils was so general that Strabo believed that the nummulites of the mountains were the fossilized remains of the lentils used by the labourers. Whenever it is possible two or three kinds of dishes must be on the table, and the inhabitant of the town tastes of them indiscriminately, taking a piece now from this, now from that.

After the evening meal our citizen either remains at home enjoying a dignified ease in his harem, or he takes up his position before his house, stretched out in the dust of the street, or squatting amidst a knot of peaceful neighbours; less frequently he visits the café again, or calls on a friend in his house or court-yard if he has a friend able and ready to gather his friends around him for a social meeting in the evening. The light of the moon and stars suffices, or if in winter they must retreat into the dark chamber, the weak glimmer of an oil-lamp. In this country nothing is known of nocturnal labours either of hand or head even among the learned, and the many blind and blear-eyed people that here wander about have not contracted their ailments through overstraining their eyes. As to-day is, so is to-morrow, and the most momentous events passing in the great world here make on most people no impression whatever. For it is only a very few that receive a newspaper, and still fewer understand it, partly because its language is too fine, and therefore not suited to the mass, partly because the necessary previous knowledge of every kind is absent. Among the ancient Egyptians the common people, such as artisans, were forbidden under severe penalties to mingle in politics. It is only the most urgent necessity that causes the citizen to take a journey, and when he does travel he makes a pilgrimage to Meccah, or, at most, goes to some other country in which Islam prevails. For in the land of the Franks something would every instant come into collision with his ideas and customs; he would have to eat, if not swine's flesh, yet dishes in which swine's fat forms an ingredient; he would have to eat carrion (that is, the flesh of animals strangled, and not slaughtered with an invocation to God); he would not have the proper conditions for the performance of his religious duties, such as his ablutions and prayer five times a day, nor any mosque or muezzin. If he ever happens to have been in Europe, or even in a town in which the Frankish mode of life prevails, he never ceases to tell his countrymen of the ridiculous and preposterous things he saw there, of course not without admitting that there was much good also, especially if there be a Frank among his audience. The ancient Egyptians had a still stronger prejudice and fanaticism against foreign people and foreign things.

LIFE OF THE WOMEN.

Though the members of the opposite sex certainly do not

groan and languish under the burden of their daily labours, yet they do not, as the common descriptions of harem life lead us to believe, recline the live-long day on the soft divan enjoying the *dolce far niente*, adorned with gold and jewels, smoking, and supporting upon the yielding pillow those arms that indolence makes so plump, while the eunuchs and female slaves stand before them watching their every sign, and anxious to spare them the slightest movement. Such slothful dames may indeed be found here and there in the harems of the great, but are not confined to this country. People fall again and again into the mistake of comparing the life of the women of our middle ranks with that of those that occupy the harems of the great! The care of house and family lies much more heavily upon the women here, and there is enough to attend to even if, being assisted by female slaves, as is the case in the higher ranks, they have not to put to their hands themselves, and confine themselves only to giving orders. Cooking, baking, sewing, embroidering, washing, and scouring must be carried on, and children must be attended to here as well as elsewhere—there is no reading nor pianoforte playing, however.

Before sunrise women and children are already awake and moving, many indeed under cover of the dark gray dawn proceed to the river to bathe and wash themselves. The toilette, however, is not usually the first thing that demands attention; the kitchen must first be attended to in order to let the husband away to his occupation. A complete toilette including combing and plaiting of the hair is not in many cases indulged in every day even among ladies of the better class. In this way time and trouble are spared, but a certain class of vermin are left almost unmolested, and establish themselves often so firmly among the black locks of the Eastern beauties that they cannot be extirpated notwithstanding the raids that are made upon them from time to time—even with the application of gray mercurial ointment. As a rule the toilette is associated with a bath, to which praiseworthy enjoyment high and low are attached, whether it be taken in the public bathing establishment, in the river, the sea, or at home by means of a shallow tub, and by pouring warm water over the body and scrubbing it with soap and date bast. In the public baths certain hours or days are set apart for the fair sex, and here many women spend half days bathing, adorning themselves, smoking, and gossiping. At these times no male, not even a eunuch would dare to set foot in the apartments.

In other respects also the women are by no means robbed of social pleasures. They visit each other often enough, if possible early in the morning, and are wont to remain half a day, a whole day, or even several days, though both parties may be in the same town. They smoke, drink coffee (the latter being less in use among the women than among the men—the opposite to what holds good among the Franks), gossip, show their ornaments and finery, tell stories and wonderful tales, sew, embroider (but do not knit), sing and dance, or better, make some one sing and dance before them (since a well-conducted lady ought neither to be seen nor heard, and therefore should not sing), laugh and make merry—in short the harem so greatly pitied elsewhere enjoy life, but on the sole condition, that no man be present! They are less often allowed to take a walk in the open air; some—and this is considered a great virtue—never leave the house after their marriage. Their lady friends come to visit them instead, and as almost every house in these regions has its court-yard or a terrace, women are by no means kept out of the open air. Moslim women are generally excused from the burdensome prayers of the men, and pious or even hypocritical women are in the Moslim female world a great rarity; indeed they scarcely know the most important doctrines of their religion. Piety in them is even looked upon with dislike.

At mid-day the husband always eats alone, or with his boys or guests. Immediately afterwards, however, the wife again comes into honour since her lord likes to enjoy his siesta in the chambers of the harem. After sunset no respectable woman must show herself outside the house, even though veiled and attended, and now, or some hours later, the husband again repairs to the sacred apartments of those denied to all but himself.

In the feeling of the Moslim the harems are not citadels of jealousy, in which the husband keeps penned up a considerable flock of luxurious indolent beauties. This representation, so current in the land of the Franks, is spurned by the Oriental with indignation. The women's apartments are rather places sacred and inviolable, where the *harîm* (singular *hurme; hárem* is meaningless), that is "the prohibited," the women, the *family*, and therefore the husband's dearest treasure must be guarded from profane glances and frivolous influences. As above remarked, they are by no means imprisoned, with the exception perhaps of the women of the highest ranks, they are merely kept and brought up, so that they may shut themselves off by their veils both in the home and outside from all strange men; among themselves they enjoy the freest intercourse. Such a harem existed already among the ancient Greeks under the less hostilely regarded name of *gynaikeion*, and even yet the Greek women are not completely emancipated, and are very strictly looked after. Besides, the native Christian women, at least in Upper Egypt, are even more than those of the Moslim "prohibited." Among the ancient Egyptians, however, they were very free, and went unveiled. In consequence of being thus shut up the oriental women have almost come to form a separate caste, whose laws the men have to respect. This caste has its female sheikhs, for which dignity the midwives and bathing women in particular are selected, has its medical art, its songs and music, its fashions, almost its own language indeed, at least so far as expressions are concerned, and unlimited rule over the little children belonging to it. From the round of its meetings even the master of the house is inexorably excluded. Of course, according to the law, the woman is the servant of the man; she has not the right to sit at a common table with her husband; on the street he shyly avoids his veiled spouse; she is even treated by religion as an object of pollution, contact with which demands a full bath before the believer can again perform his devotions; and when mention is made of her it is usually accompanied, as in the case of other unclean things, with a "saving your presence" (*essuk Allah*, literally "God honour you"); with regard to inheritance she is regarded as only a half person; she is generally excluded from the mosque, and as a rule is not required to pray, or to know more than is necessary for housekeeping. Still, in the lands of Islam, as well as in the rest of the world, the weaker sex has subjected the stronger in certain fields. Here, too, there are plenty of men who are under petticoat government. The wife is significantly called *sitt*, that is, "mistress," and even the husband calls her so. The wife has even duties to perform towards the outer world in so far as she has to manage the housekeeping. When, in the absence of her husband a guest has to be entertained, meals are served up in the name of the wife through her servants or children, she inquires after the name and health of the guest, but she herself does not appear.

Her sphere of activity is entirely limited to the house, and she fulfils her mission with all the more contentment that the pleasures of the great world are unknown to her. She is not unsusceptible to the attractions of dress and finery—her sex makes this a matter of course—but she has only her husband and her female friends to shine before, and that sets a natural limit to her desires. Her longings do not go beyond her state of half freedom, to which she is accustomed from her youth up, seclusion is not regarded by her as a restraint imposed by the tyrannical men, but as a precept of morality, and a sudden edict of emancipation would at once arouse in the harem itself as much indignation and resistance as a tightening of the reins among the ladies of civilization. It is not to be denied that only in the garden of freedom can a healthy plant thrive, and come to maturity and produce fruit a thousand fold. The greenhouse plant never feels the storm, but it remains weakly and droops at the slightest breath of unaccustomed air that gains entrance from the outside by some crevice. Yet experience teaches that a goodly number of those open-air garden plants cannot stand their freedom, and perish if they do not receive strict attention and care.

THE FAMILY.

Mohammed's dictum regarding wine is also true of love—it has many good sides, but also a great many and even more that are bad and dangerous. The Prophet has therefore cut Cupid's wings as well as he could; by the armour of concealment he protected the sexes from the swiftly wounding arrow of the god, and granted to his faithful believers the joys of domestic love in full, perhaps in too full, measure so soon, and to as great an extent as they could do homage to them. Matches are made early, and love's thirst is usually quenched in an orderly and legitimate manner. Fallen virgins, illegitimate children, bachelors, and old maids hardly exist in Mohammedan countries, although there are perhaps more unfaithful wives and husbands, and especially wives who have gone astray and been divorced, than elsewhere. Existing regulations render it difficult for these faithless members of both sexes to meet directly; but this is managed by the herd of procurers and procuresses, who are comparatively numerous in the East, though held in the deepest contempt. "Women contrive to meet their gallants, even though shut up in a box," says the Oriental himself in a very common proverb, as well as in many a tale. Adultery committed by a woman was punished with drowning down to a short time ago; among the ancient Egyptians by cutting off the nose. But the Mussulman is proud with regard to the above-mentioned state of matters, and listens with scorn to the statistical revelations made by the states of the West, which suffer from all kinds of moral sores no less than the more dignified "sick man."

Nothing shall here be said in approval of polygamy, but to those who have had lengthened opportunities for watching its effects it does not appear as a rule so black as Western imagination is accustomed at a distance to paint it. A thorough panegyric would perhaps show that it even possesses some advantages on moral grounds; and in the West also it certainly exists in some social circles. In the East it has prevailed from the earliest times, from the Bedouin to the king, even among the patterns of Godfearingness in all times and all countries. Though a man has several wives, that is not a proof of his unbridled sensuality. A man often takes an additional wife because his first one has not presented him with the heirs he longs for—sons in particular—as was the case with the Prophet himself; or matrimonial relationships have become impossible through illness, old age or incompatibility. And it always testifies to some tenderness of feeling when the husband will not put away his first wife or the mother of his children. This step, easy as the law makes it, is resorted to only in exceptional cases, especially if the children are still alive. The great ease with which divorce may be effected is a much weaker side of Mohammedanism, and there are of course a considerable number of dissolute fellows who take advantage of this and do not fill their houses with expensive, scolding, legitimate wives (the number of whom cannot exceed four), but indulge their passions by a change of wares, be they free or slaves. Some men get as far as a fifth wife without ever having had more than one at a time. This does not lower a man in the estimation of the people, if he does not do anything not permitted by religion, though it will be easily understood that such a person is often unsuccessful in his wooings. Any one may keep as many female slaves as he pleases; if one of them has presented him with children, however, the excellent custom that prevails demands that he shall not sell her, still less her children, who according to the law are in all respects legitimate. The father must always maintain the children that any divorced wife has had to him. The question of expense, therefore, forms a beneficial check upon licentiousness, and from this and other reasons it is very common among the higher classes, and among the middle and lower classes almost the rule, for a man to live his whole life long with only a single wife. Unfortunately no statistics are to be had relating to these matters, since the state does not concern itself about matrimonial affairs; these are attended to by the ecclesiastical judge or kadi.

In divorce cases this functionary, after some weak attempts

at reconciliation, has always to give effect to the expressed wish of the husband. The wife also can press for a divorce, and is not, therefore, devoid of all rights; but in this case, besides losing her maintenance, she also, as a rule, loses the jointure that would otherwise fall to be paid to her by the husband as stipulated in the marriage contract. The divorce cannot be judicially forced from the husband, he must say the words "Thou art repudiated," and if he will not do so he has to give his wife a *bêt shér 'ai*, that is, a separate dwelling and maintenance; it is a kind of divorce *a mensa et thoro*. During the continuance of this relationship the woman cannot marry again, though of course the husband can. But during the proceedings, with which a multitude of laymen, both summoned and unsummoned, mix themselves up, the husband often becomes morally pliant, or is induced by cunning to utter the words, whereupon the case at once comes to an end. The phrase "thou art repudiated" is fatally momentous, the mere utterance of it, even in the heat of a quarrel, results in separation, and "thrice repudiated" even in complete divorce (see below). If a person writes these words down and in joke asks a Mohammedan to read them, he absolutely refuses to read them aloud. The asseveration "by repudiation," or stronger "by threefold repudiation," is equivalent to a solemn oath. The greater number of disputes in cases of matrimonial separation arise on account of the children, whom neither the father nor mother would like to part with. They, together with the matter of expense, are what unites most closely the bonds of marriage, otherwise so loose. Up to a certain age, which differs among the various so-called sects of Mohammedans—among the Hanafites, for instance, being the seventh year, among the Shafaites the second—the child remains with its mother, while the father pays for its support, and in return has the right of seeing it as often as he wishes. Henceforth the father, if he has satisfactorily supported it hitherto, can take the child altogether to himself, and he usually does so if it is a boy.

The divorced wife returns to her parents, who generally soon succeed in finding another settlement for her. In a great many cases the separation is only temporary, the husband and wife make up their quarrel and come together again without any farther formalities than the consent of the kadi. When the severest form of divorce has been pronounced, however, namely, with the formula of threefold repudiation, a reunion becomes not such an easy matter. For such cases there exists the well known and peculiar law of the *mostahill* (literally "permission-maker"). A third person has formally to marry the divorced woman and put her away again, whereupon the husband can again take back his former wife. Men who are endowed with the minimum of personal advantages are usually selected to act as these middle men, and they are paid for their welcome services. Cases of this sort are certainly rare, being considered disgraceful. It sometimes happens also that the pair joined in this momentary marriage take each other's fancy, the intermediary will not give up the woman joined to him, and no power can tear them asunder if they do not wish it. The law just mentioned is said to be founded on the awakening of jealousy.

The man of the middle and lower ranks who has more than one wife usually has his harem, with children and attendants, in different houses, or in different portions of the same house specially constructed for the purpose; and in order to give satisfaction to all parties, a good polygamous husband eats and sleeps in regular alternation, the one day in the house of one wife, the next in that of another. These look upon themselves as relatives, and from time to time pay each other at least ceremonial visits. Indeed there are a great many examples of several wives living together peacefully, obediently, and free from jealousy. Of quarrels arising from jealousy much less is heard than one would have beforehand assumed. By his supreme powers the husband maintains order, and jealousy frequently takes even the form of a praiseworthy struggle how each wife may appear more amiable in the eyes of her husband than her rivals. Most women give up from the first the idea of requiring their husband to remain true to them, and jealous women are even laughed at by their female friends. The ideal romantic love is never felt by the Oriental; he condemns it, and knows only the natural sensual love, and the noblest and most practical, the love of a husband, often very true and deep. Among the ancient Egyptians monogamy alone seems to have been practised; on the other hand marriages between brothers and sisters were allowed.

To the modern Egyptians, the monogamous Copts, as well as the polygamous Mohammedans, kind-hearted and full of feeling as they are, lively family affections are not to be denied. The members of a family usually cling tenderly to each other; to them a foreign country is equivalent to misery, and a lengthy separation a misfortune. Veneration is deeply, to us as it often seems almost tyrannically, impressed upon children. In the presence of a father it would be disrespectful to smoke, to sit, and to speak more than is necessary. If there are guests the son does not eat with them but serves, it is only by the special desire of a guest that he joins the party. The younger brother has to behave in a similar manner towards his elder. Where circumstances permit, and especially therefore in the country, all the members of the family up to old age inhabit a common dwelling, living in patriarchal style. The old father or mother, no longer able to work, lives with the vigorous son, and free from care awaits the end; and additional children, instead of being looked on as a burden, are welcomed by parents as a blessing from Heaven, which thus bestows on them so many additional supporters. Living the simple and temperate life they do, great ages are common; according to the statements of the people 90 to 100 years are no rarity, but these reports are not to be depended on, since scarcely anybody knows the day or even the year of his birth. Early marriages being the rule, generations follow each other so rapidly that it is not rare for the great-great-grandfather to see his great-great-grandson.

The idyllic patriarchal life of union is on the whole the rule, but there are also many exceptions. Here as elsewhere there are cruel mothers, shrews, ungrateful children, brothers at deadly enmity, scolding mothers-in-law, husbands that beat their wives, wives that beat their husbands.

FRIDAY.

The week is over, and on the eve of Friday the muezzin proclaims, by a variation in words and melody, the day of the Lord, which begins at this hour, and consequently on Thursday evening. But neither now nor yet next morning does any change in the physiognomy of the working day manifest itself. The retail-dealer sits in his shop, the artisan knocks and hammers, the broker shouts, the countryman brings his fruits as at other times, it is but a very few that have even changed their clothes. Towards mid-day the muezzin calls repeatedly, not as at other times only once, and now the town assumes a remarkably deserted appearance, in the streets and market-places only idle boys make a stir, the whole grown-up male population hurry to the mosques. Here, sitting in rows upon the ground, the congregation listen to the exhortations of the uneducated lay-preacher in the pulpit, who but a short time ago sat in his shop and wove or worked at his trade of tailor or carpenter, while the attendants on a platform chant formulas in confirmation of his words. A short half hour and the whole service, the sermon of the preacher, his official supplication, and the genuflections of the worshippers, are at an end. The remainder of the day is also devoted to ordinary occupations, the Prophet having so permitted. Only the schools and the public offices remain closed.

As with the Friday so with many other days held sacred by the Mohammedans; the uninitiated is often made aware of them only by means of slices of bread and butter, which a friendly neighbour sends to the house, or, as at the Ashoora, by a kind of cosmopolitan cake, consisting of flour, wheat, barley, walnuts, hazel-nuts, raisins, rose-perfume, cinnamon, ginger, and all other possible fruits and spices.

RAMADAN.

But now comes the month of fasting—the sacred *Ramadan*. On the evening of the day preceding the first of this month the people begin to be in an active and excited state. Numerous groups collect in the open spaces and scan the western horizon to see if they can discover the new moon; since it is only on the testimony of a Moslim that he has seen the new moon—though he may be a man of no account whatever—that the festival can begin. Even the most accurate astronomical calculation, so far as this is possible, has not the same authority. The rising and setting of the new as well as of the full moon are not regulated exactly by those of the sun, since the synodic or lunar month contains 29 days, 12 hours, and 44 minutes, and the time of conjunction, when moon, earth, and sun are in a right line, happens at very different hours of the day in different months. The time at which the new moon, so eagerly looked for by the Mohammedans, first reappears after astronomical new-moon also depends upon the season of the year; it is seen earliest in the spring months, for reasons depending upon the position of the moon's path relatively to that of the sun. An astronomer says that he has not seen the moon earlier than forty hours after nor later than twenty-seven hours before the astronomical new-moon, but that by a combination of all favourable circumstances this may even happen within twenty-four hours, and travellers maintain that they have seen the old moon on the morning and the new moon on the evening of the same day. To these considerations one is led who every year looks on, while the Moslimin thus eagerly and for the most part uselessly watch the heavens. Since the official calendar pays no attention to this important method of determining Ramadan, it simply gives, now to one month, now to another, thirty or twenty-nine days in order to make up the total of 354. Accordingly, when the first of Ramadan occurs in the calendar, it is by no means certain whether at the same time the new moon is visible. The more scientific among the heads of the province often actually cause the fast to be altered a day till the moon is perfectly visible in the evening sky. When Ramadan falls in winter, at which season the sky is often clouded, and in high latitudes, where it is gloomy for weeks at a time, the determination of Ramadan is attended with still greater difficulties. In modern times, however, the inhabitants of the province are informed by telegraph from the capital, when the new moon became visible there, and that generally at a time before even the most sharp-sighted among the country people could descry anything.

So soon as it is believed to be certain that the new moon has appeared, in towns where there are cannon a loud report proclaims the commencement of the fast, and from this moment the Moslim becomes quite a changed man. Henceforward he leads more of a nocturnal life. In the morning during the fast only a few persons belonging to the lowest classes are seen, as in the large towns of Europe; porters, water-carriers, day-labourers, ass and camel drivers, go to their occupations; the children, who are not expected to fast, and the infidels have possession of the streets; the markets and cafés are deserted, the shops and offices shut. Gradually a person here and there rises, and, with eyelids weighed down by sleep, crawls languidly along, and the shops begin to open. Such things as are absolutely necessary are bought, but trade remains extremely dull, and when a person asks to see some goods the shop-keeper sulkily lays aside the Koran, which he had been conning over to himself aloud, moving his head to and fro, and scarcely deigns to give the customer a single glance. "When ye fast, be not as the hypocrites of a sad countenance; for they disfigure their faces, that they may appear unto men to fast" (Mat. vi. 16).

In the forenoon nature makes herself felt as being deprived of her proper night's rest; from noon onwards hunger and thirst also demand to be appeased. Not a bite, not a sup, not an odour must enter the body that is clad in the armour of fasting. The most exquisite dainties would not be able to seduce a fasting Moslim. When he passes an infidel who is smoking he carefully shuts both mouth and nose, and it is not many years yet since any one who dared to smoke before a fasting Moslim would have suffered for it. Unless he is very unwell (and then he is freed from fasting) a Mohammedan takes no medicine during the day, he even refuses to allow an eye-lotion to be dropped upon his sore eyes, and the doctor may as well desist at once from attempting a regular treatment during this month. Anointing the head, bathing, cleaning out the ears, and even looking into a mirror, are also considered sinful by some. It need scarcely be mentioned that matrimonial duties, were it even a kiss, are excluded from the labours of the day. Perjury, stealing, and lying are trifles compared with the deadly sin of cooling the parched tongue with a single drop of water during a day in Ramadan. Ramadan is the touch-stone of the true Moslim, and there are very few who openly at least venture to break the fast. Even the women, who know nothing more of their religion than the words Mohammed, paradise, hell-fire, and unbelievers, fast likewise (though not in all places); if their menses intervene, however, they become unclean, and fasting then becomes sinful. A person who is sick and travelling does not require to fast, and can make up for lost time on another occasion.

The nearer evening approaches the more does the traffic on the street increase. It is comical to see the eagerness with which the faster awaits the minute that allows him again the wished-for refreshment. One man, for instance, may be seen standing with a live coal held above the newly-filled bowl of his pipe, another holds a piece of date-bread or a cup of coffee an inch from his mouth. The cannon roars, and the dainty is at once bolted. As the thunder of the cannon clears off the clouds from the face of the sky, so does it cheer up the gloomy lenten-visages of the sons of Islam. The streets again become empty, since at home there is already an abundant repast prepared; of fat mutton, and many other varieties of dishes, of spices, and sweets of all kinds, there is abundance at the tables of the rich; while the man of the lower classes, who can seldom afford to buy meat at other seasons of the year, has been saving up for months in order to give himself the gratification of a good evening "breakfast" during Ramadan. It is a good custom among the rich to have a guest at this meal, and one is often taken in off the street. Nor does the poor beggar at this time go empty away.

Thus strengthened it is possible for the Moslim in his nocturnal devotions to perform the twenty systems of reverential bendings (*rák'a*) now demanded instead of the usual three. On the streets there is not to be sure a surging of people up and down, and there are also but a few of the dealers or artisans' shops opened, but a bustle and traffic at other times unusual on the street at night may still be noticed; numerous sellers of fruits, and especially of confectionery, have lighted up their stations, and, till far into the night, cry their wares, now so largely patronised by young and old; the cafés are all well attended, and if one pleases he can now get here besides the black bitter coffee sweetened coffee or a cup of ginger water with sugar, and sometimes also sherbet of rose-water, tamarinds, raisins, St. John's bread, or, lastly, a drop of liquorice juice. A "poet" relates to the by-standers the deeds of the hero Abuset or Antar, sometimes bursting out into song, and accompanying himself by scraping on a one stringed fiddle. In another café a master of music twangs with all the rapidity of a virtuoso the innumerable treble strings of a kind of guitar, and draws from it those weak jingling tones which recall to us our boyhood and the time when we received our first music lessons on the dingy-keyed piano of a country schoolmaster. There the guests listen to a story-teller; with voluble tongue and poetic verse he describes the enchanted princes and princesses, the excursions of the disguised Haroun al Rashid and his viziers, the man-eating monsters, the Jewish enchanters, which form the material for every one of those tales, the number of which is far more than 1001. The narrative is extempore —purely from memory.

In the houses matters proceed in the same way or even with more liveliness. Everybody who has a house to offer "prepares a couch" (*yfrish*) in order to receive guests, and treats them to coffee. On such evenings the merriest humour prevails, and at no time the whole year through does the Moslim appear in such a hearty vein as on the nights of Ramadan. He goes from one house to another and makes a round of calls upon his friends and acquaintances. In order to add life to an entertainment gentlemen often send for singers, instrumentalists, and dancers, the last of whom are generally in great request on the evenings of this month. The religious element is represented by a schoolmaster who recites the Koran in another room, and who is expressly hired for the month, or an educated slave or a son may perform this office. Other feasts, such as circumcisions or marriages, are never celebrated in the sacred month. Sittings of the courts are commonly held and the more important official business performed at night. It is not till towards midnight that quietness prevails; the muezzin calls, and soon after, a cry is heard and a warning shot sounds over the town intimating that it is time to prepare for the last meal. If any person has failed to notice this he is warned by individuals who about this time wander singly through the town from house to house beating a drum. The "vigil-meal" consists of the remains of the principal meal warmed up, or of meat fried with butter and articles made of flour, such as are at other times prepared for breakfast. Two hours after the boom of the cannon is again heard, the fast has to begin and along with it the same routine. Such is the sacred month of Ramadan, the great month of fasting and also of feasting, for which the women during the following month sing songs of regret as if for a loved one departed.

THE GREAT AND THE LITTLE FEAST.

In the three following days of the next month, Shaual, the "Little Feast," the "Little Bairam" of the Turks, is celebrated. It begins, as every day does, in the evening. The women have made ready bread and butter and sugar-cakes, the men dress themselves in their best, and the barbers are occupied till late at night in attending to their customers. On this evening three cannon shots proclaim that the fast has now come to an end. After supper everybody goes early to bed, but before sunrise all the men are in the mosque offering up their feast-day prayers, and listening to the feast-day sermon, which does not last much longer than the Friday's ceremony. This day's breakfast, the first for a month, consists, if possible, of fresh or salted fish, with all kinds of fruits and delicacies, in order that the body may be gradually accustomed to its usual course of life. People appear in their holiday clothes, and the shops are shut. On this day shirts covered with a year's dirt are exchanged for brand-new garments even among the poorest, gay silken stuffs infold those parts and members of the body that were previously exposed, costly cloths flutter round the head, and the cheerful colours of the bright red, bright yellow, green, and blue coats show vividly in the morning sun. The little girls, who are allowed to run about the streets and markets only on rare occasions, on this day flutter about like brilliant butterflies through the whole town, in their fire-red clothes, their faces carefully painted and touched up, and their persons hung with ornaments of gold and silver. A nameless joy beams in and from out the heart of everybody. No longer is there any enemy, any hateful unbeliever; high and low are all one, the whole citizens embrace each other—liberty, equality, fraternity. A round of visits is made from house to house; officials and people of the higher ranks give a very imposing reception, and everybody wishes everybody else a happy new year, though the new year will not come for three months yet. After the visitor has embraced his host round the neck, bending over his right and his left shoulder, coffee, and sherbet are brought, or the half-fermented native beer made from barley, and called *buza*. Everybody serving another in any capacity on this day receives from his master a money present or at least a new garment. The women also adorn themselves and hold receptions for each other, but this is done to a greater extent on the following day, as they have too much to do on the first day in preparing liquors for the male guests. Any other kind of work is out of the question. The remaining portion of such holidays passes quietly, the chief times of the day being proclaimed by the reports of a cannon as well as by the muezzin. As early, however, as the second day of the feast some persons who are eager after business open their shops and buy and sell;

while those who have lost some one dear to them recall him or her to their thoughts, proceed to the cemetery (especially the women), stick a palm branch into the grave mound, distribute pastry and alms, and even pass the night there with their family.

The other feast follows three months after. It is called the Great Feast or Feast of Offering, and lasts for four days, but is really the smaller feast. The baking, cannon-firing, receiving of visitors, embracing, congratulating, and dressing go on as at the little feast; the festive gaiety is, however, dulled, and is not so universal as after the Ramadan. The chief ceremony on this occasion is the eating of "offering flesh" in memory of the offering of Abraham. Every believer *must* have his piece of meat on this day, and anyone who cannot procure it for himself receives it from his richer neighbours, each of whom offers a sheep for every member of his family. The native Christians abstain from flesh on this day out of opposition. This is the most brilliant period of the pilgrimage in Mecca.

FEAST OF THE SAINTS.

In the middle of the month Shaaban, which precedes Ramadan, is celebrated the great annual jubilee (a kind of wakes), when every town that can claim to have had a saint of any note, having chosen him as its patron, honours his memory by some kind of festive demonstration—the saint having been a man gifted by God with miraculous power, not necessarily on account of great piety, but oftener as a compensation for harmless and innocent imbecility. The ancient Egyptians also had their patrons and protectors, namely, special divinities or forms and varieties of such for particular cities. In Upper Egypt the chief festival is that of the Sheikh Abder-Rahim at Keneh; it is for Upper Egypt what the celebrated fair at Tantah is for Lower Egypt. The latter is evidently a continuation of the ancient Egyptian feast of Diana at Bubastis, or is analogous to it. From the beginning of the month onwards some bustle prevails round the temple or mausoleum of the sheikh, as the saint is called, booths and tents are erected, and the spot where he is buried is crowded with devout visitors. At night the halls of the mausoleum are lighted up, all the lamps above the tomb being lighted; the citizens crowd to the spot, listen to the reading of the Koran, and give themselves up to the intoxication of the *zikr*, a kind of religious dance which will be described afterwards. Coffee and sherbet are served out in the booths, and dancing-girls, singers, and instrumental performers attract the people, the stalls of the dealers in fruits and confectionery extend far into the city; all the shopkeepers have provided large supplies of goods; foreign traders expose their commodities; the festival assumes the appearance of a fair. The nearer the feast the greater the throng of people that assembles from far and near. Every hour brings more new-comers, many of whom advance in solemn procession, horsemen and flags in front, with drums, musical instruments, and women behind, who express in a melancholy chant their longing regards towards the sainted sheikh, or utter quavers of joy. The flags and the sheep that are dragged along in the procession are intended as offerings for the saint, in fulfilment of a vow made for a prayer granted in the course of the year. When the attendants of the sheikh, as sacrificial priests, have taken as much as they want, the remainder is divided among the struggling people.

At the place where the festival is held boys and youths amuse themselves on a large swing, the smaller and the girls enjoy a kind of see-saw; on the level unused area of the graveyard the equestrian performers go through their manœuvres. Clad in a wide flowing blouse, with the sleeves thrown far back, their feet planted on the broad flat stirrups, as they sit in their saddles that rise into a high pommel before and behind, holding upright in their hands a long pole, these performers ride at full speed, one after the other, from one row of people to the opposite. They display their dexterity by suddenly stopping their flying horses when close beside the frightened crowd, in accomplishing which their pole serves as a support, and by raising the dust in clouds causes their daring to be visible to a distance. The people on the festival ground take up their positions in a number of circles, in the centre of which performers of all sorts show themselves. Here a silver-haired wise woman or female sheikh sings rousing religious hymns; there the listening people get stories of genii and of heroes told to them; here the monkey-keeper puts his red-buttocked baboon through his performances, making him show "the maiden's sleep and that of the old wife, the walk of the thief," &c.; there a group of improvisators are bawling and clapping their hands, ready at a moment's notice to make a verse for and upon every new comer. Elsewhere a buffoon is giving amusement by his gestures in theatrical representations, and his wit, which is coarse, generally obscene, and exceedingly personal. A juggler stuffs his mouth full of cotton and draws out endless ribbons instead. These he winds up together, then shuts them into his magical box, opens the box, and discovers it to be empty. He then summons the magic spirit to his assistance by blowing a large shell (generally that of *Tritonium variegatum*), opening the box again and a large serpent crawls out of it. In the meantime he goes through all sorts of antics with his boys and assistants. One of these robs him, but the thief is discovered and condemned to death. The juggler bares the culprit's belly, into which he forcibly thrusts a dagger, and in order that death may be certain, he withdraws and inserts it several times. A stream of blood spurts out, and the performance is too real and horrible for some spectators. The corpse is covered up, the magic shell is blown, the spirit awakes the boy, who gradually moves his limbs, and soon jumps about as merry as before. The handle of the dagger, as the police have learned, is hollow, and the blade is pushed up into it when brought into contact with the skin, while at the same time a bladder applied to the dagger gives out a stream of blood-red beet-root juice.

On the morning of the festival itself, as upon all the great general festivals of Islam, town and people are decorated and dressed out, work is entirely at a stand-still, and the throng upon the main streets leading to the tomb of the saint is immense. The town contains twice or thrice as many strangers as inhabitants, and these are all on foot. Camels behung with coloured cloths, ribbons, carpets, and bells, carry the *mahmel* or "ark" of the tutelary saint, which is covered with the grave-cloth embroidered in gold and silver; the main part of this mahmel, a quadrangular wooden frame with a pyramidal top, may be seen at other times on the roof of the sheikh's building. The anniversary of other saints is also occasionally celebrated at the same time, and each has his mahmel. These processions have an unmistakable similarity to those that took place at the clothing of the statues of the ancient Egyptian deities. When the camels are collected the procession starts. The advanced guard is formed by a large number of swift camels, whose riders, sitting upon rich housings, and themselves decked with gay garments, gallop backwards and forwards and display their dexterity. Others show their horses' action, while boys strive to get their donkeys to gallop. Pipers and kettle-drummers head the procession itself (it is only the military that have drums and trumpets proper), then comes the chorus of day and night watchmen, followed by the Turkish soldiers and police-officials in full regimentals. This armed body keeps up a perpetual fire, loading their old-fashioned guns and pistols to the muzzle. In their midst rides the governor of the province or his representative on a richly caparisoned steed, the procession being joined also, when possible, by a squadron of Bashi Bazouks or irregular troops, and a company of regular troops of the line. The camels with the mahmels, each led by a man, form the middle of the festal procession. Under the frames of the mahmels peep out boys and girls who have been elevated to this blessed seat, either in virtue of their rank, or by the recommendations of their fathers. Before every camel a body of men dance and sing pious odes, hymns and verses of the Koran; gay flags consecrated to the sheikh are carried alongside of the camel. Behind follow more musicians, and after them dancing-girls, who are indispensable even to such pious solemnities, and are believed not to have a disturbing effect upon the devotion appropriate to the festival. Upon a wheeled conveyance, and adorned with flags and ribbons, a small boat is pulled along, the property of the saint, and at other times hung up in his mausoleum. In it he is said to have from time to time made journeys by sea and river. The end of the procession is formed by camels bearing huge kettle-drums, which the rider belabours with a mighty drum-stick. Behind these, lastly, comes the crowd of people extending as far as the eye can reach. Thus they march away, often to some spot leagues distant in the desert, and after making the round of the town appear before the serail of the governor. This solemn moment, which does not take place till towards evening, is proclaimed by the thunder of ordnance. At some places the firing takes place at the start of the procession. With the replacing of the arks in the temple of their sainted owners the festivities come to an end, and next morning all the people are again in their working clothes.

EASTER WEEK.

It is remarkable that the bigoted Mohammedans celebrate, at least in Egypt, some days in common with the native Christians, though certainly in a peculiar and by no means Christian manner. To these belong especially the days about Easter. On Palm Sunday (*had el chus*) the women bind palm twigs round their heads and fingers. On the Monday following people eat *fagus* (a kind of cucumber) along with caraway; on Tuesday, whey with onions, this day being accordingly called "whey and onion day" (*yum el mish u el basal*). The Wednesday is universally known by the name of Job's Wednesday (*arba Ayub*). On this day the plant *ghubera* (*Inula arabica?*) said to Job in his illness, "Wash thyself with my juice, and thou wilt recover;" he did recover, and on this day it is customary for all the Egyptians to wash themselves with the *ghargharah Ayub*. Maunday Thursday has become "pea-Thursday." Good Friday is called among the Mohammedans, "cake and butter Friday" (*guma'a el mafruka*), cakes spread with butter and honey being the special dainty on this day. Saturday is named "the Sabbath of the light," from the celebrated sacred fire, which on this day bursts forth in the Greek Church of the Sepulchre at Jerusalem, and on this account the Christian brethren there annually get up a spectacle, which often terminates in deadly blows and renders the intervention of the Turkish, and consequently Mohammedan soldiery necessary. On this day the Mohammedan faithful strengthen their eyes with eye-powders; everybody has a vein opened, or gets himself cupped, a custom which prevails in many places in the West also, and in Egypt, Mohammedan as it is, coloured Easter eggs are also eaten. People take *kishk*, that is, a decoction of wheat with sourmilk, boil it with eggs, and stick it with the coloured shells of the eggs above the doors to adorn the entrance for all time coming and ward off spirits. On Easter Sunday the "great feast of the Christians" (*'id en-nusdra*) these hold a grand reception, with sherbet and holiday gifts, the Mohammedans in a friendly and neighbourly way call upon the Christians as the latter did upon them during Bairam. The Easter Monday of the Copts, whose festivals are settled by the Greek calendar, is the universal spring festival for the adherents of both religions. The night before onions, beans, and a bouquet of roses are laid under the bedcushions and slept upon. On Easter Monday the onions are crushed and stuck with some water on the door; the beans are stuck on the bar, and the roses are used as a nosegay. At the first streak of daylight everybody moves abroad, this being the day of *shimm en-nezim*, that is, "air-smelling," or more poetically "sipping the zephyr." People go to the gardens or other attractive spots, and pass, if possible, the whole day there. At the most-frequented places sellers of coffee, sherbet, buza, and cooked meats establish themselves. A company of friends may take an Easter lamb with them, kill it at the rendezvous they have selected, and prepare *tanur*, that is, they cut up the meat in several pieces and bake it in an improvised earth-oven; or they make *shauirma*, that is, the whole lamb with the skin and hair on is placed on a spit and roasted at the fire. The day is spent in conversation, ball playing, and gymnastic exercises, and those whose conscience allows it smell the contents of their dram-bottle as well as the fresh air and roast meat. Health must be inhaled to-day since the five days' period of terror, the time of the *chamasin*, is now at hand. A serpent then wanders over the earth and infects the atmosphere with its poisonous breath, leaving behind small-pox, plague, cholera ("the yellow wind"), and all other varieties of disease. The curse is not removed till Whitsuntide dissolves it.

THE NIGHT OF THE DROP.

On the 17th of June a "drop" falls (according to the ancients a tear of Isis) into the decreasing waters of the Nile, and impregnates the wonderful stream. Its effect is soon after observed in the dirtier colour of the water, then in its more rapid flow, and lastly in its increase and overflow. On this day, or on the night, the "night of the drop," young and old flock to the banks of the blessed stream.

THE NERUS DAY.

On the 10th September, the first day of the Coptic solar year, the river has reached to about its highest point, and on this day—the *nerûs*, the people give themselves up to the pleasures of the carnival. For three days it is all up with the rule of the Turks; every little town chooses for itself in its own way, and from its own midst, a ruler (*abu nerus*), who has a towering fool's cap set upon his head, and a long spectral beard of flax fastened to his chin, and is clothed in a peculiar garment. With a long sceptre in his hand, and followed by a crowd of correspondingly-dressed bailiffs, hangmen, and scribes, he promenades the streets and turns his steps straight to the hall of the chief magistrate. Every one bends before him, the guards at the door make way, the governor of the province or of the town has the humour to let himself be ousted, while the new dignitary seats himself on his throne and holds a most rigorous criminal investigation, from which even the displaced functionary and his abettors do not escape. The hangman's assistant of yesterday is sentenced to be hanged, the bastinadoer to be beaten, the *bashkatib* or chief secretary to imprisonment, immense taxes are imposed, and all decisions are set down on a sheet of paper. There is no pardon for the condemned unless on the payment of a few piasters as backshish. Thus they move from house to house, the taxes being levied in the form of backshish. Three days does the capricious rule of the ephemeral tyrant last; at length he, that is his dress, is condemned to death by burning, and from the ashes creeps out the slavish Fellah. In the times of good-natured Mohammed Ali the abu nerus is said to have ventured even to approach his throne, but the harmless jest has now fallen a good deal out of practice. The ancients also celebrated feasts when the Nile was at its height, in the month of Tût, as, for instance, that of Hermes on the 19th of this month. The anniversary of the opening of the canal is kept only at Cairo.

BIRTH-DAY CEREMONIES.

The monotony of the work-day life of the Mohammedan, interrupted by no Sunday, is richly and agreeably varied by domestic ceremonies and observances. However thrifty or niggardly he usually is, on such occasions he spares no expense.

When the time comes that a child is to see the light the midwife makes her appearance with her seat, and displays the greatest activity on behalf of her suffering charge; female relatives and neighbours also come in crowds to encourage and advise. It is often sought to lighten the difficult task by hanging opium about the mother, or making her eat the drug. The newly-born child is merely dried, not washed, and immediately laid upon a corn sieve; beside its head lies the knife with which the umbilical cord has been cut, and corn is scattered round about. This procedure is intended to drive away the *karina*, that is, the child's evil brother or sister from the spirit realm that always makes its appearance and torments the poor child of humanity till it sickens and falls into convulsions, which are therefore also called karina (see chap. vii.). Immediately after the birth the mother receives melted butter with honey and fenugreek, and instead of fasting she must daily eat at least a fowl or a good piece of meat, which her female friends and neighbours give her. On the sixth day the mother in her turn sends these a plate of *kishk* (decoction of wheat and sour milk) as a sign that they are invited for the following day. Above the head of the sleeping child is placed on this night a pitcher, hung with gold coins and lighted with tapers, the pitcher being long-necked (*dorâk*) in the case of boys, short-necked (*kulleh*) in that of girls.

On the morning of the seventh day (*yum es-subû'a*) the house is filled with female visitors. The child is placed upon a sieve, tapers are fixed upon metal plates and on the point of a sword, and the child is carried in procession through the whole house, while the midwife scatters *bissle*, that is, wheat, barley, pease, and salt as provender for the wicked spirits. The child is shaken in the sieve, being thereby believed to lose fear for the rest of its life, and its eyes are held up to the sun to sharpen them. The cymbals and small drums, the singing and trilling of the women, make the outer world acquainted with the joy within the house. The guests present the mother and midwife with money and gold, for which they distribute parched chick-peas, St. John's bread, and walnuts.

But the father must also keep the seventh day as a festival, especially if the child is a boy, though in many cases he does not dare up till this time to look upon his own child, since he might possibly, and quite against his will, do some harm to his tender offspring by a glance of his eye. He invites his friends to a feast, and entertains them with Koran reading, zikrs, and similar pious amusements, or sends for instrumental players, singers, and dancing-girls. The son is brought in a sieve and shown to the guests, who rejoice with the father, and perhaps also leave some gifts. A plate of candy-sugar is now sent to the kadi or some other theologian; he sucks it, and lets the sweet fluid trickle from his consecrated mouth into that of the child, and "gives him the name out of his mouth." This is accordingly a kind of baptism. It is well known that among the Moslim, as among the native Christians, and till lately among the Jews of the West, only personal (and not family) names are used even in public life. For distinction the personal name of one's father is joined to one's own name, as Mohammed Soliman, that is, Mohammed, son of Soliman. Many have of course a surname, but it is generally personal, as for instance, the Bald, the One-eyed, the Falcon, and so forth, and only in rare cases is retained as a family name. In recent times the desire of acquiring a family name is showing itself, especially among government officials. This custom has of course the advantage that it leaves no room for pride of noble or patrician descent. Only the descendants of the prophets, the *sherifs*, of whom there are millions, pride themselves on their birth, and generally marry only among themselves. Still more the Bedouin, who is said to be able to repeat his pedigree in personal names alone up to Abraham and Adam, like the genealogies in the Bible, and who knows the pedigree of his horse equally well.

On the fortieth day after childbirth the mother goes with the child to the bath, and gets forty dishfuls of water poured over her head if her offspring is a boy, and thirty-nine if it is a girl. The child also is now bathed for the first time, and mother and child are now clean and purified.

CEREMONIES PRELIMINARY TO FAMILY FESTIVALS.

The more important family festivals, as a circumcision or a marriage, are often preceded by a whole round of preliminary ceremonies that last for weeks, or even months, and take place every evening. The master of the house prides himself in giving a feast that will be long spoken of. Every evening he gathers together his friends in his hospitable dwelling, and provides for them amusements and entertainments of every form and kind. At present chess, draughts, dominoes, and other games are played, but not for money, or at most for a trifle, since games of chance are strictly forbidden by the Mohammedan religion, as well as wine and fermented liquors generally. The loser is often jeered, and has his forehead stamped with his own seal as a mark of disgrace; but if he then beats his opponent the latter has to wipe off the mark with his own robe, and is marked by the other.

Next day a grand *Fantasie* is held (a general name given by the Arabs to an entertainment where anything merry is to be seen or heard) in the form of a dance with music and singing. Such an entertainment has little resemblance to a Frankish ball, which has accordingly preserved its own special name of *balo*. In the court, or the space in front of the house, even though this be the street, carpets and straw mats are spread, benches are placed, and many-branched candelabra and brilliant paper lanterns or oil-lamps with coloured water are suspended above the scene of the nocturnal festivities. Soon after night-prayer everybody flocks to the spot, high and low, young and old, invited and uninvited. A number of dancing-girls step up. They take off their street mantles and display themselves in their richest attire, from the gold-embroidered skull-cap, and gold trinkets round the neck and over the heart, to the silken bows upon the polished boots; but on such a public occasion there is no impropriety. The dancing-girls of the ancient Egyptians appear to have worn a very transparent dress; they also are often represented as quite naked; even the short skirts of the modern ballet-girl are seen in some representations. The hair of our dancing-girls smoothed, oiled, and plaited, their dotted faces, their rich and gaudy dresses—all is faultless. The childish forms seem to have become filled out, the haggard faces under the mystic half light of the illumined darkness and the effects of the "Joseph's beauty" (rouge) have recovered their youthful freshness; the really pretty have become charming. The orchestra has already taken up its position on the ground; some gray-bearded fathers are strumming on the two strings of their spindle-shaped fiddles; a jolly musician blows the reed-clarionet; matrons with buckram voices sing to plaintive tunes, beat hand kettle-drums and swing cymbals or tambourines with jingling metal plates attached. Or a genuine young singing-girl (an *almeh*) has been sent for, often also a singing-boy. With elevated necks they rise up to the highest regions of the tenor, always despising, however, the feminine region of the falsetto voice; anon they let their voices sink deeper and deeper with the most delicate swells and modulations, but seldom venture down into the bass voice. All sing together in the same key; harmony is unknown, monologues and recitative choruses being generally sung. Rapid shading is strictly avoided, and, accordingly, the Arab derives no pleasure from European music, regarding it as disagreeable and ridiculous, or at best remains indifferent to it, as something foreign. From time to time modulations occur which suspend the expected close. The sound now dies away like the stroke of a bell trembling through the stormy air. A sudden outburst of ecstasy begins a new period, the most delightful sounds of which are uttered through the nose. Allah! Allah! shout the people in rapturous enthusiasm, and the singing-girls, encouraged by the applause, sing still more delightfully, the kettle-drums and other instruments become louder and stormier.

At such moments rise the dancing-girls, the celebrated *bayaderes* of Egypt, commonly called *ghawâzi* (not *almeh*, which means a singing-girl). Only a few of these form an artistic conception of their parts, and represent in pantomime the common history of a love affair—pursuit, coyness at first, victory, and lastly, entire self-abandonment.

Dancing-girl.

Their much-admired dances are, however, generally quite inartistic, having no regular figures, no keeping of time, no combined movements. In dancing the girl skips backwards and forwards before the spectators, raises the arms, clatters the inevitable castanets (like the crotali of the ancients), and casts around coquettish glances. Whatever of art is displayed consists in movements of the trunk and hips—impossible to imitate—the limbs being almost at rest. Occasionally the girl moves slowly round in a circle, gives a slight hop, perhaps swings a sword, and sinks gradually to the ground balancing a small cup on her forehead, or whirls herself round sitting on a narrow-mouthed pitcher. Yet the public are enthusiastic to the highest degree about those female performers, a popularity which no doubt they owe more to their affability than to their artistic skill, since they joke with everybody and everybody with them without any embarrassment. But dancing is given up entirely to them, and if any one were to catch them round the waist, *ala Franka*, and dance round in a galop with them, he would bring abuse and disgrace on himself, and would be set down as crazy. It is a modern and Frankish custom for members of both sexes to dance together in close contact, and such a practice was also unknown to classical antiquity. The Oriental loves dancing and music, but seldom cultivates them in person, getting people who practise these arts as their profession to perform for his entertainment; and their profession is never held in esteem, but is regarded as degrading, like that of an actor in the Frankish middle ages. For a grown-up man of the better class to sing by himself, or merely to join in with others, or even to amuse himself on a musical instrument, is regarded as undignified, and still more for ladies. At such *fantasies* the representatives of religion, the kadis and ulema, do not fail to be present, and laugh heartily even at obscenities. The priests of ancient Egypt, as also the severe Socrates, saw no harm in having music and dancing in their houses; they even practised music themselves. The higher ranks did not dance and sing themselves, but hired professional dancing-girls and musical performers as at the present day. Among the Greeks music and dancing were in high esteem, and formed a part of education—even the gods themselves danced.

The performance of the *chauel* or male dancer is not much

of an improvement on that of the female dancer. Clothed and tricked out like a dancing-girl, he goes through the same kind of motions on another evening to the delight of the spectators. Sometimes he also plays on some instrument, and sings as well; he blows his bagpipes full of wind, and while it escapes melodiously from the holes of the tubes under the play of his fingers he strikes up his ear-piercing song, which is followed by the hip-dance—a threefold artistic effect produced all at once. This class of hermaphrodites, the product of the luxurious East, also resemble the dancing-girls in their abandoned morals.

RELIGIOUS ENTERTAINMENTS.

In this round of festivities entertainments of a religious kind must not be absent, and they are commonly, on these and other occasions, the only ones that are held. They are not called *fantasies;* it is considered very far wrong in any one to call them so. The *chatmeh* or public reading of the whole Koran at one spell begins at vespers. From that until night, and from night-prayers to next morning, the whole of the Koran is gabbled over by school-masters, corpse-washers, and other similar functionaries who can read. The readers of the Koran speak and sing in the paternoster style, in a tone as if cajoling themselves and God, and breathlessly hurrying to the end; the words, nevertheless, have an imposing effect through the emphatic and melodious expression in which they are clothed, and the greater the more mystical they are. The guests, illumined by the blessing arising from the sound of the divine words, converse about all kinds of worldly matters. Indeed they do not generally understand the meaning of the words any more than the readers, and perhaps often the author himself. They do not wish to understand, since the truth of the Koran is raised above all doubts, and to reflect on its meaning, and especially to criticise it, like the *feilosufi,* were worthy of hell fire. The Koran contains mingled together dreamy unintelligible passages, platitudes, repetitions, contradictions, unexpected digressions, curses and threatenings against unbelievers, but often also deeply moral ideas and regulations, and wonderful poetry. The statutes of the Koran, the religion of Islam, are apt to lead adherents of the faith to hypocrisy and fanaticism, and interpose the barrier of fatalism and superstition to effort and progress (this, however, is contested by enlightened Mohammedans); but this religion, more, perhaps, than any other, has acted as a bond of union, has formed and united nations together, and has been able to preserve the old patriarchal virtues up to the present day, of which respect for old age, hospitality, and to some extent also female virtue, are the most to be commended.

Another religious reading is the *mulid*, that is, the genealogy of the Prophet, in which the forefathers of the latter, from Adam onwards, are enumerated and their praises sung.

Among the favourite devotional observances are those well-known religious gymnastical exercises called *zikr*. Those taking part in them form a circle or a line. At one end the leader (*munshed*) of the singing seats himself, and sings an ode, which at one time is deeply poetical and religious, at another, through images and similes, like the Song of Solomon, becomes lascivious and indeed obscene. The people sit with their legs crossed, and keep time to the melody of the singer with an uninterrupted "Allah," at first slow, solemn, in a deep bass, turning the head alternately right and left. Gradually the time and the movement of the head become quicker, the upper part of the body takes part in the movements of the head, the "Allah" becomes an "A A Allah." They then assume a kneeling posture and move the body madly about, still keeping time, however, and each like his neighbour. In the third stage the company of pious gymnasts rise to their feet, and their movements become more and more frantic. They pant, they moan, they groan, their voices sound hoarser, they stutter, they yelp out, "Ha, Ha, Allah," and thus for hours the frenzy continues. One or other of them is now sure to drop, becoming giddy, or being attacked by spasms and convulsions. This, however, attracts little attention, since the person possessed or "disguised" (*melbûs*) will recover of himself, or if it lasts too long, somebody shouts into his ear the Mohammedan confession of faith. As soon as he can repeat it in his turn the evil spirit leaves him, and he is again an ordinary man as before.

ENTERTAINMENTS OF THE WOMEN.

While during the weeks before a circumcision or a marriage the men are thus spending the nights in pleasures and amusements, the women also get up *fantasîeh* in their own manner among themselves. They meet together every day (seldom by night) in the house where the entertainments are given, where they sing, beat the darabuka or hand-drum and the tambourine, and dance too, it may be, like the professional dancing-girls, rattling their castanets. This for the most part, however, is only done by women of the lower ranks, those of the higher listen and look on. Men must not be spectators, not even the master of the house. The professional singers (*almeh*), more virtuous than the dancing-girls, generally exhibit their powers only in the harem, and the men listen to their charming songs through the latticed windows of the women's apartments.

On the occasion of festivities among people of lower rank, especially country people, a man, on the other hand, may witness a public dance of women, veils, however, being worn. The scene is the court-yard or other open space. Late at night, after the evening prayer, the male spectators who choose to come seat themselves in a circle or semicircle, a fire being kept burning near by in order to heat coffee, to furnish lights for pipes, and occasionally to dry the kettle-drums rendered damp by the night-dew. On one side of the circle stand, thronging closely together, the ballad singers or improvvisatori, who at the command of a leader repeat for hours on end a verse manufactured by himself, always in the same melody, for instance:—

"She (the loved one) has made me a cap
 Handsome as the castle of Mohammed Ali."

They also clap their hands, beat the kettle-drums, make gestures and movements of all kinds, wag their heads about, jump, stoop down, but do not move from the spot. At the same time female forms, completely veiled and enveloped in an outer robe, enter the circle and dance, but in their dancing also there is no violent galloping about, nor even hopping, but they move with varying paces, run sideways, backwards and forwards, wriggle, bend, and turn round slowly. The pantomimic motions are made with their hands, their faces not being available for the purpose. The row of singers appears especially to take pleasure in the movements of the dancers, catching up all their bendings and gestures, and repeating them. One woman steps into the circle while another vanishes, or several dance together at the same time, but never in harmony with each other. A spectator now passes through the circle, hurries up to one of the dancers, who has particularly pleased him, and twines a handkerchief round her, in which he has knotted several coins. The more actively and coquettishly the veiled damsel dances, the more admirers she gains, and she may leave the scene hung with handkerchiefs. After some time the unfolded and emptied handkerchief is unexpectedly flung to its owner by the lady, who again appears on the scene, and who has been able to find out, even in the darkness of night, who it was that decorated her and made her the present.

On this occasion a dance which has a half warlike character is also executed specially for the men. The dancer is armed with a sword or a long cudgel, which, hopping and springing, bending and wheeling, he swings as gracefully as possible, with pantomimic and gently threatening movements towards the spectators. Or perhaps two dancers enter the circle, and with similar movements engage in mock combat.

CIRCUMCISION.

On the evening before the great day of Circumcision, the "night of the henna," the women assemble. The henna leaves are kneaded into a dough or paste, which is set in pieces on a tray, a taper being stuck on every piece. The women move through the house in procession to an accompaniment of singing, trilling, and kettle-drum playing, the boy who is the occasion of the festival behind the henna tray. The mother and the singing-girls receive presents, the boy has a piece of the henna-paste tied into the hollow of his hand, the assembled women do the same for themselves, and all awake next morning with brownish-red palms.

On the day of the circumcision itself, the boy, who is now five to ten years old, is dressed in a new and costly garment, a Cashmere shawl, or it may be a woman's robe (perhaps as a sign that up to this time he has belonged to the harem), a gold-embroidered woman's cap is placed on his head, he is mounted on a horse, and rides in grand procession accompanied by musical instruments round the town. In the evening there is great feasting in his parent's house. Next morning, or on the evening after the procession, the barber performs the circumcision with a razor, an operation customary even among the ancient Egyptians. By it the boy becomes clean, and capable of performing religious exercises, of praying and entering the mosque; this religious act is, therefore, in some respects analogous to the Christian rite of confirmation.

The circumcision of girls is performed privately, and may be guessed to have taken place when, on a customary day, girls in red holiday-clothes swarm about on the streets.

MARRIAGE.

As in the case of circumcision, the preparations for a marriage, in the shape of domestic entertainments and ceremonies, commence months before. As soon as a son exhibits the first signs of puberty his parents think of providing him with a wife. In opposition to the views of other peoples these marriages of children are considered very healthy and judicious throughout the East, even among the Christians. The parents justly believe that they thus provide for the well-being of their children. Long before puberty, which follows in their twelfth or fourteenth year, or still earlier, all the girls are given away, that is, are arranged to marry some boy or other, and as soon as both arrive at puberty they are married. Men marry as a rule from their fifteenth to their eighteenth year. These early marriages appear to have by no means a degenerating influence upon the race, but on the contrary a beneficial one, the marriages being, with few exceptions, fruitful and happy, and the women being not so liable to be attacked with female ailments, such as chlorosis, hysteria, and nervous weakness. The same principles are applied also in the case of the domestic animals.

In a learned treatise by a modern Arabic physician who studied in Europe it is maintained, however, that for the men of his country the age of eighteen to twenty, for the women of sixteen, is the most suitable. The main consideration relative to early marriages, the bread question, is regarded by the Oriental only as of secondary importance, he only thinks of it when he is hungry. So long as the son is still too young the father provides for the maintenance of him and his family, when he is old enough he earns his daily bread himself, and when the father grows old the son in turn provides for him.

When their young son wishes to have a wife the father and mother set out in quest of a bride for him; by the latter the bath is often selected for this purpose, and her sober reason often brings more suitable pairs together than the impulses of the heart. Both young people have also to acquiesce in the arrangement, they cannot be forced, and the marriage is not valid until on the "uncovering and unveiling" the pair feel a mutual pleasure; but at this age a refusal is rare, and in case of after disillusion the marriage may be easily dissolved on either side. The search for a bride is generally quite unnecessary, as in two-thirds of the cases it has been previously settled that the young fellow is to marry his female cousin, and if he has none, more distant relations are applied to, and lastly strangers. If these marriages of cousins had really such a prejudicial effect upon a race as they are usually represented to have it must have been long ago noticed in Egypt; its inhabitants, however, show no inferiority either from a physical or an intellectual point of view. The low rank they hold in the intellectual world is not a consequence of want of understanding, but of want of knowledge; it is a consequence of their stagnating religion, and of the hostility of former governments to enlightenment. Besides being forbidden between very near relatives, marriage is also forbidden between such as have been suckled at the same breast. Among the ancient Egyptians, as already mentioned, marriages were permitted even between brothers and sisters.

At the preliminary betrothal the marriage contract is made between the fathers or guardians on both sides. The father agrees to pay to the father-in-law of his son a certain sum, and part of this is paid at once, the other part is always tied up and settled upon the wife in case she should happen to be divorced. These payments, however, must not be understood as if the parents were simply selling their daughter; the "bride's treasure" is in most cases spent on clothes and ornaments for the bride, and the bridegroom often gives these directly instead of money. And the bride who brings nothing to her husband except her person, lays up for herself from this bride's treasure a fund for cases of misfortune. If the wife has any independent means she does not share it with her husband—it remains her personal property. In the East, accordingly, mercenary marriages—so incompatible with manly dignity—are unknown.

On the evening of the wedding-day is held the marriage banquet, on which great sums are often expended by the more wealthy. Everybody in the place is invited to the house of the bride's parents; whole hecatombs (this is often literally correct) of sheep are slaughtered and devoured with a rapidity that has become proverbial, and with the most voracious appetite. Only the very poorest confine themselves to inviting none but the members of their intimate family circle.

In the course of the day the bride and bridegroom frequently take a bath, to which they often proceed in grand procession. In other cases the bridegroom, when evening has come, takes off his clothes in front of the house before the gaping crowds, and has his whole body soaped and bathed by the barber. The chief festivity does not take place, however, until nightfall.

Under the red glow of crackling pitch torches, amid the unmelodious noise of copper hand-drums, the joyful toot of a double reed-pipe, and the hymns chanted by the schoolmasters and other pillars of the faith, followed by half the inhabitants of the town, the bridegroom walks from night prayer in the mosque to his own dwelling. Here the procession halts. The singers form a ring and sing around the hero of the wedding, for whom the marriage torches form an illumination. A transparent vernal down is springing on his full smooth cheeks, his stature gives hope that he will grow for some years still, his voice as it is heard now and then sounds childishly delicate, or struggles painfully with the voice of manhood. The immature form of the youth is clothed in a coat of scarlet cloth, for the first time the manly turban rises on his head, and by his side hangs the marriage sword. Solemnly, seriously, and slowly he paces onwards in the midst of a few of his companions. The procession halts before this or that house, and the chief personages and musicians are regaled with sweetened coffee and sherbet, musket shots sound in the stillness of night, till at last his father's house is reached. Hither the bride has already come in another direction from the house of her parents, from the crown of her head to the sole of her foot enveloped in a Cashmere shawl, which, like the red coat of the bridegroom, is generally borrowed for this day only. She is embraced, and almost carried by two wives, and followed by a crowd of women and girls uttering cries of joy. The house of feasting is lighted up outside with gay lamps and lanterns, and here the people amuse themselves with the dancing-girls, singers, and buffoons, or, if more seriously disposed, listen to the mysterious words of the Koran, or tire themselves out in zikrs, while the bridegroom mounts to the chambers of the women, and lifts the veil of her who has been chosen for him, and whom he has never yet seen, unless, tormented by impatience, he has already, on the occasion of the procession from the mosque, gone through this momentous proceeding in the house of the bride. There she stands before him, the little, tender, lovely maiden, her eyes deeply blackened with kohl, her hands coloured red, her face dotted over with beauty-spots, her tender limbs can scarcely support all her heavy ornaments of gold and silver, her armlets, bracelets, anklets, crown, hair-chains, and other trinkets. The silken jacket falls smoothly over her breast, that scarcely as yet shows any swelling. The doll-bride blushes in childish modesty, and, instead of her husband, not seldom wishes— her playthings. He, however, intimates to her, in the name of God, the all-merciful, that he has become her husband. If the bridegroom has had reason to be satisfied with his bride, the women who have been in attendance on the pair utter cries of pleasure, and the joy passes through the whole house, and extends to the people collected below. Ceremonies very similar were customary in the middle ages also among our German forefathers.

Early on the morning after this "night of access" there is much congratulation in the house of feasting; the guests receive coffee, and are sprinkled with rose-water, which they rub on their hair, their beards, faces, and hands. The ancient Egyptians used to anoint themselves with ointments, but this is no longer practised. On this day the bridegroom takes a walk in the open air in his red coat with some of his comrades and sings pious songs; for three days or more he goes about without engaging in any occupation, and at this time displays an extraordinarily serious mien.

A man that marries a second time invites only his nearer relatives and friends, or a scribe, to the betrothal feast in his house. Thereupon the marriage contract is drawn up, the dowry paid, a prayer uttered, and he has now free access to his betrothed.

FUNERAL CEREMONIES.

A shrill cry, as loud as the female falsetto can produce, pierces the air, first one, then another, then several, then ever so many. A soul has departed. The cry was the wail of sorrow uttered by the women concerned, and at the same time the signal which brings up crowds of women to lament along with them. On the street, before the house of mourning, a long row of straw mats and carpets is laid, on which sit many men silently smoking their chibooks. Some men and boys, connections of the departed, run to and fro on the street uttering cries of grief and covering their faces with their hands. "Oh, my father," they cry (or "mother," "brother," &c., as the case may be), "Oh, my sorrow, my death; oh, despair; oh, my strength; oh, camel of my house" (camel as a symbol of strength or support). Friends show their sympathy and attempt to give consolation, but even men, at other times so undemonstrative, weep loudly and give themselves up to grief. What, then, is to be expected of the women, with their more easily excited feelings? They put on the dirtiest dark-blue dresses they can find, loosen their hair, and display their breasts, smear these and their faces with filth, pluck out their hair and tear their own flesh in a frenzy of grief. All order ceases, the loud outcry is raised again and again by the mourning-women hired for the purpose, and those who come to give consolation and show their sympathy go beyond the real mourners and join the hundred-voiced chorus. It was customary among the ancient Egyptians, and also among the Jews, to indulge in these loud lamentations, to smear themselves with filth, and to hire mourning-women. The Prophet strictly forbade it, but the Egyptian women will not let themselves be deprived of these ancestral methods of expressing their grief.

Scarcely have the eyes of the beloved dead been closed and his head turned towards Meccah, when preparations are begun for getting the corpse out of the house. The ancient Egyptians, on the other hand, retained the body at least seventy days in the house for the purpose of embalming it, before it was placed in the tomb. All the former repose and dignity of the Oriental are now gone; beside the dead body are found only loud despair and headlong haste. The doctor or corpse-inspector is first sent for before waiting for the first traces of the phenomena of death, and he must give permission for the burial of the body while it is yet warm. Other messengers have already purchased the linen for the shroud, while outside, the grave-digger is already preparing the last abode. The corpse-washer goes to work with the utmost care; he washes the body up and down, repeatedly cleaning out all external openings, including the nose and ears, and stops them with cotton; cotton is placed even between the toes and fingers and under the armpits. After the body is dried with equal care it is enveloped in the linen cloth, which has meantime been sewed together, and in such a way that no part of the dead is now visible. It is then laid on a bier without a coffin (it is only the Christians that hastily put a coffin together), and a green or red pall is spread over it. After a benediction has been said over it in the mosque, it is carried to the graveyard.

Hither the dead are borne at a rapid pace, those at least that were Mohammedans. With a haste and hurry that nothing can check the funeral procession rolls along, amid the murmur of *la ilah ill allah,* in order to carry the bier from the city of the living to the city of the dead. The advanced guard is formed by some blind and poor people and petty scribes, perhaps also some boys as a kind of choristers, and some flag-bearers. The bier is borne by four men, friends of the deceased, who are relieved by others of his friends, and thus the rapid march does not meet with the slightest interruption. A long procession of mourners and sympathizers follows, all in their ordinary working-day blouses, the relatives in the oldest and filthiest possible. Several portly well-to-do gentlemen pant behind, or have got themselves mounted upon trotting asses. By the side or at the end of the procession follows the wailing chorus of women, who on this day show remarkably little of their usual strictness in veiling themselves.

Having reached its destination, the corpse, wrapped only in its white shroud, is taken from the bier and let down without a coffin into a perpendicular excavation. During this proceeding, if the corpse is that of a female her former street mantle is held spread out over her in order to keep off longing glances—under such circumstances little to be expected. It is not the perpendicular excavation, however, that receives the dead body, which, being protected by no coffin, would be crushed by the clods of earth heaped over it. This excavation serves only as the entrance to a roomy earthen vault, hollowed out alongside of it, in which the body is placed, and is thus protected as well as if in a coffin. The entrance to the lateral vault is then built up with bricks, and during this lengthy operation the people standing around sing the melodious song "God pardon the Mohammedan men and Mohammedan women, the believing men and believing women" (*allahu mughfir el moslimin u el moslimat u el mumenin u el mumenat*). One of the scribes, an imam, a schoolmaster, or the corpse-washer, delivers himself of a short stereotyped funeral discourse, in which the deceased—who is no doubt straining his ears to listen—is instructed as to what he is to answer at the examination he will have to undergo in the coming night. Once more the confession of the Mohammedan faith is impressed upon him. For there come to test him two angels of horrid aspect, Nakir and Munkir by name, and torment him soul and body if he does not stand on the firm basis of Islam. Lastly, those present whisper the *fatha*, and amid loud invocations to the gracious and all-merciful One, clod after clod is flung by them into the grave. The male members of the family who act as mourners place themselves in a row, receive the consolatory words and hand-shaking of the people who have come along with them, and every one hastens to the place whence he has come.

In the night we hear behind the walls of the house of mourning the shrieking of women, now wound off in the trochees of a machine in action, anon in the dactyls of the steam-horse thundering along at full speed, or breaking up into the indefinite clack of a mill. Briskly is the kettle-drum beaten, and high up, from time to time, like a rocket, rises a shriek from a hundred throats. The earth gives out a hollow sound from the stamping of the feet of the filth-besmeared women. It sounds like an ungovernable outburst of joy and revelry; it is the corpse dance, through which the wife gives vent to her stormy grief.

The men, however, pass the "night of loneliness" with their friends and neighbours before the house or in a neighbouring court-yard, drinking coffee and enveloped in clouds of tobacco-smoke. At the entrance or exit of a sympathizing neighbour, though he has merely come to sip a small cupful of coffee, the mourners rise and are addressed with such customary phrases of consolation as, "Such is life; but you are still alive yourself." General and individual conversations go on, in which some of the mourners take an active part, while others, bathed in tears, sit dumb in a corner. In an adjoining room lean schoolmasters occupy themselves with chanting the "book that cannot be doubted," or murmur a three-thousand-fold "Allah," in order to induce God to pity the poor soul of him who has gone to his rest. This mourning reception with coffee lasts for three days if the deceased was grown up, and the near relatives and friends remain together even during the night and take a common meal.

On the following days we hear in the house of mourning such a sorrowful, slow, monotonous song of lamentation, uttered in a low tone by a company of women, and mingled with weeping and sobbing, that it thrills painfully through bone and marrow. Thus for years does a mother or wife bewail one whom she has loved and lost, on certain days of the week, or on certain days of the year consecrated to the memory of the dead, collecting her female friends, relatives, and neighbours, and especially practised mourning women, in order to relieve her sorrowful heart, and to have the virtues of the deceased duly sung; while the men gather round them a company of their friends and cause the Koran to be read in memory of their lost ones. Among the ancient Egyptians similar mourning hymns were sung during the period of seventy days that the body was being embalmed. The great festivals also do not pass without visits being made to the graves of dear ones, as we have seen above.

Thus does Islam honour its dead.

CHAPTER IV.

THE DESERT.

I.—RIDE THROUGH THE DESERT.

POINT OF DEPARTURE.

We take leave of what is called the Nile valley, the long evergreen oasis bounded on both sides by extensive deserts, in order to proceed eastwards to the desert tracts of the Egypto-Arabic mountain ranges on the coast. We have immediately in our eye that much-frequented caravan route, which, starting from some place in the Thebes district of Upper Egypt, intersects those mountains, following the course of their transverse valleys in an almost due easterly direction without any considerable ascent, and terminates in Koseir. In order to collect our energies for the exertions that await us, we enjoy a siesta under the overshadowing roof of acacias and sycamores in front of the caravanserai of the principal departure station Bir Amber; once more we moisten our palate with the sweet soft water of the Nile; we make a preliminary repast on the gifts of the valley, milk, pigeons, and fruit, and listen to the hundredfold twitter of the birds perching on the branches of the trees. The caravanserai is a building in the true modern Arabic style (see ch. i. p. 96), not without taste, crowned with cupolas and possessing colonnades and chambers. Like the ordinary caravanserais, called "wekalehs," it belongs to no one, but was built by the celebrated old Ibrahim Pasha for the general benefit, especially for the pilgrims to Meccah, who frequent this route so much. In winter it is sometimes used to sleep in; but in summer people avoid its neglected and almost ruinous chambers on account of the serpents and lizards that take up their abode in them, and prefer to sleep in the open air.

From a Sketch by Dr. Klunzinger.

THE CARAVANSERAI OF BIR AMBER, NEAR KENEH,
ON THE GREAT CARAVAN ROUTE FROM THE NILE TO THE RED SEA.

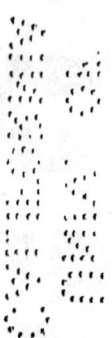

THE CAMEL.

There is a great deal of stir and bustle in the front court. The famous ship of the desert, the one-humped camel, to which we have henceforth to trust ourselves entirely, is being prepared for its voyage through the desert. This vessel, which is as unpoetical as it is much sung in verse, offers much for observation and reflection; and we cannot refrain from adding our observations on this singular animal to the many delineations that travellers have given of it. Its skull nearly always points exactly horizontally out into the wide world towards the distant goal. At the top its small erect ape-like ears stand beside the small cranium. Its eyes, at the side of the skull, stare earnestly, or even, as Brehm will have it, stupidly out of their cavities, surrounded by the protruding edges of the bones and overshadowed by high shaggy eyebrows. The fore-part of the crest of the head forms a long nose like that of a ram, the nostrils of which unite at a sharp angle. A long, broad, bearded upper lip half-divided in the middle and sloping downwards in front and at the sides, a loosely pendent but extremely mobile under lip, between which opens a slavering mouth well furnished with broad yellowish teeth, complete the very far from pleasing picture of a camel's head. The long, arched, slender, and yet powerful and very flexible neck, compressed at the sides and below, and adorned above with a woolly mane, cannot be called ugly. The fore-feet appear almost too weak to support the weight of the body when the centre of gravity is brought forward as the animal leans to the front in striding along under a heavy load; but a broad, soft, elastic sole, formed by the partial union of two thick toes, provides for security. The abdominal line rises steadily towards the hinder part of the animal from the great wart or lump on the breast; the dorsal line forms several undulations in front, culminates in the well-known single hump of fat, and then descends to the rump, from which there hangs down a short compressed tail like that of a cow, rather sparingly clothed with tufts of hair on the sides and at the end. At the lower back part of the rump a longish, smooth, ugly fold of flesh with parallel edges, the hip or thigh flesh, depends on either side, gradually diminishing in size when it reaches the lower part of the leg. This latter stiff member runs out into a very projecting heel, which is followed by a rather short ankle-bone, and then by the soft spongy sole.

The skin of the animal is covered with a kind of wool, which is longer or shorter according to the part of the body on which it grows; but as a rule it is shorn smooth, and nearly always scarred and burned, for burning with a red-hot iron is the universal remedy with the Bedouins and peasants for man and beast. The colour varies from whitish and reddish gray to brown and brown-black. A well-formed hump, the singular ornament of the *Camelus dromedarius*, is to be seen only in very young animals, and those which have been allowed to browse for a considerable time and have borne no burdens. The hard work which the animal is obliged to perform from an early age, from the time when it ceases to suck, the pressure of the burden which acts directly on the hump soon wears away the fat to which the hump owes its roundness, and there remains little more than a gristly and not very high swelling.

When in heat the male animal—which, like other domestic animals, such as the horse and the ass, is in these regions seldom castrated—acquires a peculiar coating of scales on the rump, called *samâh*. It is now uncommonly strong and unmanageable, but still continues to work and be made use of. Better known is the throat bladder, a blue and red fleshy mass which the male camel when under the sexual impulse emits from his mouth from time to time, by-and-by sucking it in again. This vesicular mass is an inflatable doubling of the palatal skin, or an anterior soft palate; its physiological purpose is still uncertain.[1] Everything is alike peculiar about the camel, and God the Lord himself, as the Moslim says, on reviewing his works after the creation, was

---

[1] The statement of Pliny, "camelus retro mingit, ergo retro coit," which continued to be repeated up to recent times, rests on mere conjecture. Observation proves the truth of the first part of it, the contrary of the second.

greatly surprised at this creature he had made. But in every part of its design and structure the animal seems as if expressly created for the purpose to which it is applied, as a machine for traversing the deserts. We shall not attempt, in opposition to its assailant Brehm, to wash the creature morally clean; but we admire in it contentment, sedateness, strength, endurance, steadiness, and in spite of occasional stubbornness, great patience and manageableness—a combination of qualities that no other animal displays, certainly not the ass or the mule, not to speak of the horse or the ox.

We soon begin to have a liking for this mongrel breed between ass and ox, and pat in a kindly way the body of one of these animals. But it suddenly turns its neck upon us, utters a short, angry, bellowing sound, and shows its open mouth. It does not care for the attentions of man, like the horse, and declines to be troubled in any way apart from its toils, as it also, on its part, when unprovoked, does not attack the human race. We remark with compassion how this animal, on the whole so peaceable, is tormented, and has its blood sucked by all kinds of small enemies. Gnats and gadflies swarm about its skin, especially round the eyes, gadfly larvæ burrow in its nose, its frontal sinuses, and nasal fossæ, and it endeavours to get rid of these from time to time by snorting and rubbing its muzzle on the body of a neighbour. To the anus whole colonies of blood-sucking bloated ticks have attached themselves, which the all too insufficient tail vainly attempts to brush off.

It is well known that in the ancient Egyptian paintings and sculptures (with the exception of the Memnon columns?) the camel has never been found represented, nor is it mentioned by the Greek writers of Egypt; from which it has been concluded that this animal, now so common in Egypt in a domesticated state, was then unknown in the country. But we learn from the sacred writings that Abraham had camels during his stay in Egypt, or received such from the king (Gen. xii. 16), and it is also objected that other domestic animals, fowls for example, are never found represented, and pigeons, which exist in such numbers, but seldom, while geese, on the other hand, are frequently figured.

We amuse ourselves, while resting in the forecourt of the caravanserai, with the proceedings of a frolicsome and very long-legged sucking camel, which is to be allowed to travel with us, but, of course, unloaded. It has not yet become acquainted with the serious business of life, it runs along at a flying trot, its fat hump swaying and waggling to and fro at a great rate, strikes out with its straddling hind legs in youthful wantonness, utters a youthful bellow, and then returns to the four-nippled udder of its mother. At a dizzy height on the naked hump of a *hegin*, that is, a camel which can jump well, a boy sits laughing, as if on a divan, without support or saddle, having only the legs slightly pressed against the shoulder of the animal, and in his hand a cord which is fastened halterwise round the head and muzzle. Trotting, seldom galloping, the dromedary measures the ground, gliding onwards in long flying strides so gently and with so little shock, that, as the Arabs say, at this pace a person might sip a cup of coffee on its back. As a rule, however, the rider sits on a riding-saddle, and besides the halter, if the animal is very wild, a ring is often passed through its nose to ensure its obedience to the rein.

PROVENDER.

Chopped straw is laid down as food, whereupon the members of the herd hasten from all sides and crouch in a regular circle round the heaps of straw. But those are far better satisfied who get a bag of nitrogenous beans fastened to their heads, covering their muzzles up to the eyes. They have now no longer either eye or ear for the external world; they are altogether wrapped up in their bag, the toothsome contents of which they quickly convey into their mouths with their soft prehensile lips. The strong jaws worked to and fro soon convert the hard beans into a pulp, which is then passed through the wonderful cells and folds of the stomach (which has only three compartments), and through the long intestines of this ruminant. Straw and beans, with the exception of a few plants which are found in the desert by the way, are year after year the only nourishment of the camel of Upper Egypt. Only in "spring," that is to say in January and February, the camel is sent for a few weeks to pasture in the meadows of the Nile valley, to feed on clover and the herbage of the chick-pea. For grass and hay do not exist in the land of Egypt. Rest and the green-fodder cure exercise a great influence, the outlines become rounded, the hump again swells out, the limbs become stronger, and these creatures, after such a new birth, again become fit for the service of man. If not allowed thus to recruit themselves, connoisseurs tell us they soon break down, and in pasture-time the owner of a camel is very unwilling to let out his camel even though a high price is paid for the hire. The camels of the Bedouins do not get beans, and such as are brought into the valley of the Nile have first to accustom themselves to this food.

After eating their fill the camels are taken to drink at a trough or water-course. They lower their long necks to the ground, the neck now making a straight line with the head, the water is sucked in with a loud noise, and is seen rising in large waves through the sloping column formed by the neck till it reaches the stomach, while the water in the vessel is visibly lowered with every gulp.

LOADING AND SADDLING.

The beast would now prefer to walk about free and un-laden, or to chew its cud in quietness, and it is by no means pleased when it is driven in between two bags or bales of goods lying there all duly packed. It makes its discontent known by bellowing repeatedly, but it obeys orders though it could easily crush the orderer. What is evidently most disagreeable to it is the moment of kneeling down; even when food lies before it it does not do this without some delay. A mere croaking guttural sound is the signal with which a person, even a young child, compels the huge animal to kneel down before him, and if this does not follow immediately he enforces his order by pulling down its head with the loose end of the halter. The stubborn beast, while expressing its displeasure by bellowing, looks once more at the path, places its fore-legs properly, and making up its mind in despair, falls at last on the callosities of its knees, that is, of its carpal or wrist joints. The hind-legs, which are still upright, are also slowly and carefully brought into position, but the hinder quarters do not drop suddenly, the knee proper, which is situated high up and close to the body, and is also furnished with a callosity, being simply much bent and allowed to sink. Some slight movements of adjustment now follow; the fore-legs are pushed forward, the elbows bent, the fore-arm (lower part of the leg) pushed inwards, the tarsi of the hinder limbs are drawn under the body. In this way the animal, which has now become quieter, crouches on the ground, touching it, too, with only a few points, and these protected with thick callosities; the centre of gravity rests on the large chest callosity.

In loading the camel the first thing is to put on the saddle, *hautyeh*. This is a wonderful thing, not less strange than the camel itself. It consists of a sausage or sack shaped pad, of coarse sacking or alfa-grass cloth, stuffed with chopped straw, and bent into a horse-shoe shape, the camel's hump resting in the hollow between. It is close behind; in front it is held together by a primitive, but ingenious, compressing apparatus of wooden bars. This consists of two narrow transverse boards, meeting above at an angle, there being two pairs of these, one behind the other, at a short distance apart. Both these angular pieces are supported and kept in their places by a longitudinal bar on each side running along the upper border of the pads, and touching the boards. Holes are pierced in the boards, and thin bars and strings passed through from the board on one side to that on the other, these cross pieces both serving to keep the boards together, and also preventing the longitudinal bars from

Camel's Saddle.

LOADING AND SADDLING.

slipping upwards. The saddle is only attached to the beast by a crupper, otherwise it is free, not even a girth being considered necessary, since the hump prevents it from shifting.

The load, which is fastened over the saddle by cords, must be accurately balanced, that is the first condition, otherwise the beast will soon be worn out. The shape of the load is second in importance, its weight third. A strong camel can carry about ten Arabian hundredweights several days in succession; the ordinary load is three or four. While it is being loaded the camel repeatedly looks round with an angry bellow to see what is being done to it behind. A person who is riding seats himself on the pad saddle, which he makes more comfortable, especially at the place where the wooden apparatus is, by spreading over it his mantle, a mattress, or a carpet, the universal couch of the rainless East. These serve him also as a bed when encamping.

Whoever does not consider this sufficient, either as not being sufficiently comfortable or for other reasons, gets a palanquin (*shebriyeh*) made, a longish, quadrangular frame, somewhat like a bed, formed of a few rough longitudinal and transverse bars, with sides and bottom formed of netting. This is laid right across the camel's back, and in the middle fastened to the saddle, projecting freely on either side. It is capable of receiving a whole family, provided that the weight is the same on both sides. It is generally taken advantage of only by women, for whom also a kind of awning is erected above it by means of some palm-branches, a cloth being stretched over these to render the occupants invisible, and protect them from the rays of the sun. There are several other kinds of sedans, for example the *shukduf*, a kind of chair, of which a camel carries two, one hanging at each side; the *tahtrudn*, which swings freely between two camels, one behind the other; these are, however, seldom employed on this route. We get on best when we seat ourselves merely on the above-mentioned carpet-covered saddle. The chief necessaries of travel, that is to say, food and cooking appliances, we pack in a basket or box, or in a kind of saddle-bags (*churg*) specially made for travelling by camel, and consisting of two large strongly-woven bags tied in the middle, hanging down on each side of the camel, and often richly ornamented with tassels.

We leave the camel-driver with whom we have concluded the travelling agreement to provide the water. He hangs a goat-skin on a camel, and, when drinking-water is required, pours it out of this into a round wooden cup or a tin dish, which he presents to his client seated high on his camel's back. Such drinking vessels, however, are inconvenient, as they can only be used when one is standing still; when in motion a very narrow necked vessel must be employed to drink from. The best is the so-called *semsemîyeh*, a leather bottle with a tube for sucking. At the watering-stations the bottle is always refilled.

If we wish to travel with great rapidity, and are not afraid of the cost, we hire a *hegin*, that is, a running or trotting camel, which carries a saddle similar to that of a horse, with a high pommel before and behind, so that it becomes almost impossible to fall off during the smooth yet rapid trot. In this way a five days' journey may be accomplished in one or at most two days, presupposing practice in camel-riding, acquaintance with the route or companions, and water and fodder stations. This mode of travelling is here very uncommon, being used at most among Bedouins; riding on horseback is still more so, and carriages are scarcely used at all in travelling.

MOUNTING.

We are invited to mount the ship of the desert. There are several methods of doing this, each of which has its difficulties. The most plausible appears to be to mount while the animal is still crouching on the ground. But we take very good care not to attempt that alone, since, long before we could seat ourselves properly, whenever it felt our weight in mounting, the camel would rise suddenly and fling us backwards and sideways. Any one who is accustomed to riding on a camel knows that quite well, and is able to seat himself firmly at once. We uneducated folks, however, while mounting and gradually trying to settle ourselves in our seat, cause the driver to tread upon the fore-feet of the still squatting camel so as to keep them from moving, or to tie them, and fix one hand upon the bar of the compressing apparatus that projects before the saddle, pressing the other upon the hinder part of the saddle. It is only in this way that we can prepare ourselves for all the changes of our centre of gravity that we have to undergo. We give the driver a signal to release the animal, and our body is now swung in rapid succession backwards, forwards, and again backwards. For the animal first springs up with the lower part of the fore-leg (it is far more willing to do this than to kneel), then brings its hind-feet, on the stretch, into play, and rears itself at last quite upright, while it now raises the lowest portion of its forelegs and stands upon the sole.

We now find ourselves high above the ground, higher than we have ever ridden before; we shudder when we think upon our helpless condition. If the animal were to become refractory what could we do? We sit far too high to be able to steady ourselves with the calves of the legs as in riding on horseback. If we sit astride upon the broad saddle, our soles scarcely touch the ribs; if we seat ourselves, as is the common plan, with our feet dangling down over the neck or over the side of the animal, our position is indeed more comfortable but is less secure should the awkward case occur in which both saddle and rider are flung off by the violent movements of the camel. The bridle is of no use, since the cord brought round its nose has little influence on the beast however hard it is pulled. The Moslim merely cries, "The name of God on you" (*bismallah 'alék*), when it turns restive or refractory. Such misbehaviour on the part of the animal is fortunately rare, however; were it not so other means of subduing it would have been discovered before now. During its ordinary running pace we are in the greatest security.

We find that the angular projections of the wooden part of the saddle on which any part of the body rests are still insufficiently padded, so that we cannot endure to ride for a quarter of an hour, and have to request the driver to let us dismount. He warns us to stick on firmly as in mounting, since the backward and forward shakings are the same, only they occur in reverse order. We can also dismount from a standing camel by grasping the projecting bar of the saddle with one hand and sliding down by means of the other on the sloping hindneck. On remounting, after our seat has been improved, we employ the second method for a change. The camel stands, we grasp with one hand that important saddle-bar, the driver forms one step with his back or his hand, the hollow of the animal's neck forms a second, and this being reached we climb as gracefully as we can into the saddle. It is certainly still better to emancipate one's self entirely from the driver, to compel the camel to lower its neck, and to get the knee upon this by swinging one's self up with one hand on the saddle-bar, whereupon the animal itself raises both neck and rider, who can now obtain full possession of his seat. During the latter operation, however, the animal is again on the march, which makes turning one's self somewhat difficult. A person should likewise learn to make the animal let him down when travelling alone, and how to bring it to the trot, and also how to dismount when on the march. But this belongs to the higher branches of the riding art; we are glad if we can mount and dismount in any manner without damage.

CARAVAN DONKEYS.

Should riding on camel-back not prove to our taste we have at our command the asses of the desert, of which considerable numbers always accompany and complete the caravans. In spite of their tender feet they are able to drag about a hundredweight over hill and dale without breaking down. With their short steps they have enough to do to keep up with the long-legged camel. It would be difficult to get the sluggish animal to go farther alone; but it follows the caravan cheerfully. It would be wholly in vain to try to get a good trot or a gallop out of these caravan donkeys—which stand in the same relation to the riding donkeys of the Nile valley as the load-carrying camel to the trotting camel—unless they should have remained till they were some distance behind the caravan. Between camels and donkeys there are many resemblances in structure, nature, and character, and they live together pretty sympathetically.

ON THE MARCH.

The caravan, consisting of from a dozen or two up to 50 or 100 camels, at last gets seriously on the march. The drivers like to go in company, less for security, since in this desert there is nothing to fear, than for convenience and society. They help each other in loading and unloading, relieve each other in driving, and at other times mount. What one has not taken with him another perhaps has; the animals themselves are in better humour and spirits, and run better; several strong good camels give the time in running, and none will remain behind. The drivers on this route are mostly Fellahs of Upper Egypt or Ababdeh Bedouins, partly the owners of the animals themselves, partly mere servants or slaves. The march generally continues the whole day without a rest; the stilted gait of the walking machine appears slow and sluggish—a pedestrian at a good walking pace easily goes far ahead of the caravan—but it is telling, uniform, and continuous, and if a person lags behind for any reason he soon sees the caravan far ahead of him, and has hard work to overtake it.

The fertile soil soon ceases, for it just reaches as far as the overflow of last harvest extended; it is only exceptionally that here and there some small gardens like oases are met with, in the desert certainly, but not far from the cultivated surface, and fed by a deep well, in which the subsoil water collects. Before us lies a widely-extended terrace land, which rises almost imperceptibly. Small undulating hills cross it transversely and longitudinally. This region is apparently devoid of all organic life; wherever the eye turns there is nothing but hopeless gray. Only in a few depressions between the hills, where the water of the winter's rain (which generally falls only once) has collected and formed a torrent, a small plant or a bush grows here and there, amid sheets of clay neatly collected and left behind it by the stream. We look backwards, and already see stretching far below us the valley of the Nile and the mountains on the west of the valley, there forming the beginning of the Libyan desert; before us we see distant grayish-white ranges of limestone mountains running in all directions, with valleys between them, which imagination might clothe with rich verdure and smiling homesteads, since in the distance they assume exactly the appearance of the fruitful fields of a mountainous region in a happier clime.

The soil on which we are marching is not loose sand, but very solid gravel and limestone. We have not to do with a sandy desert here. A light dust-cloud can scarcely be raised by a storm, and the heavy drift sand immediately collects again at various spots under the protection of the hills. The path taken by our caravan is little inferior in firmness and solidity to a regularly-constructed road, and since it is generally level, might be traversed without special difficulty even by a velocipede. The steps of the camels have marked out many lines of ruts, each the breadth of a foot, which wind along it longitudinally, and between which are so many raised lines of loose and seldom trodden gravel. Camels prefer to move along the beaten track, and the firmness of the ruts increases with the amount of the traffic. Nothing else is done to keep up the road; what it is it is in itself. Projecting stones no one thinks of removing. The animal, whose centre of gravity the load now throws forward on the forelegs, runs down smaller and gentler slopes at first slowly and cautiously, but strikes into a trot for a few steps before reaching the bottom of the declivity—a serious matter for the rider and for wares easily broken. Gullies cut by mountain torrents run abruptly across the road, forming sharp breaks which cause the camels to stumble. It crosses these with lumbering footsteps, and always at the risk of a broken leg. It is only suited for the level ground. At difficult points it turns aside of itself. On the whole, however, a fall is a rare occurrence. Pashas, who like to ride in carriages, as was formerly the custom during their pilgrimages, no longer use this route at the present day; some English ladies have themselves carried by natives in palanquins the whole long road.

On this advanced terrace the landscape offers little that is interesting. Instead of it we amuse ourselves with the inexhaustible study of the camel, including its shadow, which changes with every movement and every hour; with the rustic but eloquent language, and the rude but kindly character of the drivers, whose cudgels fall far oftener upon the donkeys than upon the faithful, or at least not unduly labour-shirking, camels; and with their fresh but somewhat monotonous mountain songs, generally religious in character; we interchange with them a short, deep-bowled desert pipe, which is filled with the coarse country tobacco, and is lighted by means of durrah pith with flint and steel. We have also enough to do with ourselves. That infernal apparatus on the saddle makes itself increasingly felt in spite of all bolstering, we sink deeper and deeper in our seat, the upper part of our body is swayed forcibly backwards and forwards with every advance of the ship of the desert, a movement which, to be sure, brings on nothing of the dizziness of sea-sickness, but is generally not long in giving the novice pains in the back. We at last become tired of riding, and take to walking for a stretch as a refreshing change.

Meanwhile the caravan has reached a spot of a brown or dark-yellow appearance, where the tread of the camels on the compact, hardened, and smoothened soil becomes almost inaudible, and a peculiar and often pungent smell becomes perceptible. This is a *urinarium (mabwala)*. The animals halt of themselves, or at a clacking cracking sound made by the drivers, and add their contribution to the keeping up of the peculiar soil. By these remarkable spots, which recur at tolerably equal intervals, and therefore serve as excellent milestones, the drivers and Bedouins reckon their journeys, and they are accordingly of some importance to travellers in the desert.

CAMPING AT NIGHT.

The caravans do not halt at mid-day, as unloading and loading gives too much trouble to the drivers; both man and beast must therefore make their breakfast last till evening. Luncheon or a drink of water may be taken while sitting on camel-back on the march; accordingly the journey proceeds with little interruption from morning till evening. The shadows become longer, the mountains and the horizon assume a ruddy hue, and the caravan begins to think of its quarters for the night, so that supper and the camp may be prepared before daylight is gone. The camels, too, are obviously tired out; they often look round about and begin to pick up and eat the balls of dung dropped by their brothers. In this operation the drivers now vie with them, but they select only the older and drier to serve as fuel. The caravan turns aside from the path and seeks out some soft and quiet spot sheltered from the wind.

We dismount, get our carpet and head-cushion spread on the soft dry soil, and lie down immediately with great satisfaction; for our back is in want of the support we have long had to dispense with, and we can now stretch and move our legs at our leisure. The carpet, or it may be only the soft sand of the camp, is, to one who travels by the ship of the desert, like the land to the sea-sick traveller by sea. In this condition a drop of brandy is a very healthy medicine in hot or cold weather, and quickly dispels all fatigue. Not less effective is a cup of tea or coffee, but these take some time to prepare. If we have no servant the driver readily attends to us, but as soon as he has made our couch ready he leaves us in the lurch in order to look after his beasts. Making them lie down one after the other, he removes their loads. They do not lie down of themselves, and if not attended to would prefer to run about with their loads in search of pasture. They are now fed in the way we have already described.

In the evening only the bag of beans is usually given them, while in the morning they are allowed to fill their bellies with chopped straw. They get water when any is to be had. In order to keep them from straying in search of pasture one of their fore-legs is tied up, so that they can only move by hopping along. The donkeys have both their fore-legs tied together. It is only now that the driver thinks of us and of himself. He is our guest and we his, for in the freedom of the desert there is no distinction of ranks, and Bedouin law prevails. The fire is either made with brushwood brought with us or picked up by the way, or with dried camel's dung, which gives a very good coal fire. So soon as it is ablaze coffee is made, and afterwards some simple dish is cooked, generally lentils, since Esau's time the favourite food of the desert, and to it we eat the biscuits we have brought with us, that is, toasted ordinary bread softened in water. If we think cooking is too roundabout a process, we content ourselves with hard-boiled eggs, dates, date-bread, cheese, or still better, pigeons, fowls, or butcher-meat roasted at home. The drivers always like to have something warm; they take out of their sacks a wooden dish, each gives his contribution of flour, they knead a lump of simple unleavened dough, spread it over a gridiron, lay this above the glowing camel's dung, generally directly, but sometimes with an iron plate between, and cover it above with another plate. In this way is made the *desert-cake*, the *kurs*, the chief and favourite food of the drivers. These now take their meal in common, inviting everybody around, travellers and Bedouins, to share with them, and we too have to try the toothsome piece of pastry and pretend to like it. On the remains of the dung fire we place once more a coffee-pot, and cause the bitter Mocha to be served out to our hosts.

Meanwhile it has become dark, one star after another breaks through the darkness, and soon—so short is twilight in these latitudes—the vault of heaven stretches in its full untroubled splendour above the camp. The company light their pipes and chat away, sitting in the well known favourite squatting position. When it is cold the groups draw more closely together, and crouch around the oft-poked fire of dung. Everybody then lies down among his baggage on the sand, or on the ever-serviceable cotton-plush, which to-day has already been used as a plaid, a head-covering, a fodder-cloth, a sack, and a basket, and now becomes a carpet or a coverlet. For the cold nights of winter one would do well to provide himself with a heavy cotton and also a woollen cover. A tent is seldom used for these short distances; carrying it, pitching and taking down is considered too troublesome by the people. As a protection from the boisterous winds of winter, a barrier is constructed with bales of goods or bags, and at night a person draws the coverlet over his head, the glare of the sun is kept off by forming a kind of awning with the ever-present wrapping cloth. No one gives his personal safety a thought, the whole caravan scarcely possesses a single firearm. For in this desert, or, at least, in this part of it, there are no robbers nor murderers, not even thieves, unless belonging to the company. Attacks by hyenas or other wild animals inhabiting the mountains are unheard of. Only when the camp is made in the neighbourhood of human dwellings one has to take care that the thievish dogs, or even the sheep and goats, do not get at the stores. since at unguarded moments they snap up bread, &c., though lying beside us and even under our pillows. Thus the whole caravan, both men and beasts, soon sink into a deep and well-earned slumber.

THE MORNING CAMP.

The coolness of the morning breeze, which ceases soon after the morning star rises above the mountain, arouses the sleepers. Packing is quickly finished and the camp broken up; the morning camp, which to the camel-driver appears indispensable, partly because the animals must be fed, partly because he must take his own breakfast, will be held at the neighbouring water-station. On the eastern horizon appears a glimmer that becomes brighter and brighter, forms become more distinct, the tops of the mountains are illumined, as the sun rises we hear a barking, and immediately afterwards we distinguish human abodes, the dog, the man, and the water. None of these four objects, in the desert at least, is to be thought of without the others.

The caravan leaders otherwise do not pay much attention to stations; the caravan marches from morning to evening, and passes the night at whatever spot it may have arrived at about sunset, human dwellings are even avoided on account of the dogs. Water is drawn at the watering places in passing, the skins are filled and the camels watered standing. The desert village Laketa, however, is not so lightly regarded as a station. There fowls, pigeons, sheep, and goats are to be had, and also company besides the villagers, as several caravans are always met with here, either resting from their journey or strengthening themselves for a fresh one; fruits and vegetables, brought by the caravans, may often be obtained from them. At the same time, on the return journey to the Nile valley, when the main portion of the difficult road has been traversed, the traveller treats himself to a little good eating here, cooks for himself at least some pigeons, and the richer individuals make a present of a sheep to their company.

DAY MARCH.

We are again seated aloft on the camel-divan; we see before us wide flat tracts, bounded by a transverse chain. One crown of hills after the other bounds the horizon, a new one always succeeds, showing so near through the clear air, though by the measure of reality so far removed. There too, at the distance of a quarter or half a league, lies a lake, there follows another and again another, a whole system of lakes, some of them even fringed with palms. But everyone knows that they are mere illusions of the malicious, mocking devil, they are the *bahr esh sheithan*, while the man of science calls such atmospheric reflections a kind of *fata morgana*, in which the ground plays the part of the silvering of a mirror, and the strata of air immediately above it that of the reflecting glass.

The sun rises higher and higher. Were we in regions a little farther to the south it would send its rays perpendicularly down upon our heads at mid-day in summer. We see and feel the twenty-sixth parallel of latitude. The glare of the sunlight on the clear gray ground dazzles the eye, which requires a pair of desert spectacles to subdue the glare. The atmosphere is extremely rare and dry, not sultry, but in this district as a rule there are no air-currents of any force, and, accordingly, the sun's rays act with full power upon terrestrial objects, and among these in the first place on our noses, faces, and the backs of our hands. After a journey in the desert these parts are always at least reddened and browned, even at the cool season. If, however, parts of the body less accustomed to the light are exposed, even for a short time, to the glare of the sun, as for instance when the trousers slip up in riding, an erythema is caused, and, in an aggravated form, an outbreak of a multitude of little watery pustules, accompanying a burning eczema that gives us plenty to do for some days, not to mention the peeling off of the sunburned skin for weeks after. The skin is the more tender the clearer it is. One would expect the opposite, seeing that a burning-glass does not light a paper cigarette. And yet the Fellah, the Bedouin of this desert (the Abadi), and the Moor, exposes the whole of the dusky surface of his body to the burning sun without inconvenience. This must be nothing but the effect of custom. According to the oriental custom, taught by experience and also adopted by Europeans, the head must be the more thickly covered the higher the temperature is, and if it is uncovered, even for an instant, a person unaccustomed to such exposure is immediately liable to the severe phenomena of sunstroke—fainting, headache, excited circulation, somnolence, extreme feebleness, and not seldom even instant death. The Abadi wears no cap on his curly head either in summer or winter, and even on the smooth-shaved poll of the Fellah, who often cultivates his field in summer bareheaded, the glowing sunbeams beat without effect. In such warm days, with the thermometer at $76\tfrac{1}{2}°$ F. in the shade, a journey in the desert is of course no pleasure, and unless people have urgent business they put off their journeys till a cooler season of the year, autumn and spring by preference. It appears a very feasible plan then to march at night and camp during the day. But this plan has also this great disadvantage, that from morning till evening a shady spot can scarcely anywhere be found. If a person buries himself among bales of goods, or keeps inside a tent, he excludes, along with the sun, such slight currents of air as there may be, and at last prefers to seat himself again on his camel, covering head, hands, and all other parts as well as possible, and holding up his white umbrella lined with green.

But the *samum* or poison-wind also blows frequently in these regions at the hot season of the year. In the afternoon the wind generally veers round and blows from the west— from the Sahara and the Libyan deserts. The atmosphere, previously so clear, becomes darkened, impregnated as it were with atoms of sand, the sky has a grayish appearance, the sun looks like a yellowish-pale or reddish disk; one sand cloud after another rolls up, lashes the traveller turned towards it in the face, and rubs his eyes till they are sore. While the air of the desert in its dryness was previously so agreeable and healthy, the glowing samum renders the body dry, relaxes the limbs, and produces a prickling of the nerves like that caused by electricity; the traveller feels he cannot go farther, and camps. The samum that came on, now gently, now roaring and storming, generally ceases after a few hours, and air and sky again become clear. This peculiar west wind breaks on the middle mountains, into the valleys of which it hardly penetrates, and it scarcely ever reaches the maritime border of the mountains and the sea.

We are now somewhat more than 20 leagues from the Nile valley. The country we have hitherto crossed has been a great, almost level terrace-land, the soil being gravel or limestone. Sandstone now makes its appearance, and the hills and mountains come more closely together and begin to form the sides of valleys, while with these at last some vegetation appears, hitherto wholly absent. The sandstone, which is yellowish or reddish in colour, rises sometimes from the valley bottoms in lofty, isolated, quadrangular rocks, water-worn on all sides; such a rock among others is the so-called Maiden's Castle (*Kasr el banât*). But soon dark, lofty, steep mountain masses show themselves and seem to bar the way. We can no longer march so straight onwards as before, a deep narrow valley winds through the hard rock which belongs to the primeval mountains. Bare rocks show themselves everywhere, torn with wild ravines and chasms, the mountain walls are covered with loose blocks, both large and small, but with no soil. These threaten to crush the traveller; a number of them have indeed fallen down into the valley and lie right in the path. At the entrance to this valley, beside the caravan route, is a cistern, the well called Hamamât; there are several such on the road, and a good many among the mountains. They are generally deep, built-up wells, from which the water is drawn up by leathern buckets, or a stair leads down to them, a structure of which a son of the country longing for coolness not infrequently makes use to descend to bathe in the cool basin below, from which others obtain their water for drinking and cooking. Along the whole road, but especially in this valley, antiquities belonging to the ancient Egyptian and the Greek periods are seen.

The route that the caravan takes lies on the whole in a single transverse valley from the Nile to the sea, and of such there are several to choose from. Here a multitude of caravans are daily encountered, embracing from one or two animals up to hundreds, and generally carrying nothing but corn from the highly-favoured Nile valley to the sea-port, the corn being thence exported to Arabia, which is poor in this commodity. It is difficult, however, to cross the watershed, which there forms a high valley 4 or 5 miles in length, sinking at both ends in the form of a steep rocky ravine. For a camel to cross such passes is just within the bounds of possibility. The camel is at home only on level ground; at such places it is apt to stumble, though it attempts with its natural caution to find a suitable spot on which to plant its every footstep; at places that appear to it very difficult it often stands helpless, till the driver leads it over by the bridle.

To go up a slope, however, is a much easier matter for it than to go down one. Slipping, falling, and broken bones are by no means rare in such circumstances, and it is always better to dismount both for our own sake and that of the animal. Animals that have fallen and broken some of their bones are left lying on the spot; some fodder is given to them, and they are handed over to the care of the neighbouring Bedouins until they have recovered, or till the butcher who has bought them for a trifle arrives from the next town. At such spots are found a multitude of stones and cairns erected by human hands; these are mementos of their presence set up by the passing pilgrims.

Thus we wander onwards in the mountains; narrow valleys and ravines alternate with opener areas more resembling plains; lofty mountains several thousand feet high, with chains of hills formed of debris; absolutely desert tracts, with oasis-like spots and steppes nourished by a visible or invisible well. Here is no longer the waste loneliness of the plantless outer terrace; the geologist admires the variety and the structure of the primary rocks everywhere laid bare, the botanist plucks the small and ephemeral plants, the zoologist hunts and collects, as well as it can be done on the march, the antiquary inspects the ruins and deciphers the inscriptions.

MARCHING AT NIGHT.

Still, these mountains are but a desert, and we strive to get out of them as soon as possible. We arrange with the leaders of our caravan to make a journey by night, and having pitched our night-camp at some suitable place, we break up about midnight and move along by the dark mountain heights. It is not pitch dark, the starlight of the southern sky shining through the transparent atmosphere lights up the path sufficiently to prevent us from making any false step, although the ruts or trodden paths appear to us to wind deceitfully up and down. The camels go faster in the cool night air than by day, and the casual highway fodder, as yet invisible, does not distract their thoughts. For hours on end we hear nothing but the gentle tread of the soft soles of our animals, and at times a "Hi!" from the watchful driver, and the thwack of a cudgel on some of the donkeys, which cannot follow the quicker night pace of the camels. Our eyes and thoughts are forcibly drawn from the terrestrial desert lying invisible around us to the infinite region of the spheres of light. We find again the constellations of the North from the polar star and the Bears to the brilliant Orion, and discover now too the great Scorpion in its whole length, the Southern Crown, and still just above the horizon Canopus. The driver, like every Egyptian, is an accomplished astronomer; but the names he gives to the constellations and his manner of grouping the figures often vary from those depicted on European maps of the stars.

From the stars our thoughts wander to the countries of that more northern region to which we belong; we recall to mind the blessings derived from the superior cultivation of the soil, the flourishing state of art and science, the mighty advances made by commerce and industry, the order in civil and political life, the power and the riches of the nations, lastly, the power of public opinion, fighting on the side of justice and morality. Directly the contrary of all this is what we see in Mohammedan states. But we find that amidst the blessings of civilization there swarm all kinds of gnawing cancerous sores and examples of glaring wretchedness; and the Frank is by no means justified in always looking down upon the Oriental as the sick man. The Moslim is essentially a natural man guided by faith in his religion, which, when rightly interpreted, is as capable of giving him the stamp of a good man as any other. That art and science can flourish also on the soil of Islam history shows, and that a Mussulman, who is a true believer, is not necessarily a fanatic, any one may convince himself who has an intimate knowledge of both country and people. To be sure, as things are at present Islam is numbed and petrified, and all high effort is wanting to its believers.

Moreover, as the Frank looks down upon the Oriental on account of his ignorance, so does the Oriental look down upon the Frank on account of a multitude of customs that to him appear strange, ridiculous, undignified, even indecent, and the Oriental is not so far wrong; indeed, the Frank who has become orientalized in his ways latterly laughs at himself for many things that he formerly did, and thought natural and matters of course. The Oriental detests above everything the emancipation of women, which he stigmatizes as indecent, shameless, and immoral; in his eyes a ball is an act by which the husband calmly allows his wife, the father his daughter, to revel in the arms of a stranger. Indulgence in wine and spirits is the other chief symptom in which the Moslim believes he detects civilization. The Frank also appears to him as unclean, because he uses as food pork, blood, and carrion, that is, the flesh of animals that have been strangled, not properly slaughtered, and because he does not wash or bathe before meals, nor generally after them, nor in connection with his devotions, and not a great deal at other times; from the throne of his dignity, clad in his long flowing robes, he criticises the goings on of the army of Frankish fops, their cravats, their stiff collars, their kid gloves, their chimney-pot hats, their tight trousers, their dress and other coats, the many different forms of their beards ("the Franks have no dignity in their beards"), and such like. And none of the strange fashions of the women escape him, any more than their falseness, unnaturalness, and want of taste.

It is the scum swimming on the top that first meets the eyes of the novice, and in indignation he pours out the whole untasted contents of the proffered cup of civilization, or he himself becomes the victim of this scum. He is only too ready to adopt the vices of the Frank without giving up his own and adopting the virtues of his model. Since, in Egypt at least, it is attempted to introduce forcibly a kind of superficial civilization from the top downwards, the people will soon degenerate if the healthy kernel which exists in the Moslims does not exercise a counteractive effect until at last true civilization, which is unceasingly spreading, shall pave a way for itself.

All at once we awake from the wild improbable dreams to

which the rocking gait of our steed has lulled us; we have slipped down a little and lost our balance. It is a wise provision of nature that in such cases the sleeper awakes just before the crisis. We hold on by something or other, fear seems to have quite dispelled sleep, and we rejoice that we are still far from the miseries of civilization, of which we have been dreaming in the ever free, unsullied desert. But in a few minutes, through the constant action of our cradle, we again fall asleep, to start up suddenly as before. In this painful intermediate state between sleeping and waking, which often means as much as between death and life—for many a man has ere now met his death by sleeping on his camel, or, at least, has fallen and broken his limbs—we look with envy upon our native companions, the drivers, who, placed aloft, snore for hours on end in the most perpendicular positions, their feet hanging down on one side, their head on the other, right across the camel. The camels march on instinctively, even when the driver has fallen asleep; but sometimes one of them, often the very one that carries the sleeper, remains standing, and it may happen that when we come to look around us we find ourselves quite alone in the wilderness, and neither shouts nor the report of a gun can reach the ear of the guide who has fallen asleep and been left leagues behind us. As a rule, however, a person joins a whole caravan, and then the driver who is keeping watch has to march behind on foot.

THE LITTORAL SLOPE OF THE MOUNTAINS.

The night march has helped our progress, and by the time it is day we have reached the littoral slope of the mountains. The air, the soil, the water, the rocks, the structure of the mountain, and to some extent also the animals, plants, and people, change their character. A fresh, pure sea breeze blows from the north, or, laden with clouds and moisture, the warm and oppressive south-east wind (*Asiâb*), which, along with the always pleasant north wind and the cold north-east (*masri*), rules the winter half-year, and which is kept from reaching the Nile valley by the intervening mountains, as the samum from the west has its progress eastwards arrested. The springs that here and there occur have a very bitter taste, and sometimes give out a smell like that of sulphuretted hydrogen. In places the soil appears loose, crusty, yellowish, moist, as it were, spongy, and impregnated with a saline fluid. A bitter, perennial rivulet, the Ambiga, makes a vain attempt to trickle farther down into the valley, and gives a verdant existence to a grove of rushes, but after a few days' rain becomes a raging, devastating stream.

Already at a distance the most striking feature of this littoral portion of the mountains is the long-stretching ridges of white limestone hills which rise youthfully between and among the dark and ancient primary rocks. The heart of the traveller, fatigued with his long journey through the desert, beats high when he sees them, since his goal, the sea, must be near.

From the bare hill-terrace that spreads out before us we perceive on the eastern horizon a bluish-black band which separates the earth from the clear blue vault of heaven. The camel accelerates his pace as we march down a valley of no great slope, that of the Ambagi. This opens out more and more, we hear behind the last hills a roaring and booming, and at last we stand before a town, the seaport of Koseir, and on the shore of the eternal sea, after traversing a stretch of 43 leagues, to accomplish which the caravans require four or five days on the "up journey," that is, when going from the interior to the sea, and three or four on the "down journey," from the sea to the Nile valley.

II.—THE NATURE OF THE DESERT.

CONFIGURATION OF THE MOUNTAINS.

The mountain mass which we have crossed is apparently a confused agglomeration of mountains and valleys where no brook nor river affords a safe guide. But abundant traces of the action of water compensate for this want, and it is generally easy to trace out the river and valley systems, even if the region is not traversed on those rare days after winter rains when the rivers really exist. Channels are seen on the sides of mountains, traces of brooks, of waterfalls, beds of rivers, some of them streams with wide valleys of embouchure. Nay, along the very summit of the mountain mass runs a regular water-shed, from which the waters must run either westwards into the Nile valley, or eastwards into the Red Sea.

RAIN AND RAINWATER-STREAMS.

During summer the sky is almost always entirely blue and cloudless; at the winter season, however, the tops of the mountains are often enveloped in clouds, especially after moist south and south-east winds. Then the soul of every dweller in the desert is filled with new hope; if the clouds become denser and blacker, the children march about with white streamers and shout, *Ya Allah idina sél, ehna 'abídak u el chér bi idak*, that is, "Dear God, give us a rain stream; we are thy servants, and blessing is in thy hand." The women and girls make a cross-shaped frame with two pieces of timber, put a shirt and a veil on it, and carry this figure about in houses and courts with singing and trilling. Hitherto the dweller in the desert town (Koseir) has had to get his fresh water brought in skins a distance of several days' journey, from springs in the mountains, and paid dear for it. But now he hopes to be able to obtain the precious liquid himself before his own door, and to fill his store vessels with a supply for months to come; the Bedouin hopes that the mountain wells will be filled, that pasture will be procured, and the deadlying desert revivified. But very often these hopes are cheated; the north wind, that rules everything, begins to blow, and in a moment the sky is again clear and blue. Two, three, even four years may pass without the aqueous vapour falling in a bounteous rain. Still the attempt of the southern sky to pour out rain is often successful, once at least on an average in every winter, and then it often does its duty in superabundant measure. In the midst of incessant thunder and lightning, as if a dozen storms had joined together, the rain pours down, being often mixed with heavy hailstones. The flat roofs of the houses of the desert city, which houses are built of unburned bricks made without chopped straw, give way "like sugar;" if they are not in good condition the water makes a hole through the ceiling, and in a short time the room, the terrace, the court-yard are converted into a lake, the streets become lagoons, filth-swamps, and streams, which sap the foundations of the houses, so that some fall at once or after a few days. In the mountains the Bedouin flees with his tent and all his belongings to the more elevated points of the valleys or to the hills. The caravans, thoroughly drenched, must come to a halt, and do not reach their destination without difficulty and danger, caused by the slippery ground, here and there converted into a torrent, or only after a very circuitous route.

Fortunately, however, these downpours do not last long, and now old and young march out of the town to look at the river that has filled the valley, many also, particularly the women, to bathe in the cool stream, not seldom to the danger of their lives. All who have strength enough, men, women, and children, convey the newly fallen fresh water in pitchers or skins into the houses; all the donkeys and camels are loaded, and the water caravans from the mountains find their labour lost, and, emptying out the mountain water they have carried so far, set to work in the river with the rest. For it is only a short time that the water of the rain-torrent remains fresh; in a few days, when the flow ceases, it absorbs salt and bitter elements from the soil, but the great bulk of the stream falls uselessly into the sea, instead of being stored up in cisterns.

At other times the clouds discharge themselves at a greater distance among the mountains, and in the town, on the seacoast, only lightning is seen and thunder heard. Then perhaps a Bedouin will come into the town the next day with the strange information that "the river is coming." If only a small quantity of rain falls it is immediately drunk up by the thirsty soil of the desert; if, however, it is greater, and the spot where the fall took place is also not very distant or very limited, the surface water gathers into rivulets, the larger valleys receive all the waters of their tributary valleys, and thus the whole is finally collected into a mighty stream in the main valley, down which it rolls like an outflow of lava, when the slope is small often very slowly. But on many occasions also the rain that follows falls on the other side of the watershed, on the Nile side, in which case the thirsty towns on the Red Sea and the dwellers in the Nile valley are equally annoyed. For the stream of fresh water then carries devastation over the laboriously tilled fields of the Nile peasant, who requires no other river than his Nile. In the Nile valley itself showers are far more seldom than in the mountains.

The valleys of the eastern slope of our mountain mass stand in the closest relationship to the sea-ports on the Red Sea, which are directly the result of the former. For in these regions the sea is fringed along the coast by a coral-reef, called a coast reef. Now, as is well known, fresh water kills the coral animals. Accordingly, where large masses of fresh water enter the sea, the coral polyps cannot continue their labours, and thus arise the *sherm*, or reef-openings which form these ports. As a rule the size of the *sherm* is in direct proportion to the magnitude of the respective valley system. Of course the stream that at present so seldom flows down these valleys, is not sufficient to account for the formation of the sherm, scarcely for its maintenance. We must go back to earlier times, when more permanent or more frequent streams flowed through, and, to some extent, formed the valleys. That this must have been the case is testified by the alluvial tracts, the heaps of gravel and pebbles transported by water, and the water-worn rocks, phenomena visible everywhere on a large scale. Under present circumstances, when at most a rivulet is formed only once a year for a few days, a thousand years would produce an equal result to that produced by a permanent stream in three years, in rounding off and wearing away the hard rocks of the mountains, and in accumulating such masses of debris. Similar observations made in the neighbouring desert of Sinai, so similar to ours, perhaps admit of the inference that such an abundance of water continued down even to historic times, seeing that the Israelites were able to maintain themselves several years round Mount Sinai, while at present only a few Bedouins roam there. Our desert also, as numerous remains inform us (see below), was formerly much more thickly inhabited. This mountain region is, therefore, essentially an *erosion desert*.

GEOLOGICAL CONSTITUTION.

The constitution of the surface, in its individual features, naturally depends upon the geological formation. In the west, towards the Nile valley, we have tertiary nummulite limestone; here the desert has the character of a plateau-desert, like that of the Libyan desert, of which it forms merely a continuation, separated by the Nile valley. This formation is followed on the east by a sandstone, which appears to belong to the "Nubian sandstone," one of the latest members of the tertiary formation. The middle, the heart of the mountain system, is occupied mainly by dull-looking primary rock, consisting of diorites (green-stones), diorite-breccias, and black or green-stone porphyries; with these are often intermingled very beautiful red-coloured granites and porphyries, and massive highly-coloured veins and lodes everywhere permeate the dark rock. The chief masses, those on which the others, so to speak, rest, are mainly composed of such granite, gneiss being less common. They rise to a height of 400 feet. These rocks are nowhere covered, as in other countries, with a layer of humus; but the geologist is not allowed to behold Earth in all her nakedness, since the superficial layer is generally traversed to such an extent with fissures, often of considerable depth, that it is not easy to break off a fragment the size of the fist showing a fresh fracture on all sides, while in ascending a mountain, from the crumbling of the surface, a firm footing cannot be obtained. In other districts, where much rain falls, this disintegrated rough-casting is washed away; here it remains, and the whole of the mountains look as if burned by the sun. The rocks in some ravines, where there are permanent waterfalls, do not show these fissures; they are firm, hard, and smooth as marble, since the water can take effect here.

It is not till towards the Red Sea that chains of stratified limestone mountains again appear, but they often advance far into the ancient mountains. They are mostly long straight mountain ridges, consisting of pure limestone or dolomite, and containing numerous flint nodules interspersed. The fossils show them to be genuine members of the cretaceous system. In the valleys isolated masses of sandstone occur along with them, often showing the action of water all round them, devoid of fossils and pretty rich in iron. The nearer we approach the sea the more readily do we find in these limestone ridges organic remains of animals that still live in the Red Sea; the transition from the chalk through the tertiary (which, however, here exhibits no trace of nummulites) to the modern period is thus, therefore, quite gradual. The interior crystalline mountain mass always stood out as dry land. The Red Sea has existed at least since the cretaceous epoch, and has withdrawn into its present limits quite gradually, and this withdrawal is still going on, as every one who has dwelt long on the coast knows, the fact being proved by many harbours, which, though celebrated in antiquity, are now dry land. Shells which are also found in the sea, for example, the well-known large Tridacna, are often found in earthy layers unpetrified, as if they had been just cast up by the sea, but upon mountain-spurs hundreds of feet above it.

Many parts of the limestone mountains, especially of the latest formation, are in process of transition to gypsum, and this is perhaps a consequence of the decay of the animal substances; the gypsum is found in all valleys that lead from the sea to the mountains, even large mountains and mountain groups are converted into gypsum. Other parts have a tendency to crumble into the form of dust, such as may be seen on walls built of bricks containing iron-pyrites; these soils, which are everywhere found in the neighbourhood of the sea, are called by the Arabs *zabach*. The cause is evidently the attraction of moisture by the salts contained in the stone. The salt often separates in thick crusts and layers as mountain salt, which is often dug for, since other salt, even sea salt, is difficult to procure on account of certain government regulations. Other useful minerals are not worked in these mountains at the present day. From many traces as well as historical notices, however, we learn that they were worked in ancient times, in those of the ancient Egyptians, Greeks, and Romans, and even the Arabs (in the fifteenth century); there were silver, gold, and copper mines, and in antiquity the emerald mines farther to the south were highly renowned, though they are now unproductive. In the neighbourhood of these, in the "lead mountain," some lead-glance is found, but not in sufficient quantity to be worked. In digging for these treasures in the deserts the great obstacle is the difficulty of communicating with the outer world, and the want of water and fuel. That was also the reason, combined with the small quantity to be obtained, why the working of the sulphur mines, which lie farther north at Gimse opposite Tor, and southwards in Range, did not pay. Coal has often been searched for, but coal proper is entirely absent, and if anything of the nature of coal is ever found it will be lignite. Petroleum is found close to the sea, near the above-mentioned sulphur diggings at Gimse, on the Gebel Set or Oil Mountain. The ancients employed stones from these mountains in making columns, sarcophagi, sphinxes, &c., which, in the neighbouring ruins of Thebes, still excite wonder, being transported there by methods still unexplained; especially the diorite-breccias from the valley of Hamamât (see above), the so-called *verde antico*, also dark green-stones and red porphyries and granite. That this valley was once a busy scene of life is evidenced by the numerous ruins and ancient Egyptian sculptures hewn in the rocks.

SPRINGS.

As in other regions in forming their settlements men followed the course of the rivers, so here in the desert mountains the springs or wells have become points of attraction, round which the nomadic inhabitants erect their huts until they dry up. The caravans prefer to halt in the neighbourhood of the wells; the town's people must get their water from them; they form the natural rendezvous of all the higher and lower animals that live in the desert. Vegetation also is usually more luxuriant than elsewhere at these moist spots, and accordingly these wells are the natural centres of life in the desert. The rain which from time to time moistens the mountains, is fortunately not all carried by the river to the sea; a considerable portion penetrates the soil, maintains itself there for a long time, and supplies moisture to the roots of the plants, and to the germs that are slumbering everywhere around. Another portion of the water penetrates deeper, and here and there appears again of its own accord as a spring, or is brought to light by digging an adit or a deep well. In order to collect and retain the water of the deep spring the well is then lined and built up. Cisterns, in the sense of rain-water being directed into a pit and kept there for years, do not exist in this desert. Immediately after rain has fallen these wells are naturally richer in water, many soon dry up, but some hold out for several years, even though they do not receive any addition from new rain. At certain places the springs are so rich in water that they form permanent brooks, which, however, lose themselves in the sand after a short course; others precipitate themselves over rocks in the form of waterfalls in wild and romantic ravines. These wells might be increased at will. On the great caravan route from Kene to Koseir, which thirty years ago was also the overland route to India, the English constructed a number of well-built wells, but these unfortunately are not kept in repair.

The quality of the water in the desert wells is, to be sure, generally none of the best; in the neighbourhood of the coasts, where limestone and dolomite prevail, it is brackish or bitter, often scarcely drinkable, in the diorite formation it becomes more drinkable, but always contains some magnesia, so that it is not very suitable for washing and cooking. Pure water springs only from the granite, the gneiss, and the diorite-breccias. But this also soon putrefies when carried in skins, and can only be purified again by allowing it to stand for several weeks in jars. Oases, in the sense of cultivated spots in the middle of the desert, do not exist in our district, but they might perhaps be produced in many places, and thus a part of the desert brought under cultivation. At Koseir, where the soil on the coast is poor and saline, a garden was laid out many years ago, and date-palms, tamarisks, Nile acacias, and in rain years many kinds of vegetables, thrive in it, though not very luxuriantly. The same would be much more easily accomplished on the better soil of the interior of the desert, if a person were only to be at the expense and trouble of sinking a deep and abundant well, and cultivating the soil by its means. Water exists wherever plants are found, and the trees and shrubs scattered everywhere do not perish even after several years of drought.

VEGETATION.

Our desert is by no means a perfect desert, that is, a tract utterly devoid of vegetation, like a great part of the Sahara; on the contrary, after an abundant rain the valleys are converted into verdant pasture-steppes. As early as January, or even earlier, a few weeks after the winter rain, green herbs and bushes sprout in every hollow, in every ravine, in every valley, while the old perennial plants put forth new leaves and flowers. The flora is at its finest from February to April, but after this the sub-tropical sun burns up one plant after the other, and in summer only the deeper-rooted trees and shrubs remain. The western plateau-like portion of our desert, however, in vegetation as well as in appearance, more resembles the Libyan desert, and is very poor in plants.

By far the most common desert plant of this region is the *zilla* (the desert-thorn), a small shrub with blossoms like those of a radish; it is this chiefly which from a distance gives the valleys the appearance of green meadows. While the ass, so highly renowned as a thistle-eater, prudently holds aloof from this thorny bush, the thick-tongued camel takes the highest pleasure in chewing large quantities of the tongue-pricking shrub without losing a drop of blood; it even swallows the strong prickles of the acacia with delight. If a caravan, after a long march, arrives at such a zilla-steppe, all order is at once lost, the camels begin tearing at the bushes and mind nothing else, and the only remedy is to muzzle them with muzzles of cord. The dry zilla, called *dris* or hay, is also eaten by the camel like straw; it gives good brushwood for fire-lighting, the dry bushes catching fire very readily, and by kindling them we can easily form a picture of a steppe-fire.

In many places the broom-like *march* (*Leptadenia pyrotechnica*) grows, a bush with long twigs and generally leafless, and which is also readily eaten by camels. The zygophyllums are very common desert plants; they are excessively salt, and are eaten only by the hungriest Bedouin camels. Though growing in the driest years and in the driest spots, strange to say, these plants are exceedingly succulent; yet dew can have nothing to do with their nourishment, as scarcely any dew falls in the desert. The Cleome, whose leaves exhibit considerable resin-glands on long hairs, is noticeable from its growing in the form of small hemispherical bushes, as round as if cut with a pair of shears, and from its strong aromatic smell, which, being disagreeable to the natives, has procured it the name of "stinking." It is disliked by all the domestic animals. In rainy years there are abundance of pasture-plants, such as the Leobordia, a highly-prized labiate plant, the scented composite plants Pulicaria and Brochia, the rough Forskalea and Anchusa, a scentless Reseda, &c. The elegant astringent *Lotus arabicus* is regarded, whether justly or unjustly, as forming a poisonous food for sheep and goats, which nevertheless eat it. Shady, murmuring tamarisk groves, enlivened with birds and insects, and consisting of hundreds of trees, astonish the traveller at all seasons of the year in the grayest and most lonely wilderness; and where the soil is saturated with moisture by purling streamlets, that last all the year round, or lagunes of sea-water, the eye is gladdened by spreading meadows of green rushes.

Medicinal plants also spring from the soil, especially the bitter colocynth, which everywhere creeps along on the borders and slopes of valleys, with its cucumber-like stems, which bear large numbers of smooth round fruits like apples, at first green and then yellow. The native inhabitants have a great fear of this purgative lying so close at hand; they scarcely touch the apples, since these make the hand bitter, and do not care to use them as a medicine; while the Bedouin fills the rind of the fruit with milk, and drinks the milk next day as a laxative. Senna, a plant having a considerable papilionaceous blossom with large wings, is common, but not here in sufficient quantity for collection, as it is farther south and in Arabia. The aromatic Artemisia (a species of wormwood) also belongs to the quarter, as well as the Calotropis tree, with its corrosive milky juice, and a shrub, the *Dæmia cordata*, to which, where it has connected itself with a saint (the sheikh Shatli, on the western border of the desert near Esneh), pilgrims make journeys of many days' length, from east and west, in order to rub their limbs with it.

Edible fruits also are not quite absent from the flora of the desert, but the date-palm is no longer found wild anywhere here, though in many places it has become wild (in the Wady Gemâl). In place of it the hegelig-tree (Balanites) offers in many places its date-like fruits, a fig-tree (*Ficus pseudocarica*) grows on the slopes of many of the mountains, but not on their bare and waterless tops, as the wonder-loving fancy of the natives of the towns believes. The juicy green caperbush bears fruits that combine sweetness with the taste of mustard, but a person has to avoid fruits that are not ripe and soft, and also the rind of the fruit, in order to remain within the limits of the agreeable. The traveller in the desert finds the agreeable acidity of the sorrel very refreshing, as also the berries of the thorny Lycium, of the trailing Ochradenus, and of the Nitraria, the latter a coast shrub; the longing palate also does not despise the chewing of the buds of the above-mentioned widely-spread *march*, which, like cherry stalks, taste of prussic acid, nor does it disdain the milky fruits of the Glossonema, both plants belonging to the family of the Asclepiadaceæ, which produces many other poisons besides.

The coast flora of the desert, which requires the saline vapour of the sea, is peculiar. A celebrated plant is the shora (*Avicennia officinalis*), which forms large dense groves in the sea, these being laid bare only at very low ebb. Ships are laden with its wood, which is used as fuel, and many camels live altogether upon its laurel-like leaves. At many places the coast is widely covered with bushes of the above-mentioned Nitraria, of the Salicornia, Statice, Suæda, and Cyperus, which, collecting the drift-sand, stand always upon a sand-hill formed by themselves. Some of these afford alkaline ashes.

The desert flora is certainly not rich, but one can soon collect in favourable years a herbarium of 100 to 150 species. Altogether 600 species are reckoned as belonging to the Egyptian deserts. They belong, in part, to families which are quite foreign to us northerners, and we find forms for which we look in vain in the Nile valley. In addition to the universally distributed families of the Gramineæ, Compositæ, Cruciferæ, Labiatæ, Papilionaceæ, &c., the foreign families of the Mimosaceæ, Moringaceæ, Zygophyllaceæ, Balanitaceæ, Capparidaceæ, Avicenniaceæ, Asclepiadaceæ, Salvadoraceæ, and Amarantaceæ make their appearance, to which, in the northern portion of the desert, Mesembryanthemaceæ are also to be added. Ranunculaceæ and Orchidaceæ are entirely wanting, and Umbelliferæ almost entirely. Fungi and mosses are rare. Some plants that are annuals in the Nile valley have to extend their roots in the desert in order to reach the aqueous stratum, and thus become perennial (see p. 145).

THE ANIMALS OF THE DESERT.

In spite of the difficult conditions of existence, a considerable number of animals of various classes have chosen our desert as their home. Where plants are, insects are sure to be found. They are hunted with most success on warm, calm, and sunny days in the spring, which begins as early as January. White and gay-coloured butterflies (Colias, Pieris, and even our common painted-lady), in company with bees, wasps, and flies, flutter about the flowers, the individuals often being in immense numbers, but the species being few; they contribute essentially to increase the idyllic effect of the quiet valleys. The pretty red and white marked *Euprepia pulchra*, a widely-spread southern form, which has even been found in the south of Germany, also often shows itself. Much more abundant are the little butterflies, on plants and about rocks, in the crevices of which they conceal themselves, but especially at night round the lanterns and the open fires. The caterpillar of the sack-spinner (Psyche) sticks to the acacia-trees, in its slender envelope shaped like a horn of plenty; another with a very short stumpy dwelling is found on the tamarisks.

The Hymenoptera are well represented. Large handsome wasps or hornets (Vespa, Eumenes) leave and enter their nests (which are stuck to rocks) and fly long distances to drink at the springs; wild bees hum about the bushes in blossom, especially the zilla and Leptadeniæ, and slender sand-wasps busy themselves in the sand and around the flowers. Ants attack the unpacked stores; their nests everywhere undermine the caravan road, and, like the holes of the jerboas, cause the camels to stumble. There are not many dipterous insects, but those that do exist are all the more troublesome; the common house-fly follows man and beast to the very heart of the deserts; mosquitos swarm in the larval form in all waters, and those that have wings sing round and sting the travellers camped by night round the wells. A flesh-fly flies continually round the camel, probably on account of the galled places, which are seldom absent. The fly most common on plants is the wasp-like but harmless hoverer-fly (Syrphus).

The Neuroptera, whose larvæ live generally in the water, are represented by numerous and beautiful forms. The dragon-flies often swarm in the greatest multitudes, like locusts, and often miles away from water. In many rocky basins with clear water the well-known case-inhabiting larvæ of the caddis-flies (Phryganeæ) are also found.

The desert is a highly favourable field for the Orthopteræ, especially for locusts. These are found everywhere, and the whole year round. In certain years, and in early summer, a large species (*Acridium peregrinum*) resembling the wandering locust, but distinct from it, appears in immense multitudes that destroy everything; in other years it appears, like our cockchafer, in smaller numbers, without, however, being entirely absent. Crickets (especially *Gryllus bimaculatus*) in the summer nights or in late spring chirp in such numbers that one might imagine that every stone was singing. The starved-looking Empusa and the predatory praying-insect (Mantis), called by the Arabs the Prophet's mare, may be shaken off bushes.

Hemiptera (bugs, &c.), large and small, are found on and under bushes and trees. The genus Centrotus is represented by insects very common on acacias, on which they stick firmly and look like thorns.

Many spiders are found on bushes, especially on the abovementioned aromatic Cleome, others hop over the surface of the water; there is also a pretty large bird-spider. One of the most common insects of the desert is the camel's tick (*Ixodes dromedarii*); at every season of the year it runs about upon the ground, especially under bushes, and attaches itself to the anus of the camels as they lie at rest; here it sucks itself full of blood, and then has the appearance of a seed of the castor-oil plant. The poisonous tick (Argas) is also found. In waters the red water-mite may be seen swimming about. Numerous large scorpions live under stones and bushes in the desert, as also in dwellings; and in limestone reefs, especially on the coast, the small book scorpions.

Among the beetles there is a black beetle (*Adesmia cothurnata*) more noticeable than any other; this is the merry-andrew of the desert, often turning itself over, with its somewhat disproportionately long legs, in the air, and it always keeps its back dusty; on account of its quiet and peaceable life with the scorpions the natives call it the "scorpion's servant." Cicindelas (*C. aulica* and *C. circumdata*) hop about in wet sandy places; and in brackish pools sport water-beetles of considerable size. There are a large number of other coleopterous insects, including Buprestidæ, Carabidæ, Longicornes, Weevils, &c.

Of the large class of Crustacea, which is so richly developed in the Red Sea, there live in the waters of the mountains, especially after rain, only small Branchiopoda (Daphnia, Branchipus, Limnadia), Lophyropoda (Cypris), and on the moist earth in groves of rushes Amphipoda (Orchestia) leap about. The Mollusca are represented in this part of the mountains only by a small water-snail, the cosmopolitan *Melania fasciolata;* of land-snails, so common in the desert near Cairo, there is no trace.

Of reptiles there are plenty of serpents, venomous and non-venomous, small and very large, but it is difficult to collect them, as the Bedouins of this desert are afraid of them, and there are here no serpent charmers, who are so useful to the zoologist. Small lizards (Eremias, Acanthodactylus) are uncommonly numerous; ground-agamas (*Agama Sinaites*), Mastigures (Uromastix), and the mountain-monitor (Psammosaurus) also occur; and geckos (Stenodactylus, Ptyodactylus) glide over moist rocky walls and the sides of cisterns.

Among the birds the great-eared vulture (*Vultur auricularis*) reigns supreme; he wings his way upwards "in the eye of the sun," and often swoops down in dozens where a large supply of carrion, such as a fallen camel, is lying. The small vulture (*Cathartes percnopterus*) is much more common; in the desert town it in some respects occupies the place that the stork holds in parts of the European continent. No one thinks of injuring this harmless and useful sanitary agent, who keeps shore and mountain clear of putrefaction. His favourite post in the town is the highest point of the minarets, to which, like the weather-cock on a church steeple, he gives a picturesque termination. He is by no means shy, but does not venture into the streets of the town. Falcons and owls are constant residents in the deserts, and the osprey

(*Pandion haliaëtus*), that lies in wait for the fishes of the sea, also shows himself in the mountains. The bird that forms a figure in every desert picture, however, is the "Noah's raven," which Noah sent out of the ark. It is a large deep-black raven, similar to the common raven, but a different species—the *Corvus umbrinus*. In the Nile valley (see Chap. III.) it shows itself but seldom. It is not to be shot with impunity, for it is the "uncle" of the black Sudanese, and these demand for their slaughtered relative the indispensable blood-money. (See Chap. VII.) Other characteristic desert birds are the rock-hen (*Ammoperdix Hayi*), the sand-grouse (*Pterocles exustus*), the desert larks (*Ammomanes deserti* and *Calandritis macroptera*), and the stone-chats (especially *Saxicola leucocephala* and *Isabellina*). Wagtails are found at every well, swallows (*Cotyle obsoleta* and *Hirundo rustica*) flit through the tamarisk groves, the common hoopoe may be seen in the very heart of the desert. The rock-pigeon (*Columba livia*, var. *Schimperi*) nestles in the rocks above the caravan-road, and arrives in great numbers from the Nile valley when this is inundated. The courser (*Cursorius Isabellinus*) is half a desert half a shore bird; like many other desert-birds and desert-animals generally, it is "desert coloured," that is, grayish-yellow or isabel-coloured. In winter the sea-shore is enlivened by a multitude of water-birds, among them also flamingoes and giant herons. A fine bird's song is not to be heard in the desert, only the twitter of the stone-chats, the peep of the larks, the croak of the raven, the scream of the birds of prey, and at night the eerie hoot of the owls.

The largest and most formidable among the carnivorous mammalia is the hyena (*Hyæna striata*). It is not nearly so bad, however, as its cry and its appearance; a case of its attacking and mangling men, or even children, is scarcely heard of; since, fortunately, cowardice and a depraved taste have, so to speak, been bestowed upon this wild beast, which might rival the tiger. It prefers carrion to anything else, and when this is not to be had it extends its nocturnal peregrinations to the sea, and breaks open shells for itself. The native inhabitants universally regard it as a wicked enchanter metamorphosed, and its flesh, hair, and teeth, are things for which there is a great demand. The lynx (*Felis chaus*), which pursues the gazelle, and hisses at its enemies, is less common.

A small species of fox, the *Canis famelicus*, almost white, with a red stripe down its back, and with large ears, is by far the most common carnivorous animal. It forms a connecting link between the common fox and the still more elegant fennec, which represents it in the Libyan desert. Both belong to the sub-genus Megalotus, while the Nile fox is quite different. The fishermen that catch fish on the coast and salt and dry them ashore are never tired complaining of the audacity of these animals, which steal their fish and provisions, though they do not venture into the town. Like the other Carnivora mentioned, this fox spends a nocturnal life. Foxes kept in confinement are morose during the day; they either disregard altogether the food that is set before them, or their pupils contracting to a perpendicular slit do not enable them to see it properly, so that they have to sniff in order to convince themselves of its presence. By day even ducks, fowls, and cats have the boldness to snap up the food of a fox before his very mouth. By night, however, such captive foxes always make a frightful uproar; a fox that had got loose at night was once caught as he had just seized by the neck a duck that had stolen from him during the day. The eyes shine at night like balls of fire. In this country also the fox passes as the very type of all cunning, and fables similar to those in which our Renard figures are in the mouths of all, the part played by him being usually that of a kadi or judge.

The jackal only occurs on the border of the desert next to the Nile valley. The hare also (*Lepus ægyptiacus* or *abyssinicus?*) passes the active part of its existence chiefly in the night; its droppings are found in great abundance, especially in tamarisk groves. The elegant jerboas and sand-mice (Haltomys and Meriones) dwell in burrows that run obliquely into the ground, and by them and the ants the caravan roads are everywhere undermined; they come out mostly by night and gather the camels' dung. A pretty little animal, but one very difficult to catch, is the daman or Hyrax. The only antelope that occurs is the graceful and beautiful-eyed gazelle (*Antilope dorcas*), which is common; it browses by day on bushes, and seems not to despise the thorny zilla. It is not till we go farther south that more species of antelopes begin to appear. The Steinbok (*Capra beden*) is not uncommon, but the Bedouins of this desert have not the courage and the dexterity to hunt it, while the Sinai Bedouins produce specimens to order. On level ground it is said to be easily captured; but when there is danger it makes immediately for the sides of the mountains, where it dexterously clambers about, and can only with difficulty be reached.

Among domestic mammals the one-humped camel plays the chief rôle in the desert; the ass accompanies every caravan as sack-carrier; the horse is not employed. Sheep and goats are kept and pastured by all the Bedouins. All Bedouin settlements have dogs, which are generally red-haired and make faithful guardians.

THE NATURALIST IN THE DESERT.

We have crossed the desert from west to east, but must restlessly continue to wander, in order to reach our distant goal as soon as we can. But we now perceive how rich in natural treasures it is, and these must be sought for and collected on special scientific tours. It were best, of course, if in such unexplored regions as our desert still continues to be the division of labour could be introduced, the geographer observing exclusively his routes, the geologist his stones, &c. But when one is alone he has to turn his attention to everything, and that also has its charm; and it is more easily accomplished in the desert than elsewhere, since there is not a confusing and overwhelming number of objects to be observed. Thus regions apparently so wearisome and monotonous become a field of perpetual activity, and, so far as results are concerned, of rich enjoyment. Here the route must be laid down with chronometer and compass; there is a plant which has never been seen or collected before; there we see a quadruped or a bird that call the gun into operation, a bush that must be shaken for insects, a swarm of insects, a lizard that must be caught with the hoop-net, a peculiar mountain formation, or a layer rich in fossils, where hammer and chisel have to work; or a sketch is to be drawn of a landscape, a Bedouin, or a tent. Lastly, as there is not time on the march to make observations of any completeness, it may be recommended as an excellent plan to select certain places as central points, from which one can at leisure investigate the surrounding country, now for one scientific object, now for another. The best season for this region is the spring, from the middle of February, or even from January, to the middle of April. Above all, years are to be selected in which life has been awaked by rain. In addition to all this labour, baggage must be prepared, which is as necessary to the shortest tour as to a great expedition. For, however simply one lives, he will require large supplies of provisions for himself and servants, water-skins, a cooking apparatus, wrappings and a carpet for the night, and a camel to carry the whole. As driver and guide an Ababdeh Bedouin is hired, who may also act as attendant and assist in collecting; it is still better if one has a special servant who understands hunting and collecting, and can set the traps. The investigator had better walk the greatest portion of the way on foot, since it is not easy to make observations on camelback, still less to write. At intervals he will get tired out, and then he can rest on the back of the camel.

As one of the most widely useful implements for a journey in the desert, the butterfly hoop-net cannot be too highly praised. Besides its original purpose, namely, for catching winged insects, it may also be used to receive them when shaken from a bush, as a net for water-animals, serpents, and lizards; also as a sunshade, and thrown over the head as a protection for the eyes against the strong glare, against sandstorms, and against bitter winds, at night as a mosquito net, in drinking wormy and muddy water as a strainer, also as a sack for provisions that require sifting (lentils, for instance), and as a flagstaff for the scattered company. Lastly, it lends the traveller the nimbus of a pious pilgrim, since these are in the custom of hanging out white pennons behind their seat on the camel.

The day's labours being over, towards evening a spot is selected for the camp, after which supper is cooked and eaten with huge appetite. After supper the company seat themselves in a circle under the wonderful star-bespangled heavens, or in the moonlight, warming themselves at the fire when it is cold, and now, puffing away at his pipe, one man retails all the wonderful stories he has, another strikes up a song, the Bedouin blows his shepherd's flute, or executes a wardance for our amusement.

III.—INHABITANTS OF THE DESERT.

HISTORY OF THE DESERT.

These mountains were inhabited and visited by men from the very earliest times. This is attested by monuments, inscriptions, and antiquities of various kinds, as well as by the accounts of the ancient geographical and other writers (Strabo, Ptolemy, Diodorus, Agatharchides, Pliny). The inscriptions at Hamamât (see above) go back to more than 2000 years before our era (sixty-fifth dynasty); Ramses III. of the twentieth dynasty (thirteenth century B.C.) opened here a new road by which the treasures of India and Arabia (the land of Pan) were brought by way of Koptos to Egypt. Under Ramses IV. 8368 labourers and officials (among them also Hebrews) were daily employed in the "Bechen," that is, the modern mountains of Hamamât, in quarrying the fine stone of the locality for the works of art at Thebes, perhaps also in mines, and they were supplied with provisions from the Nile valley, the provisions being drawn in carriages by oxen (so that there were no camels!). We find here, too, inscriptions of later date containing the names of the Persian kings. These mountain roads became of still greater importance in the time of the Ptolemies—to some extent also of the Romans—when the great emporia of the Red Sea, Philoteras, Myos Hormos, and Leucos Portos, were in their glory. The stone camping-places standing at intervals, constructed of rough blocks without mortar, as well as the watch-towers on the mountain peaks, probably belong to this period, although inscriptions seem to be wanting. The ancient Greeks called these erections *hydreumata*, the Arabs call them *wekalat en-nusara*, that is, "caravans of the Christians." Many such are found also in other localities in the mountains, especially at watering-places; a number of these ruins are probably to be regarded as camping-places of miners. In any case, this desert was very much frequented in these ancient times. In the later times of the Ptolemies, when Berenice became the principal port, the chief route ran more towards the south, also, however, terminating at Koptos. In the early times of Islam, too, the route for both trade and pilgrims ran more southwards, to the once important place Aidâb, near Suakin; in the eighth century of the Hejra (fourteenth after Christ) this road was entirely given up on account of the plundering of the caravans by the Bedouins, and this caused the downfall of Kûs, where the road terminated, and which rose to importance in place of Koptos or Koft. The Kene-Koseir route next rose into notice, especially since the conquest of Egypt by the Turks in the sixteenth century. The French held this road in their possession for several years. In the time of Mohammed Ali it was much frequented by pilgrims, and by caravans with corn for export; at this time it was also the overland route for the English to India. After the opening of the railway to Suez, and that of the Suez Canal, the importance of the road has continued to decrease, and now it is scarcely used except by pilgrims from Upper Egypt to Meccah, and a few corn caravans. We must also add that the caravan route above described is not the only one; on the contrary, the mountains are intersected by a number of such, all more or less frequented, and generally following the valleys and easier passes, not to mention a number of smaller footpaths and bridle-paths.

THE ABABDEH.

The inhabitants properly belonging to our desert are Nomads or Bedouins; they call themselves *Abábdeh* (sing. *Abádi*). This name occurs very early; the inhabitants of the coast range on the western shore of the Red Sea (corresponding to the locality at present inhabited by the Ababdeh), being named *Gebadei* even by Pliny (A.D. 70). The nomadic peoples inhabiting these coast mountains south to Ethiopia are also called Blemyes or Troglodytes by the ancient geographers, those dwelling on the sea, in particular, being named Ichthyophagi. The old Arabian geographers and historians, such as Makrizi, call them *Bedya*, a name which, as *Bugaites*, even occurs in an ancient Roman inscription, and at the present day is especially applied to the Bisharin, a race closely allied to the Ababdeh, and dwelling south from the tropic. These peoples accordingly have inhabited the same country from the earliest times. The Ababdeh themselves maintain that they are descended from the *Gin*, that is, a kind of mountain-spirits, the statement probably being the same as if they called themselves autochthones.

In appearance, manners and customs, and dress, they are entirely distinct from the *Semitic Arabs* proper who inhabit the northern portion of the desert, from Syria and the peninsula of Sinai to the southern borders of Middle Egypt. These are here called *Máasa* (also *Atuni* or *Hauadát*), and exhibit the genuine Semitic-Arabic type—a clear, pale colour of skin, thin, somewhat longish face with non-projecting cheek-bones, broad and lofty forehead, thin and sharply cut nose, strongly curved eyebrows, small mouth and small lips. They shave their heads, wear a turban or a parti-coloured head-cloth, never go naked, and possess firearms and short swords.

The Ababdeh, however, who in former times lived in constant feud with these Mâasa, have a skin varying in colour from deep-brown to black, along with an almost Europæo-German expression of countenance, and are, generally speaking, a race possessed of extraordinary beauty and noble forms.

THE ABABDEH. 251

All travellers give great prominence to this impression, which is certainly heightened by the long waving hair of the head, whereas elsewhere in these regions only heads rendered artificially bald are to be seen. The Ababdeh are dolichocephalic and orthognathous; the face is a fine oval, not so long as among the Arabs, the eyes large and fiery, the mouth and lips neither large nor small, the nose straight and rather short, broad and blunt, than long. The neck is long and thin, the ear small and roundish, the hair naturally straight or curled, but not woolly; it is artificially twisted into cork-screw ringlets, and worn long and uncovered. In these peculiarities they agree with the Bisharin, Nubians, and Abyssinians, who dwell farther to the south, and to whom also the general name of Ethiopians is given; they are not to be confounded with the negroes, from whom they are as different as from the Arabs and Egyptians. The Bisharin very closely resemble them, but are somewhat more prognathous, as well as more muscular, and have also a fiercer expression than the slim and gentle Ababdeh; they wear their hair also, but shave the moustache, while the Ababdeh let it stand. The Bisharin and Ababdeh are very closely related, and along with some other races dwelling farther to the south are classed together as "Bedya."

An Ababdeh Man.

The long black hair, which is twisted into large curls like those which the painters give to Christ, or. plaited into braids, flows down to the shoulders and back, while on the front part of the head a short and very curly tuft projects. The hair is the pride of the Ababdeh youth and man, and the object of the most careful, even effeminate attention, as is easily seen by the curling-pin stuck in the hair behind or at the side. This is also evidenced by white lumps and smears of grease, which, not being properly rubbed in, appears between the raven-black plaits, and is often carried in such quantities that the hair seems as if powdered. A small soapstone cup,

Ababdeh Boys.

in which the by no means odorous pomade is worked up, is indispensable to the travelling-bag of an Abadi. This luxuriant crop of hair he always wears without any covering, as well in the glare of the subtropical summer sun as in the chill storms of winter. The Bisharin, the Abyssinians, and a portion of the Nubians have the same practice. The heads of very small boys are first prepared by the razor, small tufts being left for the later national adornment. Sometimes the excessive increase of vermin renders it necessary to give up the ornament of manhood for a time, and the graybeard must cover his baldness with a quilted cap of linen.

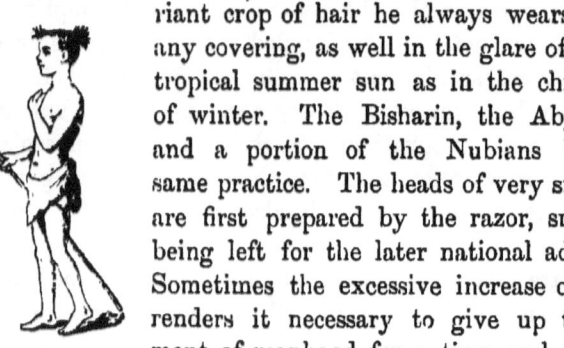

Small Ababdeh Boy.

DRESS OF THE ABABDEH.

For clothes the Abadi wears besides the loin-cloth a long white coat or shirt (never blue as among the Fellahin), and in winter perhaps also a light coloured and generally striped woollen mantle. When he becomes too hot or uncomfortable he even wanders through his lonely rocky valleys without a coat, quite naked. His naked body is protected from the heat of the sun by the brownness of his skin, which is generally smeared with fat for the purpose, but still more by custom, since he generally passes his childhood in perfect nudity. In other respects he has already, both in dress and customs, adopted much from the Fellahin; the Ababdeh of former times, like the Bisharin of the present day, wandered about half naked, clothed only with a leathern apron and wrapper, and without a shirt. The male Abadi is also fond of wearing a ring in his ear. He walks either barefooted, his feet being insensible to the stones, or in sandals; in his hand he often carries a lance; round his upper left arm a short knife stuck in a sheath is always fastened; and sometimes also he girds on a long straight sword. He seldom carries a shield now-a-days and never a gun. These weapons are more for show than for actual combat; he likes to appear as warlike as his forefathers. At the present day, however, perfect peace and security have long prevailed in his country. Occasionally he may also kill some game, but the noble art of the huntsman is by no means his forte.

Ababdeh Woman.

The women clothe themselves with a white cloth drawn under one or both armpits, so that one or both shoulders and the arms remain free, and over this a large outer wrapper, also generally white, which can conceal the whole form; in winter, instead of this a mantle of brown woollen stuff is also worn, as among the female peasantry of the Nile valley. They plait the hair from the crown down into many rows of plaits, the foremost of which, in front of the ear, has more freedom of movement than the others. Like all other women they believe that they are not attractive without ornaments; they wear ear-rings, necklaces, buckles on arms and feet, and above all the inevitable nose-ring, like their camels, an ornament they consider charming. Instead of gold, silver, and pearls, however, their poverty compels them to limit their ornaments to brass, coloured glass, and shells. The smaller girls often wear the *raad* or girdle round the loins, as is customary among the negresses, and nothing else, except that round their head and neck they hang white shells and glass beads, which show wonderfully against their nut-brown skin. An almost idyllic scene meets the eyes of the traveller when, in wandering over these mountains, he suddenly, in some lonely valley, comes upon a few boys and girls of the Ababdeh in their almost paradisiac nakedness tending their sheep and goats. Though shy at first they soon gain confidence, and give the best information regarding the road and every little plant. Among the Ababdeh women, classically fine, elegant, and slender figures are often seen, seldom bulky, but in old age usually as lean as a rake, and on overcoming their first shyness they allow themselves to be looked at and spoken to, and they are less fond of playing bo-peep than the women of the cultivated regions and the towns.

OF THE ABABDEH IN GENERAL.

The country that the Ababdeh possess is the mountain desert between the Nile valley and the Red Sea, as far as it corresponds to Upper Egypt, accordingly from the latitude of the town of Siout to the Cataracts of the Nile or the tropic. They are also, however, scattered over the Nubian desert to near the Soudan, and in the Nile valley itself a number of them have settled in villages of their own and practise agriculture. The whole number of this people may amount to 30,000. They are under a chief of their own race, who again nominates the sheiks for the principal localities. The dignity of chief is hereditary in one family according to patriarchal law, that is, it passes to the eldest of the family; the sheiks nominated are quite dependent on him and may be deposed. The grand sheik is a vassal of the Viceroy of Egypt, but has no tribute to pay; on the contrary, he receives something, viz. a certain share of the road dues, which the Egyptian government levies on the caravans.

Internal quarrels among the Ababdeh are arranged by the family elders, by those under-sheiks, or by the grand sheik. The Egyptian government takes no part in them, nor does it raise any taxes or levy soldiers among the Ababdeh. On the other hand, the prince must pledge his life and property for the security of the desert roads; he must when required provide camels and guides for payment, but sometimes also without it, and he is bound to live in the Nile valley; he is thus to be considered as a kind of hostage. This hostage system was first introduced here and among other subjected Bedouin peoples by the great Mohammed Ali, and it has kept its ground. The consequence of this permanent state of war is profound peace and absolute security in these inhospitable tracts. Before his time these and all other Bedouins were much dreaded robbers; during antiquity and the whole of the middle ages they made inroads from time to time into the cultivated territories, and the merchants and pilgrims (as late even as the time of Burkhard) only ventured to pass through the desert when armed and collected in large caravans. All this is now quite different, and now even articles that have been lost may be recovered on giving intimation to an Ababdeh sheik.

An example of how desert justice is administered is told as having occurred within the last few years. A camel which had strayed from some caravan and was laden with fruit was found by a Bedouin in the Nubian desert, the important trade routes in which are also intrusted to the Ababdeh. As in duty bound he immediately brought it to the nearest station, uninjured, with all its load on its back, but not without peeping in to see what was in the sack it carried. This was noticed, and the Bedouin was condemned to death for his curiosity, "for," said the sheik, "if there had been gold in the sack you would have stolen it and not brought back the camel."

The Ababdeh prince must also, however, have something to live on, the more so that he is no longer externally a Bedouin, but has become entirely Egyptian. A regular system of taxation cannot be carried out among nomads, and accordingly the Abadi must contribute a considerable mite for his chiefs from everything that he brings to market and from payments that he receives for his services as guide, for conveying goods by his camels, &c. Even that seems not to be sufficient, since from time to time a sheik of the second or third rank, on commission from the patriarch-prince, undertakes a little trip to the chief settlements of the Ababdeh and into the desert, and the good shepherd carries away with him whatever seems to him good among the possessions of his flock, such as camels, sheep, or goats, and also lays claim to be honourably and hospitably received by those of the same rank as himself. The approach of such an expensive visit or *razzia* is, to be sure, soon well known throughout the mountains, and the Bedouin withdraws with all his goods into the interior, so that the sheik only finds abandoned stations. At such times no Abadi is seen far or near, in the markets no sheep, no wood, no fodder is to be obtained; occasionally, however, some ignorant Bedouin or other, or one who has been urged by necessity, is laid hold of, and he must pay for the others.

DWELLINGS AND HOUSEHOLD MATTERS.

The Ababdeh have no tents, but only huts, and these of the most wretched sort. These consist of a few poles, round and over which old straw mats are stretched to form the walls and roof, which is generally sloping. The whole is of a longish quadrangular form, one of the long sides, namely that turned away from the road, being open or partially closed by a hanging piece of cloth, and forming the door. The internal space is generally only two or three paces long and about four feet high, so that a person can only sit or lie inside; but indeed, the inhabitants of these regions generally cannot imagine that there is any pleasure or domestic comfort in standing.

Into this the family creep, for in every hut there is room for a pair to live comfortably, together with a swarm of children. An Ababdeh settlement generally numbers only four to eight

Ababdeh Tent.

such huts, with as many families. It is only in a few settlements, such as the desert village of Laketa (see above), which contains about fifty dwellings, in the villages of the Nile valley, in the Ababdeh suburb of Koseir, the inhabitants of which have partially given up their nomadic life, that we see hole-like houses of clay or rough stones, in the style of those of the Nile peasantry. Many dwell also at times in natural caves, and are therefore "Troglodytes," as the ancients called them. Dwelling in these caves is here somewhat dangerous on account of the serpents. In the caves are found remains, such as cinders, ashes, blackened stones, &c., which generally show them to have been tenanted, at least temporarily, by men. The caravans often stop at these for their siesta, and perform their cooking in the inside, whence the sun and wind are excluded. It is possible that if excavations of sufficient depth were made traces of the ancient Troglodytes might be found.

Other household appliances are quite in keeping with the wretched abodes. They consist of a few cooking utensils of clay or soap-stone, skins for water and milk, leathern buckets, drinking-cups of wood, a wooden or leathern bowl for eating out of, a few grinding stones, a straw mat or a coarse woollen carpet, and, for a fire-place, a few stones picked up at random. Everything has the provisional, nomadic character. For cutting they make use only of an iron knife; they do not

17

use flint (of which their limestone mountains are so full) for this purpose, employing it only to strike fire.

A LIFE OF HUNGER.

The food of the Ababdeh is chiefly milk and durra. The latter they enjoy either raw or roasted, or in the form of unleavened cakes baked on a glowing fire of camels' dung. The few fruits that the desert affords are also made the most of. They seldom allow themselves to indulge in flesh meat, since they sell their cattle, and are not great hands at hunting Any wild animals that they can get hold of, however, they consider dainties, including hyenas, hares, jerboas, foxes, and gazelles. Those dwelling on the coast live chiefly on fish and molluscs. The better sorts of these they sell fresh or dried, and content themselves with those that are despised by other people, and are always easily caught, even in the time of storms; coffer-fish, sea-eels, rays, globe-fish, wrasses, crabs, and polyps. The ground round an inhabited or a deserted Ababdeh dwelling is always covered with the remains of these, especially with the heads of the globe-fish (Tetrodon), which are considered very poisonous, and are therefore always thrown away. These denizens of the sea are generally simply roasted on the open fire. Yet the Ababdeh are not in such a wretched state as were the ancient Ichthyophagi, according to Strabo. "These," he says, "roast the fish at the sun, and tread the roasted flesh into cakes; the back-bones, however, they gather together, and when they cannot fish, as for instance during storms, they eat these bones stamped into cakes; the fresh bones they suck. And when they suffer from thirst, they travel with their houses journeys of some days' duration to the wells, and flinging themselves on the ground gulp down the water like cattle till their bellies are swollen like drums."

The modern Ichthyophagi or coast Ababdeh catch their fish generally with a spear, on reefs laid bare at ebb tide; some also catch them with nets, especially the ring-net; they do not know how to use the hook and line. They do not possess any kind of vessels, not even fishing-boats, and on the whole are not fond of venturing on the sea. Their territory is altogether on *terra firma*, including the coast reef. Their neighbours, the Bisharîyeh, on whose coast are many islands, make use of a raft in order to reach them.

Such being their scanty fare it is not to be wondered at that the Abadi is always hungry. When a caravan is doing its cooking some son of the desert always makes his appearance, having smelled it from a distance. He does not beg, but regards the persons eating with such a dog-like and piteous air that they cannot but invite him to partake, especially the Moslim, who when he eats can never allow a stranger to stand without giving him an invitation. And when the camp is pitched beside an Ababdeh settlement the least signal brings the hungry and naked Bedouin children bounding up, who, with amusing eagerness, stuff their mouths with the left pieces of bread and meat offered them, and for which they never beg. As soon as the camp breaks up hungry creatures of the desert of all classes forthwith fall upon what it has left; the children of men vie with the dogs in gathering the bones and crumbs, with the sheep in scraping together the straw, with the pigeons in picking up the grains of corn, with the ravens in making use of the balls of dung. The Ababdeh are also able to use, as their daily beverage, the worst water, a pure solution of Epsom salts, when good water is too distant.

EMPLOYMENTS.

The chief employment of the Ababdeh is flock-keeping and camel-driving. They keep camels, goats, and sheep, but never horses or cattle. Some also possess an ass, and they all have a dog. Pasture is only available for a time, when winter rains have fallen, and called the vegetable germs into life; in the dry season, and in dry years, the herdsman must often make long journeys in the mountains in order to find pasture; nay he must then diminish his herd, and is even obliged to hire himself out for a time in the Nile valley as an agricultural or other labourer. But when his desert valleys are once more verdant he is sure to return again to his beloved fatherland. The value of the plants of the desert as nutriment is certainly small, and, accordingly, the cattle of the Ababdeh, like the people themselves, are lean and hungry, notwithstanding that they browse continually the whole day and the night too. In making a journey with an Ababdeh camel, one would require to take into consideration the delay caused by its almost constant eating. The water caravans from Koseir to a well 10 leagues distant require about thirty hours, those of the Ababdeh from two to three days. The Ababdeh camels pass no bush without stripping it, and they are not disturbed in doing so, since they get nothing else to eat; while the camels of the Fellahin in journeying through the desert, besides being allowed a little pasture, are always fed at camping time with straw and the nourishing beans. The Abadi at most scatters before his camels a sackful of dry zilla stems which he has collected in the course of the day on the route. The camels of the Ababdeh are, therefore, always lean, and not adapted for carrying heavy loads, but for the same reason they are excellent and celebrated runners. A good running camel, over which it is the custom to hang a splendid sheepskin as housings, and a double saddle-bag with long tassels, performs a journey of 40 leagues in twenty to thirty hours, including the necessary stoppages. All the Ababdeh are excellent dromedary riders.

Some of the Ababdeh that live on the coast are called Shora Ababdeh; they have settled at one of the well-known shora groves (see p. 240), that grow in and close to the sea, and their camels and other live-stock feed the whole year round almost entirely on the leaves of this tree, while they themselves cut it down and sell its timber. Like the other coast Ababdeh they also catch great multitudes of fish of medium size, especially parrot-fish, cut them up, salt them, and sell them. Fish so prepared form a not unimportant article of trade. Ababdeh who live a more settled life also keep pigeons and fowls.

The Ababdeh derive their livelihood from converting the

products of their country into money, as well as from stock rearing; in particular, they supply excellent fuel in the shape of timber, brushwood, camel's dung, and excellent charcoal made by themselves from acacia wood; they are therefore also charcoal burners. They also collect fodder-plants and medicinal herbs, such as senna leaves, colocynth, a kind of wormwood, and gum Arabic on the acacias so common in the desert. Others support themselves by carrying water on camels or asses. In Koseir for every camel-load of water, which consists of six goatskins, and which, as already mentioned, occupies them three days, they receive, according to the market price, which varies with circumstances, from 1s. 6d. to 6s.

The people dwelling on the Nile are now more frequently employed than the Ababdeh as camel-drivers in large caravans, but according to the accounts of travellers the Ababdeh seem formerly to have mainly conducted the traffic. Some live close to the caravan route, and besides keeping stock, earn something from the services of various kinds which they render to caravans passing by or camping near, fetching water, branches, and wood, watering the camels, loading and unloading, &c. For these services they receive from the camel-drivers a few handfuls of corn or durra. They are also placed here as road-watchers, and are said to receive payment for this duty from their chief, but they do not appear to get much. If there is a cessation of the traffic (which consists on their roads chiefly in the export of corn from Egypt), even the road-guards break up their huts and remove somewhere else. A few Ababdeh are attached as dromedary riders to the stations of the carpenters who have to keep the *desert-telegraphs* in repair. For these carpenters the government has already erected stone-dwellings of a somewhat more solid character. Lastly, many live as camel-drivers in the service of others as masters, or they accompany through the desert herds of cattle bought up by merchants, or are fishermen and shell-gatherers by profession. A considerable number, as already mentioned, have settled in the Nile valley and practise agriculture. There also they prefer to stick to each other, building villages for themselves, and not mixing readily with the Fellahin.

Their trade with the settled country is carried on by money, but among themselves more by barter; the women in the interior accordingly scarcely know the value of money, and when one wishes anything from them, such as wood or milk, they do not give it though offered a great deal of money, but readily give it for a piece of bread, some corn, or a piece of cloth.

INTELLECTUAL QUALITIES AND CAPACITIES.

As the Ababdeh, looking at their bodily characteristics, are a well-built race but bear the stamp of hunger, so also from the mental point of view they are, like most races living in a state of nature, very intelligent within the circle of their wants and conceptions, but at the same time "poor spirited" (*fakir*), as the Egyptian expresses himself, that is, in the good sense of the word, not stupid, but well disposed and harmless. According to the accounts of older travellers (Burkhard, Bruce) they were formerly the opposite, being represented as "dishonourable, faithless, vicious." Either they were confounded with the Bisharin, to whom these three words apply only too well, or it is only since that time that their character has been so much improved. More recent travellers cannot sufficiently praise them as peaceable, honourable people, rather too shy and timid. Considering their poverty they are not to be blamed if they eagerly lay hold of a gift offered them, but they *do not beg*. Their country is as yet too little traversed and corrupted by Europeans, who accustom the natives to beggary, as the Fellahin are accustomed to backshish. That they do not, like other Bedouins, practise hospitality towards strangers is not to be wondered at, since they have scarcely the barest necessaries of life for themselves. If misfortune has thrown in their way a person who has lost himself or been shipwrecked, and who in want of food and assistance has been forced to have recourse to them, they do not certainly rob or murder him, but they give him nothing to eat unless he has money in his pocket or can give certain promise of payment. When, on the other hand, a man of rank belonging to their tribe comes to them, pride and honour demand that a member of their herd shall be offered up to show their regard for him; nay, if the guest comes exactly at the time when a sheep has been killed for the family, yet a second must fall for him—the guest.

The Abadi has a most accurate knowledge of his country and its products; he knows every little plant and every animal by name, and all the paths for a wide circuit round; and their skill in following a trail is celebrated and is really extraordinary. In the arid desert, where there is no drift sand, the trail remains impressed for a long time on the ground. An animal that has run off, a man that has fled or lost his way, is sure to be brought back by the Ababdeh in a short time; wild beasts are pursued up to their holes; even in inhabited cities they can point out the trail. A few Ababdeh specially skilled in this art are even kept in the pay of the government in order, in case of a crime, to track out the perpetrators, and the results are often wonderful. The people even relate that the parties really guilty have been found by a comparison of the footsteps of a large number of accused persons.

Arts and manufactures there are naturally none among these Bedouins, except that rude utensils are made, and vessels carved out of soap-stone, serpentine, and wood.

Sickness is left to the healing power of nature, or treated with herbs growing in the desert. Of small-pox these Bedouins have such a horror that they pitilessly expose persons affected with this disease, and only throw to them every day the necessary food and drink until they die or recover.

LANGUAGE.

The language of the Ababdeh, strange to say, is the Arabic. When they speak with strangers they always—even the children—express themselves very well in Arabic. Among themselves, however, they speak a jargon almost unintelligible to strangers. Many words and expressions in it are decidedly Arabic, although twisted about so as to be unrecognizable; others, however, as well as many names of places, seem to belong to a language of their own, which may be a branch of the Bedya tongue spoken by the Bisharin, so closely allied to them. Strangely enough they make their language a matter of secrecy; the Abadi cannot be brought to speak of it. The singing or interrogatory tone, which the Ababdeh always employ when speaking, is peculiar. It is also reported that the Ababdeh sheiks have a kind of secret language, which, however, is a modern invention; it is said to be formed by the insertion of the consonants k and r into words already in use; for example, they turn the Arabic *yôm*, day, into *arkelyerkom*, *gebel*, mountain, into *gerkeberkel*, just as when boys we made a kind of artificial language for ourselves by inserting *rf* between syllables, as *gorafold* for gold, &c.

RELIGION.

The religion of the Ababdeh is the Mohammedan, but little more than nominally so, its rules being very loosely observed. These dwellers in the desert, indeed, never perform the first duty of the Moslim, the well-known prayer in a bending attitude. Even those living among other Mohammedans seldom go to the mosque. A pilgrimage by an Abadi is almost unheard of. As already mentioned he eats without religious scruples very unclean meats, such as foxes, mice, and hyenas, but only if they have been duly slaughtered beforehand. For him to fast at Ramadan, as will be understood from what we have said above, is a thing impossible. If an Abadi is asked whether he is a Mohammedan, he often answers, "No; I am an Abadi," of course meaning this more in a national sense, and in contradistinction to Arabs and Fellahin. Some make themselves known in confidential conversation as freethinkers, and hold that at death everything is over; but they openly reckon themselves among the believers of the Prophet. Their chiefs, who always live among the Moslimin, are generally even bigoted adherents of the Prophet. They have also adopted many usages from the Moslimin, and accordingly there are saints, whose tombs are distinguished with pennants, and they practise circumcision, divorce, early marriage, and polygamy like other Moslimin. Some even rig themselves out with a rosary, which, however, serves rather for a tooth-pick than for counting off their prayers. For it must be mentioned that to the rosary is attached a piece of wood from a branch of a tree growing in the mountains (*Salvadora persica*), which is highly thought of as furnishing excellent tooth-cleaners. An implement of this kind (*misvak*) is well known to have been among the objects left by the Prophet, and this explains its position on the rosary. While the orthodox Moslim is always superstitious this is not the case with the Abadi, at least he does not believe in spirits, and makes game of the camel-drivers of the Nile valley, who do not venture to encamp by night in a desert valley which is reputed "uncanny." The Abadi fearlessly wanders quite alone both by day and by night in tracks where there are no men, but a Moslim would not venture to do so. For this reason the Moslimin accuse the Ababdeh of practising the black art; they are said to be able when at a distance to bring moving objects to a stand-still, their glance is said to be very dangerous, &c., but this the Ababdeh themselves will by no means allow.

FAMILY LIFE.

The family life is not essentially different from that of the Moslimin, since, as already mentioned, they have the same laws and usages, including early marriage, divorce, and polygamy. The last, on account of its expensiveness, is seldom practised except by the sheiks. The violation of the marriage vows, so rare among the Bedouins, sometimes occurs; the Troglodytes who love in secret meet each other in the stillness of night, in lonely mountain gorges and caves miles away from any human dwelling. This, however, is a risk to run all the greater that the injured party is sure, by means of his skill in tracking, to discover the betrayer. On the caravan route and on the outskirts of the larger villages there are even a few Ababdeh prostitutes.

When a woman has been married she must never see her own mother afterwards. The young husband always removes far away from the parental family of his bride, chiefly in order *to avoid his mother-in-law*. This fear of a mother-in-law is spread among many peoples; it may be traced throughout the whole of Africa, America, and Australia, and perhaps naturally arises from the relationship itself, being expressed also in our proverb, "Mother-in-law—tiger-mother," or "Devil's lining."[1] Among the Ababdeh, too, the brothers and nearest relatives of the wife must not eat with her after the marriage.

WEDDING FESTIVITIES.

When a young Abadi is about to marry, which he is always allowed to do whenever the first down appears on his cheeks, for a week before the marriage, at least in the larger settlements, preliminary festivities are carried on every night, without the Koran, but with drums, singing, and hand-clapping. Here the Ababdeh execute their weapon dance in full equipment, that is, naked and armed with shield, lance, and sword. A dancer or two warriors step into the circle, swing their spears, and make a number of leaps and bounds; the dance is much more violent than the similar dance of the Egyptians, with its studied grace. The dancer often rushes at a spectator, and giving a loud shout makes a thrust at his breast with his lance or sword, to which the latter gives for answer, "Abadi." The former then retires. According to the statements of travellers, others sing a national song, in which they praise the bold and celebrate the Ababdeh race, while joy, fear, suffering, or anger is depicted in the features of the spectator. Others, using a double-toned reed flute, play for hours on end tunes impossible to imitate; or the dance of veiled women, already

---

[1] *Schwiegermutter—Tigermutter oder Teufelsunterfutter.*

described (Chap. III. p. 193), is executed, the whole being done in the darkness of night, only very partially dispelled by an open fire, at which the drums are occasionally dried when they become wet with the dew. Round the fire sit the sedater men and smoke their serpentine pipes, which have the form of a short tube bent at a right angle and without a wooden stem, or are of the usual form of a pipe, with a heavy massive bowl of serpentine.

FUNERALS.

When the last hour of an Abadi has struck loud lamentations resound through the mountains; the body is buried with usages similar to those practised by the Moslimin, and over the grave stones are heaped up, some of the higher of them pointing towards Meccah. The ancient Troglodytes are said to have thrown stones at their corpses, laughing and rejoicing all the while, till they were covered from view, and then to have set a goat's horn on the top.

Ababdeh Tobacco Pipes.

CHAPTER V.

ON THE RED SEA.

THE RED SEA.

The waters of the sea are murmuring against the sandy shore of the wide bay that penetrates westwards; towards the south-west the foremost billows of the open sea strike with greater power, advancing in long rolling swells. At a greater distance towards the south the shore surf ceases, and as far as the eye can reach, a streak of foam separates the deep dark sea from a lighter, shallow coast lagoon, which is almost dry at ebb-tide. On the north of the bay, which is open towards the east, another similar lagoon is seen, soon disappearing from sight behind the northern hills. A dull, hollow, thunderous booming and roaring, in which the listening ear imagines that it can from time to time distinguish a singing and whispering, called by the natives "the weeping of the sea," mixed with the howling of the north wind, brings to us from that quarter intelligence of the wild war of the waves against the firm land. The bottom of the lagoons just mentioned is a coral bank and the bay an opening in the same, a natural harbour. We are standing on the west shore of the Red Sea at 26° N. lat., in Koseir, the sea-port town of Upper Egypt.

Until a recent period the Red Sea was known to the public at large almost entirely through the tragical death of the Jew-persecuting Pharaoh, and it is only within the past few years—since the opening of the Suez Canal—that it has had the honour of being again in the mouths of all. "But why is this sea called 'red?'" is the question commonly suggested when the sea is mentioned. The inhabitant of the desert finds an answer when the sun rises in his dull-gray morning robes; the reappearance of the rising day-star awakens on the top of the waves and ripples a millionfold, glancing and glittering, and the rambler on the shore now sees his shadow doubled, it being produced by the sun himself and again by his equally brilliant image in the sea. The higher the sun rises the deeper becomes the blue of the waters, changing from royal blue to slate blue, and in places where there are underlying rocks all at once to grayish-green. As the sun sinks, late in the afternoon and onwards, the blue becomes paler, rising to sky blue, and with sunset loses itself in a white or sometimes rosy-tinted surface. At night it is black like other terrestrial objects, and only the stars seem to bathe in it. The full moon throws a long narrow silvery trail of light across the waters to the horizon. At night, when the water is disturbed by a stick or an oar, the drops, which contain decomposing animal substances, glitter like sparks of fire; or some swimming creature gleams spectrally in the nocturnal water; while a similar general luminosity of the watery mass, the "sea-light," is here a rare occurrence.

The cause of the name is by some assigned to a microscopic alga (*Trichodesmium erythræum*, Ehrenberg), which sometimes communicates a blood-red colour to certain stretches of the sea; or to red mountains on the coast; but these are only local and limited occurrences. The coast mountains are generally white. The corals of the reef are mostly brown, yellowish, or bluish, the red ones being less numerous; lastly, among the fishes, crustacea, &c., there are only a few that are red. There is, therefore, hardly anything that is red connected with the Red Sea, and the name was probably chosen capriciously by the ancients, or by way of *lucus à non lucendo*.

THE DESERT SHORE.

The shore and country adjoining it, often for miles into the interior, is a howling wilderness, with an arid or saline and friable soil, here and there covered with white salt flowers, as if with snow or hoar-frost; the subsoil water is brackish and bitter, almost undrinkable. There is scarcely any vegetation except a few salt plants. It is not till we approach the mountains that the soil of the valleys becomes capable of sending up herbage after rain. A more desolate strip of coast is hardly anywhere to be found unless on the shore of the Sahara or the Arctic Ocean. "Oh wherefore then is the water of the ocean not fresh!" with childish peevishness exclaims the wanderer on the boundaries of the desert of land and water; "into what luxuriant fields might not these subtropical shores be converted!"

ANCIENT SETTLEMENTS AND SEA-PORT TOWNS.

Here one would think that a human being could no more get on than on the waterless moon. And yet man is here; to this locality too has he been brought by the struggle for life. Round the wells and springs in the mountains he has settled as a herdsman, passing a wretched existence, and to the coast has he come as an ichthyophagist, a fisherman, a mariner, a trader. Even the peoples of antiquity had populous towns here, the entrepot of an active trade carried on by Egypt with Arabia and India. In the time of the Ptolemies there were, beginning at Suez, the ancient Clysma, and going south: 1, Philoteras, probably at the bottom of the bay of Gimse and on the Wady Enned; 2, Myos Hormos, or Portus Magnus, probably on the bay of Abu Somer; 3, Leukos Limen, perhaps the present Old Koseir; 4, Nechosia, at Ras Moghek; 5, Berenice, the chief trading town, at Ras Benas. But they flourished only for a short time, one town rising as the other sank, partly because the trade took a new route or ceased altogether, partly because the harbours became sanded up or left by the sea (see Chap. IV. p. 234), or were reduced to small dimensions by the ceaseless operations of the coral polyps. The towns then fell into ruins or vanished without leaving a trace. In the first centuries of Mohammedanism the only point of importance on the coast was the port of Aidab, in the neighbourhood of Suakin, opposite Jeddah, where the pilgrims took ship from Africa for Arabia.

HISTORY OF THE SEA-PORT OF KOSEIR.

The Turkish conqueror of Egypt, Sultan Selim III., appears to have been the first who again directed the route for trade and pilgrims to the Egyptian coast: at least he built a small fortress, the modern Koseir, principally for a protection against the Bedouins, erecting others of the same kind also on the east coast, in Moilah and Wudj for example. But no inhabited town arose under the protection of this fortress, Koseir being only a periodical trading-place. The road through the desert was so dangerous, on account of the plundering Bedouins, that only large caravans could venture to pass through it. The merchants attached themselves to the pilgrim caravans, and crossed the sea with the pilgrims as well in going as in coming; the Arabic merchants, chiefly belonging to Yemba, at this time transacted their business in Koseir, and then returned home. There were only a few houses standing inhabited by people from Yemba. In this condition the place was found by the French on their conquest of Egypt; as a point of strategic importance they kept it garrisoned during the three years (1798–1801) that they possessed Egypt, and cannon and mortars still remain ornamented with the Jacobin cap and republican inscriptions of the year III.

Koseir first became a permanent settlement of importance under Mohammed Ali, and under the favour of this pasha soon rose to a flourishing position. The fact of its having a comparatively good harbour, at least for smaller vessels, in a situation that could be reached from the Nile valley more easily and in a shorter time than any other port, and enjoying a climate celebrated as being temperate and healthy, appeared to justify the selection, notwithstanding the want of fresh water. The viceroy was, as he still is, bound by treaty to pay a portion of his annual tribute to the Porte in the form of deliveries of grain for Arabia, with which the Sultan, on his part, had to supply the Turkish soldiers and officials there, the chiefs of the Bedouins, who would not allow the caravans to pass unmolested through their territories unless on this condition, and the sherifs or descendants of the Prophet. These deliveries, called *dachîre*, consisted of about 180,000 ardeb annually—wheat, barley, beans, lentils, and also oil, biscuits, and the like. Koseir was selected as the place where these were to be collected. At that time, when there was no railway, Suez was as difficult to reach from the fertile regions as Koseir; from it a long and dangerous sea voyage had first to be made to the Arabian ports of Yemba and Jeddah, and the corn of Upper Egypt was better and cheaper than that of the Delta. The distance by sea from Koseir was considerably shorter, and through the energetic measures of the viceroy, who had effected treaties with the Bedouins, the desert route had been rendered quite safe. The hope of deriving a large profit from the transport of this grain as well as from the then flourishing private trade, and from the passage annually of a large number of pilgrims to Meccah, as well as certain privileges specially granted to the place (freedom from military service and direct taxation), soon attracted a multitude of people both from the neighbouring valley of the Nile and from the Hedjaz, especially Yemba. Thus in a short time (in the first thirty years of the present century) Koseir acquired a settled population of 6000 to 8000 souls. It obtained the title of *bander*, meaning pretty much the same as "good town" or "good trading-town," and had a governor of its own (*Muhâfiz*) of the rank of a bey, who was directly dependent on the central government at Cairo, as those of other sea-ports, Alexandria for example, still are. Correspondence with the central government was partly carried on by messengers mounted on dromedaries, who set out at least once a week, and, taking the most direct route, traversed the desert in five days, partly by a system of towers and semaphores running through the Nile valley to Cairo. At this time there were at Koseir about sixty persons employed by government, including, besides the governor, a port-captain, a doctor, two superintendents of police and customs, three overseers for the grain-store (*shuna*), nine Coptic clerks, eighteen soldiers, with two corporals, for the fort, hospital-superintendent and male attendants, custom-house officers, &c. Every

HISTORY OF THE SEA-PORT OF KOSEIR.

month these received as pay sixty-four purses (1 purse = 500 piastres = about £5), the governor alone claiming sixteen purses. Extensive public buildings arose for the government, the customs, and the grain depot. The citadel was repaired and additions made to it, a quay faced with stone and a wooden mole projecting into the harbour were built. The inhabitants on their side filled up a portion of the beach and built houses, mosques, and the bazaar. The prosperity of the place increased to an unusual degree; almost all the trade between Egypt and Arabia went through Koseir, every year there passed about 30,000 pilgrims (12,000 going to Meccah, 18,000 returning), and among them many men of rank and wealth from the whole Mohammedan world. Numerous inns served for the reception of these pilgrims, though the greater number of them encamped in the open air or in tents; all round the town a still larger town of tents was pitched. The passage of this multitude of people, who could leave Koseir only by ship or camel, occupied nearly nine months of the year. If it is considered also that every day several hundreds, nay thousands of camels arrived from the Nile valley, that another hundred or two brought water from the mountains and were quartered in the neighbourhood, and also that the Ababdeh settlement outside the town numbered about 200 persons, a conception may be formed of how busy a scene the town and environs must have been. Entertainment and amusement were also provided for; there were thirty coffee-houses, three spirit shops, and more than fifty dancing-girls, who inhabited a special quarter of the town. At that time, too, the overland route for the English to India passed through Koseir, and twice a month Anglo-Indian steamers entered the harbour and brought numerous European travellers who, from Koseir to Keneh in the Nile valley, rode on camels, or, perhaps (especially the ladies), had themselves carried this distance in palanquins, a journey of four or five days. For these steamers a coal depot was formed. An English, a French, an Austrian, and a Persian consul—all natives of the country—looked after the interests of the travellers belonging to the country represented by each.

Hundreds of vessels entered the harbour every month; for the transport of the contributions of grain, and perhaps also for certain warlike purposes, the Egyptian government itself possessed seven large three-masted vessels of European build, of from 4000 to 7000 ardeb burden, with European captains and officers, as well as eleven one-masted vessels of Arabic build; but even these were not sufficient, and had to be always supplemented by many ships hired from private persons.

Under Abbas Pasha, and up to the beginning of the government of Said, Koseir still continued to flourish. An English company undertook to lay a submarine telegraph to India, and in the Red Sea it was to run along the west coast. At Suez, Koseir, Suakin, Massowa, and Aden stations were established, with four or five Europeans attached to each. After steamers had become less common at Koseir, in consequence of the establishment of the overland route to India by way of Suez, they were again often seen, being partly engaged in the laying of the cable, partly in bringing supplies for the employees, who were allowed to want for nothing belonging to English comfort. These well-paid individuals also spent their money freely and brought no little life into the town— a subject spoken of long after. While these Englishmen were staying at Koseir, the massacre of the Christians at Jeddah took place in 1858. A war-steamer sent by the English government for the purposes of observation and giving security to its subjects created a panic; but in peaceful Koseir there was nothing to avenge. The telegraph soon began to cease to work; when a thorough inspection of it was made, the cable was found to be damaged throughout; the coral rocks had chafed it; and after scarcely two years the telegraph was entirely given up.

The severest blow, however, and one from which it has not yet recovered, was received by Koseir in the same year (?) —the railway between Cairo and Suez was completed. By this means the traffic, including the pilgrims, was almost entirely removed to Suez, for which Said Pasha had as great a favour as Mohammed Pasha had had for Koseir; all kinds of advantages were granted to it, the Meccah pilgrims must go by way of Suez to make the line pay, and the *dachîre* were managed at Suez. It thus happened that Koseir was deserted by the greater number of its inhabitants almost at once, and it sunk more quickly than it had risen.

Koseir only retained the grain trade with the Hedjaz, which, however, was of some importance, and sufficient to prolong the life of the town. The profit from the pilgrims became rather negative than positive, as with the exception of a few persons from Upper Egypt it was generally none but begging pilgrims that took this route, over the whole of which they could beg. The number of the government employees was greatly diminished, that of the inhabitants sank to 1500, whole streets were deserted and fell into ruins. But still more blows fell. The year 1864 was a year of scarcity, and in order in some degree to lessen this the export of grain was strictly prohibited by an edict of Ismail Pasha. For the town this was a mortal injury. The prohibition was so sudden and unexpected that a large quantity of grain had been already stored up. A deputation of merchants to the government received the answer that of the 11,000 ardeb of grain found to be in the town (in any case, therefore, a considerable quantity) 8000 might be exported, as the corn could not be taken back again to the Nile valley; 3000 were to remain in the place in order to support the inhabitants for six months.

After the year of scarcity the trade again went on, but no longer as formerly. The prices of grain, like the prices in Egypt generally, were no longer so low as formerly, and the cost of transport and customs dues made them still higher for the opposite coast.

Hitherto Father Nile had almost exclusively supplied arid Arabia with corn; but now also the Euphrates and Tigris, even the Indus and Volga, began a dangerous rivalry. By the steamers, which, since the opening of the Suez Canal, traverse the Red Sea in great and increasing numbers, grain can now be brought to the Arabian sea-ports from the distant but cheap countries on the above-named fertile streams at a lower rate than is possible for the Egyptians. Occasionally, in years of extraordinary abundance, or when high prices rule in these countries, a short time of improvement is again induced, but after those injuries formerly received mainly at the hands of the government, the town is now in the condition of a sick person wasting away through some internal complaint; it can neither live nor die, but every year becomes worse and weaker, and will hardly as such last more than half a score years. The government has, to be sure, given it a strengthening medicine by causing the *dachîre* to be again exported from Koseir, after finding that the Suez route was too expensive; but the contribution now amounts to only 24,000 ardeb, far from sufficient to bring about any improvement. The remaining trade, exclusive of the grain trade, is also too insignificant to keep up the town; and while the sources of income are drying up, taxes are enormously increasing; provisions, being generally brought from a distance, are usually higher than in the Nile valley, to which must be added the cost of water, amounting for a considerable household to from 1s. 6d. to 6s. a day. At present, therefore, everybody is now leaving his native town, formerly so dear, and the population can now scarcely amount to more than 800.

The history of the town of Koseir, as we received it from the mouths of natives, we have given in some detail, partly because it is not uninteresting in itself, partly because it shows what an ephemeral existence the waterless sea-ports on the Red Sea have and always had.

Even Suez is not secure against a blow to its prosperity, in spite of its canal. Some time ago the project was brought forward of bringing the traffic, which merely passes Egypt through the canal, and brings nothing to the country, more into the country itself, and on the Egyptian west coast of the Red Sea a good harbour which could be easily provided with fresh water was sought for. The harbour was then to be connected by a railway with another railway to be constructed in the Nile valley, and it was hoped that at least a portion of the trade with India would be attracted to this quicker route, much in the same way as the route to Egypt *via* Brindisi is often preferred to that *via* Marseilles or Trieste. All

KOSEIR ON THE RED SEA.

Drawn by Karl Girardet.
From a Sketch by Guillaume Lejean.

these advantages, it was believed, were to be found in the good harbour of the anciently celebrated town of Berenice, but the project was quite given up.

Perhaps recourse may once more be had to the unfortunate town of Koseir, which, though it neither has a good harbour nor yet fresh water, possesses the advantage of being near the Nile valley, and of being connected with this by a road along which a railway might easily be constructed. A good harbour would be found at Shurum, 18 or 19 miles farther south, and the want of water might be remedied by cisterns. If a more active race than the indolent unenterprising native Moslimin inhabited these regions, town after town might now perhaps rise even on these barren shores, as in the time of the Greeks, and in the adjacent desert garden after garden might perhaps be made by the digging of wells. The town of Koseir has at present produced at least one garden, though, certainly, this cannot be called luxuriant.

THE TOWN.

The picture of our sea-port town essentially resembles that which we have already drawn of a provincial town of Upper Egypt (see Chap. I.), but many Arabic elements from the Hedjaz also present themselves. Here also the houses are generally of one story and built of sun-dried bricks, and they stand in straight rows, the streets being remarkably clean. A few handsome government buildings of stone, some mosques and sheik-cupolas, rise above the other houses, and the whole is commanded by a citadel occupying a considerable area, but of no use for modern warfare. On Sundays and feast-days many flags are hoisted. In the foreground lies the bay with the shipping, in the back-ground rise picturesquely the mountains of the desert.

POPULATION.

The population, as in other sea-ports, is remarkable for the diversity of races it exhibits, while here also there is a still more striking diversity of colours. The chief body consists of the free proud offspring of sacred Arabia, who for the sake of gain have bowed themselves under the rigorous sceptre of Egypt, and have accustomed themselves to behave like the submissive slaves of the land of the Pharaohs. These "Yembauiyeh," or Bedouins, as they like to be called, still continue to look proudly down upon the Fellahin. They love to clothe themselves in bright and gay-coloured attire instead of the blue blouse of the Fellah; round their heads they wind a bright-coloured cloth which hangs down over their shoulders behind; their naked feet carry thick sandals. These Yembauiyeh are generally connected with the shipping, especially as owners, captains, and sailors. The Egyptians are more important numerically; they are the petty traders, artisans, and porters, though many are also excellent sailors, or have become merchants and ship-owners. The greater number have come from Upper Egypt, only the younger having been born in the place. There are also a number of Copts among them. Of genuine Turks there are only the governor and a féw officials; the half-dozen soldiers in garrison are of Turkish descent, but have been born in the place and are quite Arabified.

The negro slaves form an essential constituent in the population, acting mostly as sailors. To these are to be added— besides the deep-brown Upper Egyptians—the almost black Ababdeh, so that the prevailing shade of colour among the people of this place is very dusky. In keeping with the etiquette of the neighbouring holy land, the women here are more strict than elsewhere in closely veiling themselves. When ladies of position arrive by sea they are not put ashore until late at night, and also when they come from the desert they choose the night for their arrival if possible. Men whose business takes them to both shores of the sea alternately like to keep a legitimate wife on each side.

THE MARKETS.

In the town we have a bazaar in which the retail dealers, in their primitive booths, sell the products of three quarters of the globe, and of the Red Sea to boot, such as coffee, frankincense, pepper, ginger, rice, tobacco for the hookah, crushed dates in skins, cocoa-nuts, fancy wooden boxes, and textile fabrics from the East; oil, sugar, rice, dried dates, tobacco, pipe-bowls, camel travelling-bags, shoes, wooden utensils, and fruits from the Nile valley; textile fabrics, cigar-paper, lucifer-matches, tapers, tin, metal plates, and porcelain dishes from Europe; plaited-leather thongs, leather pouches, confectionery, bread and biscuit as industrial products of the town itself; and, lastly, dried fish, dried molluscs, the opercula of molluscs, cuttle-fish bones, porcelain shells (Cypræa), shells of the pearl-mussel, and other shells from the sea. Here too the broker runs up and down the market with all kinds of auction-wares: clothing, amber mouth-pieces for pipes, carpets, chairs, goats, sheep, asses, and camels. Large objects for auction, such as boxes, trunks, and other furniture, are exposed in different parts of the market-place, and if they cannot be sold they remain all night under the charge of the night-watchmen that sleep there. In the fish-market the strange forms and brilliant colouring of the Red Sea fish are exhibited as they hang in bunches by means of a cord of alfa grass drawn through their gill-openings; the large ones lie on straw-mats waiting till they are cut up with the hatchet and sold in pieces, while the parts that are not eaten, such as the entrails, gills, and ovaries, are flung to the cats, multitudes of which always collect here. In the fruit-market the parched inhabitants struggle for the fresh fruits and vegetables which the camel-drivers bring from the Nile valley, and are prevented from plundering only by the switch of a police-soldier. The cargo is generally sold to the retail dealer that offers most, after the doctor, who has been summoned for the purpose, or his agents, as overseers of the markets, have passed the goods as not being injurious to health, this being soon managed if a few first-fruits are presented for their families, either gratis or at a low price. Any objections on the part of the police or the "sheik of the vegetables" are also removed in this manner. Many citizens, however, in their longing for green food, set out very early and go a long distance to meet the expected camels, getting their wants supplied on the spot. In the cattle-market are exhibited various varieties of sheep descended from the fat-tailed breed; the brown-wooled shaggy-headed Nile sheep, the lean sheep of the Ababdeh, and the long-legged, smooth-haired Arab sheep, transported from Arabia by sea, besides the goats of these regions, all of them with large ears. A portion of them are immediately slaughtered on the beach, which is employed as a slaughter-house, by a transverse cut across the throat, in the name of God the all-merciful, according to the rules of the Koran, sea water being plentifully poured over them; others are previously kept and fed in the yards of the corn-dealers, in order to give milk and produce progeny. The latter object is promoted by the public he-goat, who has the market-place allotted to him as his home; here he remains day and night in the midst of the numerous consorts provided for him, and forms an essential feature in the scene. From the sellers of the high-priced drinking water, who set their commodity before them in casks, compassionate souls buy for him the delicious refreshment; but his food he procures for himself, penetrating into the court-yards of the corn-dealers, plundering the baskets of the children that sell bread, or biting unnoticed a hole in a skin containing dates. He even contrives to find entrance into the government grain warehouse by means of his commanding walk and stately horns. The wood-market is provided by the Ababdeh with the excellent wood of the acacia and other trees of the desert, as well as with wood charcoal, and by ships with the same articles from the opposite shore, or with shora-wood. A very cheap fuel, and one in general use, is also brought hither by the Bedouins, viz., balls of camels' dung in sacks, collected on the caravan roads; they also occasionally bring all kinds of desert plants as fodder for cattle. At other times the cattle kept in the town receive the bran arising from the grinding of grain, barley, among the grain-dealers also wheat, and always beans, without which they do not thrive; the latter take the place that oats occupy in other regions.

THE WATER.

The peculiarity of our desert town is the water market. Every morning arrives a stately water caravan with a supply for the wants of the citizen from the springs and wells of the desert. The better springs are from 8 to 10 leagues distant. Each camel carries six tanned goatskins, which are always rubbed with oil after being used in order to keep them from cracking with the heat of the sun on the up journey. This gives to the newly brought water that disagreeable flavour which has made the water of Koseir famous, and causes it to appear undrinkable to the new comer; we must also mention the impurities and insect larvæ that are always found in the basins of springs, and when the water is carelessly filled enter along with it into the skins. For this reason the water becomes putrid in a few days and still more undrinkable. All attempts at purifying it, even filtering and throwing in live coals, are of no avail, though, perhaps, allowing it to stand for several weeks in large reservoirs would have this effect. The water is brought partly by Bedouins, partly by inhabitants of the town itself, who make that their special trade. They require at least two nights and one day, the Bedouins three days. Some of the townspeople who have a large household keep special camels for carrying the water. The water being dear, a full goat-skin, which is by no means large, always costs from half a franc to 2 francs; it is dearer than usual at the pasture season, when the camels are sent into the Nile valley and only those of the Bedouins remain, and also at the time when many pilgrims are in the town. Government officials get their water paid for or delivered by the government; several water camels are at the orders of the governor. The poorer people provide themselves with water from less remote springs, but these are all saline, bitter, and hard. The domestic animals are watered with water from springs in the closest proximity to the town; this water is still worse, and is just drinkable for human beings only for a few months after a fall of rain. The soil is then turned up to the depth of a few feet, and the water collecting in the trenches is carried by women and girls into the houses in clay pitchers with handles, as on the Nile. The joyful excitement among the townspeople after a plentiful fall of rain that produces a river has already been described in Chap. IV. p. 231. There has been much talk for years about the construction of a cistern; everybody considers the scheme decidedly necessary and even profitable, but from the utter want of enterprise nobody will contribute the money for it. A good cistern, which would have to be well cemented and plastered in order to keep the water sweet, would, in any case, cost a large sum of money; and all sorts of apprehensions stand in the way, such as of the possible drying up of the water after several rainless years, and the damaging of the cement thereby, of competition, of its being forcibly seized by the government if the enterprise should turn out to be profitable, and the like, and the desire was always cherished that the government should take the matter in hand. So the project was always shelved, to be brought again upon the carpet every winter when the stream of rain-water once more ran unprofitably into the sea. Now when the town is lying almost at the last gasp there is no longer any hope of such a work being carried out. Others were enthusiastic about an aqueduct from the mountains, and petitioned the government for it, but naturally in vain. The production of freshwater from sea-water by distillation, as is done by the government at the Egyptian village of El-Wudj on the opposite coast of Arabia, where the pilgrims must submit to quarantine, obtains least approval; the Moslim will not readily look upon such an artificial product as a true gift of God, and will only drink it when forced.

INDUSTRY.

Manufactures are limited to articles the most indispensable for household use and for navigation, the division of labour being carried to a very small extent. There is here a shoemaker, or rather a cobbler, who is at the same time a tanner and a leather-sack maker; a few blacksmiths who work chiefly for the shipping; a locksmith who understands gun-making thoroughly, and is also a corpse-washer and Koran-reciter; a turner and pipe-borer, who, when his business as grain merchant allows him a few spare hours, drives his original trade; a joiner or general worker in wood, who, when business is dull, does not think it beneath his dignity to split wood; a number of ship-carpenters; a house-builder, who is also a stone-cutter, a mason, a bricklayer, and a plasterer, and makes room-floors of sand and earth; a tinsmith, who is also a tinker and a coppersmith; and so forth. At the pilgrim season workmen of various other trades gather here, such as cutlers, cover-makers, lace-workers, tailors, shoemakers, &c.; these find employment for a few weeks and thus procure means for carrying them farther on their journey. In addition to the manual occupation he may be engaged in, everybody with a few dollars capital does a little bit of trading; he travels in the Nile valley or to Arabia, and buys a few goods, such as cloth, utensils, fruits, live stock, and sells them in the needy desert-town; even the "fortress-commandant" or corporal takes every year a furlough-trip to Cairo and brings back with him various kinds of wares, which have always a rapid sale.

The ordinary citizen passes a large part of his time in the coffee-house, which also serves as an exchange for the mercantile class. Here important affairs are arranged; here the ship-master engages his crew, while others play, sleep, or smoke their hookahs in quiet satisfaction. Greek dram-shops, on the other hand, have not been able to maintain their ground since the glory of the town passed away; in the little town no one has the courage publicly to appear such a sinner as the drinker of spirituous liquor is considered to be.

THE "COURTS" AND THE TRADE.

No little activity manifests itself when the trade is being carried on in the "courts," the magazines of the wholesale dealers or grain-dealers. These are partly independent merchants, who have their business friends, their partners, or agents in the Nile valley and the sea-ports of Arabia; but the greater number are only agents of Arabic or Egyptian merchants on the Nile. The camel-drivers so soon as they arrive call at one court after another with samples of their goods, especially grain, carrying these in a knot of their shawl or their turban, or in a little bag for the purpose; others who have brought corn on the order of a partner, show the person addressed a sealed packet, also containing a sample and a letter. When the business has been concluded, or everything found correct, the camels that have been waiting outside the town are brought in, the grain is poured out on the smoothly cemented floor of the court and measured. The caravans generally remain over night at a well some miles from the town, which they enter at early morning; all day long business is transacted, and in the evening the caravans start on the return journey, intending to reach the same well again. The treasure-heaps of grain are now prepared for shipment, being remeasured and filled into sacks of coarse canvas or alfa-grass. If a vessel is ready the sacks of corn are placed upon a hand-barrow, consisting of two beams with cross-pieces, and carried by four men singing and tripping along to the custom-house, and thence to the mole, from which it is taken off by a large boat and conveyed on board the ship. But, besides grain, there are also a number of other articles of trade, which, when exported or imported, pass through the courts. Several frequently unite together in one business, but only in the form of partnerships, not of large companies; in these concerns either every member is active, and contributes money as well, or the one contributes the money and the other carries on the business, so that in the calculation of profit and loss the capital reckons as one factor, the personal activity in the business as the other. Others prefer to have agents or brokers, and the latter receive about 2 per cent. of the profits. The taking of interest being forbidden by their religion is not practised by the natives in their dealings with each other; the rôle of usurer, however, has been assumed by Europeans and Greeks, at least in the Nile valley, and they take a high rate of interest (2 to 5 per cent. monthly).

They now lend only upon personal security, since they have learned by experience that otherwise the money is certain to be lost; mortgages upon land are not recognized by the government, at least not willingly, as by this means all the land might soon come into the possession of the Europeans. On the whole pretty sound principles prevail in the commercial transactions of the native inhabitants with each other, and the percentage of European swindlers would probably be far higher than that of Arab swindlers.

CUSTOM-HOUSE.

Goods exported and imported are strictly examined in the custom-house, especially the former, which have here to pay the customs dues, while on the latter the dues have generally already been levied in the Turkish sea-ports of Arabia, and if a clearance sheet obtained there is brought with them nothing more is demanded in the vassal-land of Egypt. On all goods an *ad valorem* duty of 8 per cent. has to be paid; for some, such as common tobacco and nargileh tobacco, far more, up indeed to 80 per cent. In the case of grain that is being exported every twelfth sack, selected at pleasure by the inspector, is opened, and its contents poured out and measured by the measurer appointed. There is generally found to be a surplus over the stated quantity, and this is immediately swept off to assist in keeping the custom-house officials spruce and in maintaining their families and domestic animals. The goods have to go through a series of examinations and investigations by the various customs officials—measurers, weighers, enumerators, valuators, inspectors, clerks, and collectors of dues. The governor has the general supervision. How far these publicans are also sinners we leave to the conjecture of the reader; who may easily imagine also that on such a length of uninhabited and unwatched coast smuggling cannot be prevented.

The exports consist chiefly of grain and leguminous fruits, wheat, barley, millet, beans, lentils, chickpeas, also onions, eggs, fowls, and molasses. Most of these goods go to Jeddah and Yemba, also the places still belonging to Egypt on the opposite coast of Arabia, viz. Wudj, Moilah, Debba. The imports are much more unimportant than the exports, most vessels returning empty. The number of the articles imported, however, is much greater. The principal are coffee (the most important of all), carpets, spices (such as pepper, cinnamon, cloves, and ginger), essential oils, frankincense, myrrh, mastic, gum Arabic, henna, tamarinds, indigo, nargileh tobacco, cocoa-nuts, rice, cotton, and silk stuffs, and household furniture and utensils. All these are brought chiefly from Jeddah, which is the emporium for all the products of the East, from Arabia and Persia to India and China. From Yemba come—dates in skins, honey, hides, grease, and also sheep and camels; from the places on the opposite coast, sheep, goats, camels, grease, wood, coal, and salt, though the last is strictly prohibited. Asses and horses are sometimes brought from Nejd. Lastly, the pearl-oyster shells, which the Bedouins of the Egyptian coast bring in their vessels, must also pay duty here, and these form an important article. Slaves are scarcely ever brought into the country by this route now. A short time ago, when the grain trade was carried on, the customs dues are said to have amounted to about £5000 annually, to which must be added the tax for the road to the Nile valley, amounting to £2000 (?). The latter tax is levied for the security of the road, which the chiefs of the Ababdeh have to guarantee, and therefore receive about one-eighth of the money raised. Special officials are appointed for the collection of the road-tax.

THE GOVERNMENT GRAIN-STORE.

There is much activity in the large court surrounded by high stone walls of the *shûna* or government grain-store, in which the *dachîre* (see p. 272) are stored. At many places in the Nile valley there are also many similar grain magazines, at which the peasants of the Nile can deliver their tribute in kind. From these the government draws its supplies for the military, &c., or it sells the corn; a portion of this, however, goes to make up those consignments of grain that, as already mentioned, are sent to the "sacred land," and a multitude of camel-drivers have to convey it to the granary at Koseir, either being paid directly for their services or by a remission of taxes. Every driver receives a written statement of the quantity of grain delivered to him, and a sealed sample to show the quality. In the granary the corn is now poured into boxes of a basin or sand-glass shape, from which it runs by a small aperture into the measure of the grain measurer; like the dictating scribe, with whom we have already become acquainted (see Chap. I. p. 63), this functionary proclaims, in a peculiar monotonous melody, the numbers he obtains from his measurements. These must agree with those on the invoice given by the granary officials in the Nile valley; but they often do not agree, and the matter does not terminate without much noise and wrangling. The grain measured off is carried into the corners of the warehouse, where it rises gradually into great mountains to the tops of which the carriers ascend at every round by means of boards planted against their sides. The stored grain is now conveyed to the vessels, into the holds of which it is poured loose till they are full to the gunwale. No one is in the granary during the night, and the great door is sealed every evening with a large seal of clay. The superintendent is responsible for the quantity in the store between the time he leaves and the time he enters. When the grain has been conveyed by ship to Hedjaz, it is there measured afresh and compared with the sealed sample sent along with it—so that there is check upon check, and yet every grain of corn that has reached its destination would have plenty to tell of brothers lost, one after the other. It is not very easy to convict the camel-driver of putting a few handfuls of earth into each sack and taking out the same quantity of corn; and if he has a bad conscience he knows how to make the corn-measurer keep quiet, who, by a certain method of placing the measure and other dodges, has it in his power to make the grain turn out more or less. It is a common saying that the grain-measurer may heap up treasures in this world, but will never attain a high place in paradise. The ship-master, too, is not readily detected if, on the high sea, or even while in port, he allows his vessel to ship a sea or two so as to wet the cargo and cause the grain to swell. When subsequently measured, it will still be of the full bulk, but will contain fewer grains. From the surplus produced by thus levying such small requisitions or large quantities, many a person supports himself and his household the whole year round. The pigeons, too, cannot be altogether prevented from the more innocent thefts committed by them on the corn-heaps early in the morning. In storms many a bushel has to be thrown overboard from the deeply-laden vessel, and then the whole crew has to swear that this was done from necessity. Oaths are readily taken by the Moslimin, if they square with their interest, and the storm need not have been a very severe one.

THE PORT.

The harbour is a wide bay open towards the east, or rather a *sherm*, that is, an opening in a coral reef stretching along the coast and connected with it, not separated by an atoll. This opening is wider than in the case of other sherms, which generally occur at intervals of a few miles and afford direct access and shelter for small vessels. The entrance is perfectly safe, and not rendered dangerous by rocks that are near the surface, though always covered by water. The harbour is available as such, however, only in the northern part of the bay, where it is deeper, and is protected against the north winds, which prevail by far the greater part of the year, by a coral reef running out in the form of a curve. Towards the south the bay becomes shallow through the accumulation of sand, and as no dredging-machine is employed the sanding up goes on year after year. The larger sized European sailing vessels and steamers cannot venture into the sheltered space behind the reef, and must anchor at a considerable distance out in the roadstead, exposed to the violence of the sea. Accordingly they prefer not to visit the port at all, especially as they are not attracted by commercial advantages. Even the Egyptian mail and other steamers do not touch at Koseir, though they regularly visit the other ports of the sea, Suez, Jeddah, Suakin, and Massowah. Other steamers that call occasionally have generally met with some accident, or are brought by the want of coals.

Against east and south-east winds, which very often blow in winter, the harbour is quite unprotected. The bay, at other times so peaceful, now throws up high waves, washes the soil away where it consists merely of shot rubbish, makes breaches in the stone walls, and damages the wooden mole, while wave after wave rolls up over the bank of sand that forms the beach, and leaves a salt lagoon to remain until it dries up and forms a white streak of salt. The vessels pitch and roll in a dangerous manner, and, snapping their cables, run aground and go to pieces in the shallow harbour, or perhaps come into collision and smash each other. On such occasions it is by no means uncommon for the greater number of the vessels in the harbour to be wrecked. The whole shore is then strewed with grain and fragments of wreck. One can foretell the approach of such a wind by the rise of a small white cloud in the eastern horizon, after a period of almost perfect calm. A slight breeze, gradually increasing in strength, then rises, the suspicious little cloud approaches with astonishing rapidity, and in a brief space a raging, howling tempest prevails. With the noise of the wind are mingled the shouts of the sailors, who must be at their posts in order to secure the anchor and keep everything in order; while above all are heard the orders of the shipmasters and the cries of the women, anxious about those at sea belonging to them.

THE MOLE.

The wooden mole running out into the sea is always an animated scene. It is supported on wooden piles that are perpetually eaten into by the ship-worm, and always require renewal from time to time. Recently the government refused to repair it, or any public building of the province, and the consequence was that the half of the mole was carried away by an easterly storm. The fishing vessels and passenger-boats lie beside the mole; on it boys angle for the fishes that swim in multitudes between the piles; here the ship-owner watches from a distance the labours of his people, while others take here their siesta, fanned by the cool breeze. Everything that comes and goes by sea has to pass the mole, where the custom-house officers examine with a searching look every passer-by. Goods to be shipped are brought from the custom-house to the mole, and thence are conveyed by boat to the vessel, those to be landed going through the reverse process.

ARRIVAL AND DEPARTURE OF VESSELS.

Much animation is exhibited when vessels are arriving or departing. This always forms an event. As soon as a vessel appears in sight, the fact is announced by the boys with a loud *Hariyeh! Hariyeh!* Others then look in the direction indicated, and if they can confirm the report they join in the cry. The news is thus carried through the whole town, and forthwith on the roofs or terraces of the houses appear female figures, the relatives of mariners or passengers expected. Arming themselves with telescopes the merchants or ship-owners proceed to the beach or to neighbouring heights in order that they may find out, as soon as possible, what ship it is that is approaching. On the entrance of a vessel an inquisitive crowd always collects on the mole, but they require to exercise their patience for a little. The sanitary officers must first take a boat and go on board the vessel to inspect it. At no time do the inhabitants show greater respect to the sanitary officials than at such moments, when it is a question of discharge or quarantine. If on account of the suspicious illness of a single individual the vessel is ordered by the sanitary officers to go into quarantine, or if the higher authorities have ordered quarantine to be enforced in the case of all vessels whatsoever, then communication with the vessel is prohibited, a quarantine watchman is put on board, the sanitary agent takes possession of all letters and papers, fumigates them and pierces them through and through according to the professional practice, and finally distributes them. If pratique is given, a custom-house officer must go on board and inspect the goods before anyone can land. When the letters, which are rolled up like ribbons, have been distributed, there may be seen stretching along the mole, and up into the town, a whole host of readers, whose countenances and gestures plainly tell whether their business affairs are in a satisfactory state or not. The sailors and passengers hasten to their houses, after submitting to the embraces of all their acquaintances on the way, and appear in public several hours later dressed in their best clothes. The more important of them, however, are followed even into their houses; they have scarcely time to speak to their families, still less to wash themselves and change their clothes. Their reception-room is immediately filled with a crowd of people who come to pay their respects and hear the news, and who are treated to coffee. People arriving after a journey through the desert have also to hold such a reception, however fatigued they may be, such being the etiquette; they have not to pay visits themselves. Some time after the arrival of the vessel, generally the next day, the ship is unloaded. Perhaps a few camels have been brought by the vessel, the poor beasts being tied up in the hold so tightly as often to stiffen their necks. These are now pulled up by ropes and pulleys and let down into the water, and half-swimming half-wading they have to find the way ashore themselves.

The departure of a vessel is accompanied with a like amount of ceremony. Vessels that are about to cross to the opposite shore always set sail in the forenoon, never in the afternoon or evening. When the ship's papers are all in order, in particular when a declaration that he will not desert has been written for every sailor, and when also a bill of health has been drawn up, the vessel is boarded by a deputation from the governor, and by the sanitary officers in company with the owner, and other persons who wish to see their friends off. The papers are now handed to the captain, who gives a gratuity to the officials. Intimate friends and relations embrace each other, exchange affectionate farewells, often with tears, and beg each other's forgiveness in case either has offended the other by word or deed. When people are setting out for the Nile valley also, it is the regular thing for their friends to accompany them for some distance, and take an affectionate leave of them. At last those that intend to remain re-enter their boat, wishing everybody a good voyage, the great sail is unfurled, a *fatha* is uttered, and the vessel now sails rapidly out to the open sea, followed by the gazes and good-wishes of the women, who assemble on the beach that they may also witness the departure of those belonging to them.

THE VESSELS OF THE RED SEA.

The native vessels trading in this sea have something antiquated and bizarre in their appearance. They are usually disproportionately short; the hinder part is remarkably broad and high, terminating abruptly in a sloping stern, and containing the cabin, which, being only between 5 and 6 feet in height, scarcely permits one to stand upright, and is not provided with berths or any kind of furniture. Behind, and sometimes also in the sides, the cabin has a few open air-holes; towards the forepart of the ship it is quite open or provided with a door, but the entrance is generally so encumbered with bales of goods that only a small aperture is left. The women and children are packed into the cabin, it being thought better to expose them to all the horrors of sea-sickness—which in this close stuffy hole is sure to attack them—than to the gaze of the crew and passengers. The roof of the cabin, or the hinder-deck, forms an open platform elevated high above the rest of the vessel, and is called in Arabic *kursi*, that is, seat or stage. As is also the case in the Nile vessels, this is the station of the steersman, who overlooks the whole ship, and governs the helm by means of a long lever projecting towards him. In a box before him, and lighted by an oil lamp, swings the antiquated compass, of Frankish origin but with Arabic improvements, and with stars in place of the points on the card. The after-deck is also the best place for the passengers, since in these regions it is most agreeable to live in the open air. The sea breeze tempers the scorching heat of the sun, which may also be avoided by awnings, and in winter sufficient warmth may be obtained by the use of woollen wrappings, the sea breeze at this season rendering the cold less severe. The large space amidships is without a deck, and when the vessel is empty—as it usually is on the return voyage from Arabia—communication fore and aft is only maintained by means of planks, carelessly laid down lengthwise and crosswise, which cannot be traversed without danger, at least by the inexperienced. There is less danger when the vessel has a full load of grain in sacks or lying loose; but the vessel then rises only a few feet above the surface of the water, and, when the sea is high, the waves break over her, and drench both crew and cargo. The prow of the vessel always terminates in a curiously-twisted beak of varying length. The fore-part is covered with a short deck, on which the fire-place is situated, an earthen vessel or wooden box filled with clay serving for a grate. A sailor or ship-boy, who knows something about cookery, here cooks the daily food of the crew—the bruised barley and lentils—in a large narrow-mouthed copper kettle, and bakes the thin cakes of unleavened flour. The drinking-water is kept in a large quadrangular wooden trough. When water collects in the bottom of the vessel it is simply baled out, there being no pump. One man passes on the baling pitcher to the other, and the uppermost empties it into a wooden gutter laid crosswise over the ship.

The huge triangular or trapezoidal sail is hoisted on the mast by means of a system of pulleys. Whenever the sail is to be braced round, the ropes which are attached to the mast and impede the movement of the yard have to be unfastened, while the sail is let down a little. During this operation, which is quite different from that practised on board the Nile boats, the weight of the sail causes the vessel to heel over dangerously to one side, especially if a strong gust of wind has suddenly come on. Larger vessels have also a smaller auxiliary sail at the fore-end of the hinder-deck. The flag is attached either to a rope belonging to the small hindermast, or to the top of the mainmast. The flag used is the Turkish—a white crescent and a few stars on a red ground. Vessels belonging to sherifs or descendants of the Prophet have the right to carry a green flag. The numerous native consular agents of foreign powers may show, and indeed are bound to show, on their house the flag of the country they represent, but for some time their vessels have been strictly prohibited from carrying it, "since they do not know the usages of the sea."

The greater part of the materials for the Red Sea vessels are brought from Jeddah and "India," the latter name as used by the Arabic seamen of these regions comprising also Yemen. The ropes and cables are made of palm and cocoanut fibre, the anchors never having chain cables. Teak, from "India," is the timber most highly prized in shipbuilding, and forms the planking of the vessels. It is very strong, and is said by its bitterness to prevent the attacks of the shipworm, which is here very destructive. Partly on account of the ravages of this creature, partly to renew the water-tight coating, vessels are careened every five months at least, and are smeared with grease and lime, or sandarac and oil, and thoroughly caulked with raw cotton. From time to time also vessels are painted with a variety of angular figures, streaks, and stripes in order to improve their appearance, the colours used being chiefly white, black, and red. The after portion of the vessel in particular is the part thus decorated. Oak and pine from Syria and Greece are also used in shipbuilding.

The vessels receive different names according to their form and size. These names are quite different from the Arabic designation of vessels commonly used in the Mediterranean; some of them do not sound like Arabic at all, and might, perhaps, be traced back to Indian or Frankish roots. *Range* or *gange* is the name of a large vessel with a capacity of over 3000 ardeb,[1] and having a long beak; *dhow* is the name

---

[1] 1 ardeb = 5 English bushels, and corresponds to 8 *kele*.

of a similar vessel with a very large stern; a *baghleh* is similar but wants the beak. The most common form is called *sambuk;* it is somewhat smaller and has a short beak. *Katéra* is a smaller vessel, such as is used in the coasting trade and the pearl fishery; *feluka* is a ship's boat, *gurdi*, a fishing-boat, *eshkif* (French *esquif*), a cargo-boat for harbour service, *húri*, a canoe made out of the trunk of a tree.

THE SHIP'S COMPANY.

The captain of the vessel, *reyis* or *nachude*, has only to attend to matters of administration. He is responsible for order being kept in the vessel and for the money required in managing it, he has to account to the harbour-police and the sanitary authorities when required to do so; but of seamanship he is often quite ignorant. The son or a relative of the owner may hold this post, or the owner himself when he accompanies the vessel. The professional shipmaster is the steersman (*ruban*), but generally the steersman and the captain are one and the same person. The crew (*taifa*) is generally numerous relatively to the size of the vessel, since the defective equipment must be counterbalanced by the number of the men. The common number is from six to ten, but larger vessels may have eighteen or twenty; among these, however, are generally a few passengers who have got themselves booked as sailors in order to avoid the numerous formalities and expenses imposed by the authorities. Over the common sailors is placed a mate or boatswain (*mokaddim*), and under them are one or several ship-boys. The sailors are either free natives of the sea-ports on the east and west coasts, with some Egyptian Fellahin among them, or black slaves either belonging to the owner or hired from some one else. Their dexterity is wonderful, especially that of the blacks. Having nothing on but a cloth round the loins and a quilted skull-cap, they leap with truly monkey-like agility and ease over the planks that serve as gangways above the hold; with a spring or two they scamper up the mast, seizing a rope with their hands and pressing their feet against another near it; they even practise the still more monkey-like habit of seizing the latter with their big toe. In addition to this quadrumanous faculty, the black monkey-like race of men are distinguished by their long arms, slender feet, small calves, projecting jaws, low forehead, and flat nose, as well as by their fondness for bellowing and grinning; but the Semites likewise, and, as the sculptures of the ancient Egyptians show, the Hamites also adopted to some extent this quadrumanous habit. Unlike the European sailors, whose strong point is said not to be swimming, the Arabic sailors are as much at home in the water as on shipboard. Not having first to take off their clothes they are at all times ready to jump into the water (which is always comparatively warm here) in order to stop a leak, or to dive down and put the anchor to rights, or to swim ashore though the vessel is a considerable distance from land; and it is said that when in quarantine they frequently visit their relatives at home under cover of night.

It is pleasant to see and hear them at their work, as they always lighten their toils with singing when engaged in any common task. When rowing they sing, like the mariners of the Nile, but the words and the airs are different. If the sail is to be hoisted, for instance, a leader will begin by singing, in the highest falsetto he can produce from his throat, a meaningless word or two, such as *moluchiyeh* (the spinach-like plant already mentioned), and at once the chorus of seamen at work follows with "moluchiyeh" in the deepest bass, giving the sail a heave up at the same time. The same thing may be seen when a ship is to be launched, an operation which always requires a large number of men, since there is no machinery for the purpose. Such scenes exactly resemble the transporting of colossal figures as depicted on the ancient monuments. There an overseer may be seen posted at some elevated point and giving his orders by clapping his hands, hundreds of naked workmen tug at the ropes in order to bring forwards the sledge upon which the colossus is placed, and among the ancients, too, the work always went on with singing. When, however, a work of considerable magnitude is finished, say, for instance, that a ship has been built, or that a vessel has safely landed after a long and perilous voyage, or that pratique has been received after some days' quarantine, then the naked and many-coloured chorus of sailors execute a *fantasie*. The strange quavering falsetto of the leader is again heard, the chorus chimes in with a hoarse, Tartarean, hollow, roaring voice, one or two of the sailors beat the small sieve-like hand-drums, another prepares with a mallet one of the skins of his drum while he strikes the other with his hand in order to leave no means of producing music unemployed; the rest grin, and dance, and clap their hands. The artists are able to continue for hours on end with the same aria. This certainly innocent fantasie is too barbarous to have been an invention of the Arabic sailors, who, however, join in it with as much heartiness as if it were their national song; it can only have come from the land of the bellowing blacks, but seems to have been used on this sea for hundreds of years, and is likely to continue for as long. In moments of leisure, especially on quiet moonlight nights, the sailor takes his lute (*túmbara*), an instrument to be found on board every vessel, and sings and plays the peculiar languishing Arabic airs, surrounded by a crowd who earnestly listen or join in themselves.

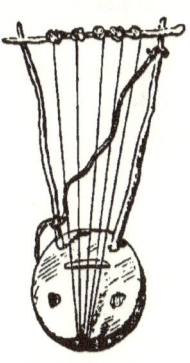

Mariner's Lute.

The lute consists of a hemispherical body, which was originally a drinking vessel or a melon, having a skin stretched across it, and two diverging bars projecting from it and united at their ends by a cross-bar. To this several strings of gut, generally five, are attached; these converge towards the lower part of the body, to which they are attached, and in the middle of which rises a bridge, as in the violin, to keep them tight. The entire instrument is made by the sailor himself.

NAVIGATION.

The native vessels in the Red Sea are almost exclusively employed in the coasting trade. It is only vessels of a certain size and tonnage (about 800 ardeb) that venture to take the open sea and cross from one shore to the other. But such a voyage is always a risk; the mariner waits for a favourable wind before venturing on it, and it often lasts eight days, and sometimes as much as fourteen. No Moslim sets any value on time, however. Vessels always try to make the opposite coast as soon as possible, and to select the shortest run, keeping well inshore for the rest of their voyage, at some distance from the coast reef, to be sure, but always in sight of land. They regularly pass the night in one of the numerous harbours or sherms. With a favourable wind the opposite coast comes in sight in the course of the next day after setting sail, or if the nearest point of the opposite coast is to be reached, the port of destination being, for instance, El Wudj, then land may be seen early in the morning of the next day, that is, in about twenty hours. Vessels sailing from Koseir to Jeddah or Yemba usually endeavour to make the island of Gebel Hassan. The voyage from Koseir to Jeddah usually occupies from six to twelve days, from Koseir to Yemba three to five. The return voyage lasts much longer, since in summer north and north-east winds almost constantly prevail in this part of the sea, becoming less violent, or ceasing to blow altogether only after it is well through the afternoon; in winter they are often interrupted by southeast and east winds. The return voyage from Jeddah to Koseir therefore occupies from sixteen to forty days, from Yemba twelve to twenty-five, from El Wudj three to ten. As the last-named port lies a little further to the south than Koseir, vessels have to work their way northwards along the coast for several days in order to get the north wind to take them across to Koseir. From Suez to Koseir is a voyage of three to eight days, from Koseir to Suez of as many weeks. This prevalence of the north wind (at the mouth of the sea it gives place to the south wind), combined with the numerous reefs and currents, is one of the chief impediments to navigation on the Red Sea, rendering it almost unnavigable for large sailing vessels, which always go round the Cape of Good Hope, notwithstanding the opening of the Suez Canal. These obstacles can only be overcome by steamers and the smaller Arabic sailing vessels. The ancients always started on their voyages in the summer months and returned in winter when the winds are more changeable and favourable. Like other seas the Red Sea is also subject to storms. They are fewest in summer and most common in the beginning of winter, especially in November. Storms from the north often last a fortnight, those from the east and south-east only a few days. In a violent storm the captain does not hesitate too long before causing part of the cargo to be thrown overboard in order to lighten the vessel, vessels being generally overloaded and sunk almost to the water's edge. Native vessels are very liable to meet with this misfortune, and the owner of the goods, like a good Moslim, after a few lamentations, resigns himself to his fate. Marine insurance is unknown. Among the citizens, accordingly, there are many ups and downs of fortune. When the ship is thus lightened, and after the large sail is furled, it pitches about and drifts with the waves; but there is generally time to take refuge in some sherm or other. If, however, the danger of sinking is too great; if a leak cannot even be stopped up with a flour-bag—a tried and approved method; if, as is very often the case, there is no boat on board; and if, lastly, there is no time to build a raft, then the bold skipper, after calculating the draught of his vessel and the height of the breakers, in despair steers straight for the coral reef, which is always flat and with shallow water above, and runs his vessel aground on it. The vessel must now go to pieces; but it is almost high and dry. The men jump from the wreck, and at once, or after swimming towards the land, get a firm footing in the still water on the reef. But this does not always happen; some even maintain that it is impossible. However, it is very rare in this sea for Arabic vessels to founder with all their crew, and so far as bare life is concerned there is more safety in a sambuk, miserable as it appears, than in a fine European steamer, constructed and fitted up in the most substantial manner.

USE OF THE COMPASS AND STARS.

The larger vessels generally carry a compass, having stars marked on the card as already mentioned; but the steersman does not make much use of it, and mere coasters that never cross the sea, but always keep to the same side of it, have no compass at all. The mariner, so ignorant generally as not to be able to read, directs his course much better by the stars themselves, which are seldom obscured by clouds; and since he usually remains near the shore, and sails only by day, except when crossing the sea, the mountains form excellent landmarks. Local knowledge is therefore his chief requisite. In this quarter practical astronomy generally speaking plays an important part in seamanship. Besides the north star there are also certain other guiding stars. A vessel's course is to be directed to a point directly south-east, for instance. Well, the Scorpion rises here, and accordingly the mariner keeps this constellation continually in his eye, even after it is high in the heavens. The compass-card also is marked in accordance with this system. It is divided into thirty-two segments by lines drawn through the centre, the chief of which passes through the north and south points, and separates the right or eastern half of the circle from the left or western. On the former are marked the points of rising, on the latter the points of setting. Another important line passes through the east and west points, marking the rising and setting points of the sun at the equinoxes. Then come the names of the following stars, going from north to south: —1, *Gah* or the north star; 2, *Farkad* or the Little Bear; 3, *Naâsh* or the Great Bear; 4, *Naka*, corresponding to Cassiopeia; 5, *Ayuk* or Capella; 6, *El Uâkaa*, corresponding to the Lyre; 7, *Lahêmir* or *Semâk*, Bootes; 8, *Tureya*, the Pleiades. Then follows the east point and the southern constellations: —9, *Gauza* or *Ozi*, Orion; 10, *Mirsam*, Sirius; 11, *Eklil*, Antares in Scorpio; 12, *Akrab*, Scorpio; 13, *Hamarén* (?);

14, *Suhêl*, Canopus; 15, *Sindibar* (?); 16, *Kutb*, the south polar star. The two last are not to be seen outside the tropical zone. The stars of the zodiac that do not correspond with those just mentioned are known only by the learned.

MARINER'S CALENDAR.

In calculations relating to the seasons of the year, and the winds that are so regular in this quarter, the Arab mariners also go by the stars. Their usual calendar, which perhaps has never before been written down, is as follows:—

1. *En nadm es-sogheyer* or *Robêj*, "the little sun," corresponding to the 20th or 21st of February. No skipper will set sail on this day, but will wait for the strong winds, the *Husumât*, that blow about this time. In the time "between the suns" a calm called *Haudl* prevails, though it is varied by south-east winds called *asieb*. At the end of this period, or at the beginning of the following, strong winds blow for some days, receiving their name from the constellation *El 'Aua* that rises at this time. This constellation is said to be one of the twelve resting-points (*mensil*) of the moon according to the Mohammedan theory.

2. *En nadm el Kebir*, also called "the great sun," the vernal equinox, that is, the 20th or 21st March, is regarded as the beginning of summer. The thirty or forty days following bring alternately calms and strong gusts of wind, *chafkat en-nadm;* there are also high tides at this time.

3. *Dufûn et-tureya*, that is, the setting of the Pleiades. Orion and Sirius also set about the same time, that is, towards the end of April. This period lasts for forty or fifty days, and is called also *Arbaintet es-sef*, or the forty days of summer; it corresponds to the period known as Chamasin in the Nile valley. It is characterized by frequent calms and south-east winds.

4. *Modelli* and *Mogelli*, literally, "the sinking" and "the brightness giving," an expression originating in the Nile valley. At this time the date twigs sink, while the fruits are forming, and the latter soon become brightly coloured. This period begins with the reappearance of the Pleiades (3d June). Moderately strong north winds blow at this time, and sometimes hot west winds (the simoom), especially in the mountains. The latter, however, are rare on the coast, being intercepted by the mountains.

5. *Tuêba*, that is, the Hyades, and *Kurûn*, the horns or foremost stars in Orion, now rise, that is to say, about the beginning of July. North winds prevail for twenty days. Then the whole of Orion appears, and there is about a fortnight of calms; this period is called *Gezaui*, and is much taken advantage of by the pearl-fishers.

6. Time of the Great Bear or Wain (*Nadsh*) and of Sirius, correspond-

ing to our August and the dog-days. North winds generally blow, though there are a few calm days between the rising of the third and fourth stars of the Wain, while Canopus (*Suhêl*) shows himself. This period is divided into several, named according to the stars of the Wain that rise in succession, *el aueltên*, that is, the two first, being followed by the periods of *Suhêl*, and *er-raba*, that is, the rise of the fourth star.

7. The remaining stars of the Great Bear, that is, those of its "tail," follow in due order. *El Châmis*, the fifth star, brings a calm and great heat. The rising of the sixth star, *Es-sadis*, corresponds with the Nerus day or beginning of the Coptic year (11th September), and brings on a few days of brisk, or often stormy, north winds. The seventh star brings a calm, *Haual es-saba*, that lasts for about a fortnight. This seventh period corresponds nearly to our September. During the whole two months governed by the Great Bear there are very low ebb-tides; according to the proverb, as the Nile rises the sea falls.

8. Time of *Kakêa* (?), corresponding to the beginning of October. North winds generally prevail at this time.

9. Time of *Lahêmir*, that is, Bootes, a portion of October and a portion of November, the time of the setting (?) of the star just mentioned, which is dreaded as a mischievous divinity. At this time sudden and irregular storms, especially from the east, often burst forth after periods of perfect calm. Thunder and rain are also frequent.

10. *El Akrabiyeh*. The Scorpion now appears, and after this period of seven days follows the *Arbaintet esh-shita*, or the forty days of winter, with frequent calms and moist south-east winds. It occupies part of November and part of December, and has a character similar to the Arbainiyeh of summer.

11. Time of the *Nasr* and *Nusêr*, that is, of the Lyre and Eagle, in December and January. This is the chief winter season; cold cutting north-west winds (*Masriyeh*) now blow, alternating with milder but often stormy north winds.

12. *Es-sâada* (?) begins on the 18th January, the day of the "baptismal feast" of the Copts, well known as the coldest day of the year. The winds at this period are irregular, the north and cold north-west being the most common.

Acquaintance with these periods, which the experience of mariners has established, is, perhaps, not without practical value, even although the dates do not always coincide with the phenomena actually observed. Besides the winds the mariner has also to contend with powerful currents that defy calculation; this greatly increases the difficulty of navigating the Red Sea. The currents are called *medds*, properly the name for "flood," and it is common to speak of a *medd yemâni* and a *medd shâmi*, that is, a current towards the south or Yemen, and one towards the north or Syria. They are always changing. There are also currents from east to west and *vice versa*.

TRAFFIC.

The following table, taken from the books of the sanitary office, shows the amount of shipping that entered the port of Koseir in the year 1863-64, when trade had not sunk so low as it has since done:—

Vessels under 1000 *kele* (at ⅛th of an ardeb),	180
Vessels of 1000 to 4000 *kele*,	154
Vessels of 4000 to 12,000 *kele*,	79
Total,	413

Of these 74 came from Yemba, 84 from Jeddah, 64 from El Wudj, 7 from Suez, 5 from Moilah. Of small craft 123 came from Gúeh, 21 from Safaga, 13 from Abu Munkar, 5 from Ras Benas, 3 from Suakin, 2 from Gebel Hassan, 2 from Gimse, and 1 from each of the following places—Wadi Gemal, Jafatineh, Tor, Lassat, Umm Muhammed, Tuer, Sheikh Hamed, Gad umm Mohammed, Shurum, Debah. The number of passengers, including pilgrims, was 5954.

FISHERMEN.

From the mariner to the fisherman is but a step. In moments of leisure, and in the evening, when he comes close in-shore, the mariner casts his line, and tries to procure in this way an addition to his scanty supper. The fisherman, when he sails out to sea in his boat, must be acquainted with the elements at least of the mariner's craft; and when he is the owner of a boat of considerable size he makes longer and shorter runs along the coast, carries millet to the Bedouins, and returns with a boat-load of fish and pearl-oysters. The fisherman who fishes in his boat in the bay, and not far from the shore, contents himself with a stone for an anchor; instead of using a sail he rows. If, however, the wind is too enticing, he sometimes erects an oar as a mast, and, pulling off his shirt, extends it as a sail; or he may take a small sail along with him. With this he often ventures far out into the open sea. His longest voyages on the coast are made by preference towards the north, and he works his way northward by taking advantage of a calm or a south wind, and also of night, when the sea is generally quieter than by day, so that, having reached his destination, he may be able to return quickly by the aid of the north wind. He does not care to sail to the south, because the prevailing north wind renders his return difficult or too uncertain. Accustomed to the duties of a sailor, the fisherman occasionally engages himself in this capacity on board a large vessel, in order to repair his finances, which his calling of fisherman alone does not keep in a very flourishing condition. For as the tax on fish is high he has to give up to the government a third of what he obtains by the sale of what he catches; in stormy times, too, he has often to remain in enforced idleness for weeks on end; and if he does make a large catch the profit he derives from it is not very great, fish being cheap in the small town, especially during calm weather, when everybody catches fish for himself, and the demand of the inhabitants is soon supplied. The fishermen also maintain that there is not now the same abundance of fish as formerly. Except for the tax referred to, fishing is free to every one who understands the business. Everybody, as a boy, has practised the angler's art once in his lifetime, and even in riper years the well-to-do citizen, who at other times has nothing in his head but buying and selling, or it may be the soldier, will sometimes feel a longing come over him to cast a line once more. Accordingly he takes up his post on the mole, or in a boat in the harbour, or on the edge of the coral reef, and sets to work. On the reef there may often be seen, especially when the lowness of the tide allows ready access, whole rows of fishers of all ages, complexions, and conditions, amateurs and professionals, in the costume of Neptune, that is to say, having a cloth round the loins and one round the head, the latter being the blue shirt of which they have divested their bodies.

FISHERMEN.

When the fishing is interrupted by storms at sea the fisherman spins thread for nets and lines, using a conical spindle which he causes to revolve by rolling it on his knee.

In spinning stronger cords he uses for spools two longish pieces of wood with a small cross-piece at top. Sitting on the ground he twirls one spool with his right hand while he holds the other with the sole of his right foot, the thread passing through and up between the great and the second toe. Round the knee, which is bent at right angles, the thread is several times wound. With the left hand the fisherman twists the two strands together. The twine for his nets is spun in this way.

Black Fisherman making Thread with the Spindle.

The usual method of fishing practised by the towns-people

Native Fisherman spinning Twine.

is with hooks and lines, the cast being made by the hand

alone without the assistance of a rod; the fish-eating Bedouins, however, use the spear. The bait attached to the hooks consists of fishes of various sizes, or morsels of fish, crabs, worms, sea-weed, &c., according to the kind that are being angled for. As many fishes only seize living prey, the fishes that are to serve as bait for them are taken alive in a basket, which hangs over the side of the boat and dips into the water; and if they are dead, an attempt is made by rowing rapidly to deceive the predacious fishes by giving the bait a plausible appearance of life. Some fishes can only be caught by night, but the usual time is early in the morning, when the sea is generally calmer than at other times. The fisherman is afoot even before the morning-star in order first to provide his bait and then to catch the right fish with it. Nets are much less frequently employed, the kinds used being the casting-net, ring-net, and trammel-net, but only in shallow water—in the harbour or on the reef. A hoop-net, such as is often used in rivers, is useless in the transparent water of the sea. When the splendidly-coloured fishes are seen swimming about in multitudes near the slope of the coral-bank, a person is apt to think that he has only to plunge in his net, but he would find that no fish will enter it. Besides this, a hoop-net or a trammel would soon get entangled among the shrub-like and branching corals. When the fishermen discover in the harbour some spot which is much frequented by a shoal of fish they spread a net between their boats, while some proceed to attack the shoal, and try to drive the fishes against the net by throwing stones at them, hissing, and making a noise. The casting-net is generally employed from the shore. Stooping down close to the ground the fisherman lies in wait for a shoal of fish swimming towards the shore, then leaps quickly into the water and throws the net, which is loaded with pieces of lead, towards the fish, so as to make it entirely envelop them. The ring-net is set upon the reef. The fishes that swim towards the shore when the tide is rising turn back towards the deep water again when it is falling, and in this way pass into the labyrinth, the entrance of which is turned towards the land; entangling themselves in its mazy folds they soon fall a prey to the fisherman. The beautiful and large parrot-fishes, in particular, are caught in this way, and being cut open, salted, and dried, become a commercial article. Some fishes are also caught by a basket with a funnel-shaped entrance projecting inwards above, and which allows the fish to get in, but prevents them from finding their way out. The basket is baited inside, generally with dough, and then set at some particular spot.

The larger marine animals, such as dolphins and the remarkable "mermaids" or "sirens," are caught by the harpoon, but people do not care much to kill the dolphins because they appear such amiable animals, and groan in a human sort of way. The sirens are cetaceous animals of moderate size, whose teeth are prized as ivory, and their thick hide as leather for sandals. According to some commentators the Jewish ark of the covenant is said to have been made of the hide of this animal. The preferable way is to take them by a large strong net, and to watch until they pay their nocturnal visits to the clefts and ravines of the coral-reef, where they browse like cattle upon the marine herbage. As soon as one has entered a narrow gully the entrance is blocked by a net. Feeling itself imprisoned, the beast plunges about, but entangles itself more and more in the net, in which it is now drawn towards the reef. When brought within reach it is beaten to death, or, according to the more common practice, drowned, for being a mammal it requires to come to the surface every now and then to breathe, and dies if forcibly kept too long under water. But these animals are exceedingly shy and wary, and not many people understand how to capture them.

PREPARATION OF THE FISH.

A common method of cooking fish is simply to fry them in oil; another method is to roast a whole fish on the open fire without oil or fat, or the fishes may be boiled with onions (called *seyadîyeh* or fisherman's food) either with or without rice, but they are never simply boiled in water. The flesh of the larger fishes is also chopped up and made into dumplings (*kufta*), or with the addition of onions and garlic into fish sausages (*semak mahohi*). The smaller fishes, as sardines, are packed up in layers with salt and kept until they have become quite tainted; when in this state they are highly prized by many and considered very wholesome and appetizing food. Fish that have been dried and salted are either boiled or are eaten raw, when they are as hard as stone. Fishes that have peculiar shapes, such as globe-fish, sharks, rays, and eels, are an abomination to the inhabitant of the town, who can easily get other sorts; the ichthyophagous Bedouin, on the other hand, prefers these as being cheaper and sells the dearer sort. The flesh of the sea-cow, being that of a mammal, rather resembles beef than fish, and is readily eaten by the Moslimin although it has not been slaughtered *secundum artem*. For, says the doctor of the law, everything that comes out of the sea is fish, and may lawfully be eaten without being slaughtered in the proper way. The flesh of dolphins and turtles is similarly treated. Most fishes collect in shoals at the spawning season, and are then taken in multitudes, especially a number of those of the mackerel and tunny kind. They often come in such vast shoals that a Greek, for instance, who understood better how to catch and cure them might drive a thriving trade. The native of the country knows no other method of preserving them than the rude methods of drying and salting already mentioned.

OTHER MARINE ANIMALS MADE USE OF.

The Red Sea is very rich in invertebrate animals, but of this class of products it is only the pearl-oyster and the black coral that are made any use of, except now and again by a European naturalist, or perhaps a wandering Greek trader. The natives seldom trouble their heads about such things. The only marine animals used as food are the gigantic *Tridacna*, large molluscs of the genus *Strombus*, and others of that of *Pteroceras*. These are gathered on the reef by Bedouin women, who boil and eat them themselves, or sell them to the merchants of the place, and thus they reach the Nile valley. It is only the bodies of the animals boiled and dried that are met with as articles of commerce, and very indigestible these fleshy lumps are. The eating of any others of the invertebrate animals uncooked, such as oysters, mussels, sea-urchins (the ovaries of), limpets, cuttle-fishes, crabs, and even the lobster elsewhere so highly esteemed, is regarded by the Mohammedans, and generally also by the Christians of the place, as a barbarous practice, and one of which only the unclean Frank is capable, while the flesh of hyenas—slaughtered in accordance with the rules on the Koran—is eaten without remark. However, these opinions or prejudices regarding the value of animal foods are mostly of a local nature, crabs, and even the man-murdering shark, being eaten every day at other places on this sea; just as in the Nile valley field mice are at some places looked upon as dainties (they were so also among the Romans), while at others their flesh is regarded with disgust.

To pay money for mere rarities is considered ridiculous by the inhabitants, though the pilgrims purchase some pretty shells as souvenirs, namely, porcelain shells (*Cypræa*), oliva shells, cone shells (*Conus*), and the beautiful Pharaoh's shell (*Monodonta Pharaonis*). The well-known Triton's-horn shell is blown as a horn by jugglers and merry-andrews, as well as used for holding water, the shells of the *Cypræa anulus* are commonly used as counters in games, the valves of the tiger's tongue shell (*Lucina tigerina*) as castanets for girls. Large quantities of the *Columbella mendicaria* are collected on the reef—generally by Bedouin children—and being sold to the merchants of the place are sent in bagfuls to the Soudan, where they are used for necklaces, and have a money value. In this quarter shells are worn as ornaments only by children, especially little Bedouin girls; but they are frequently hung about children, and animals also, as amulets. The opercula of univalves are of some commercial importance, being burned by way of incense when spells and incantations for summoning spirits are employed, the smell being supposed to attract them. The thick chalky operculum of the round-mouthed shell (*Turbo*) is laid upon scorpion stings. Sponges also are articles of trade, but their quality is inferior, and they cannot compete with those of the Mediterranean. They are gathered on the reef, and are then washed and macerated by being buried for some time in the sand. The use of the sponge, however, is unknown in Egypt, the inner bark of the palm being employed instead. The red organ-coral is sometimes collected by Greeks; it is said to serve as a colouring material for painting houses. Blocks of the kind of coral that forms reefs are frequently used as building material in the coast-towns, as it is easier to carry them from the sea than to transport stones from the mountains.

THE PEARL-FISHERY.

The pearl-fishery is an industry of some considerable im-

Vessel used in the Pearl-fishery.

portance. It is not a government monopoly, being free to every one, but on the goods being landed the customary import duty of 8 per cent. on the value must be paid; a certificate to this effect is then given, and must be shown when the goods are taken to Cairo and other important marts as well as when shipped at Alexandria for exportation to Europe. The pearl-fishery is almost exclusively carried on by Arabic Bedouins, who have settled at various parts of the coast as well on the African as on the Asiatic side. The chief place where the trade in pearl shells and pearls is carried on is Jeddah; but Koseir also is not without importance in this respect.

In the middle of March or beginning of April, when the atmosphere and the sea have become sufficiently warm to allow of diving being carried on, the Bedouins start with their light barks and a number of *huris* or canoes, and proceed north and south to places which they know to be productive. The crews mainly consist of black slaves, three or four to each vessel, the owner, and another Bedouin or two, also going along with them in order to superintend and direct. The vessel takes shelter in one of the numerous *sherms* or harbours. The divers seat themselves in the canoes, which, being easily capsized, cannot carry more than two men; but they are skilfully managed with the oar, which terminates in a circular plate. For diving and navigating the canoe, the one thing needful is calm water. Those engaged in the business accordingly take advantage of the periods marked as calm in the calendar already given. The first and chief fishing season is from the middle of March to the end of May —*En-nadm el kebir* and *Dufûn et-tureya*. In the windy periods following the vessels return and disembark their take, which is mostly sold at once. The second fishing season is the calm period *Gezâui* in the end of July, and that of *Nadsh* in August; the third is the time of *Lahemir* in October. The last two are very far behind the first in productiveness. In the winter months the fishery ceases altogether. The best time of the day is the quiet early morning. The diver in his canoe then peers down into the depths, and perhaps assists his vision by dropping a little oil on the surface of the water—hence these vessels always carry a supply of oil with them. The pearl shells (*Meleagrina margaritifera*) are found between the corals, to which they are attached by their byssus, the smaller sized ones also on the reef, the larger in deep water on the slope of the reef, and in front of it. They have accordingly to be brought to the surface by diving, in which these Bedouins, and more particularly their black slaves, display an extraordinary dexterity, using no apparatus. As soon as the diver spies a shell he leaps into the water, swims downwards head foremost, tears off the shell, and swims up again with his booty in his hand. When the shell is situated at a great depth he often hangs a weight to his feet in order to get down more quickly; this he throws off immediately he is at the bottom, and he either swims up himself or is drawn up by the cord attached to the weight. These divers render the greatest services in recovering packets of money and other articles that have been lost through shipwrecks, they can even employ the crow-bar at the bottom of the sea to enable them to get things out of narrow crevices in the rocks or similar positions, when the spot where they have sunk is in some degree known.

But to attain this skill they must practise diving from their youth up. The Bedouins are too fond of their comfort to dive themselves, and therefore train their slaves to it, whom they buy when boys and often treat with great cruelty until they learn. The slave, while still new to the work, will be shown a shell at the bottom and told to fetch it. If he does not bring it up he is beaten, bound, and flogged, his life is even threatened, and his scanty food is his only reward when he brings up the most valuable shells. The pearl-fishery in which slaves are thus employed is in a highly flourishing state, but it exhibits one of the worst aspects of slavery, and one which it is time steps were taken to abolish.

The shells when collected are exposed to the sun, when the animals soon die and the valves open. The fleshy tissue is now detached and carefully examined to see if it contains any pearls. The valves are next separated from each other and heaped up singly on board the vessel; for this reason it is seldom that a fine and complete specimen of a pearl oyster is met with. A good pearl is always a rarity, and it would not pay to fish for pearls alone if mother-of-pearl were not at the same time obtained. The Bedouins know the value of pearls only too well—they can often be bought cheaper in Europe. Here, however, they may sometimes be got at a low price in an underhand way, the slaves having secreted them and sold them behind their masters' backs. The yellow pearls, which are more highly prized in the East than in Europe, are said to belong to a different species of oyster —the *Meleagrina cocca*. The genus *Tridacna* also produces pearls, but these are ill-coloured and worthless. The very small pearls are pulverized by the natives and used as eye-powder.

A rational method of proceeding is not to be expected of the Bedouins. Thus they take quite young shells as well as old ones, since all add to the weight and bring money; and though one person were inclined to leave the smaller ones in order to let them grow larger by next year, he might be sure that some one else would take them in the interval. It is no wonder then that they are now obtained in smaller quantities than formerly, while the demand for them has increased. It is extremely rare for the divers to meet with injuries from the attacks of large fish. The hammer-headed shark and the saw-fish are most dreaded.

When diving cannot be carried on on account of the wind, the Bedouin occupies the time in fishing with the ring-net on the reef, the fish being salted and dried in the manner already alluded to. Such salted fish always form a portion of the cargo of a vessel engaged in the pearl-fishery. Turtle-fishing is also carried on as an accessory occupation, the kind chiefly caught being the *Chelonia imbricata*, which affords the valuable tortoise-shell; sirens also are harpooned and eaten.

The Bedouins sell their pearl-shells to the native merchants and other inhabitants of the towns, who follow them to their settlements, so great is the demand for their goods. Some of them have a regular contract with a merchant, who is called their *amil*, and who advances money to them, supplies them with rice, corn, &c., looks after their business matters in the town, provides lodging for them when there, and so forth, while they hand him over at a low rate all the shells they get. The merchant sends the goods on camels to the Nile, and then down this river to his agent in Cairo, or he brings them there himself, where they are bought up by European wholesale dealers. The Bedouins sell them at so much the hundred or the thousand, but in Cairo they are sold by weight. Three sorts are distinguished in commerce:— the large old *moghâs*, which have the layers of mother-of-pearl very thick, especially near the hinge; those of medium size; and those of small size (*adda*); a few very small ones are thrown in with every hundred. Of the larger-sized sort one to three double shells weigh an *oka* (that is about $2\frac{1}{5}$ lbs.); in 1874, when there was a great demand, the *oka* cost 12 to 15 government piastres according to size, that is to say, 2s. 6d. to 3s. Many of the shells have worm-holes bored through and through them, and are worthless. In other cases certain boring worms (?) have made a lodgment under the uppermost layer of the shell, penetrating from the border inwards, and producing a slight elevation which is known as the "water." This imperfection is of little consequence, as no perforation is made through the shell. If the mollusc has been dead for a considerable time the shell loses its mother-of-pearl, becomes of a dull chalky appearance, and is worthless. Among the ordinary pearl shells there is generally found another sort with a bluish border; this belongs to a different species, the already mentioned *Meleagrina cocca* (Arabic *bulbul*). It always remains small, and affords a mother-of-pearl that is of little use.

The black coral (*yûsr*), which belongs to the genus *Antipathes*, is also obtained by diving, but with greater difficulty than the pearl-oyster, as it is usually situated in very deep water, and is so firmly attached that it requires to be sawn off. The fleshy coating of this shrubby animal-plant is stripped off, and the black, ebony-like, horny axis is converted by native turners into rosaries, mouthpieces for pipes, and the like, and is rather high-priced. The red coral is not met with in this sea.

THE COAST BEDOUINS.

The coast Bedouins, of whom mention has repeatedly been made, are genuine Semites, pure Arabs, who, coming from Arabia, have settled at several places on the African coast of the Red Sea. These settlements, which are likewise ports for their light vessels, are called Gûeh and Safageh, one and two days' journey northwards from Koseir. They seem to have existed only for two or three generations, the oldest inhabitants saying that they crossed over from Arabia with their fathers. There are three tribes—Absi (plural Abs), Asmi (plural Anâsim), and Irêni (plural Irenât)—which prefer to live apart though they are not at enmity with each other, and even sometimes intermarry. The cause of their emigration from Arabia seems to have had something suspicious about it, since the Bedouins of Arabia call them "refuse" (in Arabic *achass min el arab*); still they continue to keep up a friendly intercourse with the Bedouins of the Arabian coast, who have similar settlements there (Gebel Hasan for instance), and occupy themselves in the same way. Their dialect is a genuine Bedouin dialect of Arabic. To the Ababdeh Bedouins, however, they remain strangers; and intermixture with them through marriage is never thought of, though they sometimes take wives from Koseir.

These Bedouins are exclusively engaged in seafaring pursuits on the coast, especially in pearl-fishing. Their habits are no longer nomadic, they do not even keep camels, but hire them when necessary from the Ababdeh. At most they have a few sheep and goats, but these they do not take out to pasture, but keep them and feed them at home. Their country is the sea and the coast, and they are still so far nomads in that they are absent from home a great part of the year. In the winter months, however, they return to their native tents at Gûeh or Safageh, where their families have meantime been keeping guard. In winter they occupy themselves in selling their pearl shells, and in felling and conveying in their vessels to the market at Koseir the shorawood which grows luxuriantly in the neighbourhood of their settlements. It is strange that, although they are skilful in catching the larger marine animals, such as sirens, turtles, &c., they are so poor hands at angling for fish that the Ababdeh in their neighbourhood, and even fishermen from Koseir, catch fish and sell them to them in exchange for corn, while the stranger who hopes to regale himself there with fish is disappointed. In modern times, when so many steamers have been wrecked on the innumerable reefs of the Red Sea, or have had to throw cargo overboard, the wreckage thrown up on the beach has been a rich source of income to these Bedouins. Through this and the fishery for pearl shells, which in recent years have risen immensely in price, these Bedouins have become very wealthy, and the goldsmith at Koseir finds his time more than taken up in manufacturing gold and silver ornaments for their women.

The chief food of these Bedouins is not millet, as among the Ababdeh, but rice. Of this unleavened cakes are made, either with or without fat; baking, properly so called, they

Tent of Coast Bedouins.

do not understand. They also indulge in flesh meat more frequently, and altogether do not live in such a miserable manner as the Ababdeh. Notwithstanding that they have adopted such a settled mode of life they live like their forefathers exclusively in tents, but these are far better, cleaner, and more habitable than the tents of the Ababdeh. The perpendicular side-walls and the sloping roof which are formed of a firm woollen stuff, are supported by posts and stretched by cords. Every tent has several divisions, the *divan*, in which the men meet, being strictly separated from the harim or chamber of the women.

The Bedouin of the coast exercises the genuine Arabic

hospitality. After the usual lengthy greeting coffee is brought for the guest as a first refreshment; but it would not be good manners to serve up the liquor ready made, the custom being to bring the beans raw, roast them, pound them, pour them into the pot, and boil them before the eyes of the guest, so that he may be convinced that the operation is properly performed.

After some time a luncheon, consisting, perhaps, of rice or sugared pancake, is served up, and is eaten of course in company with the host, who dips into the dish, or the leather vessel serving as dish, along with his guest. When a visit has lasted for some time, however, the guest, especially if he is somewhat of a stranger, is no longer hindered from consuming his own provisions, and the host, though on his own ground, is very glad to receive some coffee or tobacco from the stranger.

The guest sleeps in the divan of the tent, in which in cold weather he may have for companions the slaves, sheep, and goats of his host; the latter sleeps in his harim, which is separated from the rest of the tent by a curtain.

Safageh has about thirty, Gûeh about fifty tents, so that since each tent stands for a family the population of the former may be estimated at 100 to 150 persons, of the latter at 150 to 200. A considerable number of these consist of slaves, but the Arabs never mingle with the black race.

These coast Bedouins are skilful navigators, the experience of years making them acquainted with all the reefs on their portion of the coast, that is to say, between Ras Benâs and Gimsheh; they are, therefore, much sought for as pilots.

Between both their settlements and Koseir there is also a rather active traffic by land. The Bedouins often come by land to Koseir when they have business matters to arrange, and the people of Koseir give them wheat, rice, fat, and molasses in exchange for their pearl shells or the plundered goods of steamers. It is only large consignments that are sent by sea.

Administratively the coast Bedouins of Gûeh are under the jurisdiction of the sheik of the Ababdeh at Koseir, while those of Safageh are under the sheik of the Gimsheh-Ababdeh. Quarrels among each other, however, they settle themselves, and endeavour to avoid contact with the government as much as possible. When the latter adopts any regulation that does not please them they "go on strike," that is, they cease to bring in goods, or remove to another part of the coast where they are out of reach. We need hardly mention that they do not practise any art or industry, and no one in both settlements can even read or write. They celebrate their marriages with an amount of ceremony that always attracts guests from Koseir. The women are kept out of sight, at least before strangers. The dress of the men is a white or yellow shirt, their heads being covered with a large brightly-coloured cloth, which is picturesquely fastened with a woollen cord. The women wear mantles of white cotton or dark woollen cloth.

THE PILGRIMAGE TO MECCAH.

Ramadan is over, and men of all zones of the pious world of Islam make themselves ready to set out on a pilgrimage to the sacred, but by all reports very sinful city of Meccah, the centre of the world and of all worlds; for it very closely concerns the soul's health so to do. A tiny branch of the great stream that annually pours towards that point also touches our little sea-port town. As already mentioned this tributary was formerly of much greater volume; it now brings only a few hundreds or thousands of pilgrims. The main stream, however, does not seem to have become weaker either through want of faith or through the numerous sanitary obstacles interposed to its disease-pregnant course. The number of pilgrims that every year climb Arafat is said to amount to at least a hundred thousand, and if there are fewer than this the number is made up by angels in the guise of pilgrims! But even the pilgrimage, this grand institution of Islam, has not been able to withdraw itself from the influence of the age of steam. The well-to-do pilgrim, instead of traversing huge deserts in the midst of dangers and difficulties, and voyaging in a small sailing vessel for a month or more on the treacherous sea, can now have himself conveyed safely and comfortably on the wings of steam, so as to arrive close to his destination in a few days after leaving his native land, and the facilities for his return are equally great. The old routes are followed only by those who remain true to the old traditions, by those, therefore, who go in solemn procession from Cairo and Damascus through the desert, bearing with them the arks or *mahmel*, by those, also, who are afraid of the sea, and by those for whom the land journey is the shortest and most natural. Among people possessed of means the natives of Upper Egypt are now almost the only persons who take the route by Koseir and Jeddah, in addition to the pilgrims who cannot or will not pay the expensive steamer fares, and above all the mendicant pilgrims. At the time when the pilgrims are going or returning Koseir is filled with foreign figures, who have to encamp here for a time and await an opportunity for proceeding farther. On the outward journey vessels must be hired, passports visé'd, and clean bills of health obtained, the baggage must pass the custom-house, and a favourable wind has to be waited for. All this may occupy several weeks, and meantime all those arriving from the desert gradually assemble here. When the "great pilgrimage" occurs, that is, when the climbing of Mount Arafat falls on a Friday, which, according to the Mohammedan method of reckoning by lunar years, happens only every eleven years, the number of pilgrims assembling in the town is even yet considerable, since the pilgrimage is then considered specially blessed and the number of pilgrims is much larger than in other years. The town is now, as formerly, converted into a great pilgrim camp. On the return journey, also, the crowding is often great when a number of vessels arrive at once and there are not enough camels to carry the pilgrims farther. On such occasions there is often a scarcity both of water and provisions.

At these times there is a wonderful medley of races in the town. Here is the thrifty Fellah for instance; he loves to travel along with his whole family—wife, mother, grandmother, child, and child's child, down to the infant at the breast, all accompany him. With the exception of his house and land, which he leaves to be attended to by his brother, cousin, or neighbours, he takes the whole of his goods with him. His wife cooks his edibles for him, which are the produce of his own fields and are carried with him in

Fellah Pilgrims at Koseir.

sacks; for the provisions of the market he never longs: they cost money. He also takes his own camels and fodder along with him if possible, one of them carrying his whole family in a kind of frame fastened across its hump; he builds his grain bags round about him in the manner of a tent, and thus avoids paying for lodgings; he does everything for himself, and thus the expense of the journey is to him by no means extraordinary. The Fellah pilgrim has usually enough for the needs of the journey, and does not beg unless he has lost his money by the way or travels as a dervish. His behaviour is generally decorous. Until late in the night the Fellah women incessantly fill the town with a peculiar monotonous pilgrim song expressive of their longing after the Prophet and the holy places.

More simple in style is the Takruri or free negro from Darfur, Kordofan, and Takru, from the heart of the Soudan, and the farthest west where Islam prevails. He has seized his pilgrim staff earlier than the other pilgrims, years ago indeed, and wanders towards the rising sun almost naked, without money, without baggage, and on foot. He receives his daily bread from the gracious God, that is, he begs, or he hires himself out for some time as a labourer. Thus he moves slowly onwards farther and farther, always on foot; even the long and arid desert does not frighten him in his strength and health that nothing can impair. Others travel in companies accompanied by their wives, who, like the gypsies, carry their children in a sack on their backs. Thus they march into the town, singing their *la ilah ill Allah* to a Soudan melody, and the women quavering a Soudan air. The first visit they make is usually to the governor, who assigns them the court of a mosque as the place of their sojourn. They have also had for a long time an agent among the citizens of the town, a "sultan" who attends to them, and in return receives from each a small tribute. These blacks all beg, create a great deal of disturbance, and not unfrequently rise against the authorities. At night they amuse themselves in the fore-court of the mosque with strange dances, which have something of a religious character and correspond to the zikrs of the Arabs, but appear to be a combination of the old heathen dances with these. The black ladies, who by no means seek to conceal their charms, also take part in it and mingle their quavers in the barbaric airs of the Soudan. On such evenings there are always a few who fall into convulsions, for the devil is always inclined to take possession of the bodies of the blacks. The domesticated black slaves of the town also execute wild Soudanic dances from time to time, in which they rage, stamp, bellow, and beat drums, but all in harmlessness. Rich people do not come so often from the Soudan, especially from Darfur. Suakin is the chief place where the Soudanese take ship to go across. The Moghrebins, that is, the inhabitants of North-west Africa, who have strayed here from Marocco, Tunis, Tripoli, and the Sahara, are also a crew of sordid beggars. The classically handsome figures of the Bedouins of Algeria are less seldom seen, with their clear skins, their blazing eyes, their sharply-cut profile, their white woollen mantles, and their hoods closely wrapped round their heads. Their government (the French) does not allow them to wander without means into the wide world to become a burden upon their fellow-men; on the outward journey it is said they have to leave a portion of their travelling money at the French consulate in Egypt, in order that they may have something to fall back upon on their homeward journey. The barbaric governments of the other Mohammedan provinces of North-west Africa have never thought of such a thing. The pilgrims from these regions set out either without means or take an insufficient sum with them, which is spent on the way or at any rate at the gold-absorbing holy places, and if not all spent still on their way back they generally live by begging. Besides begging many of the Moghrebins make something by conjuring, writing curative mottoes and talismans, prophesying, astrology, and other mystic arts. In these matters the greatest confidence has long been placed in a "Moghrebi;" it is only the learned Fellati of the Soudan, "whose hand-writing is blessed" that can rival him. These Moghrebins are a quarrelsome, dangerous, and disorderly crew, dreaded by other people, and difficult to keep within bounds. Their devotional exercises or zikrs are still more barbarous than those of the negroes: the pious frenzy to which they excite themselves when practising them is not always harmless; and it sometimes happens that, in open day and in the public street, they seize a lamb, tear it to pieces with their teeth like beasts before it is quite dead, devour the still palpitating heart, drink the warm blood, and chew the tough fibres of the raw meat!

Besides these main contingents, the misery of all the rest

of the Mohammedan east meets here; the Turk, still proud
in his poverty, the broad-cheeked, thin-lipped Tartar or
Daghestani, the Bokharian, the "Suleimani," or East-Iran-
ian (?), the well-bred and talkative Syrian, the native of
Mesopotamia (Aerâk), the Caramanian or Anatolian, even
the meagre brown-skinned Mohammedan Hindu, but seldom
the heretical Persian. The Persians have, however, a consul at
Koseir, who every Friday hoists the Persian flag. It is only
the Persians who are regarded as heretics, being Shiites, all
the other peoples are orthodox, and the Mussulman, looking
at the state of matters among the Christians, is extraordinarily proud of this uniformity of faith, though certainly it
has not always existed in the lands of Islam.

Many of these pilgrims, whose route should be quite different, come this way in order to make a pilgrimage to Jerusalem, the third sacred place of pilgrimage; this is often done,
for instance, by the Christian inhabitants of Abyssinia and
the Jews of Yemen. Others, however, are simply carried
away by the stream, and come here without being able to say
why and wherefore. Gay and well supplied with money at
their departure, they land like a wreck cast up on the shore.
Their travelling companions, protectors, or relatives have been
lost in the crowd and confusion, or have been carried off by
death, and those left behind now attach themselves to some
band or other, in order that they may be able to continue
their journey, even though it be by a round-about way. The
fatigues undergone, the over-crowding, the dirt, exposure,
hunger, thirst, and sunstroke every year cause a number of
diseases, particularly dysentery, typhus, intermittent fever,
and virulent ulcers, often also deadly epidemics to which
many thousands succumb. It has been estimated that the
number of persons who have died on the pilgrimage since the
beginning of Mohammedanism is equal to the whole number
of Moslimin at present living (200,000,000 ?). The sick and
the aged are often cruelly left behind in the burning desert
by their own people, and die of hunger and thirst with no
one near them. The great pilgrim caravan moves pitilessly
onwards, and whoever remains behind is plundered by the

Bedouins, who are always lying in wait. But the Moslim who dies on the pilgrimage thinks little of death, being sure that he will immediately enter paradise.

When the holy places have been visited, the pilgrims who have money return home by steamer or with the pilgrim-caravan; those who are to go by way of Koseir embark in native sailing vessels at one of the Arabian sea-ports, such as Jeddah, Yemba, or Wudj. There the begging pilgrims also gather in crowds, and the respective governments compel every vessel that sets sail to take on board a quantum of this troublesome crew. These pilgrim-vessels are truly a wretched sight, no better than a slave vessel. A comparatively small vessel will carry 80 to 120 persons; men, women, and children, the sick and the healthy, animals and goods, are all packed and jumbled together in a disgusting manner, and the voyage in this confined space often lasts for several weeks. No wonder that death always reaps a rich harvest here. The dead are thrown overboard as soon as possible. The government provides the begging pilgrims with a supply of food enough to keep them from starvation, namely, biscuit or black bread simply dried, and during the whole of the long voyage they have nothing but this to live on, unless such of the passengers as are better off contribute something from their stores.

Arrived at the port of Koseir these wretched begging pilgrims, half starved and parched with thirst, pour through the streets and lanes of the town, and importunately demand an alms, knocking at the doors almost in a threatening manner. At the same time they sing a begging formula they have learned, some of them accompanying themselves on a primitive lute or dancing in their wonderful tattered costumes, and holding in their hand their bread-bag or a water-vessel, such as a cocoa-nut shell. They pass the night in the street, on the floor of a mosque, or in some ruinous shop. The sick lie down there too, and receive food and drink from compassionate souls. It is only when they are reduced to extremities that they make up their minds to allow themselves to be taken to the hospital, where they are cared for, and receive more suitable food and medicine; many have to be brought there by force.

But all the begging pilgrims are not really so poor. Many of them may be very well-to-do citizens at home, but here they act the begging pilgrim, partly from avarice, partly to pass themselves off for persons of superior holiness. When an inspection is made by the custom-house officers, or when one of these begging pilgrims has died, it is by no means rare for a roll of fine gold pieces to be found in his wallet, or sewed up in his clothes, or even in a bag between his thighs, though he had previously affirmed his poverty with the most solemn oaths. At the same time he will be clad in the filthiest rags, he will hunger and starve along with his companions for weeks, till reduced to a skeleton, will allow himself to be fed and carried gratis by the government, and will live the whole journey by begging.

The authorities never think of checking these parasitical on-hangers on the body of pilgrims, they rather encourage them. To be sure there is a clause in the sanitary regulations according to which the authorities can forbid the departure of persons entirely unprovided with means; but, like most ordinances that do not refer to money and taxation, it exists only on paper. Such begging pilgrims are not sent back before setting sail, but are imposed upon the first and most convenient vessel in order that the town may be rid of them as soon as possible. On the return journey, if they are put in quarantine, they are supplied with food and water; on the journey through the desert to the Nile valley they are handed over in half-dozens to the camel-drivers so that they may ride by turns, and for this the government pays the camel-drivers, giving the pilgrims also a supply of biscuit to take along with them. The sick are cared for in the hospital free. Sometimes, when the public health seems to demand it, and in order to guard against epidemics, the government sends steamers of its own to fetch these beggars from the Holy Land, and to convey them through the Suez Canal to their own countries.

A strange class of men are every year to be met with among the crowd of pilgrims of all nations; these are the travelling dervishes. Travelling, and making pilgrimages in particular, is their profession. They are always alone, without family and without companions. Many appear regularly every year at the time of the pilgrimage, and continue to do so all their lives. A few of them are learned men, and are often taken under protection and kept for weeks and months by wealthy and God-fearing individuals with a thirst for knowledge, till they go to some other place to receive similar treatment. Others are a kind of mendicant monks, who dress themselves in bizarre costumes, for example, a mantle consisting of an immense number of many coloured patches sewed together, with a towering head-covering or a cap something like a Jacobin's cap. A great many let the hair of their head grow long in order to distinguish them from other Moslimin, and wear a patriarchal beard; many go almost naked. They also exhibit some strange customs and peculiarities. For instance, one of them will run up and down the streets without uttering a word and without any object; another carries a club and beats his breast with it; a third from time to time shouts out the confession of faith, or the call to prayer, or a chapter of the Koran; a fourth, without any reason, from time to time works himself into an ecstasy (as in the zikrs) by repeating the name of Allah a thousand times, while he foams at the mouth and his eyes water; a fifth leads a crowd of children through the streets, with a flag in his hand, shouting out something or other which the children repeat in chorus. Many act the buffoon, and play all sorts of foolish pranks, but always in their sacred dresses. They do not take money, but only food and drink, in which they are very moderate; some of them gnaw bones they find on the street, and invite the passers-by to share with them. These persons venture to take great liberties, since they have a reputation for sanctity, and are regarded as *valis*. They seat themselves boldly in the place of honour in the divan of the rich, and high and low eagerly seek their blessing. Since they enjoy the special grace of God, God has denied them in this world the ordinary human reason, they are therefore without sin, and will be favoured in the next world; moreover, they can work

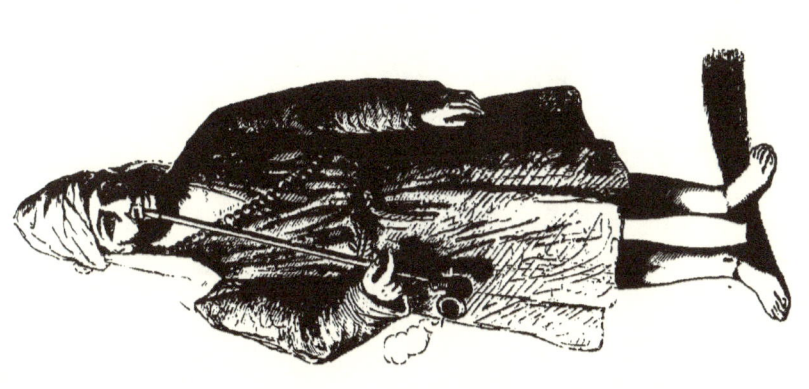

TRAVELLING DERVISH FROM THE FAYOUM.

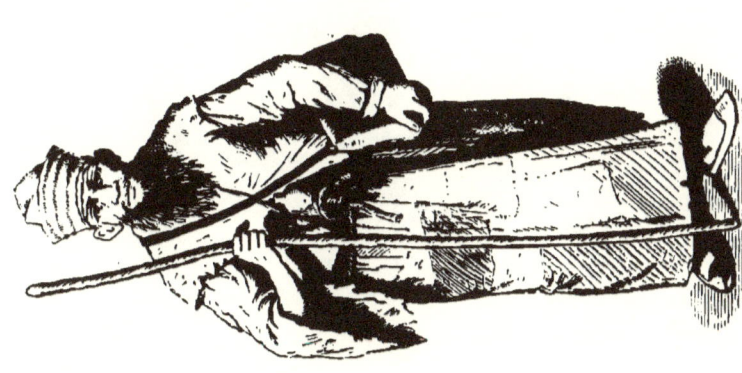

TRAVELLING DERVISH FROM KHORASAN.

TAKRURI OR FREE NEGRO OF DARFUR.

miracles even in this world or after their death. Generally speaking they do no one any harm, though their jokes are sometimes disagreeable enough. These men would afford an interesting study for a doctor of the insane. Their condition is that of a peculiar, harmless lunacy, or partial simplicity, perhaps caused by long-continued ecstacies. Some also are possibly mere pretenders.

The pilgrim season, however, does not bring merely sorrow and wretchedness; there is no want of amusements and sights worth seeing. It is very interesting to watch the crowd of people collected from all the zones of the earth, to note their behaviour and their dresses, to listen to their narratives and adventures, to go through the inns and the areas now converted into encampments, in doing which we may have an opportunity of looking more deeply into the large oriental eyes of many a foreign child of the fair sex; for when on the journey they are not so strict in veiling themselves.

We examine also the foreign utensils and goods which come to light under the inspection of the customs-officers, or which the pilgrim sells for a trifle through the broker—if he does not act as auctioneer himself—in order that he may be enabled to continue his journey. Here we may see weapons, books, perfumed woods, pieces of black coral, and rosaries made of it or of aloes wood, leathern and metal vessels filled with water from the famous Zemzem well, sheets of pictures giving views of the holy places, packets of sacred earth from Meccah or Medinah, dates from the tomb of the Prophet, toothpicks and other relics. Lastly, there meet here jugglers, athletes, musicians, male and female dancers, snake-charmers, conjurors, astrologers, story-tellers, poets, learned men and soothsayers, retail-dealers, and all kinds of handicraftsmen of all sorts and all countries. By working at their trades and occupations these earn at least enough to pay the expenses of the journey, while they at the same time obtain the blessing that belongs to those who have made the pilgrimage.

QUARANTINE.

Closely connected with the pilgrimage is the institution called quarantine. In the Egyptian ports of the Red Sea there were quarantine officers long ago, every vessel had to subject itself to a sanitary inspection, and in the time of epidemics, such as cholera, typhus, or small-pox, universal quarantine was imposed. But sanitary arrangements on the whole were incomplete, on the opposite coast people would hear nothing of sanitation, and certificates were never exhibited. Then came the cholera year 1865. Conveyed from India its source, and brought into fermentation by the huge multitude of people that were then engaged in the "great pilgrimage," the disease spread quickly over the whole world in spite of quarantine. It was brought to Suez by returning pilgrims, and thence travelled northwards, especially to the countries on the Mediterranean, as well as southwards by way of the Nile valley as far as the Soudan. After this evil year an international sanitary congress was held, as is well known, at Constantinople, for the purpose of consulting as to what measures should be adopted for guarding against and preventing the further progress of the devastating disease. An important resolution of this conference to compel the pilgrims to travel by land should have been put in force the following year, since the cholera again broke out among the pilgrims, although with less virulence. But the quarantine establishments were then defective in their organization, and that led to great confusion. The Egyptian sanitary authorities on the African coasts were strictly commanded to compel every pilgrim vessel to sheer off and withdraw to Tor on the Sinaitic peninsula, in order to undergo a quarantine there. To support this command a division of Turkish Bashi Bazouks was sent to Koseir. Whether the order to sail to Tor did not reach the vessels leaving the Turco-Arabic sea-ports, where a portion of them had already undergone a four weeks' quarantine, or whether they intentionally evaded it, we cannot say, but at all events one day eight pilgrim vessels appeared at once in the harbour of Koseir, crammed with more than

800 moneyless and starving human beings, a great many of them sick. With the passengers in this shocking state sailing immediately to Tor was out of the question, a brief space must at least be granted in order to provide them with a supply of provisions necessary for a voyage which, in the face of the prevailing north winds, might occupy three or more weeks. The total prohibition against landing was also broken through. But the pilgrims would have nothing to do with Tor, they would remain here, however long they should be kept in quarantine. Wringing their hands some of them begged for compassion, the others threatened. The provisions which were being put on board in view of the voyage ordered were partly thrown into the sea. When at last the captains were earnestly entreated to set sail, a general pilgrim-revolution arose; the pilgrims bound the sailors who were willing to obey, beat the captains, cut the ropes, took possession of the boats with the intention of landing, or jumped into the water to swim ashore. But the beach was already occupied by soldiers and watchmen, and the pilgrims who attempted to land were driven back. The authorities, however, saw the impossibility of executing the command of the government. To use firearms against pious pilgrims seemed a doubtful proceeding. And who could hinder such desperate men from landing at one of the uninhabited sherms, and returning by land or penetrating through the mountains into the Nile valley.

It was accordingly resolved to send a special messenger by dromedary to the nearest provincial town, and thence to telegraph the state of matters to the government in Cairo and Alexandria. This resolution gave hope and comfort to the pilgrims, who now remained quietly waiting. But the capital is a long way off in spite of the telegraph. The pilgrims had in the meantime to get their food and drink, and the latter especially was difficult to provide, while the supply of biscuits was soon exhausted, particularly as the number of pilgrims soon rose to 1300 by fresh arrivals of vessels every day. During the whole of this time the town was in arms, there was a constant dread lest the pilgrims should quit their large fleet and force their way into the town, soldiers and workmen kept guard night and day on the beach, keeping watch-fires burning and loudly challenging each other to give the watchword. At last—after thirteen weary days—the message was received that the pilgrims were to be allowed to land, but in quarantine, the proper quarantine to be held at Bir Amber, on the borders of the Nile valley, whither they were to be brought in travelling quarantine under an escort of soldiers. In the circumstances this intelligence naturally caused great joy. The pilgrims were now at least allowed to leave their prisons, the vessels, for the dry land. A week was still required, however, before all the pilgrims could be conveyed away by camels, and the difficulty of providing food, and particularly drink, caused fresh revolutionary scenes every day. Besides this, more than seventy sick persons—the most of them suffering from dysentery—lay scattered around polluting the air, while fresh cases of illness were being caused by the piercing rays of the sun above and the burning sand beneath, for the quarantine place is only fenced round with ropes and poles, straw huts having been provided only for the officials and the sick, and that not without difficulty.

Gradually sanitary arrangements grew to be better organized. Instead of the distant Tor the Egyptian sea-port El Wudj, situated on the Arabian coast, was chosen as being in every respect the most suitable quarantine place for all pilgrims, both those returning with the great caravan by land, and those going by sailing-vessels or steamers to Suez and Koseir. Every year during the time of the return of the pilgrims, quarantine is now held there for about two months after the Great Beiram, a special quarantine commission being sent there by the Egyptian government. If cholera is not prevalent it lasts only five days as a quarantine of observation; should a suspicious case of sickness occur it is prolonged. No vessel that leaves an Arabic harbour, not even the European steamers, is admitted at this time into the Egyptian harbours of Suez and Koseir if they have not passed through quarantine at El Wudj. At other times also, if a suspicious illness is notified from Arabia, quarantine is established there; thus, in 1874, when cases of the plague were said to have occurred in the country of Asir, and near Meccah, not at the pilgrim season, although most people denied the correctness of the report, vessels had for months to undergo quarantine for three weeks. According to circumstances vessels may be ordered for security to pass through a short subsequent quarantine in the Egyptian ports, or they may be discharged at once after a regular inspection by a medical man. At all the principal ports on the Red Sea there are now permanent sanitary officers who grant regular certificates, and the pilgrim caravans are accompanied by government doctors (of course Mohammedans), who have to send in reports on the general state of health of those under their care to the supreme sanitary authorities, and to take measures in serious cases. Since the terrible time experienced in 1865 Meccah itself has had a certain sanitary organization; numerous channels, for instance, are said to have been dug in order to carry away the blood and other remains of the sacrificed animals, the heaps of such matters having formerly polluted the air.

Will now the cholera and other epidemics be prevented in future from spreading by these important regulations? That an epidemic may be confined by quarantine regulations within a cordon or the walls of a lazaretto, that the methods of procedure prescribed, such as fumigating goods and papers with aromatic substances, or keeping at the distance of a gunshot from infected persons, are of great value there is very good reason to believe, especially in the case of cholera, which, by means of excrementitious matters, is capable of acting at some distance. But to carry out the system a number of quarantine officials and doctors are required, all of whom are exposed to the infection, which is also liable to be conveyed by provision sellers or by gossipping friends, not to mention the numerous possibilities of contagion through the carelessness or corruption of those appointed to see the regulations strictly carried out, and the repugnance of the fatalistic Arabs, physicians included, against all regulations of the kind. The only perfect safeguard against contagion would therefore be to prevent all communication whatever between a vessel and the shore, but of course this is impossible. On land it has been found decidedly advantageous to have several quarantine stations, all of which must be passed through, one after the other. The utility of this was proved some years ago when the cholera, in a virulent form, was spreading from the Soudan towards Upper Egypt; it was stopped at a third quarantine cordon on the southern frontier of Upper Egypt and did not invade the country itself. The detection of the disease by the medical men is also a matter of no small difficulty. It is not easy to perceive that a person is suffering from choleraic diarrhœa in its early stage, or to detect the beginnings of any disease the instant a vessel arrives and is inspected, particularly as the new-comers do everything in their power to avoid being recognized as ill and forced to go into quarantine. At the decisive moment a sick person will put on a cheerful air however ill he feels, he will even cut capers, and will chew a morsel put into his mouth as if he had a ravenous appetite; he considers it, in short, a patriotic duty to deceive the doctor and save his companions from quarantine. There is no use in putting questions, for the answers are certain to be false. To feel pulse and skin is not allowed, and the general appearance and tongue are the sole remaining criteria. A certain diagnosis, therefore, is only possible in cases of admitted illness.

Still the value of quarantine stations is not to be denied; they impede the movements and render slower the progress of those who carry the disease, which gradually becomes less and less virulent, while by the isolation of those attacked, which can only be brought about by a quarantine, so many sources of disease are kept apart from the general body. But quarantine inflicts severe wounds upon trade and navigation; even in the case of the small native vessels the fees that fall to be paid through a single quarantine often amount to as much as 100 francs, a large percentage of the total returns of a voyage, Of course quarantine causes the government also a great deal of expense, which is far from being covered by the fees. But why should the inhabitants of the maritime districts, whom it is sought to protect, be exempted, and the expenses fall upon the travellers and mariners already sufficiently annoyed by quarantine? If the expenses of quarantine were to be paid by a general tax on the country, the amount falling upon each individual would be very small. By the abolition of the quarantine fees many an incentive to corruption would be removed and the regulations more strictly observed, for the Egyptian does not dread loss of time but expense. But as things are, quarantine is universally regarded as an institution for taxation and extortion, and no one believes that it is of any real value in preventing the spread of epidemics.

CHAPTER VI.

THE NATURAL TREASURES OF THE RED SEA.

The arm of sea which springs from the great Indian Ocean and bears the name of Red Sea or Arabian Gulf is a genuine tropical sea, although it stretches northwards far beyond the tropic. Though it is separated from the Mediterranean Sea only by the isthmus of Suez, in the character of its animal life it is sharply distinguished from the former sea, and only a few cosmopolitan forms are common to both, a proof that in recent epochs at least there has been no communication between the two. Recently this neck of land has been cut through by the strong hand of man and the waters of the north have been wedded to those of the south. Perhaps a certain emigration and immigration of the animals of both seas may take place in time, but from their union up to the present time nothing of consequence on this subject has been made known. The conditions of life in both seas are still very different, and the canal lying between offers many hindrances.

We get up betimes in the morning in order to observe, in all its freshness, the active life that prevails in the warm and briny deep. And this is a very easy matter for us; we do not need to wade in mud and sand up to the middle, nor do we require Moses' rod to lay the sea dry; we simply wait until the moon passes over our heads or that of our antipodes. At such times the sea sinks a yard or sometimes two, and we can reach almost dryshod the rocky surface of the fringing or coast reef, which here, as a rule, is not separated from the shore by a lagoon. Over this we may venture a long way, as far as the edge, indeed, where the breakers are raging, without fear of being swallowed up like Pharaoh and his host by the billows of the returning flood.

The naturalist will do best to choose the summer months, especially those of the late summer. "When the Nile rises the sea falls," says the inhabitant of these parts. During this time, that is to say, especially before and at the autumnal equinox, the surface of the sea is at its lowest level at ebb tide. During the winter, on the other hand, from October to the vernal equinox, the sea never sinks far enough (except about the New-year) to expose the whole surface of the reef, though this is frequently the case in summer. This lowness of level, which is also noticeable at high water, may be a consequence of certain currents, or of the north winds that almost exclusively prevail at this time, and drive the waves southwards; it may partly also be due to evaporation, the sea being closely shut in by burning coasts, and having a dry and heated atmosphere above it.

ON THE SHORE.

The sea is still standing like a shallow lake above the surface of the reef, which, with a breadth of about a hundred paces, extends far along the shore; the powerless waves, their strength being broken on the slope of the reef, beat against the fearfully desolate sandy or rocky shore. The naturalist, however, finds it by no means so desolate; numerous bones of vertebrate animals, bleached shells, and branches of coral lie about, and these he picks up as he chips them out of the rocks into which the might of the eternal elements has baked them. He has no intention of adding these weather-worn and broken specimens to his collection, he wishes to compare them with others which he will obtain fresh and uninjured from the sea. Perhaps some of the forms may no longer exist as living forms, and in this case they must remain in the collection as evidence of the former existence of an extinct species. The shore on which we are wandering is under the influence of puzzling forces; it is rising while the sea is withdrawing, as already mentioned in Chap. IV. p. 234. The geologist calls this phenomenon "the secular elevation of the land."

But also living children of the sea display their activity on the arid coast. We never tire of watching the comic behaviour of the sand or mouse-crabs (*Ocypoda*), which run about in immense numbers on the sandy beach, especially on summer evenings. Beyond tide-mark, and often a considerable distance from the sea, but never so far as that the sand below is not moist, they dig burrows of the size of their bodies. They do not take long journeys by land like the West Indian land crabs (*Gecarcinus*). The holes penetrate for 3 or 4 feet either obliquely or in any direction, and are inhabited by a single crab, or by a pair of the same or of different sexes. The sand that falls down as the animal is digging is carried out between one of the nippers and an anterior foot, in which operation the hairbrush existing on the second pair of feet may be of service, the other side is left free and enables the animal to crawl out of the hole. On reaching the entrance the crab flings the sand to some little distance from the hole with a sudden jerk, and having performed its toilet by cleaning its jaws with its arms, as with a tooth-brush, slips back again into its dwelling. After an interval it reappears and acts in the same manner. The sand cast out gradually rises into a pyramid a span high, which the active crab climbs with each new parcel of sand, and dexterously forms the top into a fine point. A field containing a thousand of such pyramids gives ample testimony to this activity. Every act is carefully weighed and considered beforehand. When it comes out of its hole it remains standing, the feet on one side still within the threshold of its domicile; it then elevates its wary club-shaped eyes, assures itself of the state of matters in the vicinity, and if convinced of the absence of every danger, continues its work. The observer must, therefore, remain quite still at a little distance. It is not very easy to get hold of this shy and light-footed crab. It perceives us long before we can get near it, and scuttles off with inconceivable rapidity, always keeping one side foremost, towards its well-known dwelling; into this, however, it does not at once disappear, but remains on the threshold to take a survey, and having maliciously allowed the enemy to come quite close to it dives in at the last moment with the quickness of lightning. If we come upon it and intercept it when on one of its excursions, and at a distance from its hole, it eludes us by a hundred turns and crafty movements, running on occasion almost as well forward as sideways, and always making for the sea, by the waves of which it allows itself to be carried away, and in an instant has disappeared under the sandy bottom or in some hole in the rocks. If we prevent this by driving it away from the sea, it presses itself in despair in among the sand, throws a covering of sand over itself, and our eyes can often no longer distinguish the dull yellowish-gray carapace of the crab from the similarly coloured sand. We may find it again, however, and think there is no escape for it this time; but if we incautiously seize it we shall in all probability have to fling it from us, with a lively feeling of the effects of its sharp and powerful nippers on our fingers, so that after all we may ourselves give it its liberty. The simplest way is to throw a cloth over it, and this we do when, after some hard work, we dig it out of its deep hole in the sand.

The rock crabs (*Grapsus*), swarms of which enliven the shady rocks, walls, and stones near and in the sea, are no less clever. They are also very swift runners, but their forte is climbing and hiding. It is a trifle to them to clamber up and down perpendicular rocky walls 50 feet high, provided these have inequalities enough in which to insert their pointed claws and spiny feet. They also make game of the crab hunter, allowing him to lay his hand over them, but when he attempts to grasp them, suddenly darting off to hide in the nearest crevice. When they are caught it is somewhat difficult to tear them away from their position, and to avoid letting the hand be injured by their sharp claws. There is less reason to fear a pinch from their nippers, which are blunt and spoonshaped. It is advisable to use a cloth in laying hold of them too.

A hermit-crab, by name *Cœnobita rugosus*, is an important inhabitant of the coast. It might lay claim to be considered sacred, since, like the vulture, it clears the coast of carrion; but it is also an audacious thief, and with the utmost effront-

ery takes advantage of every unguarded moment in order
to attack the stores of the traveller. Its number is legion.
We hear behind a stone or rock a mysterious, rustling, clat-
tering sound. Stepping up to the spot we perceive a fish or
some other unfortunate creature of the deep, half reduced to
a skeleton, and closely covered with a great number of univalve shells of all shapes and sizes, but chiefly the round-
mouthed shell (*Turbo radiatus*). Everything is as still as a
mouse, and if we lift up or move the putrefying carcass all
the shells fall off. Some of them are fresh and clean, but the
majority are worn, damaged, and discoloured; in many of
them we notice a little round hole. Picking one up we see
that the mouth is tightly closed by the operculum, and thinking that it will suit our collection we keep it in our hand
and continue our investigation. In a little we feel a scratching and pinching in our hand; we open it, but see nothing
except the shell with its aperture tightly closed. But we
now notice some peculiarities about the operculum, and soon
find that it is no operculum at all, but the claws and anterior
parts of a crustacean—a pale-coloured crab with long feelers,
bulbous eyes, and well-sized nippers, but with only two loco-
motive feet visible on either side. We endeavour to rescue
it from its prison, but it draws itself back and remains
motionless again in its chamber. The last joints of its feet
and its nippers close together so as to form a smooth surface
shutting up the aperture. We try to pull the animal out,
but it will let its head and feet remain in our fingers rather
than allow us to get possession of the soft and shelless
hinder-part of its body, which is only brought to light by
smashing the shell. The animal can be made to crawl entirely
out by putting it in a liquid which is disagreeable to it,
such as putrid sea-water, or by the somewhat cruel joke of
heating the shell with a live coal or a cigar. As a rule it
lives in its shell like Diogenes in his tub (it is sometimes
called the Diogenes crab), runs about with it, not actively to
be sure, but unweariedly, and even climbs rocks, walls, and
trees. It often goes a long distance from the coast, and like
the mouse-crab digs for itself holes in the ground. These

holes are shallow, being only about half a foot deep, and are not left open like those of the crab just mentioned. The fishermen, who use it for bait, discover its dwelling by a circular or horse-shoe shaped linear depression round a little heap of loose sand or round a flat sandy surface. In selecting a shell as an abode in which it can protect its soft and easily injured tail, the crab seems to prefer those of which the original inhabitants have perished by some external cause, such as the piercing of the shell by other animals—a faculty possessed by many molluscs and annelids. This explains why so many of the dwellings inhabited by the hermit-crabs have holes in them.

Another hermit-crab is the black and yellow striped *Clibanarius signatus*, which also occurs in immense numbers. It also leaves the water to feed on putrefying substances with the previous species; but as it requires more moisture it does not go beyond the shore, nor does it dig holes for itself. It cannot place its feet so as to closely shut the aperture of its shell. It is not so large as the other species. Very young specimens inhabit the tiniest shells, especially the needle shells (*Cerithium*), and it does not despise worm tubes and other habitable articles. This species inhabits the reef up to the immediate vicinity of the surf, and is here one of the most abundant animals; it conceals itself among stones, and at spots which are first laid bare at ebb-tide, but still afford shade and moisture.

If we stir up the sand on the beach within flood-mark we shall be sure to find at the depth of a few inches some species of mollusc, such as the *Cytherea arabica*, with its many markings, or the *Mesodesma glabratum*, called by the natives "sea-egg." Under stones creeps a little flat crab, the thorax of which is marked with all shades from milk white to raven black. Once discovered, it does not know how to rescue itself like its relative and associate the grapsus and the little *Doto sulcatus*. In these localities, which, though wet, have yet a sufficiency of air, land-slaters and millepeds live a kind of amphibious life along with water-slaters, and molluscs, and salt-water worms. Flat-worms (*Planaria*) glide rapidly over the rock, and when cut in pieces each begins a separate life as lively as before. There lie a transparent white holothuria (*Synapta*), and an inextricable tangle of thread-worms (*Borlasia, Meckelia, Nemertes*). Where the soil of the beach is muddy, long, many-jointed rose-red sea-scolopendras wriggle; these are sought by the fisherman as bait for his hooks. Thousands of sea-fleas (*Orchestia*) hop out when we disturb the sea-weed on the beach or turn up the damp sand; they are as active as the little guests that derive their food from our bodies, and to bring a dozen of them together is a work of much patience and circumspection.

Until the reef is entirely uncovered with water we may contemplate the winged inhabitants of the air and water, who find their food (perhaps also their drink) in the briny deep. Only a few of them are permanent residents; in order to get a drink of fresh water they must fly a long distance into the mountains. Most of them are birds of passage, or perform at least local migrations. The flocks increase in spring and autumn, when the birds seek a more congenial climate. Then appear all kinds of plovers, snipes, herons, and water-hens, also ducks, cormorants, gannets, gulls, and sea-swallows. They are generally the same species as are found in the north in summer; but some are peculiar to these regions, or are more southerly forms, such as the courser (half a desert, half a shore bird), the giant heron, and the gulls and sea-swallows belonging to the Red Sea. The migrations last the whole winter through. In summer, on the other hand, bird-life in this region of the sea almost entirely ceases, the only birds remaining being the fishing eagle and a few plovers and sandpipers; even gulls, sea-swallows, and herons disappear. The vulture is a permanent shore-bird. The hyæna and the dog are nocturnal visitors to the shore and the reef.

PREPARING FOR A VISIT TO THE REEF.

The waters have begun to withdraw, the outermost shore-zone of the reef becomes passable, and we prepare to set foot on it. We could get on very well with boots, by choosing the higher and drier spots, and perhaps under favourable conditions might reach the edge of the reef next the sea without wetting more than our soles; but the sea-water, when assisted by the jagged surface of the rock, has a very destructive effect upon leather. Even water-boots of Russian leather are not to be recommended, as they soon burst and shrink; nor are the best patent soles of any service. Besides, who could repair this foreign foot-covering here? It is best then to follow the custom of the country, and put on sandals of a kind of leather prepared for holding water, and called *zemzemiyeh*. We also wind a piece of cloth turbanwise round the tasselled cap to prevent the rays of the sun from causing sun-stroke. In other respects we have no need to fear the heat; the sea-wind fans us and keeps us cool, becoming stronger the higher the sun rises; in this warm zone, indeed, the mid-day hours in summer cannot be spent more coolly and agreeably anywhere than on the reef and in the sea. We have an attendant with us carrying a basket divided into compartments, and containing tin cases of different sizes, a good steel hammer, and a steel chisel, also perhaps some hoop and other nets and a pair of pincers.

THE REEF.

Thus equipped we wander over the jagged rocky surface of the shore zone. A glance on the dark-coloured rock, which here is generally bare, teaches us that it is no ordinary rock, but a conglomerate formed of lime, shells, worm-tubes, and especially coral blocks, like the rocks that we saw from the land projecting towards the shore. The reef, a so-called coast-reef, commences immediately at the shore-line and extends seawards for 200 to 400 paces, presenting on the whole a flat surface, and running along the shore for miles without a break except opposite the entrance of some valley, which formerly brought down fresh water and sometimes does so still. When more closely examined, however, some differences of level present themselves. A slight elevation of the shore zone is generally noticeable, the consequence of which is that it is the portion first left dry when the tide is going out and last covered when the tide comes in. The main surface, which at ebb-tide is laid bare at once, besides presenting various projections and irregularities, embraces a number of larger and smaller depressions, the bottom of which becomes filled with sand, and in these hollows the water is retained even at ebb-tide, forming pools that receive the name of *kalaua* from the Arabs. Only in the shallowest depressions does the water evaporate. At ebb-tide, then, the reef presents the appearance of a net-work with lagunes as meshes, or when they communicate with each other, and are very numerous, a kind of archipelago is formed. At spots here and there large blocks of stone, similar to erratic blocks, rise from the surface of the reef. These are regarded by the common people as "petrified vessels." They are continuous with the surface of the reef, and consist of the same kind of rock as this and as the rocks on the shore. Other blocks are loose, not joined on to the rock below, and are moved about by the violence of the waves. In other respects the surface of the reef is, generally speaking, level. The formation of the reef surface is only to be explained by the hypothesis that the secular elevation of the land withdrew the coral polyps next the shore from their natural conditions of life, thus causing them to die out, while next the sea the formation of the coral was still continued. In the Red Sea, accordingly, this reef-formation is not brought about, as Darwin and Dana claim to have shown in the case of the islands of the Pacific, by the sinking, but on the contrary by the elevation of the sea bottom.

OUTER SHORE ZONE.

The outermost zone of the reef, as remarked above, enjoys the refreshing influence of the cool sea-water only for a few hours. In summer, therefore, the water in the small shallow pools becomes so hot at low tide as to compel the sudden withdrawal of the naked foot. On several days of the year high water can scarcely be noticed at all, the reef remains dry for one or two days, and this occurs, as a rule, once in winter and once in summer. When this takes place the temperature of the water in the pools becomes so high in summer and so low in winter that the animals living in them, fish in particular, die in great numbers. Some kinds of worms that are never seen at other times now come out of their deep lurking places in the sand and die on the surface. In this zone thrive gasteropodous molluscs of the genus Nerita, species of which are found also in brackish and in fresh water. One species (*Nerita polita*) has always a smooth and polished surface, that of another (*N. albicilla*), which exposes itself more to the sun and air, has generally a weather-worn appearance. The holes and crevices in the porous rock afford welcome hiding-places to the beckoning-crab (*Gelasimus tetragonon*). Its dwelling is here and not on the beach. It does not dig holes in the sand as is said to be the habit of the Brazilian species (*G. vocans*), but the sand that accumulates in its rocky dwelling through the rise of the tide is rejected in the form of small round balls as soon as the water withdraws again. It is not a particularly quick runner, and therefore cautiously remains in the neighbourhood of its abode. Its eyes are supported on long footstalks. The full-grown males carry an enormous nipping-claw compared with the animal's size and that of the other claw; the young ones have it of more moderate dimensions. The females have two small nipping-claws both of the same size. It is often said that they block up the entrance of their hole with this large claw, but this is not correct, as they almost always hold it before them when crawling in. A pair are generally found in the hole. When running the males have a habit of holding their claw aloft, or of keeping it before them like a boxer on guard, the powerful nippers always ready to pinch. It is this position that has gained for it the name of beckoning-crab.

A similar skulking mode of life is practised by the large-eyed crabs (*Macrophthalmus*) and the *Chlorodius Edwardsii*, which is common all over the reef, but especially here. The latter varies greatly in its colouring, and often has a cross and other figures painted on its back. Small black mussels (*Mytilus variabilis*) are attached by their beard (byssus) to the coral rock, and surround the pools and clefts in the rock like a wreath. As their valves gape slightly the fine green edge of their mantle may be seen. Under the stones and in the pools are found a multitude of periwinkles (*Littorina*), and large and small needle-shells (*Cerithium*), together with Nerita, as well as the hermit-crab that takes possession of their shells (*Clibanarius*). On ridges of the reef that have become dry and warm a Purpura, known as the horse-chestnut shell (*Purpura hippocastanum*), crawls about with the others just mentioned, while limpets (*Patella variegata*) and chitons as long as the finger (*Chiton spiniger*) have attached themselves by suction to the rock, surrounded by little balls of dirt formed by them. When taken by surprise they may easily be detached by a flat instrument and used as food (at least the Patella); but if the danger is noticed in time they stick so close that they cannot be removed without rupturing their bodies, unless a chisel is used and they are chipped off along with the piece of rock below them. The chitons roll themselves up like wood-lice after being detached. These two sorts of molluscs are not altogether condemned to one spot, they can crawl, though certainly not much more quickly than a plant grows. Being exposed to the rays of the sun and other influences, their shells have generally a coarse and worn surface, like the *Nerita albicilla*.

In the sandy pools we may observe, after the water has run off, a multitude of little hills with a crater-like hole in the top, from which at intervals a jet of water shoots; fine threads enveloped in sand radiate from all sides of the crater, and even from the sides of the hill, but they are only observed when they are being withdrawn. Occasionally a thick fleshy thread is projected from the crater. On digging into the hillock we find tubes winding about in many directions and formed of particles of sand and fragments of shells. The inhabitant of these is a tube-worm (*Terebella*); it withdraws so deeply into the sand that it can scarcely be got hold of. Out of one hole, in front of which there is an eddy in the water, we notice, after a little observation, a crab peering and waving its upper feelers; in another, out of which a stream of water is forced, we see the long feelers and the nippers of a small long-tailed crab, an Alpheus. Holes with small round balls in front of them belong, as already mentioned, to the beckoning-crab. Many little hillocks of sand are surrounded by a multitude of small sand-cylinders; these are the fragments of a long round sand column which is forced out at intervals through a hole in the hillock, like vermicelli from the tube in which it is formed; the author of this phenomenon cannot be laid hold of. There lies a smooth sheet of sand rolled up in a spiral form; after drying it crumbles at the slightest shock; it is the spawn of a species of Natica. The delicate thread-like algæ (*Phycoseris reticulata*) of the pools are covered with myriads of the spat of Cerithiums, Patellas, and other molluscs. The bright-green fronds of the Phycoseris swarm with the lively-coloured, almost microscopical, Cyclops. Almost the only fish found here during the ebb are young gobies and sea-leapers (*Salarias*), and the remarkable *Cyprinodon dispar*, belonging to the fresh-water family of the toothed-carps (*Cyprinodontidæ*). The male and female of the latter appear to be quite different fishes. When the pools threaten to dry up these fishes slip under stones and into crevices of the rock, or work their way over a piece of dry ground into hollows better filled with water. Here flourish also in many inlets of the sea thickets of the laurel-like shora shrub (*Avicennia officinalis*, see p. 240). But on the whole this part of the shore zone is poor in forms, and the animals that do exist withdraw from the investigator into the unfathomable clefts of the hard rock which lies below the slight deposit of sand that covers the bottom of the pools, and somewhat annoyed we proceed a little farther towards the sea.

THE INNER SHORE OR SEA-GRASS ZONE.

The pools among the rocks, which are either bare or covered with a blackish and red mucilaginous sea-weed, are now filled with greater quantities of sand, and on this soil grow green phanerogamous grasses of the family of the Naiadeæ (*Halodule australis, Halophila ovata* and *stipulacea,* and *Cymodocea ciliata*). By stripping the hand through them a person may fill it with the very small but pretty shells of the *Neritina Rangiana.* Here creep and feed sea-hares (*Aplysia*), pleurobranchs (*Pleurobranchus*), bubble-shells (*Bulla physis* and *B. ampulla*), the gigantic conical Dolabella, all sorts of sea-lemons (*Doris*), and other nudibranchiates (*Eolis*). A number of species of wing-shells (*Strombidæ*) knock against each other in hopping about; one of the commonest is *Strombus gibberulus,* white, with a beautiful carmine-red mouth. It is found thrown up in quantities on the beach. The allied finger-shell (*Pteroceras bryonia*) is almost a foot long, and its flesh is boiled and eaten. These Strombi cannot crawl, they can only hop by planting and suddenly extending the slender arm-like and very protrusible foot, which is furnished with a toothed and claw-like operculum. By this method of locomotion the animal can turn its shell round at pleasure, and hop forwards, backwards, and sideways.

Among the grasses small shrimp-like crabs—the transparent Palæmon, green Hippolyte, and almost microscopical Mysis—swim about. A species of shy-crab (*Calappa*) skulks along the sandy bottom and conceals itself under a slight covering of sand, pushing itself in sideways or backwards. Similar habits are displayed by the swimming crabs (*Lupea, Thalamita, Portunus, Matuta*). They are common enough also near the shore in the sandy and muddy bay forming the port, and conceal themselves under stones and mud. They are good runners, swimmers, diggers, and climbers, and can, in addition, escape from their pursuers by stirring up the mud and rendering the water turbid, an artifice which enables them to hide themselves or swim from the spot without being noticed. The rare grayish-green *Lupea Tranquebarica* is one of the largest crabs of this sea. Deep in the sand of the grassy pools, their byssus attached to the underlying rock, the brittle Pinnæ hide themselves, one species (*Pinna nigrina*) reaching a length of 2 feet. In these

THE INNER SHORE OR SEA-GRASS ZONE. 347

are found the celebrated Pinnotheres or pinna-guard, a little crustacean, which, in former times, when poets and singers rode upon dolphins, carefully guarded the entrance to the house of the blind pinna, but has now sunk to the level of a despicable parasite. If we clear out the sandy pools we find, besides various kinds of worms, a multitude of shells of the genera Tellina and Lucina come to light, though generally only the empty valves; the living shells are down in the cool depths. The rare watering-pot shell (*Aspergillum*) also lives here, as well as a peculiar annelid that hides itself in a conical tube. We had expected to find more bivalves here, but beyond the ones just mentioned and those named before, some Venus-shells (*Cytherea*), ark-shells (*Arca*), heart-shells (*Cardita*), and the like, there are not many regular bivalves in this sea. Both in number of species and of individuals this section stands far below the univalves or snails; the greater number of its forms belong to the Monomya, Heteromya, and Dimya with unequal valves.

On the rocky projections of the reef between the pools sit large numbers of limpets, chitons, and all the shore molluscs. Leaving the grassy pools the pear-shells (*Pirula*), large-sized navel-shells (*Natica*), sharp-pointed needle-shells (*Terebra*), in numerous species, and the hoop-net shells (*Nassa*), which can creep quickly for a snail, enjoy the sun and air. The majority of the clefts and crevices have been taken possession of by gray, brown, and black serpent-stars (*Ophiocoma erinaceus* and *scolopendrina*). They have some of their arms or rays at rest and extended to the upper surface of the rock, which is covered with a thin layer of water, while they sit with the others twined up together in the hole; or their arms are stretched out from the hole and rest in the numerous gaps in the rock. It is only when they feel themselves seized that they withdraw their arms, pressing these pliant and prickly appendages more and more firmly to the rock within the more their assailant pulls, till at last, instead of the body of the animal, a few fragments of its broken arms come away in the hands of the astonished star-fish hunter. Since they are constantly liable to the attacks of fishermen (for bait), fish, and other enemies, some of their rays are generally broken, or they exhibit various other marks of injury. The lost members soon sprout and grow again, but the new portions remain for some time not fully developed and brighter in colour than the articulations nearest the body disk. A collector who wishes complete Ophiuras must carefully pull the disk-formed body itself, or hew the animals out of the rock, or surprise them when detached and bathing themselves in the water.

Side by side with the serpent-stars star-shaped egg-urchins (*Echinometra lucunter*) peep out of narrow holes. When it depresses its prickles voluntarily this animal can easily slip out and in, like a vessel that lowers its mast when passing under a bridge. When it is violently pulled, however, it elevates its pretty strong prickles so as to make it even more than fill the hole, and all attempts to move it are useless, especially as the prickles, which are not very hard or sharp, do not afford a good grasp for the hand. These animals would seem often to bore holes in the rock for themselves.

THE DIVISION INTO ZONES.

Our division of the reef, from the shore seawards, into zones that correspond to various depths or horizons is not an arbitrary one. Here, to be sure, as in nature generally, there are no abrupt transitions. In different districts some one or other of the zones may be hardly represented at all or may preponderate over the others, and the inhabitants of one zone often extend into others. But these zones force themselves upon the notice of the explorer again and again; each has its own peculiar character and its prevailing species. New forms appear in the second zone that were not met with in the first; forms that have already occurred become rarer or vanish altogether; the external aspect changes.

STYLOPHORA OR CORALLINE ZONE.

We have passed through the shore zone, and have found an outer girdle, followed immediately by the subdivision of the sea-grass pools. The genera prevailing here we have seen to be Clibanarius, Gelasimus, Nerita, Litorina, Strombus and Pirula. The second chief zone begins with a moss-like alga which covers the rock, and forms, with the sand retained in the midst of its fronds, a soft covering which is far more comfortable for the feet than the sharp ridges of the shore zone. The pools are deeper and larger, filled with pure transparent water, and resembling wells. A characteristic feature is the occurrence of corallines, and the first appearance of corals, the earliest forms of the latter appearing in the branchy Stylophora. Everything that lives here loves pure, fresh, and not too hot water, which is not apt to be much disturbed. At many points this portion of the reef is somewhat higher than the shore zone, and wide stretches of it are almost entirely clear of water at every low tide, the only water remaining being that in the deep pools or wells. This elevation probably arises from the fact that the surf waves, already broken on the slope of the reef, are able to throw the foremost portion of their water up here and deposit their sand. In other places this zone lies lower, and even at low tide extends for the most part as a lake until close to the shore. But also in this case there generally remains behind the surf of the outer slope a higher surface which assures the quietness of this zone, and in spite of difference of appearance the moss-like Algæ, the Corallines, the Stylophoræ, and the forms to be mentioned below, at once tell us where we are. This portion of the reef we call the Stylophora zone. It may correspond to the quiet lagoons behind the reefs of the Pacific Ocean.

JOYS AND SORROWS OF THE NATURALIST.

The fauna and flora of the portion of the reef occupied by this coralline zone are exceedingly rich. For years one may make an excursion to this zone at every low tide, may wander over its soft surface, turn over and shatter the stones in the wells and the blocks of coral broken off the slope of the reef by the violence of the surf, strip off the Algæ, smash the living polypites, empty out sandy holes, and try to catch the fish;

something new will always be found. If a person, believing he has exhausted one district, examines another and more distant district, he will see essentially the same things. There is no use, therefore, in going very far, since the good things lie so near, but still the toil and trouble of larger excursions are not quite unrewarded. The naturalist is more easily satisfied than the treasure-seeker; the latter, on finding after a long search an old copper coin, throws it away in a rage, but the former, if he finds to-day a single species previously unknown to him, carries it home quite contented. During his investigations he will also have collected in his phials some species previously known to him, but rare; he will have made some new observation, or cleared up some phenomenon about which he was previously in the dark. His realm is boundless. To-day the fishes obtain the most of his attention, to-morrow he prefers the crustaceans; at one time he studies the mollusca, at another the annelida; and, lo! in the very cavity that he has examined a hundred times he finds some entirely new members of that kingdom to which to-day he has specially devoted himself. But what he takes with him he must always study thoroughly at home; he must know what he has, and what may still remain to be got, otherwise he will not distinguish nearly allied animals, but let them lie: an unscientific person, therefore, one who does not study, will never make a good collector. It would be very agreeable to be a specialist on this teeming sea, to devote one's whole life, as European naturalists do, to a small section of the boundless empire of Nature; but in truth the feelings rebel against this, and the strictest determination in this direction brought from the clear-headed North melts away amid the magnificence and variety of the tropic sea. Who could disregard this Doris so beautifully coloured, or simply put it in spirits without investigation in order to investigate the habits of a worm? Who could refuse a remarkably formed fish which a fisherman brings, and which, possibly, has never been seen by naturalists, simply because he is studying the crustacea alone? The fauna of this sea, although brought to light by many distinguished naturalists, is not yet, so to speak, ripe for one who is purely a specialist. Here the naturalist collects everything that comes into his hands, though paying more attention to those classes in which he is specially interested, and which are most richly represented, and he leaves it for time to decide when his labours are to be finished. Accordingly the naturalist remains banished for years, not merely for months, if he can prevail on himself to spend so much of his existence among the semi-barbarous inhabitants of these uncultivated tracts.

No occupation is free from its disagreeable concomitants, and the harmless role of the naturalist is no exception to the rule. Long rambles on the jagged surface of the reef, some excoriations of the skin, a sun-burned nose, an often very painful erythema on the naked arms and feet, exposed at once to both sun and salt-water, an involuntary bath, uncomfortable postures in investigating and observing, are trifles that the naturalist makes no account of. A gigantic eel, of serpentine aspect, that endeavours to bite his fingers and toes, a crab that pinches him with its claws till the blood comes, a fish that hovers round his naked feet and is provided with a half-poisonous sting, are bugbears that prove their reality but do not disturb his composure. But sometimes his patience and endurance are sorely tried. For example, on a warm summer afternoon the naturalist, after hammering and grubbing for hours on the reef, returns heavily laden to his house, and finds on his threshold a crowd of children who offer him the marine wonders that they have found to-day in greater numbers than at other times, while fishermen bring him some remarkable fishes. This very day the whole has, if possible, to be carefully examined, determined, taken note of, separated, washed, prepared, placed in spirits, or probably skinned and drawn, for in the aquarium the half would either eat each other or die and become putrid. Scarcely, however, is he begun when some other urgent business turns up, or a loquacious friend finds it necessary to waste his time, and to his chagrin he is interrupted in his self-imposed task. Or it may happen that he examines his treasure-chamber and observes with despair that cats, dogs, mice, and insects have taken anything but a benevolent interest in his collection.

Sometimes the out-door labours of the naturalist are altogether interrupted, as on the short, gloomy, and stormy days of winter when the ebb-tide uncovers as a rule only the highest projections of the reef, against which the stormy winds dash the waves; when the storm ripples the surface of the lagoons and wells, and the eye cannot penetrate their depths. It is not without an effort that the foot is now planted in the cool, not to say chilly water, and an arm that has been dipped shivers in the winter's breeze. Even the native fisherman avoids entering the sea that is now so reduced in temperature, and angles either on the shore or from a boat; or giving up all thoughts of catching fish, he mends his damaged nets at home. At such times the naturalist also must either give himself up to idleness, or examine, study, and arrange his collections, and see to the packing of them, this last and most difficult labour. And such days of leisure extend to weeks and months, until the sun rising higher in the heavens calms the sea and warms its waters.

THE INHABITANTS OF THE STYLOPHORA ZONE.

But we are standing in the Stylophora region. The abovementioned serpent-stars now spring forth in greater luxuriance than ever from every crevice; on the dry ridges of the reef living and extinct clam-shells are immured in the rock, their coarse shells, which resemble their mother soil, giving one rather the idea of chance-formed nodules than of organized beings. The *Clibanarius signatus* here gives place to a green-spotted hermit-crab, which now becomes the leading crustacean. The Neritas are now replaced by the pearly Pharaoh's shell (*Monodonta Pharaonis*), the most charming of this sea, and by elegant Columbellas or pigeon-shells, of which a black and yellow striped species (*C. mendicaria*) is collected for the market in order to be imported into the Soudan (see p. 309). Limpets and chitons, and the horse-chestnut shell are still everywhere to be met with here. In shallow pools the swelling tentacles of a sea-anemone (*Cereus*) of considerable size display themselves, the rest of the animal being generally invisible. If an attempt is made to seize it it withdraws itself quickly, and is found only at some depth, and after the surrounding sand and stones have been removed. It can only be obtained uninjured when it has fixed itself upon stones lying loose in the sand, and not upon the surface of the rock. In many of the smaller water holes another slender Actinia (*Heptaktis*), similar to the Edwardsia, stands upright and displays its starry crown; it withdraws itself even deeper, and is still more difficult to dig out of its narrow hole.

LIFE IN THE POOLS.

We lift up a stone that lies loose in one of the well-like pools. How it teems with life both externally and internally! Over its surface move quickly great numbers of the pretty univalves known as Stomatellæ, with their varying markings and colours; we saw these also in the sea-grass pools of the previous zone. Here sit also highly coloured sea-lemons (*Doris*), with their branchy waving anal branchiæ, yellowish red Pleurobranchi, small five-lobed disc-stars (*Asteriscus*), needle-shells (*Cerithium*), pigeon-shells (*Columbella*), tower-shells (*Pleurotoma*), and so-called shore-shells (*Eulima, Rissoa*); among bivalves may be seen small wing-shells (*Avicula*), pouch-shells (*Perna*), and young pearl-shells (*Meleagrina*), as well as ark-shells (*Arca*) and mussels, attached by their byssus, and everywhere oysters are attached to and growing on the rock, sometimes planted one above another. The latter are generally too small to be worth the trouble of picking them off and eating them. Besides, the native-born inhabitants consider oyster-eating as a barbarous practice. The old pearl-shells, with their celebrated oriental pearls, occur at greater depths, and are obtained, as already mentioned, by diving.

And the porous interior of the stone, which may often be broken up by the hand! Not an opening in it but is occupied. The most important and preponderating tenant here also is the serpent-star (*Ophiocoma erinaceus*). It rapidly detaches itself from its lurking-place when this is broken into, allows itself to fall, and creeps into the first suitable hole it can find. This species is associated here with another species, the *Ophiocoma Valenciæ*, somewhat more slender and spotted with green, and with a very small reddish scaly-star (*Ophiolepis*). Green or brown spotted grasshopper crabs (*Gonodactylus gonagra*), the length of one's finger, make their appearance, but draw back and make haste to get out of the way as soon as the explorer notices them. They run quickly on the dry land, are adepts at hiding themselves, and if they fall into the water they paddle away, shooting rapidly along by a series of jerks. When they are seized they bend themselves round, make their large nipping claws fly out from their body with an audible noise, and dig them into the fingers of their persecutor, who lets go his booty more from astonishment than pain. Of similar habits are the already-mentioned small long-tailed crabs (*Alpheus*), the species of which are very numerous, and generally have fixed abodes. On the stones here the *Alpheus Edwardsii* is the prevailing form. The joints that bend inwards the disproportionately large nipping claws are very tender, and the latter are detached with the slightest pull; in catching the animals, therefore, they are not to be laid hold of by these.

In the blocks of stone there also conceal themselves those small or middle-sized crustaceans in which the Red Sea is so rich, belonging to the genera Zozymus, Actæa, Actæodes, Pilodius, Actumnus, Chlorodius, Pilumnus, &c. The most common among them are the hairy *Actæa hirsutissima* and *Actæodes tomentosus*. Motionless sponges, lively coloured simple and compound ascidians, and the cell-colonies of the Bryozoa form with corallines and nullipores brightly coloured coverings, disguises, and ornaments. The tiny mussel-like or coin-shaped calcareous shells of the Rhizopoda or Foraminifera, of which a considerable proportion of the sea-sand consists, cover the surfaces of the stone like white points or dots, while the little tubes of the tube-worms (*Serpula*) form wavy streaks on it; the serpentine dwellings of the worm-shells (*Vermetus*) penetrate the block in all directions. In the smallest vacancies and passages of the labyrinth Annelidæ, Sipunculidæ, and Nemertinæ have established themselves, whether by simply crawling into holes already existing or excavating them in the stone for themselves.

Some worms, such as Clymene and Terebella, build their dwellings by cementing together fragments of bivalve shells, grains of sand, and shells of foraminifera, and retain possession of these until their dwellings are destroyed by violence. Others, the predaceous worms, namely, employ the holes merely as hiding-places, and seek their prey abroad. A worm of considerable size often met with (*Notopygus*) at the least touch brings into play its stings, which resemble silky tufts; these bore with their barbed points into the skin of the person touching it, and produce a sharp stinging pain. Flat annulose worms with "wings," or imbricated worms of a brick red or green colour (*Polynoe*), attach themselves to the stones as if by the force of suction, like the limpets. A large round rose-coloured annelid (*Dasybranchus*) lies in the rock wound up in a clew, and almost always gives off pieces of its body when it is pulled or even disturbed, like the ribbon-worms (*Nemertes*). Still more sensitive are the nimble Syllis, each joint of which gives out in the darkness, and often even in the daytime, a splendid green or blue light. Like the flat-worms (*Planarida*), these live when divided into pieces, each piece commencing a separate existence.

The upper surface of the rocks in these pools is generally covered with shaggy sea-weed, among which live small amphipodous crustaceans, as well as crabs with remarkable beaked carapaces belonging to such genera as Menæthius, Pisa, Cyclax, Huenia, &c. The uneven or hairy surface of the carapace and feet of these forms is covered with a flourishing growth of sea-weed or grasses, or if clean and smooth it takes on the colour of the plants among which these crabs live, and in one and the same species will vary from dark-brown to emerald-green. From the sand that lies scattered among the sea-weeds project crabs (*Micippe*) of a hideous form and grayish colour, scarcely to be recognized as living creatures,—so ugly, indeed, that in an æsthetic system of classification they would be at the bottom of the scale when compared with other representatives of the animal kingdom. These animals that take on an appearance assimilating them to their surroundings are surpassed in cunning by the woolly crab (*Dromia*), which covers the naked parts of its somewhat hairy back with a piece of sponge bent into shape or a frond of sea-weed which the far extended hind-foot has constantly to keep in position, and thus the animal deceives its greedy enemies by counterfeiting the appearance of an object which they do not use as food.

A NOCTURNAL VISIT TO THE REEF.

A nocturnal promenade on the reef at ebb-tide, when the stick stirs up a thousand sparks in the pools, and every footstep leaves a phosphorous track behind, is truly a wonderful experience. This phosphorescence is mainly due to the destruction of worms or gelatinous animals of a very low organization (*Noctiluca*), and doubtless also to scattered particles of animal matter of various kinds in a state of decay. When the surface of the sea is thickly covered with such animalcula over a considerable area the celebrated "luminosity of the sea" is produced. It is well known that when it is filtered, and the animalcules thus removed, the sea-water is no longer luminous. Here and there, too, at a greater or lesser depth, slowly swims a large luminous body which proves to be a medusa; the great cat-like eyes of the Priacanthus also gleam upwards; and large shining balls probably belonging to the corals appear.

A BLOCK OF STONE.

A huge block of stone which has been detached by mighty storm-waves or by the hand of man from the region of the reef-slope, and has been rolled into this quieter zone, rests in a slight depression of the reef, the edges of which now afford it a secure support. Its upper surface, only occasionally washed by the waves at high water, rises naked, gray, and dry above the surface. On this surface needle-shells, shore-shells (*Eulima, Rissoa*), and tiny hermit-crabs sun themselves, and the small but active rock-crab (*Nautilograpsus minutus*) clambers about. The last occurs in the greatest abundance over the whole of this zone where it is laid dry, popping out of one hole and into another; it is the representative here of the larger Grapsus of the shore. If we examine the holes and crevices of the block that still remain under water, a few small fishes dart out, chiefly belonging to the families of blennies and gobies (*Salarias, Blennius, Gobius, Eleotris*), while small and often strangely-shaped long-tailed decapods also hop into the light of day (*Palæmon, Lysmata, Hippolyte, Athanas*). The sides of the crevices are behung with hairy trumpet-shells (*Tritonium pileare*), frog-shells (*Ranella*), sea-ears (*Haliotis*), small sea-cucumbers (*Holothuria* and *Sporadipus*), and ark-shells (*Arca*); here, too, may be obtained in particular abundance the inexhaustible sea-lemons (*Doris*), already mentioned repeatedly. Oysters, ascidians, and sponges cover and colour the walls of the clefts. One after another certain bodies let themselves fall down into the water; these are the inevitable serpent-stars (*Ophiocoma erinaceus*), which are also accompanied by certain other species (*Ophiocoma elegans* and *Valenciæ*), by a scaly serpent-star (*Ophiolepis Cincta*), the already-mentioned egg-urchin (*Echinometra*), and common apple-like sea-urchins (*Echinus*) either white or brightly coloured. If we roll the stone over we will often find, in addition to the above-mentioned creatures, some very large-sized lobsters (*Palinurus*). The latter, however, are best caught at night when they leave their lurking-places. Such stones also afford a hiding-place for the brownish-red octopus or sea-polyp, which, when discovered, swims off at once, and if the danger is imminent discolours the water with its ink. It is not easy to master this powerful and slippery creature; it is almost impossible to bear the clinging of its sucking arms to the skin. Under the block we are sure to find also some beautiful though common porcelain-shells (*Cypræa*). Of these there are in this sea more than a dozen species, from the large marketable

Cyprœa pantherina or panther-shell, to the small *Cyprœa trivia*. With these the cone-shells (*Conus*), which are found from a line to a span in length, vie in variety, and in some cases also in beauty. Provided with a strong shell these sluggish animals withstand the assaults of the waves as well as attacks from other quarters. They love the hottest water, and therefore seldom conceal themselves at low tide, but lie exposed and almost motionless in small shallow depressions in the sand.

REEF-POOLS.

Let us give up work for a time, and gaze quietly into one of the 2 to 4 feet deep pools or wells. The circular edges of these are overgrown with algæ of all kinds—flat and crust-like, high and bushy, soft and watery, cartilaginous, or hard as a stone, green, brown, and reddish, moss-like or fern-like, fruit-bearing and fruitless. Here and there sprouts the coral known as Stylophora, yellowish-brown or reddish in colour, in many cases small and slender, but forming stronger and broader stony bushes the nearer it approaches the breakers and the open sea. While in the cells of the upper branches life is exuberant, and new matter is rapidly formed, the coral animals die out gradually towards the root, and dark, dirty algæ and corallines cover the extinct generations like a winding-sheet. Between the walls of the pools we see zigzags and waves, some of them a span and a half long, blue, green, or spotted with bright brown, gleaming out in a wonderful manner from beneath the water; they belong to the mantle of the large Tridacna, which, fixed in some crevice of the rock, opens its valves very readily. Half hidden under the overhanging walls of the pools lie deep-black gleaming spheres, from which radiate lances a span long and as fine as a needle, while between these appear sky-blue gleaming lines and points running perpendicularly over the surface of the sphere. Above, at one of the poles of the sphere, a black club with a cinnabar-red extremity turns round. This is the diadem sea-urchin (*Diadema Savignyi*), and the revolving club its rectum. Raised and enlarged by the transparent covering of water above it, this creature affords, with all these attractions, as beautiful a sight as its pointed, brittle spines, with their almost microscopical circle of prickles, produce violent burning pains when they have penetrated the skin of the fingers. The long spines remain always under water, and accordingly the body lies at a certain depth. Unfortunately the spines fall on drying, and are very difficult to keep uninjured, so that these animals are little adapted to transportation. The bottom of the pool is covered with loose stones of various sizes with sand between, and here, too, there sometimes rise phanerogamous grasses, algæ, and corals. This is where the sea-urchins (*Echinodermata*) are found in greatest abundance. Here, stretched out openly, lies comfortably at rest, a sea-cucumber (*Holothuria vagabunda*) which appears black, but, as the stain on the fingers that touch it testifies, is in reality purplish-black; it is surrounded by grains of sand either single or closely adhering together, and grows to the length of two spans. Another and still larger Holothuria, with great yellow lateral spots, from its plasticity appears quite a prodigy, in turns assuming a sausage shape or that of a disc or loaf of bread. All these holothurias are disposed to commit suicide; as soon as they are withdrawn from their usual conditions of life they force their intestines out at their anal opening, diffusing at the same time a rank disagreeable smell, or they divest themselves of their epidermis only, a proceeding which brings about their dissolution with equal rapidity. The black species of holothurias are so rigid and motionless that they are readily confounded with the species of bathing sponge that occurs here, which is quite black in its fresh state, and assumes all possible forms. The sponges of commerce are yellowish or gray in colour because they have been subjected to repeated washings and bleachings. Here we see also the Synapta, which at one time resembles a water-skin filled with water, at another hanks in its body at intervals, so as to make it resemble the large intestine in man, and according to the extent of the contraction it subjects itself to, appears as a wide bag the length of one's arm, or as a thin cord. When touched by the fingers its upper surface clings disagreeably to the skin, by means of little anchor-shaped projections. It can cover itself up with sand and rubbish on occasion. In its company are found also various kinds of beautiful echinodermata, in some cases lying exposed, in others under stones or in crevices of the rock; we may mention the "bride of the sea" or the comb-star (*Asteropecten*), the sea-turban (*Cidaris*), the shield-urchin (*Clypeaster*), and the warty-star (*Acrocladia mamillata*), as well as the *Ophidiaster Ehrenbergi*, which, from the abortion of individual arms, often assumes singular shapes, and the Scytaster, which is of a beautiful scarlet colour, like the star of some order of knighthood, but unfortunately soon fades.

FISH OF THE POOLS.

As in the shore zone the fish in these pools still continue to consist chiefly of gobies and blennies. These fish are very cautious and cunning, and on the approach of any person conceal themselves immediately. It is only when one approaches slowly and seats himself quietly that they allow themselves to be looked at, as they nibble and feed upon the sea-weed, or half swimming half leaping dart this way and that on the surface of the water, sometimes also slipping into crevices and worm-holes, and roguishly showing their heads peeping out; while, at the last extremity of danger, as we have seen in the case of various other animals, they spring out of their pool and scramble somehow over the dry ground into another. The short arm-like and stunted ventral fins may stand these leaping fishes in good stead when they engage in such gymnastic feats. The best leaper is the *Salarias tridactylus*. In these pools we also meet with several of the finely-coloured coral-fish of the family of the ctenoid-scaled labroid or wrasse-like fishes (*Labroidei*, *Ctenoidei*, or *Pomacentridæ*), especially young Glyphisodons, gray or black and yellow striped, and the small golden Colibri among fishes, the *Glyphisodon antjerius*, with its gleaming blue or green dorsal stripe. These small fishes are shy and difficult to catch. Small silvery fishes, scarcely an inch in length (*Myxus*), keep circling about constantly at the surface of the water, and rival in brilliance the ripples that glance under the rays of the sun. Here we see a serpent-like creature winding through the pool and hiding itself in a crevice, from which it peeps out after a little with its long-snouted head, and gives a steady gaze. It is no serpent, however, only an eel, but the pet aversion of the reef-fisherman for all that. From pure enmity the natives condemn to death every individual they meet with; to eat them they could never bring themselves. These creatures can also wriggle their way very well over dry ground.

FAUNA OF THE STYLOPHORA BUSHES.

A piece of work still remains to be done, one of the most profitable of all the labours that can be carried on on the reef, viz. to disentangle and break down the corals known by the name of Stylophora. The spaces between the branches and twigs of these are selected as places of abode by marine creatures of all kinds, but more particularly by small crabs and other crustaceans. Besides many of the sorts that we have already noted as inhabiting the stones of the pools (such as Gonodactylus, Alpheus, Actæa, Zozymus, Chlorodius, besides Columbella, Cerithium, small Cones, Ascidians, and sponges) there lives here a peculiar and characteristic fauna which can be met with scarcely anywhere else. It consists chiefly of certain species of small square-shelled crabs belonging to the genus Trapezia, which cling so closely with their claws to the branches of the corals, or climb about among them so cleverly that a person can get hold of them only by breaking down the corals. Here also sits the slimy and sluggish crab Cymo, which adheres still more firmly to the corals. The observer will seldom miss the small long-tailed crabs, Harpilius, Palæmon, Athanas, the fantastically ornamented Hippolyte, and especially a bright red Alpheus. Here also the small univalve *Purpura madreporarum* makes for itself a small protuberance, on which it sits closely adhering. The serpent-stars so often mentioned (*Ophiocoma erinaceus* and

Scolopendrina) are here remarkably rare; instead of these we find in abundance the black and yellow *Ophiocoma elegans*, and the green *Ophiocoma Valenciœ*. If we lift up one of these bushes quickly and let the brittle mass fall on the ground and break in pieces, a multitude of small fishes are sure to hop out, such as Eleotris and Gobiosoma, and the *Gobius echinocephalus*, which is a form very characteristic of these bushes. It is not an easy matter to get one's hands on all these little creatures at the right time and in the right place, especially the crabs. Unless caution is employed the collector will see with sorrow that these have suffered the loss of an arm or a feeler. When the branches of the corals are broken, in the central mass of a great many, indeed the most of them, a flattish cavity is seen, which a date-shell fills so completely as to have but very little room to move. Only a comparatively small aperture leads from the outside into this strange abode.

TRANSITION OR PRÆ-CORAL REGION.

We move across the reef a little farther in the direction of the sea, and enter upon a region which bears to the Stylophora zone the same relationship as the sea-grass zone to the shore zone, that is, it is a transition district. Its external appearance is still essentially the same, only this region is almost always covered by the sea, and can only be walked upon at the very low tides of the after-summer. The water is in greater commotion, and serves as the fresh source of an active coral-life; the waves of the surf reach as far as this, but their strength is already broken on the edge of the reef. The Stylophora corals continue to prevail universally, and thrive still better than nearer the land. The other corallines generally form layers, spheres, and protuberances, which, like a frieze, adorn the borders of the pools that now become deeper and deeper, or they grow up from the bottom of the pools, or spring here and there from the upper surface of the reef. To this region belong many star-corals (*Heliastræa, Solenastræa, Leptastræa*), mesh-corals (*Porites*), honey-comb corals (*Favia*), brain-corals (*Mœandrina*), many millepore corals (*Millepora*), and the well-known organ-pipe coral (*Tubipora*), with its purplish-red stone pipes. The rest of the fauna of this region is characterized by a mingling of the fauna of the previous with that of the following zone.

CORAL ZONE PROPER OR SURF ZONE.

The appearance and conformation of the reef now show a remarkable change. The ground is now to some extent converted into a slippery sea-weed steppe, and the naked feet, as they slip among the luxuriant vegetation, are everywhere threatened by the sharp edges of the apertures of the worm-shells, the tubes of which grow as it were in a piece with the rock. Among the plants we are struck by a sea-weed that gleams with a blue colour; but when it is withdrawn from the water the gleaming ceases, and, like most other sea-weeds, it appears brown. The pools now become deeper, and often form abysses with overhanging edges, to the bottom of which the eye cannot penetrate. These abysses have often subterranean communications with one another and the open sea, and this portion of the reef for the most part manifests itself as the rocky covering of a grand system of caves opening to the upper world by clefts and circular crater-like holes. The swell and heaving of the open sea, though broken to some extent, is continued through these ocean caves, and produces in the openings of the rock an alternate rise and fall of the water at regular intervals, combined with a frightful hollow gurgling and hissing. When the sea is at rest, however, the water in these dreadful abysses also remains at rest, and from some secure stand-point on the reef the eye can penetrate unimpeded far down into the transparent depths. Nowhere can one contemplate the life of the corals and what belongs to it more quietly and comfortably than here, although he has to lie on his belly—a trifling matter for the naturalist—and hold his magnifying-glass at the point of his nose above a coral bush. Such days, however, when the tide is so low as to lay the reef quite bare even to the outer edge, and when the wind at the same time is still, are extremely rare, and do not occur even once a year. In order to examine the coral world on the large scale it is better to make use of a boat. For the present we only remark that on the accessible portion of the surf zone the madrepore coral has become the prevailing coral, without, however, completely crushing out the Stylophora, and we take advantage of the time during which the reef is uncovered to investigate the remaining fauna.

FAUNA OF THE SURF ZONE.

The serpent-star (*Ophiocoma erinaceus*) has now entirely disappeared, and instead of it we find curling about among the rocks the already-mentioned *Ophiocoma Valenciæ* and other genera of serpent-stars, such as Ophiothrix and Ophionyx. The green-spotted hermit-crab is still also found, but never the *Clibanarius signatus*. On the other hand, many miniature species of this genus of the Paguri are common. A giant species (*Pagurus tinctor*) is often found in large univalve shells, such as the tun-shell (*Dolium*) or the triton's horn (*Tritonium*), on the outside of which there is regularly seated a certain kind of sea-anemone (*Adamsia*), sometimes in large numbers, while between the anemones are frequently shells of the family Capuloidæ. Here, therefore, we see a colony of several different creatures living together. Between the two regular inhabitants of these shells there is a remarkable bond of connection. With regard to the northern species Mr. Gosse has made the interesting discovery that the crab lifts with its nipping claws the sea-anemone on to the shells in which it wishes to live, so that the latter animal must be of service to it in some respect or other, though we do not yet know in what. The sea-anemone seems to make use of its dwelling-place as a means of locomotion, so that it may be carried to places where there is food both for it and the crab, or may also, so to speak, enjoy change of air; the crab, on the other hand, may allow the actinia to catch parasites that would annoy it, though this certainly remains to be proved. The Adamsia cannot live free, however, and is found sometimes on stones, though less frequently than on the shells inhabited by the hermit-crab. At small depths and in clefts lie large and small species of the genera Ricinula, Fasciolaria, Turbinella (chank-shells), Turbo and Trochus (angular and round-mouthed top-shells), all with thick shells which, without protection, set at nought the breakers. A large and beautiful blue arcuated crab (*Zozymus æneus*) is common here, exposing itself without protection to the wash of the surf. The higher rocks, which on the retiring of the waves are periodically exposed to the air, are often covered with a multitude of sea-acorns (*Balanus*). Under the covering of sea-weed new forms of pointed crabs conceal themselves (*Cyclax, Stenocinops, Pseudomicippe*). Over crevices in the rock gigantic sea-anemones, such as *Discosoma giganteum*, spread themselves out along with the social *Thalassianthus aster;* it is only with difficulty that they can be extracted from the rock. The rare gigantic annelid, *Eunice gigantea*, here occasionally shows itself, rapidly crawling out of sight again like a serpent, and the collector considers it quite a master-stroke to lay hands on it before it disappears into its unfathomable hiding-places.

The best spots for the collector here also are under stones and between the branches of the corals. Loose stones that would only require to be turned over in order to get at the booty beneath are not found here at all, being hurled back to the Stylophora zone by the force of the waves, or flung into the depths of the rocky chasms. To be sure numerous blocks of stone with masses of living and growing coral lie mingled together in wild confusion, but all are solidly attached to the rock and to one another, no doubt by the action of the superabundant calcareous elements contained in the sea-water, which supplies the material of which the coral rocks are built. The attachment at first is often only a loose one, many holes and crevices remaining between the block and the rock beneath, and furnishing shelter for a multitude of living beings whose tender bodies could not withstand the unbroken force of the waves. Here is the home of a multitude of small round crabs, generally of different species and genera from those inhabiting the preceding zones. New annelids of changing hues, and various genera allied to the shrimps now make their appearance. Sometimes by the removal of the blocks a narrow cleft is disclosed, the sides of which are closely covered and overgrown with moss-like Bryozoa, mossy sea-firs (*Sertulariæ*), small polyp-colonies of chalky or leathery consistence (Cœnopsammia and Cilicia being of the former description, Zoanthus and Polyzoa of the latter), a small red Gorgonia (*Mopsia Erythræa*), small social actinias, sponges, and ascidians. Oysters, ark-shells, and thorny-oysters (*Spondylus*) have also attached themselves to the walls, and here have taken refuge the delicate feather-stars which live free but do not swim.

THE INHABITANTS OF THE CORALS.

The fauna for which the Stylophora corals afford hiding-places is not much altered here, and with it that of the bushy cup-star corals (*Pocillopora*) agrees. Similar, but still with distinct characteristics, is the madrepore coral (*Madrepora*). Instead of the quadrangular-shaped crabs (*Trapezia*) we find here the similar genus Tetralia; the shrimp-like crustaceans are also represented by different but allied genera. Between the branches of the fragile bush-corals (*Xenia*) a small crab of the genus Camptonyx is seldom absent. The massy corals are not well suited for hiding-places, but nevertheless a number of creatures of very diverse forms have obtained a lodgment in their interior. To these belong the Magilus, which prefers for its abode certain star-corals (*Leptastræa*) and mæandrine corals (*Cœloria*), and along with these is already found in the transition zone. The young Magilus, a grayish dome-shaped shell, lies loose in a smooth dome-shaped cavity not much below the surface of the coral colony, like the date-shell in the Stylophora, and this cavity communicates with the surface, where the coral-stars open, by means of a small hole or narrow canal. The older ones, such as are seen in particular in the mæandrine corals, lie deeper, and through the solid substance of the mass, from the shell proper to the surface, a thick tube variously bent and twisted extends. This tube also lies loosely in its canal; it is very brittle, and difficult to procure whole by breaking up the coral rock. After the animal has once penetrated the coral, accordingly, no farther boring takes place, it simply adds to its tube according as the surface of the coral rises, and as the shell grows larger the hole in which it lies also enlarges.

Another parasite on, or at least dweller in, the coral is an abnormally-shaped crab, by name Cryptochirus, which not long ago was brought into notice by Heller. It ensconces itself, like the worm-shell (*Vermetus*), in a short cylindrical tube made by itself, and penetrating perpendicularly from the surface of the coral. Its similarity with the worm-shell is all the greater from the fact that the shield-formed head of the crab forms externally a kind of operculum closing the aperture. Its abodes are almost always observed in the rounded masses of coral, whether it be that it chooses these, or that it disturbs the life of the corals in its vicinity, and so produces this rounded conformation.

The dwelling of a Serpula of considerable size is similar; but the latter penetrates much deeper into the rock, and is found in bushy and massive corals. The living animal forms a beautiful sight when, protruding the anterior part of its body, it bathes its brightly-coloured spiral gills or branchiæ in the water. In radiate corals (especially *Goniastrœa*) a cirrhipede of the genus Pyrgoma has imbedded the tubular portion of its shell; the upper portion forms elliptic warts which much resemble the stars of the corals.

THE CORAL SLOPE.

In order to inspect the realm of corals and the treasures of the deep sea leisurely and at our ease, though our glance must be somewhat unsteady, we step on board a boat and proceed to the reef. The sea must be perfectly quiet, otherwise no boatman would be so rash as to voluntarily steer his craft towards the breakers of the reef, and the surface must be as smooth as a mirror, the least ripple rendering it impossible to see down into the depths. The lower the tide is too, the better objects are seen, and it will contribute to the same result if a little oil is poured on the surface.

The line of the declivity runs on the whole pretty nearly parallel to the shore; where the latter exhibits an indentation of any size there is also a corresponding one in the slope-line. At particular points, to be sure, there is not such a close correspondence, the breadth of the reef varying between 200 and 400 paces. The slope-line also is much more winding and indented. Where the reef is interrupted by a harbour, the slope-line forms a bend so as to almost reach the shore, while the slope gradually diminishes in depth and coral life ceases. The slope is at some points steep and precipitous, perhaps even forms an overhanging cliff, at other points it sinks gradually, or in the form of terraces, towards the open sea. The depth of the water, measuring from the surface of the reef, may average from 5 to 8 fathoms, so that the eye can generally perceive the sandy bottom immediately in front of the reef; the bottom rapidly sinks, however, and at the distance of a few paces from the reef seawards we see only what for the eye are blue unfathomable depths.

This slope, then, like the staging of a greenhouse, is entirely covered with those brightly-coloured many-formed animal growths which we call corals, or, to speak more correctly, it entirely consists of these or their remains, bare and lifeless blocks on which new generations begin to build, while around them swarm and browse the coral fishes, so distinguished for splendour of colouring and strangeness of form. "As humming-birds sport around the plants of the tropics, so also small fishes, scarcely an inch in length and never growing larger, but resplendent with gold, silver, purple, and azure, sport around the flower-like corals, on the leaf-like prehensile arms of which feed beautifully tinted shell-less and strangely-shaped snails (*Æolidæ*), like the caterpillars and garden-snails on the leaves of plants."[1] All this is enveloped in the magic mantle of the transparent briny flood, which, by peculiar effects of refraction, raises and magnifies the distant forms, and lends

[1] Ehrenberg *Ueber die Korallenbänke*, 1832.

them colours so deceptive that, when taken from the water, they can scarcely be recognized. We feel drawn downwards as it were by a mysterious power towards these objects, apparently so near, yet rendered by the foreign element so distant and unattainable, and we gaze dreamily into the depths, sunk in nameless feelings and dim impressions regarding fairy beings flitting about in the gardens of some marine paradise. Against such ideas even the Arabian fisherman, unsentimental as he is, is not quite proof; apart from the elephantine "sea-maiden" (*Halicore cetacea*), which can be caught and skinned, for him, too, there are below the waters charming genii who are eager to marry human beings, though, to be sure, only when the latter have mortified themselves for months previously with unsalted bread and water, so as to give to their flesh and blood a half-ethereal character.

The naturalist, however, cannot allow himself to be allured by dreams and phantasies; he insists upon seizing and taking to pieces those forms to which the water lends such an indistinct and magical effect. He wishes he had a diving bell and a diving helmet in order that he might get down to the bottom at once, and he would fain catch the fishes with a net. But the former appliances are unknown here, and the water is too clear and the bottom too uneven and treacherous. The gallant divers, however, that sit in the boat are able to fulfil every desire, quickly bringing up the corals to which they are directed by a stick or by description, and by means of baited hooks catching one after another the finny denizens of the deep. They use hooks of various sizes, and different kinds of bait, such as small fishes, or morsels of fish, worms, serpent-stars, pieces of crabs or other shell-fish, and algæ, according to the size and likings of the fish. It requires a practised eye to distinguish the corals on the spot where they grow; it is indeed difficult, and often scarcely possible, with the microscope to make out the species at home and by the study table. If the divers are left to their own choice, they will be sure to bring a limited number of species, but of these as great a number of examples as possible. The same species often exhibits very different external forms and colours, and *vice versa*, different species often exhibit the same general forms and colours. In catching fish much depends upon the appetites of the fish, but the fisherman knows the tastes of the several fishes, and can pretty accurately determine beforehand what fish will take such and such a bait.

THE CORALS.

In multiplicity of species and forms, and in the number of its individual colonies, the great genus of crown-corals (*Madrepora*) characterizes before all others the outer slope of the coral reef. The colour of the animals and their dwellings varies generally from dark brown to yellowish and greenish, the points of the branches being usually conspicuous from their lighter shade, which sometimes passes into bluish and rose-red. The coral structures or colonies assume sometimes the appearance of a sward of grass, stems comparatively low, and with few branches rising in tufts above the general flat surface; sometimes they resemble a net-work of leaves and grass with a rounded or gyrate periphery, the branches and twigs uniting to form a much broken surface; or, lastly, they grow to a considerable height, with a bushy or tree-like form. Of these three typical forms, the first is found especially on the higher part of the reef, the species of the second often cover large areas on the slope and form tabular prominences and terraces, the third form belongs mainly to the deep water. Many such madrepore trees reach a height of three or four feet, some form bushes, which, growing in great numbers beside each other on the bottom in front of the slope, appear like extensive woods or steppes. The thistle-like bushes of the Seriatopora, with its delicate and much interwoven stems, have a habit similar to the latter.

But these loose and brittle corals, in regard to which we cannot but wonder how they withstand the force of the breakers, are not proper rock-building corals. The blocks of which the reef is built are produced by the massive forms, and in particular by the mesh-corals (*Porites*), which are consolidated together into huge bluish, brown, or black spheres, bosses, and columns, and to the meandrine or brain corals (*Leptoria, Coeloria*), which have polyps with shimmering green flesh, and which fringe the prominences of the reef in rounded wavy masses. Rocks are formed also by the great family of the star-corals (*Astræa*), which form convex expansions, and also balls and bosses. The stars or openings of the individual animals have a certain size according to the species, from the large Acanthastræa and Prionastræa to the elegant Goniastræa and peculiar Astræa. The flat crusts of the flat Montipora shimmer in light, yellow and violet colours. The urchin-coral (*Echinopora*) spreads itself out as a half free crust, or as an undulating brown or yellow table, with a very rough surface, the substance rising here and there into knobs and pillars. The solid Hydnophora grows similarly and exhibits a bench-like appearance. The millepore corals (*Millepora*), called by the natives "fire-corals" from the sharp stinging nettle-like pain they cause, and classed by some among the Medusæ, sometimes rise in the form of upright, thick, abruptly terminating tables and walls, or they form variously-shaped crusts on worm-tubes, shells, &c., or lying free they form themselves into knotty protuberances. Some, lastly, rise in the form of thin net-like plates, which readily fly in pieces and terminate above in yet more fragile twigs. One of the most beautiful corals, and one that at once attracts notice on account of its cherry-red colour, is the cup-star coral (*Pocillopora*), which grows mainly on the upper part of the slope, and generally in tufts, though also forming beds. The colour belongs to the stony structure, though only to its extremities, like the blue colour of the madrepores; the lower portion and the polyps themselves are brown. The Stylophora still continues to be well represented on the upper part of the slope alongside of the Pocillopora, and, like it, varies from a brownish to a rose-red colour. Besides those mentioned there are many other corals, which, from their smallness or scarcity, however, are of subordinate importance in the formation of the reef; such are the Coenopsammia, which forms a little tree, sometimes of a deep black at other times of a blackish-green appearance, the mushroom corals (*Fungia*), which are attached only in earliest youth, and afterwards lie free on the ground, sometimes having a flat round body (*Fungia patella*), sometimes having a lengthened elliptical shape with a longitudinal furrow, and then assuming the deceptive appearance of a petrified roll of bread (*Fungia Ehrenbergi, Herpetholitha*). The sight of rosy-rayed and pretty rare Galasea always excites joy and admiration in the discoverer. At a great depth grows the well-known black coral (*Antipathes*), a six-rayed sclerobasic coral. In the Red Sea there are but few representatives of the numerous family of the eight-rayed sclerobasic corals so richly represented elsewhere, especially in American seas, and to which the well-known red coral belongs. While the reef is so thickly overgrown with algæ up to the line where it sinks into the surf zone, vegetable life appears to cease altogether when we approach the deep water. Instead of plants leathery corals or Alcyonaria now flourish luxuriantly, and by an ignorant observer would be at once mistaken for them. The polyps of these, however, generally project considerably, and are easily noticed; they are distinguished from the animals of most other corals by possessing eight rays and as many feathery tentacles, while other polyps have generally only six rays. The colour of these animals changes very remarkably according as they expand or contract themselves, and a person might easily think that a colony or bank when disturbed belonged to quite a different species from the same when not so disturbed. From particles of lime interspersed throughout their entire tissue, some of these "flesh corals" possess a leathery consistence, as is the case with the cork-corals (*Alcyonium*), while in others the calcareous particles are reduced to a minimum, and the stems remain almost soft (*Xenia, Sympodium*). The Ammothæa is a coral that has a remarkably plant-like appearance, often forming lofty stalks and bearing "catkins."

THE FISHES.

The Red Sea is extraordinarily rich in fishes, the number of species at present known amounting to about 520.[1] They are most plentiful on the slope of the coral reef. Whether there are real coral-eating fishes is still doubtful; the hard substance of the corals at least can only be nibbled at, and the soft animals withdraw into their cells on the slightest disturbance. Many fishes eat plants, others subsist on the numerous worms and molluscs that live here, or on decaying animal matter; the greater number are predaceous, and eat other fishes. The slope of the reef, with its crevices and deep pools, affords admirable hiding-places, and since the locality exhibits a number of bright colours, the fishes do so likewise, according to a law which generally prevails in nature (that of *mimicry*), although not without many exceptions.

In splendour of colour and diversity of form the fishes of the coral region do not yield to the most brilliant birds. As among birds the parrot takes the first rank for brilliant plumage, so among fishes the same rank is taken by the parrot-fish (*Scarus*), the jaws of which have a remarkable resemblance to the beak of a parrot. It is rivalled by the remaining members of the great family of the wrasses (*Labroidei*), especially by the rainbow-fish (*Julis*), as also by the squamipennes with their disk-like forms, their very small mouths, and their delicate teeth, the most remarkable of these forms being the genera of the brittle-teethed fishes (*Chætodon*), the opercular-spine fishes (*Holacanthus*), the whip-thong fishes (*Heniochus*); we must also add the sea-surgeon (*Acanthurus*), the unicorn thorntail (*Naseus*), with its sharp tail-spine, the trigger-fish (*Balistes*), and lastly, the elegant, though generally small, Pomacentridæ, the humming-birds among the fishes. These fishes are for the most part comparatively poor swimmers, and do not venture far from the slope of the reef, being also met with frequently in the deeper pools on its

[1] See on this subject my complete "Synopsis of the Fishes of the Red Sea" in the *Transactions of the Imperial Royal Zoological and Botanical Society of Vienna*, 1870–71.

surface. Many fishes of the sea-bream family (Sparoids) also love to frequent the slope, though less exclusively, and their colours are commonly not so brilliant. The nearly allied fishes of the genus Cæsio, which swim about in shoals in front of the slope, at once attract the spectator's notice by their beautiful sky-blue colour.

The predaceous species among these coral-fishes are the perches (*Percidæ*), especially the saw-perches (*Serranus*), so numerous in species and so rich in colouring, the notched-perches (*Diacope*), and the thorn-perches (*Myripristis*), that generally lead a nocturnal life, the toothed-perches (*Priacanthus*), the spiny-gilled perches (*Holocentrum*), and the Chilodipterus. The sea-eels (*Murœna*) show themselves more on the reef itself and in the pools; a gigantic species, *Murœna Javanica*, reaches a length of $6\frac{1}{2}$ feet or more, and occurs also on the slope.

Among the inhabitants of the reef surface, in the zone of the breakers, are the repulsive-looking mailed-cheeked fishes (*Cataphracta*), such as the dragon-head (*Scorpœna*), and the most hideous of all fishes the Synanceia. They lie here motionless and hidden between stones and grass, and as they can imitate the colour of their abodes in the most surprising manner, the invader of their haunts is often not aware of their presence until, having set his foot on them, they suddenly start up and inflict on him very painful wounds with their spines. The stings of the Synanceia, at least, are almost as painful as those inflicted by the scorpion. This hideous creature has usually the points of its dorsal spines concealed under a thick skin like the claws of a cat. It can voluntarily withdraw this skin, however, whereupon, according to the fishermen, a milky drop exudes, a kind of eating poison, which makes the wound so painful. One of the finest sights in this sea is afforded by the winged-fish (*Pterois*), when it swims about in a pool or creek with its large brilliant and delicate fins. But care must be taken not to let it touch the naked skin, as the sharp and slender dorsal spines form weapons capable of inflicting very severe wounds.

The balloon-fish (*Tetrodon*), which generally occur in bays, are also remarkable creatures. When danger threatens they quickly rise to the surface of the water, in doing which they are assisted by their large swimming-bladder, and here they gulp up air with a certain noise. The air passes through the gullet into a sack (an extension of the peritoneum), which lies between the peritoneum and the skin, and in ordinary circumstances is in a state of collapse; as the sack becomes inflated the fish thereby gradually assumes the form of a sphere, which floats on the surface of the water like an inflated bladder. The back being the heavier portion turns undermost with the belly above it. The surface of the sphere is almost everywhere closely beset with prickles, which this procedure causes to stand stiff and erect. In the case of the urchin-fish (*Diodon*) these prickles are very large and strong. In this state these fishes have no active means of defence; they can no longer swim at pleasure, since their fins have become withdrawn, and they are altogether at the mercy of the waves. But as the hedgehog among mammalia is safe against attacks when curled up in a ball, so, too, these piscine hedgehogs are protected by their spiny armour, the more so that a bladder when swimming is by no means easy to lay hold of even though unprotected by spines. According to the magnitude of the danger they inflate themselves much or little, and when they are very greatly disturbed their bodies swell almost to bursting. When the danger is over they let out the air gradually and with some noise, and then they resume the appearance of an ordinary fish and swim away. All the species are not equally inflatable, however. The beak of these fishes has some resemblance to that of a parrot, but while the bite of the latter is comparatively harmless, these globe-fish bite severely whatever comes into their neighbourhood. Their heads are looked upon as very poisonous, even for cats, while the rest of their bodies are much eaten, at least by the ichthyophagous Bedouins. Their bite is not poisonous, nor are there any other poisonous fishes in this sea, though several, when eaten at certain times, cause pains and purging, as, for example, a mackerel (*Scomber Kanagurta*), which otherwise is not bad eating.

The trunk-fishes or coffer-fishes (*Ostracion*) have a form which apparently marks them off from all other fishes. They possess a hard, rigid, and box-like coat of mail, composed of separate polygonal plates joined together, and out of this only the fins, the mouth, and the tail project as movable extremities. Accordingly they swim very badly, and may be even taken with the hand. A closer examination of their structure, however, shows the greatest similarity with the globe-fishes. The bases of the spines of the latter have, in the case of the coffer-fishes, become broadened out into the form of simple plates, and are grown together, while the spines have diminished in size or disappeared altogether.

Other strange forms which swim about in the creeks and pools are the tobacco-pipe fishes (*Fistularia*), the sea-needles (*Syngnathus*), and the well-known, though here rather rare, sea-horses (*Hippocampus*).

Rays and small sharks may sometimes be met with on the surface of the reef, though mainly as casual visitors. Colossal specimens of the former are sometimes thrown up dead on the shore, of which the genera Cephaloptera and Ceratoptera may be mentioned. Such a monster of the deep is also the so-called swimming-head or sun-fish (*Orthagoriscus*), which is closely allied to the globe-fish.

The sea-grass meadows (*Gisua* of the Arabs), which we have already often mentioned, and which are met with partly in depressions in the surface of the reef, partly on the bottom of the sea (especially in harbours), afford concealment to a special class of fishes, many of which are distinguished by possessing a green colour. To these belong several sea-needles (*Gastrotokeus*), the knife-fishes (*Amphisile*), several of the sea-bream family, especially Lethrinus, the Percis, young broad-fish (*Platax*), and some of the genus Diagramma.

On a sandy bottom in front of and on the reef, as well as on the bottom of the harbour, live the flat-fishes (*Pleuronectidæ*), or, as they are here called, the Moses-fishes, half covered over and generally lying quietly in wait for their prey; along with these we also find the flat-heads (*Platycephalus*), which belong to the mailed-cheeks; and, lastly, rays, especially the Torpedo, which gives slight electric shocks. These ground fishes have this in common, that they are flat, and have the under surface, or, as in the case of the Pleuronectidæ, one of the sides, pale and colourless. It is only the *Gerres oyena*, which sometimes, though rarely, makes a trench in the sand with one of its sides, that has scales gleaming like silver all over its body.

A number of species of fishes are always on the move. The shoals of these are met with in the harbour and on the reef, but do not go far out into the open sea. At high-water they swim over the reef towards the shore, always making for the shallows, probably from fear of the predaceous fishes, and at low-water they return to the harbour, if they have not allowed themselves to be imprisoned in the pools by the receding tide. Such wandering fishes are the barbels, the mullets, the members of the genera Gerres, Therapon, and Pristipoma, and these are accompanied, especially at night, by some of the coral fishes, such as the parrot-fish, and several of the genera Chrysophrys. They are mostly good swimmers.

The open sea also is not poor in fishes, though by no means so rich as the reef region. They are all excellent swimmers, able to make long journeys, and accordingly have generally a wide geographical distribution. Many of them are not only spread over the whole of the Indian Ocean, and as far as Japan and Australia—which is also the case with many of the previously-mentioned fishes, even the coral fishes proper—but also over the Atlantic Ocean to the American coasts, and into the Pacific Ocean. Some few are even found in the North Sea and in the Mediterranean. These strong-swimmers are almost all of a monotonous colour, which becomes paler on the belly; and members of the same species, though inhabiting regions widely separated, differ from each other in no respect, not even by a mere shade, while the reef-fish proper generally exhibit race differences at least in colouring.

The fishes, and the fauna generally, of the East African coasts and islands, up to the Mozambique, are most closely connected with those of the Red Sea, as well in the number of species possessed in common as in similarity of colouring, while farther towards the East the species and races gradually become more and more different. Of the 520 species of fishes found in the Red Sea 140 are known from this sea alone up to the present time; 26 are common to it with the East African sea, while the remainder, that is the greater number, are spread over the Indian Ocean, and as far as Japan and Australia. In the Atlantic Ocean, also, live 19 species, being confined chiefly to the tropical portion of it; only 7 are found in the Mediterranean. Of the latter one species (*Caranx trachurus*) is a citizen of the world, being found from England to New Zealand; the others belong to the above-mentioned strong-swimmers or fishes of the high sea, namely, the well-known pilot-fish (*Naucrates ductor*), the remora (*Echeneis naucrates*), the coryphene or dolphin (*Coryphœna hippurus*), the hammer-headed shark (*Zygœna malleus*), the long-nosed shark (*Lamna Spallanzani*), and the smooth hound (*Mustelus*).

The fishes of the open sea belong chiefly to the families of the mackerels and tunnies (*Scomberidæ*), the mackerel-pikes (*Scomberesocidæ*), the arrow-pikes (*Sphyrœnidæ*), the sharks, and the herrings (*Clupeidæ*). Among the first may be mentioned the scad (*Caranx*), remarkable for the number of species it presents; these are predatory fishes, and prey especially on herrings and allied fishes, the periodical shoals of which they follow, like them appearing periodically. The tunny-fishes proper do not make their appearance here in shoals of any size, but the single individuals are often of large size. A remarkable fish, closely allied to the tunny, is the large and rather rare sail-fish (*Histiophorus*), the swordfish of this sea. It has an extraordinarily high dorsal fin, and laying itself on its side, and forming an arch about 12 feet wide, it is able to make several leaps to the height of 3 or 4 feet above the surface of the sea. Other leaping-fishes are mackerel-pikes (*Scomberesocidæ*), the half-beaks (*Hemiramphus*), the mullets and the herring-like Chirocentrus, while the flying-fish proper (*Exocœtus*), by means of its large and wing-like pectoral fins, can support itself in the air for considerable distances. The flying-gurnards (*Dactylopterus*) have not yet been observed in the Red Sea, but, on the other hand, a fish which is here met with, viz. the *Apistus Israelitarum*, closely allied to the scorpion-fish or dragon-head (*Scorpœna*), is capable of flying, according to Ehrenberg's observation. The sail-fish or fan-fish (*Pterois*), formerly mentioned, has pectoral and ventral fins so large as to resemble wings, and some persons have believed it able to fly, but this is not the case, as its fins are too delicately constructed. It is strange to see how shoals of these leaping and flying fishes suddenly leap from the water and take the same direction, all rising together, as if at the word of command, or as if impelled by the same external influence, the same thought and will. This community of feeling is, generally speaking, peculiar to fishes that move about in shoals.

The pilot-fishes (*Naucrates*), as is well known, swarm around the sharks, greedy as these are for most sorts of animal food, without the latter doing them any injury, and in company with the sharks they often follow ships for long distances. By means of the sucking-disc which it has on its head and shoulders, and which is nothing else than a modified dorsal fin, the remora (*Echeneis*) attaches itself to the skin of a shark, and often to the bottom of a vessel, and thus travels over the whole world. Herrings and sardines appear periodically and in great shoals, and are always accompanied by a multitude of fishes of prey. They are generally small, though some allied forms (*Albula*, *Chanops*, and *Elops*) grow to a large size, and these occur in both the Indies without it being possible to make a specific distinction between them. All the fishes mentioned are strong-swimmers, travel far out into the open sea, and are found also in the harbours, but only a few of them seem to care for living on the reef. Here the perches ply their predatory trade.

Some fishes remain almost always close below the surface of the water, as the sea-pike or garfish, and the half-beak (*Hemiramphus*); others love only shallow water, or keep at a moderate depth; while others again only feel comfortable at a great depth, and seldom make their appearance above.

This diversity of habit depends upon the species, and often upon the age of the fishes. Many species are never met with except of a large size, as is the case with species of Serranus, Plectropoma, Diacope, Holocentrum, Sphærodon, Pagrus, Dentex, Aphareus, Sphyræna, Thynnus, Caranx; such species may pass their youth in localities where they cannot be caught by the hook, probably in deep water. Some species retire to greater depths as they grow old, while the younger ones are met with nearer the surface; this is the case with several of the genus Serranus. The fishes that are hooked at great depths present this peculiarity, that their bodies are distended, and their throat and æsophagus forced forward to their mouths. This is evidently a result of the diminished pressure on the gases of the body, and analogous to the swelling up of a frog under the air-pump. When the fish voluntarily comes up it can gradually restore the equilibrium by means of its swimming-bladder. The lower animals that live at great depths have their water-vascular system, or something corresponding, as a means of equalizing the pressure. Many fishes that live deep down "in the purple darkness" have, strange to say, a bright red colour, while other similar species and individuals that live higher are darker and grayer, or are brightly coloured. Besides the locality they live in (the coral reef or the open sea), sex has some influence on their colours; this probably accounts for the striking diversities of colouring exhibited by some of the parrot-fishes and rainbow-fishes, which do not have the slightest difference in form; but too few observations have been made, and the sex cannot be easily detected except at spawning time. At this time some of them, as in the genus Caranx, show more lively colours, afterwards becoming lean and gray. On this subject also further observations are desirable.

Many fishes show themselves only at night, and these night-fishes, as well as those living at a great depth, have generally large eyes. There are, to be sure, large-eyed day-fishes also. The "eye-fish" (*Priacanthus hamrur*) has two very large eyes, with wide cloudy-looking pupils which, when it is alive, shine in the dark like the eyes of a cat. To the luminous fishes belong the genera Scopelus, Maurolicus, Astronesthes. They have peculiar round corpuscles or glands in their bodies, and these often gleam like precious stones, amethyst, for instance, and are said to be luminous at night. A considerable number of Red Sea fishes produce sounds, and especially when they are taken out of the water.

But we have already ventured with our frail boat too far in the billowy open sea with its cruel sharks and saw-fish, its companies of sportive dolphins, its sirens, and its gigantic turtles; we might come too near a gigantic sperm-whale, and accordingly we prefer to return to the quiet harbour. There we may, perhaps, have the good luck, rare in this sea, to catch some of the Medusæ or a chain of Salpæ, which creatures sometimes cover the surface of the water in the harbour, generally about once in two years, and especially after east and south-east winds. Or we may catch some of those gleaming sepias that swim with a succession of jerks. If we dip into the sea a fine-meshed net, such as is used for catching butterflies, and drop what it retains into a glass of sea-water, we shall be sure to find various minute creatures, such as Polycystina, Infusoria, and larval forms. If we have a trawl-net we may let it down and hoist a sail, and then we shall, no doubt, catch some of the rare inhabitants of the bottom The trawl-net cannot be much employed here, however; it soon becomes frayed and torn on the rocky bottom of the harbour, and still more on that of the sea in the neighbourhood of the coral reef, where also the depth is generally too great.

We finish our labours by collecting a few gnats that were dancing above the water, some of the sea-runners (*Halobates*) that run about upon the surface of the sea, sand-beetles (*Cicindelæ*) on the sandy shore, and tiny spring-tails (*Poduræ*) under stones in the water; these assure us of the existence here of the insect world, so sparely represented in the sea, where the numerous varieties of crustaceans take its place. Thus we return to land laden with the treasures of all the zoological kingdoms, from the mammals to the Protozoa.

CHAPTER VII.

POPULAR BELIEFS AND SUPERSTITIONS.

In the ancient wonderland of Egypt, according to the almost unanimous testimony of its inhabitants, there are still at the present day wonders upon wonders; and phenomena from the region of the supersensual, which extends without any obvious boundary from the dominion of faith to that of superstition and folly, are still of daily occurrence. At the present day it is generally considered superfluous to treat of these matters, but whoever has had an opportunity of mixing with the Moslimin for only a short time will admit how deeply penetrated by superstition *the whole people* are, and how they *cannot really be understood* unless by one who has a knowledge, not only of their religious beliefs, but also of their superstitions.

THE GINN.

Like the other countries of Islam (so the Koran teaches) Egypt is inhabited by a vast number of ginn or spirits (genii) in addition to the ordinary human race. These ginn are not spirits of the dead that have to "walk," as in other regions, but a distinct kind of beings, a sort of cobolds or elves, beings intermediate between angels and men. Like men they are born, grow up, become old, and die; they are male or female, black or white, high and low, free and slaves, Moslimin and Christian; they have each a personal name; there are among them kingdoms and governments, with rulers corresponding; in short, they are exactly parallel to mankind, from whom they are distinguished only by the want of flesh and blood, and by reaching a great age, namely, 300 years or more. To the human race they stand in the closest relationship. Every child of man has a companion belonging to the realm of the ginn, who is born at the same hour with him, and attends him as his guardian angel, but more frequently makes him the victim of malicious tricks, nay, even renders him sick and causes his death. This companion, the *karina*, is female in the case of a male child and *vice versa;* and when the child dies of spasms or the like while still receiving suck from its mother, it is generally the karina that kills it. Even in the official registers of deaths kept by the physicians the karina was till lately a regular variety of disease, exactly corresponding to our convulsions. As people grow up these companions lose more and more their influence over them, and latterly they only visit their human mates now and again when the latter are asleep.

Usually these beings are invisible, but they can assume all kinds of intangible and shadowy forms, with the outlines of persons, animals, and monsters, and as such they appear to many people. When a proper view is obtained of them they may at once be distinguished by their perpendicular eye. Many of the inhabitants of the country, indeed the majority of them, have experienced such encounters, and can tell gruesome stories about the "afrit" exactly similar to our ghost-stories. If any one wishes to be sure of seeing these beings he must impart to his material earthly fleshy nature a kind of half ethereal strain by preparations for months beforehand, by mortifications, and fasts, and by eating nothing but unsalted bread and water.

THE MAN OF SCIENCE AND THE MAGICIANS.

The "man of science" is able to call up these beings, to drive them away, and to make them do his bidding by invoking them by name,[1] by reading certain chapters of the Koran (especially the *Kurzi*) a certain number of times— perhaps several thousand times—by writing down mysteriously arranged letters, figures, words, and numbers (taken from the so-called *Abged*). This science, although not recommended by the Prophet, is cultivated throughout the whole

[1] These names generally sound unlike Arabic, and may afford the philologist not uninteresting hints regarding the origin of this "science."

of the Mohammedan world by a great number of men, and also by women. The Moghrebins or Moors and the Fellatah of Soudan are reputed the most learned and skilful in it. They draw their knowledge from tradition or from written books, which form a great body of occult literature; in scope, importance, and popular esteem only the religious literature proper can vie with it. By the instrumentality of the ginn, the "servants of the secret," or by the knowledge, however gained, of one of the "secret names of God," those acquainted with occult lore can perform all sorts of miraculous feats, though it is very remarkable that they are generally as poor as beggars. Poverty, however, we are told, is in many cases the essential condition in a compact with a genie, in others celibacy, or such like self-denial. With regard to some, however, it is maintained that, although genuine men, they are formally married to a ginnee or female ginn, and perform their wonders by means of this wife, who is invisible to other people; they themselves, of course, do not admit this.

Men are sometimes met with who spend a great deal of money, though nobody knows how they procure it. Such persons are also said to have a compact with a ginnee, who supplies them with money. A few years ago a mysterious Mohammedan gentleman of this kind travelled about in Egypt, calling himself the Seyid Abd er-rahman el Adaros from India. He sailed up the Nile with a vessel and a large retinue, had a medical attendant of his own, and intended to travel in the Soudan. Travelling without a definite object is something extraordinary among the Mohammedans, and accordingly he attracted a great deal of notice, especially as he worked wonders, and was very open-handed. Eye-witnesses asserted and swore that he could take pieces of money from below his carpet whenever he wished, that he could with a breath change silver coins into gold ones, salt into sugar, &c. This was quite enough, he was denounced to the government as a magician, and the authorities courteously requested him, instead of going to the Soudan, to change his route to the nearest sea-port (Koseir), and there embark for some other country, supplying him at the same time with an escort.

These people maintain that they practise only the higher and innocent kind of magic, and that their ginns are good, and not given to commit evil deeds, such as robbery and murder, while the "magicians" are in alliance with devilish beings, wicked ginns. The good ginns, who are all Moslimin, serve Moslimin only. Such Christians and Jews as practise magic are able to do so only by the assistance of the evil and degraded ginns or devils (*sheitan*). These unbelievers, on the other hand, charge the Mohammedans with enchantment and exorcise their genii with psalms. "Let a Christian beware of calling up a Moslim ginn," is the warning given by an old authority, "the ginn will revenge himself for this affront and immediately put his summoner to death."

Maskat is regarded as the home and native country of magic. There at the present day men are still changed into animals, especially donkeys and apes, as in the times of the Caliphs and in the Thousand and One Nights.

THE MAGIC-BOOKS.

The written books of magic teach how a person must proceed in order to gain any one's affections, to awake at will, to unloose chains, to bring back a fugitive, to keep a wife from faithlessness, to meet with any one, to keep birds away from crops, to cause the belly of a thief to swell up (!), to make a man or an ox run after him; but above all, to discover buried treasures, to find out a thief, to summon up ginns, or to find pieces of gold under one's pillow. In these books there are also a multitude of receipts against sickness in general, and against headache, restlessness, terror, wakefulness, fever, stoppage of milk both among women and animals, and scald-head in particular, as well as against serpents, scorpions, bugs, and other vermin, and for and against pregnancy.

THE COMPACT WITH IRON AND LEAD.

The triumph of this science, however, is due to the "compact with iron and lead," and we believe that we have earned for ourselves the eternal gratitude of war-tormented mankind in copying it out of the magic-book and preserving it for the good of both friend and foe. Since every one will make haste to wear this talisman on his breast, henceforth no sword will cut or pierce, and no bullet penetrate, and the golden age has arrived. The celebrated Ibrahim Pasha, as any of his subjects will testify, came out of every battle uninjured, and reached an advanced age through wearing such a talisman, and the head of one of the ringleaders in the massacre of the Christians at Jeddah could not be struck off until a talisman that he had sewn under the skin of his arm was removed.

The following receipts occur among many others.

RECEIPT FOR SUMMONING SPIRITS.

Fast seven days, and let body and clothes be clean. Read first the chapter of the Koran called "the angel," to the word *hazir*, fourteen times after the night prayer; then pray with four genuflexions, uttering the *fatha* seven times at each genuflexion, and when in the seventh night you have read that chapter fourteen times, ask of God what you wish to receive. One of the spirits, who are the servants of this chapter, will now appear, and will give you information as to the treasure, and how you may get possession of it.

"And if you wish to see still more of the wonderful powers of this chapter, fast seven days in a lonely place, and take incense with you, such as benzoin, aloes-wood, mastic, and odoriferous wood from Soudan, and read the chapter 1001 times in the seven days—a certain number of readings, namely, for every one of the five daily prayers. That is the secret, and you will see indescribable wonders, drums will be beaten beside you, and flags hoisted over your head, and you will see spirits full of light and of beautiful and benign aspect. Enter into friendship with some of these, and they will show you treasures and reveal to you secret knowledge, and will initiate you into the mysteries of religion."

An interesting and characteristic remark was made by one of our acquaintances, who asserted that he had undergone such a course of self-mortification and spirit-seeking; he said he really saw all kinds of horrible forms in his magic circle, *but he saw them also when his eyes were shut;* at last he got quite terrified and left the place.

A LOVE-CHARM.

" On a Wednesday after the vesper prayer, and when your shadow measures twenty paces, write the following formula (*chátim*) with rose-water and sesame water on paper or parchment. Roll this up and throw it on the ground. Then write the formula on the palm of the left hand and fumigate with mastic, benzoin, and coriander. Say over the chapters, *Amran* and *Ichlás,* while your hand is held above the smoke, and then pick up the talisman from the ground. Touch your body with it, and that of the person on whom you have designs. Hang it to the members of your right side, and you will see something wonderful; God's protection is with thee. But use the talisman only for what is lawful!"

The formula consists of certain words written so as to form a hollow square with words also written across the corners. Inclosed within the square on each side are the words *bil hák ansilnah u bil hák nésil,* that is, "in right (not unallowed) we have made him (the spirit) descend, and in right he descended." The words *Gabraíl, Mikaíl, Israfíl, Israíl,* the names of the four archangels, are written so as to form the sides of the square; across the corners are *Abu békr, Omr, Otman, Ali,* the four chief companions of the Prophet. Outside the square on each side is *Biduh,* the name of a ginn, which is very often written on the addresses of letters, or else the corresponding numbers of the Abged, 2468.

THE MAGIC MIRROR.

The magic mirror is much employed. A "pure" innocent boy (not more than twelve years of age) is directed to look into a cup filled with water and inscribed with texts, while under his cap is stuck a paper, also with writing on it, so as to hang over his forehead; he is also fumigated with incense, while sentences are murmured by the conjuror. After a little time, when the boy is asked what he sees, he says that he sees persons moving in the water, as if in a mirror. The conjuror orders the boy to lay certain commands on the spirit, as for instance to set up a tent, or to bring coffee and pipes. All this is done at once. The conjuror asks the inquisitive spectators to name any person whom they wish to appear on the scene, and some name is mentioned, no matter whether the person is living or dead. The boy commands the spirit to bring him. In a few seconds he is present, and the boy proceeds to describe him. The description, however, according to our own observation, is always quite wide of the mark. The boy excuses himself by saying that the person brought before him will not come right into the middle, and always remains half in the shade; but at other times he sees the persons really and in motion. When a theft is committed the magic mirror is also sometimes questioned, as we ourselves were witnesses on one occasion. (This is called *darb el mandel.*) The accusations of the boy fell upon a person who was afterwards proved to be quite innocent, but whom the boy, as it appeared, designedly charged with the crime out of malevolence. For this reason such experiments, formerly much in vogue, were strictly prohibited by the government, though they are still practised.

OTHER MAGICAL RITES.

Another magical rite is that of the revolving pitcher. Into a pitcher filled with water are murmured certain magic formulæ. Two persons, sitting opposite each other, hold the pitcher lightly with the fingers and the thumb, and after some time it begins to turn either towards the right or towards the left, giving an affirmative answer in the former, a negative in the latter case. This reminds us of table-turning, and also of the key which turns when held by two people, who have a very slight grasp of it, or when it is hung between two books, &c. The latter experiment succeeds as well when performed to the accompaniment of a merry song as to that of a pious psalm.

A proceeding similar to that of table-turning is often practised by the Egyptians. Those engaged in it squat round a man who stretches himself out on the ground as if dead; they join hands, and each two sitting opposite each other lay the hands or the points of the fingers under the man. Every one then whispers to his neighbour *er rágel mât*, that is, "the man is dead." After a little time it is said that though the parties have only their fingers placed beneath the man they can raise him from the ground. It is said that other heavy weights may be easily lifted in this way also—an application of force which, in spite of faith, has not yet been adopted in practical life.

From this species of magic we must distinguish the *natural* magic (*zîm*), which acts by natural means and sleight of hand, but differs from the ordinary art of the juggler. A master of this art, we are told, was able so to deceive the senses of his audience that he appeared to go in at a camel's mouth and come out at its other end. Another, however, is said to have played a trick upon him, and made use of means to counteract the delusion, so that the spectators saw him really passing along by the side of the camel.

FEAR OF SPIRITS.

Very few of the inhabitants of the country display much eagerness to come to close quarters with the spirits, but all firmly believe in them. Nobody ventures, therefore, to live in a house alone, to go out alone late at night, or to remain alone in a room at night; and when the husband wishes to go out in the evening to visit his friends, the wife takes refuge with her neighbours or relatives if she has no children or servants. It is only the night-watchmen, sextons, and soldiers whom familiarity relieves from the fear of the spirits, though certainly not from belief in them. On Friday, the Mohammedan Sabbath, the spirits are particularly fond of stationing themselves on the thresholds of doors and gates, and nobody will then venture to remain at such spots. It is not considered as permissible to sweep out a house at night, since a ginn might be struck and injured, and so induced to revenge himself. For similar reasons people do not care to have anything to do with cats, as these may be ginns in disguise. A Moslim is never heard whistling a tune or anything else, especially at night, since the spirits are attracted by whistling. The respect with which the people regard the ginns is evidenced by the exclamation, in universal use, "with permission, ye blessed ones," when a person enters any room or pours out water. The intention is to attract the attention of the ginns, and warn them to get out of the way, so that nothing may happen to them.

TALISMANS.

For the most part, however, people try to protect themselves against these beings, as causing sickness; and popular medicine is based almost entirely upon this view. Whoever feels himself unwell gets a schoolmaster, a scribe, or any other person who has a "blessed hand" to read a chapter or some verses from the Koran over him, and the seat of the disease in particular; or he gets such a verse written down on a piece of paper, and, tying it up in a little leather bag, perhaps sewing it in, attaches it to his person. He may also get a text written with ink in a plate or other dish, when, having washed off the writing with water, he drinks up the nauseous inky mixture, and sometimes recovers. If this religious cure proves of no avail he has recourse to magic. There is scarcely a town, scarcely even a small village, in which there is not one "doctor" at least who professes this art, and who, for a trifle, will write out a valuable talisman for the invalid, after having first determined whether the sickness proceeds from spirits, from the evil eye, from God, or from some material cause. Most people do not allow matters to go so far, but wear themselves, and make their children wear from the first day of their existence, one or more amulets against all evil influences in general.

THE ENVIOUS EYE.

In working mischief the evil eye competes closely with the ginns. Many men go about who are by no means sorcerers, and who have eyes like other people, but "empty, hollow." They cannot bear to see anything fine in the hands of another, and their envy falls with a blighting effect upon any creature they admire, which suddenly or gradually becomes ill, or meets with some accident, and often dies. This power of throwing an evil glance upon anything is by no means always voluntary, for even a father may cause the death of his own child by looking upon it with admiration! It would be impossible to quote all the proofs that the people bring forward in favour of this theory. If a she-goat retains its milk somebody will at once remember that an old woman (in other countries called a witch, a conception which is almost entirely unknown among Mohammedans) went out of the house a little ago; if an object that has not been put in a secure position falls down, the accident is caused by the eye of some person who covets it. The envious person can cause the dates to fall from his neighbour's trees, or even bring down the birds in the air. *A great number of the customs of the people are directed against this secret danger.* The dirty state in which children are kept, the usages of hospitality to some extent, such as the urgent invitation to a person present to partake of a repast served up, the practice of carefully concealing provisions while they are being carried home, the readiness with which an object is handed to the person that admires it, are based on this view; even the seclusion in which women are kept is the result, not merely of Mohammed's commands or of idle jealousy, but arises from the fear lest the evil eye may injure the beloved beings. Texts from the Koran and talismans are employed with success against the effects of the "eye," also both before and after its influence falls. When a person wishes to express admiration without causing injury the words of praise are concluded with the name of God—*ma sha Allah.*

THE PEOPLE OF BLESSING. THE SAINTS.

In opposition to these envious people, to these goblins and devilish magicians, there are fortunately men of such a character that they spread around them good luck and blessing; they are known as the *ahl el baraku* (people of blessing). These consist of the sheikhs or saints, especially silly, childish, crazy people, as well as ascetics and hermits. Most of them have no occupation, but live on alms, which they do not require to ask, since every one considers it to his interest and advantage to bestow something upon them and receive a blessing in return. Others support themselves by some occupation, and do not appear different from other people, but they belong to a family of blessing. Respect is paid to them as to a sherif or a man of position, and they are saluted with a kiss on the head and hand. These saints are usually harmless creatures who do no harm to anybody, and whom no one thinks of injuring. They presume upon this, and do many things that an ordinary man would not venture to do. Sometimes they offend against police regulations, but they are allowed to do as they please, their displeasure being dreaded as much as their blessing is sought for. The people believe in their power of working miracles. Such a saint, we are told, was caught breaking into a shop and was apprehended by the police and placed in confinement. Next morning, as a punishment for this forcible detention, every one of the officials awoke with an eruption over his whole body. Another saint set fire to the shop of a merchant. All the goods were burned, but the blessing of the wrong-doer enabled him in a few months to acquire three or four times as much as he had lost. An extraordinary personage of this kind, an old man, the celebrated Sheikh Selim, sits quite naked, year after year, at a certain spot on the bank of the Nile in Upper Egypt, and lives on the voluntary tribute of the passing mariners. If they give him nothing his curse arrests their vessel on its course, even though it be a steamer, and farther progress is impossible till the saint's tribute is paid. Another possesses the gift of omniscience, and will answer a stranger accurately as to the latter's previous life, his name, and his family, though he never saw him before. Still greater is their miraculous power after death. The body of such saints, when on its way to its last resting-place, has such a mysterious power on those that carry the bier that they can do nothing of themselves, but are compelled to follow a certain route, and bury the saint in whatever spot he may choose. An old negro slave in Koseir, well known for his long, harmless, pious life, having died towards evening, would not, on any account, have himself buried the same evening, and the bearers, in spite of all their shouting of *la ilah ill Allah*, could not bring the corpse to the graveyard. It remained, therefore, all night in the house (though the people do not like to keep a corpse a night), watched by a multitude of people praying. Next morning also it could not be buried for a long time; the blessed dead compelled the bearers to go through all the streets of the town, till at last, on the recommendation of the more enlightened governor, the higher officials carried the bier to the grave; even the Turkish soldiers could not accomplish it. The whole town was in uproar. The Mohammedans say the angels exercise this coercive power, the Christians believe it is the devil. Deceit or practical joking is not always to be surmised in such cases; on the occasion just mentioned almost the whole male population tried what they could do, and among them many staid and serious men. It is the firm belief of these people that the deceased saint or the angels cause the pressure, and then they feel it too. Even in Cairo such occurrences are common as well as in the other parts of the country. Among the ancient Egyptians also the processions of the images of their deities did not direct themselves at pleasure, but by divine inspiration.

After burial the saint appears in a dream to some well-to-do persons and commands them to build a tomb for him, whereupon he gives them an effectual means for the cure of their diseases. When he obtains a temple wonder follows upon wonder. People stream to the spot to perform their vows, their wishes are granted, and offerings are brought, of which the worthy sacrificial priest or saint's attendant (*nekîb*) claims a half or a quarter, the rest being distributed among the poor. From gifts made to it the tomb gradually acquires costly ornaments, and a great jubilee is celebrated every year. In short, the worship of saints has gradually risen into importance, and now is not behind what is practised in the Christian-Catholic Church. It is unknown to the Koran, and therefore the Mohammedan Puritans, the Wehabites of Arabia, would have it expunged from the pure religion of Mohammed along with much else. It is very gratifying to some to stand in the odour of sanctity, to be honoured and feasted by everybody. Such prophets move from place to place, getting their former wondrous works proclaimed abroad, and playing the quack and mountebank. One of these men, whose father is said to have been able to satisfy a whole assembly with a meal that had been served up for himself alone, had the impudence to swindle some £7, 10*s*. out of a man who wished to have children, under the pretext that this preliminary outlay was necessary to procure drugs, whereupon the favoured of God set sail with the next ship and was never seen again.

STATES OF ECSTASY.

Among the Mohammedans, and perhaps throughout the East, it has always been an everyday occurrence for people to fall into a state of ecstasy. Such states are also ascribed to the ginns, who take possession of a person, transform his appearance or "ride" him, and speak and act through him. In the nature of all peoples lies an irresistible tendency towards intoxication, and if wine or spirits are strictly forbidden, as among the Mohammedans, they induce this state by means of opium and hashish, or if their religious scruples cause them to reject these also, they intoxicate themselves with religion itself. The religious dances or *zikrs*, of which we have repeatedly spoken, seem to have been invented for this purpose. After these exercises, which are accompanied by much flinging about of the head and body, and by innumerable repetitions of the name of Allah, it is a common occurrence for one or two to fall into an ecstasy. As in the case of alcoholic intoxication one will be in high good humour, another dull and silent, a third quite frantic. Those possessed in this way foam at the mouth, while laboriously persisting in trying to stammer out the name of Allah; at last they fall to the ground in a swoon, or remain standing as stiff and rigid as a pillar, or they rush frantically about and strike at whatever comes in their way. Certain dervishes are said on such occasions even to eat fire, glass, and serpents. The Soudanese are the most addicted to these strange performances; in their leisure hours they know of no better amusement than putting themselves into a state of ecstasy by songs and dances which have always a religious basis. They set some store by the reputation of quickly working themselves into this condition. Though here and there one or two may succeed in becoming really possessed, others merely pretend to be so, and accordingly it happens, that when the police appear upon the scene, the whole of those who immediately before were lying rigid and in ecstasy at once start up and take to their heels.

This ecstatic intoxication has no ulterior consequences. Those possessed awake either of themselves or are roused by the call *la ilah ill Allah Mohammed rasul Allah*, and they then appear as if nothing had happened. Many of the saints that are seen wandering about may have contracted their imbecility through their repeated ecstasies, and people of this sort are more disposed than others to fall down during these pious exercises.

THE SAR.

Among the women zikrs are not indulged in, but the tendency to ecstasies is even much greater among the more nervous sex, and to gratify this inclination they have adopted a practice which is said to have been introduced by Abyssinian female slaves, and which gradually spread to such an extent that the government felt itself called upon to forbid it. Nevertheless, it is still common among high and low, especially in Upper Egypt. The sâr, a certain ginn, is the powerful genie of sickness, who throws himself upon the women by preference. Whenever a woman is affected by any illness, the causes of which are not as clear as day, the sâr is blamed —'aleha es-sâr. It is immediately made known that the sâr is at so-and-so's house to-day, but the day must be a Saturday, or a Tuesday, or a Thursday. A multitude of women and girls stream to the house of the sick person, and are treated to buza, the half-fermented Arab beer, the favourite drink of the Abyssinians, and to tripe. Songs are now sung, and drums beaten, and the sâr-dance is danced—the women placing themselves in a squatting posture, or with their limbs bent under them, and rocking the upper parts of their bodies and their heads this way and that, as is done in the zikrs. Some of them are soon seized with the frenzy, and leap frantically about. All the proceedings are under the superintendence of the shêcha of the sâr, who is a person well known for her tendency towards ecstatic states, and generally a slave, and who earns a good deal of money in this way. When she, as well as others, is in a state of ecstasy she is asked as to the means to be employed to remove the disease. The cure always consists in a simple thick silver finger-ring without a stone, sometimes also bracelets and anklets, and as soon as the greedy sâr is satisfied with this the sickness is said to cease. So great is the faith in this remedy that many spend their last penny to procure these silver ornaments, and in entertaining their numerous female visitors.

Like the tarantella dance of the middle ages, the sâr is contagious. One woman after another in the company rises up and seems to begin dancing involuntarily, and boys and even men, who are sometimes admitted to these orgies, are affected in the same way. The features of some become altered, they slap their own faces, knock their heads against the wall, weep, howl, and try to strangle themselves, being difficult to restrain; they also give themselves out for other persons, for saints, and especially for the sâr himself. They may be asked what it is they wish, and may be shown a silver ring, some henna paste, or buza. They fix a furious glance upon them, seize them suddenly with wild haste, put on the ring, clutch the henna-paste in their hand, or drink buza. With this as a rule the sâr is satisfied and appeased, the party possessed wipes off the perspiration, and now speaks quietly and reasonably as before. On a day appointed for the sâr the attack is often repeated, ending as at first when the person's wish is gratified, and that is often strange enough.

These states are not pretended, that is clear—why indeed should the parties beat and often seriously injure themselves? They are cases of acute delirium, of ecstasy. The spiritualist will call these persons mediums, the believer in animal magnetism will say they are "magnetized." We remember reading in the report of a doctor attached to the English Abyssinian expedition that a girl suddenly conceived the idea that she was a wolf and ran off at such a rate that no one could catch her till at last she found a bone. This she devoured with the eagerness of a hungry wolf, whereupon she instantly returned to her senses. This case is quite similar to that of our sâr-possessed women, and Abyssinia is the native country of the sâr.

POPULAR MEDICINE.

Since all diseases cannot be cured by talismans, reading, dancing, and vows, an extensive system of popular medicine has developed itself side by side with these, which is based upon more tangible remedies. That a number of these are effective enough is not to be denied, and they agree pretty well with those that experience has taught physicians. For example, zinc or alum is a chief ingredient in all eye powders, compounds of lead in drugs applied to wounds and eczema, as well as astringent vegetable substances, especially fenugreek (*Trigonella fœnum-græcum*). Among those much used are "good oil," that is, olive-oil (used as a lotion in rheumatism and skin diseases), fennel, coriander, caraway ("corn of blessing"), mallows, mint, opium, saltpetre, sal-ammoniac, sulphur, green and blue vitriol, and litharge; as purgatives are used, epsom salts, senna leaves, tamarinds, rhubarb, scammony, and gamboge, the native colocynth being less frequently employed and considered dangerous. As already mentioned, the Bedouins fill the rind of the last-mentioned in the evening with milk, which they drink in the morning. Bleeding with the lancet is common, as well as cupping by means of the razor and the horn, setons made of the chick-pea, the actual cautery, to cure a headache for instance (perhaps performed by a hot nail), boiling oil for fresh wounds, the seeds of the fenugreek for ulcers, the warm steam-bath in rheumatism, syphilis, and skin diseases; the use of the leech is less common, and the native leech (*Bdella nilotica*) causes painful wounds. When there is a pain on the left side blood must be taken from the left arm. Veins are also opened in the hand, the foot, and even the nose.

The majority of the medicines, however, are grossly empirical, and they contain the most absurd ingredients. Animal matters, some of which formerly flourished also in our *materia medica*, are very common, such as a goat's bile, dogs' and monkeys' dung, black-beetles, pearls, the bones of dogs and fishes, lizards, mummies, and the opercula of univalve shells, and all these either raw or boiled, baked or burned as incense. Many vegetable matters from all countries, and often with very unintelligible names, are also held in high repute for their curative properties. We give a few recipes: Burned dogs' bones, along with copperas and ox-gall, are good for piles, if the mixture is applied with a little saliva. Another specific for the same disease consists of black-beetles baked in oil, the hard covers, the head, and the intestines being then removed, and again softened in oil over a gentle fire. These black-beetles are looked upon as a universal panacea. Thus the soft white substance found in the inside of these insects, the flesh indeed, is rubbed on the eyes, and puts away spots on the cornea that are not yet hardened. It is good also against night-blindness. Similarly prepared scarabæi (*Ateuchus sacer*) inserted in the ear along with a little cotton, and blown out a day or two after by the pressure of the air of expiration expelled with closed mouth and nose, are considered an excellent remedy for difficulty of hearing. The following is a recipe to enable women to become fat: Take some black-beetles, burn them and grind them down, add beef fat, sesame oil and *mufetta*, that is a mixture of all the various wares sold by grocers, boil the whole together, and drink a cupful of the liquor every day. Earwigs are driven away by sprinkling onion juice (a very plausible remedy). A good preventive against abortion is for the woman to carry at the small of her back a small scorpion and a little piece of amber tied up together in a little bag; pearls or red coral may also be used instead. Women that do not wish to become pregnant must take fasting three mouthfuls of the powder of burned porcelain shells (*Cyprœa*). When a hair of the eyelids grows inwards, it is pulled out with a pair of tweezers, and the spot is rubbed with a fly, the head of which has been pulled off, or with St. John's-bread powder made into a paste with oil. "No hairs will afterwards grow there." Eczema of the head or other parts is put away by aloes dissolved in vinegar, and well rubbed in. Ginger, preserved or unpreserved, is used as an aphrodisiac, as well as ambergris (a fatty waxy-like substance found in the intestines and bladder of the sperm whale, and sometimes floating on the sea) and honey, or cinnamon and carrot or radish seed boiled with honey, also the gall of a raven, and burned Tridacna shells with honey. To cure a scorpion's sting a piece of garlic is rubbed on the place, or the dirt from the ear of an ass; another common cure is to lay on the wound a polished gem, as jasper, ruby, or turquoise, or the operculum of a Trochus shell, or some remarkable coin, these things being said to adhere to the spot which has been stung. Others maintain that they are caused to adhere by rubbing with an ass's hoof. These gems have a high repute for their curative properties generally, and are often sold at high prices. The different varieties are credited each with special effects, and have as many names; thus the jaspers with red spots, and marblings that look like spots and streaks of blood, stanch blood. The bezoar-stone (a concretion found in the stomach of various animals, ruminants in particular) serves as an antidote to all poisons, that of serpents included. The bezoar-stones from apes are in most repute. A cup made of rhinoceros horn also counteracts the effects of any poison that may happen to be drunk.

THE ANIMALS IN POPULAR BELIEF.

The frequent employment of animal substances as medicaments or talismans arises to a great extent from the belief in a metamorphosis, not allied to the Indian or Pythagorean transmigration of souls, which is quite foreign to Mohammedanism, but caused by magic. Many common stories of this kind may pass for myths or fables among the people themselves, but many are firmly believed by the majority.

While in the scientific circles of our more civilized countries man is held to be an ape modified by natural selection and time, among the Egyptians of the present day the ape is a metamorphosed man. The baboon, it is generally maintained and believed, was a wicked fellow who stole the Prophet's red shoes, and hid them behind him under his coat. The prophet noticed it, however, and uttered this curse over him: "Thief, may your form become a caricature of that of man, and may your buttocks, above which my shoes are hanging, be coloured red like them for all time coming, in memory of your evil deed." For the Moslims in general, the world properly begins only with the Prophet, and no one thinks whether the baboon existed previously, though it is frequently figured on the Egyptian monuments. To keep an ape in the house " is not good," it brings ill luck. Ape's dung, however, is a valuable ingredient in many medicines.

The hyena is generally regarded as a vile enchanter, transformed by the anger of God; and for this very reason its hair, teeth, skin, and flesh possess miraculous powers. The animal having been slaughtered according to the rules of the Koran (such a slaughtered animal is always a rarity, however), the flesh is sold in the market, and goes off rapidly, and at a good price; the ulema, who are at the head of religion, are the chief lovers of it. It imparts strength, especially masculine strength. Lying on a hyena's skin drives away pains in the back. The teeth also are highly esteemed, and are used as amulets for young and old. The tufts of hair from the mane are particularly prized, and whoever has a skin requires to guard it well from the covetous multitude, for the possession of this hair secures love and faithfulness on the part of a husband or wife, as well as the favour of the great.

The cunning of the fox has caused thousands of wonderful stories to pass current regarding him, but these are not believed, being regarded as fables. In the stories Master Reynard generally plays the rôle of a kadi. One story may be given as a specimen:—A man is carrying a basket of fowls to market. A fox who is anxious to get at the fowls lays himself down on the road and pretends to be dead. The man with the fowls is surprised, but passes on. Somewhat farther on the man finds a second fox lying dead, and farther on again a third. "Now," thinks the man, "three fox skins are worth the trouble of taking with me to sell," so he sets down his basket and goes back to pick up the foxes. Of course he finds nothing, and when he gets back to his basket the fowls have disappeared.

Like the hyenas, other animals also, especially injurious animals, are looked upon as transformed villains—serpents, scorpions, and the large pinching ants (*Myrmica*) for instance. The serpent charmer makes a business of enticing out serpents concealed somewhere in houses, and summons them in the name of some of the patriarchs, as Adam, Enoch (Edris), Noah, Abraham, Ishmael, and even David and Christ, but he does not fail to bring along with him a basket containing serpents. Scorpions are brought to a standstill with the cry *homâr*, that is ass, so as to let themselves be killed. People may have themselves rendered proof against the poison of scorpions and serpents through the initiated, but after this they must never kill one. An Abyssinian slave once brought us a scorpion in his hand, and on being told to do so dropped it into spirits himself. After some days the same slave was stung by a scorpion and wanted to get spirits of sal ammoniac. He had broken the conditions laid down.

Another sort of transformation is that which produced the flat fishes. Moses was once cooking a fish, and when it had been broiled till it was brown on one side, the fire or the oil gave out and Moses angrily threw the fish into the sea, where although it had been half broiled, it came to life again, and its descendants have preserved up to the present day the same peculiar appearance, being white or colourless on one side and coloured on the other. In Constantinople a similar story is told of the flat fishes there, but in this case the actor was the Sultan Mohammed II., the conqueror of Stamboul.

To certain animals instincts and senses are ascribed for things that the human senses do not take cognizance of; for instance, at the time of the rising of the *Tureya* or Pleiades, the camel is said to see this constellation before it is visible to human eyes, and at this time (beginning of June) it is said not to lie down in any other direction than with its head towards the east. Fishes also are said to see this constellation first.

While some animals, namely, those that are mischievous or held to be so, and those that are regarded as game, are pursued and killed upon every opportunity, and others, such as the dog or the swine, are regarded with the deepest contempt as unclean, and are kept as far from the person as possible, the purposeless slaughter of harmless animals is generally regarded as a sin. On one occasion when we were preparing specimens for our collection, and had flung away some worms and other marine animals as useless, a Turk, rude enough otherwise, carefully picked them up and carried them back to their native element. By strictly orthodox theologians the formation of a collection of animals is condemned; for them natural history is not a science but a mere amusement. To shoot the useful and harmless vultures is looked upon as a piece of great barbarity.

But the person who kills the great black raven or raven of the desert (*Corvus umbrinus*) does not get off unpunished. This bird, called Noah's raven, as being the bird that he sent out of the ark and that did not return, is the *uncle* of the blacks, the Soudanese. On one occasion a hunter had been commissioned by us to procure a raven, which he did, and after carefully barring the door, proceeded to pull it out with the utmost caution from the pocket of his coat. The affair had got wind, however, and we began to hear the sound of kettle-drums, accompanied by shrill cries, coming nearer and nearer to the house. In a short time the whole crew of the blacks were outside the door. For a long period the black Soudan slaves have formed a union for semi-religious semi-national entertainments. They now began drumming, clapping their hands, bellowing and yelling, and also performed a dance, in which the dancers had girdles of goats' horns. On our asking the president or sheikh of the blacks what was the matter, he replied in a friendly, but serious and decided tone, that blood-money must be paid, their "uncle," who from time to time brought them news of their relatives far separated from them in the Soudan, had been killed, and we ourselves were morally his murderers. The hired murderer in the meantime had fled, but was soon discovered and brought back to the house. We gave them a few coppers, believing the affair settled, and went on with the skinning of the bird. But the noise before the house, the lamentations for the dead, and the dance in his honour became more and more demonstrative; their uncle was worth more blood-money. At last, after long negotiations with the sheikh, who, from his solemn manner of conducting the business, appeared to be really in earnest, we were let off for three francs. Their uncle's body, minus the skin, was handed over to the horde, and being laid in a bier covered with coloured cloths, was solemnly carried to the graveyard, accompanied with flags and shouts of *la ill Allah*, as if it were some person's funeral, and finally was formally interred. The kadi himself having shot a raven was once treated in a similar way. At first he would pay nothing, but the blacks walled up his house-door, and at last he gave the blood-money demanded. Even a pasha at Jeddah is said to have been forced to pay blood-money.

ALCHEMY.

Alchemy, or the art of making gold from substances of little value, is intimately connected with popular medicine.

There are still people who occupy themselves with it, but none of them have as yet made their fortunes.

RELIGIO-ASTRONOMICAL FANTASIES.

Astrology is practised to a much greater extent. The astronomical conceptions of the people, and even of the educated, are those of the Prophet, and if any attempt is made to impress them with others, they shake their heads proudly or incredulously. The unfortunate sun still continues to revolve every day from east to west round the earth, which is of a disc-shape, and surrounded by a circular mountain inhabited by the ginn (Mount Kaf). Above it lie seven heavens and paradise, through which flow precious brooks of water; here the believers lead a life of rapturous bliss in the company of the virgin houris, "whose large black eyes resemble pearls that are yet concealed in their shells." These and the boys of paradise present them with cups of precious wine, "which neither causes headache nor clouds the reason." On the other hand unbelievers, condemned by anticipation from the beginning of the world, will suffer deep down in the fire of hell, howling and gnashing their teeth, and only when they have led a pious life are the pains of hell somewhat lessened. The sun and moon have their abode in the fifth heaven; in the course of their revolutions they rest at certain stations (*mensil*). In the uppermost of the seven heavens God sits upon a throne held by four archangels, namely, Israfil, Gabrail, Michail, and Israil.

Under these according to the secret books are the following great angels of heaven:—Zemzemaîl, Kasfeail, Zarfeaîl, Rangeail. The following rule over the earth:—Moshab, Murra, Ahmar, Baragan, Shamharish, Zaubaa, and Maimun. They take the government in turn, each ruling one day of the week; on Saturday, the unlucky day, the ruler is the malignant Maimun. Among the ancient Egyptians also Saturday was the day of Typhon, or the evil principle. Each of these angels has as many attendants as the Abged can get numbers out of their names; Moshab, for instance, has 747.

Other angels or kings of the ginn (*mélek*) are—Leltahtilin, Mahtahtilin, Kahtahtilin, Fahtahtilin, Nahtahtilin, Gelhatahtilin, Lamakfengel—the last being the greatest. The initial letters of the others give the name of the last.

A certain angel or king of the ginn is called Meitataru; he dwells in one of the seven heavens. When incense is burned on the earth he smells it, and waving his rod, he commands his subjects to attend to the matter and stand at the service of the person offering the incense. Another, like the Christian ginn-king Kim, is attracted by the smell of the opercula of shells burned as incense.

Falling stars are wicked angels or devils hurled down by God. It is they who teach men the black art, the evil kind of magic. Accordingly it is a matter of duty for every believer to say, when he sees a shooting star, "I take refuge with God from the stoned devil."

ASTROLOGY.

The ever visible splendour of the tropical or subtropical starry firmament is a powerful inducement to its study. The stars also serve people in general as a nocturnal clock; to the traveller, and especially the mariner, they serve as guides. As in these latitudes the winds have a very regular course, corresponding to the season of the year, and the stars show what season it is, the seaman is perhaps right when he is afraid of such and such a star in a certain position (Lahemir, for instance, when in the west at evening), and looks upon it as an unlucky star, while he considers others lucky stars. Such views, however, lead gradually to the fantastic domain of astrology, and there are few who would venture to deny the influence of the stars upon the fate of mankind. Both Christians and Mohammedans occupy themselves with astrology. A special literature teaches how to detect this influence, one of the books among others being "the true and accurate book of the renowned Greek (?) philosopher, Abu Moshaër, the great astronomer." More important for this science, however, than the knowledge of the starry vault is that of the Abged. Every letter of the alphabet corresponds to a certain number; B, *biduh,* for example, corresponds to 2468, but the letters are not arranged as at present, not A, B, T, Th, &c., but A, B, G, D (hence Abged).

There are twelve constellations for men and twelve for women. The Abged number of the name of the man on whose behalf astrology is to be consulted has to be found, together with the name of his mother. From this number subtract 1212, and if the remainder is 1, the Ram is his constellation and his planet Mars; his temperament, therefore, is the sanguineous. If 2 is the remainder, his constellation is the Bull and his planet Venus; his temperament is "earthy," that is, phlegmatic; and so on. This art teaches also to know whether a sick person will die, whether something lost will be found, an affair turn out well, or what will be the general course of the coming year. Many earn their bread by making such calculations, and there is no lack of believers even among the higher ranks; numbers of people allow themselves to be guided in matters of the highest importance by these astrologers and calculators, who often have the effrontery to take a sum of money in advance, and when the time arrives for the fulfilment of their prophecy they are far enough away.

GEOMANTISTS AND GYPSIES.

Geomantists, who practise the *darb er-raml,* are generally Soudanese. At every yearly market may be seen a few of these black and half-naked prophets squatting on the ground, making holes and lines in the sand, throwing upon these a few stones as dice, and predicting therefrom for a few coppers the future joys and sorrows of the people. Gypsy women, too, may be seen sitting there, telling fortunes in their usual manner by the lines on the palm of the hand, or by shells, which here serve instead of a pack of cards.

THE FUTURE.

Of all prophecies those of the Prophet are the most important. They are not openly set forth in "the perspicuous book," but the wise understand how to extract them from it, and everyone knows and believes in them, Islam will complete a thousand but not thousands of years (*el elf u la el ulûf*); others say not twelve hundred years. We are now at 1292 after the flight (or emigration, as the Mohammedans will have it that Hejra should be translated). Accordingly the world must soon come to an end, and the signs of this are always increasing, witness the railways, telegraphs, and balloons, and the ever-increasing preponderance of the Franks and Frankish ideas. Towards the end of this period the world will be in a sad condition—sovereigns will make war against each other, there will be great dearth, unbelief and profligacy will prevail. The hordes of the king of Abyssinia will descend from their mountains, and will subdue the sacred land of Islam and Egypt. The Mohammedan world accordingly watched with the most lively interest the last Abyssinian wars with England and Egypt. The sultan will be driven out of Constantinople, and will take refuge in Egypt. Then comes the Muhdi[1] (Reneg of the Koran?); from his Abged number (4253) he should be already born. The Muhdi, a kind of Messias, will be sprung of an obscure family in Yemen, but will raise himself by his abilities, not, however till his fortieth year, and will soon acquire dominion over the whole world. During his reign Mohammedans and Christians will be reconciled, and all men will share their goods like brothers. An antichrist will, however, appear, and attempt to sow mistrust and dissension, but will be slain by Christ, who will now come upon the scene. After this the Moslimin will all die of plague and other diseases, and only Christians remain alive. These finally die also, and the earth is no longer inhabited by men.

DAY OF JUDGMENT.

At the end of all things the archangel Israil blows his trumpet, and the whole earth becomes a firm and level field. A

---

[1] A false Muhdi who gained many adherents, and in a short time set all Egypt in an uproar, was shot about ten years ago. He was the Hâg Theyib of Gau in Upper Egypt.

rain falls which causes the remains of the dead of all times and peoples to begin to grow, like the seeds of a plant. As soon as the bodies are again formed, all human souls, who from the time of their death had been collected in a well at Jerusalem,[1] rise and reanimate their respective bodies, and the day of judgment comes. The judgment, as we are assured by authorities on the subject, will be held at Damietta in Egypt!

[1] Regarding the abode of the souls between death and resurrection there are various views.

END.